NEW DAY/NEW DEAL

Recent Titles in
Bibliographies and Indexes in American History

American Puritan Studies: An Annotated Bibliography of
Dissertations, 1882-1981
Michael S. Montgomery, compiler

Free Trade and Sailors' Rights: A Bibliography of the War of 1812
John C. Fredriksen, compiler

America on Film and Tape: A Topical Catalog of Audiovisual Resources
for the Study of United States History, Society, and Culture
Howard B. Hitchens, General Editor
Vidge Hitchens, Associate Editor

The Immigrant Labor Press in North America, 1840s-1970s:
An Annotated Bibliography
Volume 1: Migrants from Northern Europe
Dirk Hoerder, Editor
Christiane Harzig, Assistant Editor

Index to Puerto Rican Collective Biography
Fay Fowlie-Flores, compiler

The People's Voice: An Annotated Bibliography
of American Presidential Campaign Newspapers, 1828-1984
William Miles, compiler

The Immigrant Labor Press in North America, 1840s-1970s:
An Annotated Bibliography
Volume 2: Migrants from Eastern and Southeastern Europe
Dirk Hoerder, Editor
Christiane Harzig, Assistant Editor

The Immigrant Labor Press in North America, 1840s-1970s:
An Annotated Bibliography
Volume 3: Migrants from Southern and Western Europe
Dirk Hoerder, Editor
Christiane Harzig, Assistant Editor

NEW DAY/NEW DEAL

*A Bibliography of the Great
American Depression, 1929–1941*

Compiled by
David E. Kyvig and **Mary-Ann Blasio**
with contributions by Dawn Corley
*and assistance from Frank A. Caulkins,
Richard J. Cherok, Ned R. Delamatre,
Lin Guo, and Mark S. Harmon*

Bibliographies and Indexes in American History, Number 9

GREENWOOD PRESS
New York • Westport, Connecticut • London

Library of Congress Cataloging-in-Publication Data

Kyvig, David E.
  New day/New Deal : a bibliography of the Great American
Depression, 1929-1941 / compiled by David E. Kyvig and Mary-Ann
Blasio with contributions by Dawn Corley and assistance from Frank
A. Caulkins . . . [et. al.].
  p. cm. — (Bibliographies and indexes in American history,
ISSN 0742-6828 ; no. 9)
  Includes index.
  ISBN 0-313-26027-3 (lib. bdg. : alk. paper)
  1. Depressions—1929—United States—Bibliography. 2. New Deal,
1933-1939—Bibliography. 3. United States—History—1919-1933—
Bibliography. 4. United States—History—1933-1945—Bibliography.
I. Blasio, Mary-Ann. II. Corley, Dawn. III. Title. IV. Series.
Z1244.K95 1988
[E784]
016.97391'6—dc19   87-37568

British Library Cataloguing in Publication Data is available.

Library of Congress Catalog Card Number: 87-37568
ISBN: 0-313-26027-3
ISSN: 0742-6828

First published in 1988

Greenwood Press, Inc.
88 Post Road West, Westport, Connecticut 06881

Printed in the United States of America

The paper used in this book complies with the
Permanent Paper Standard issued by the National
Information Standards Organization (Z39.48-1984).

10 9 8 7 6 5 4 3 2 1

Contents

Preface

In 1928 Republican presidential candidate Herbert Hoover proclaimed that, if he were to be elected, the coming years would represent a "new day" for the American people. Four years later when Hoover ran for reelection, his Democratic opponent, Franklin D. Roosevelt, declared that the time had come for a "new deal" for the United States. With the onset of the Great Depression in 1929, the unintended irony of his campaign phrase was used to mock the beleaguered Hoover. In contrast, Roosevelt's phrase was seized upon by journalists as an upbeat label not only for FDR's active, innovative government but also for the decade which it dominated. Brief labels are of course inadequate to express the full reality of complex periods of history, but "new day" and "new deal" serve as well as most to capture the essence of the years between Hoover's inauguration on March 4, 1929, and the Pearl Harbor attack of December 7, 1941.

This bibliography lists retrospective books, articles, and doctoral dissertations having to do with American government, law, and politics; economics; regional and local affairs; society; thought and culture; and foreign relations during the new day/new deal era. General histories of the period, bibliographic and historiographic studies, and discussions of the impact of the era on subsequent American development are also identified. More than 4600 individual items have been located, including approximately 1300 books, over 2500 articles and essays, and 800 dissertations. Of course no compilation of this sort is flawless, and no doubt we have missed items that ought to have been included. To begin with, we were obliged to limit our coverage to works published in English. Furthermore, M.A. theses and newspaper feature stories, many of which contain unique information and insights, were beyond our reach. Our coverage extends to mid-1987, but is not as thorough for the final months as it is for 1986 and earlier. Nevertheless, this is by far the most extensive bibliography of the depression decade ever published. It reflects the impressive and ongoing interest in this era by scholars and non-academics alike.

The bibliography is organized topically in thirteen chapters, with most chapters divided into several sections. In all, there are forty-four topical categories, each of which is subdivided into lists of books, articles, and dissertations. The chapter devoted to biography contains listings for 167 noteworthy individuals of the period. Within sections entries are arranged in alphabetical order by author.

Readers need to be aware that, in order to accommodate the large number of entries, items could only be listed once. Each entry was placed in the category which seemed to reflect its principal focus. For instance, an essay concerning an individual's involvement with a particular issue would have been listed under the appropriate topical heading, while a general discussion of the same individual's career would have been placed in biography. Of course many entries could have been located in two or more categories. Readers will therefore find it useful to examine not only the principal category of interest but related categories as well. In almost every instance, broad, logical searching will pay dividends.

For example, a reader interested in Great Plains agriculture would want to begin with 7.2, the agriculture section of the chapter on the economy. He or she would probably find it well worthwhile to look at other sections of the chapter, including 7.1, general; 7.3, banking, finance, and monetary affairs; and 7.5, labor. The same reader might profit from examining chapter 3, participant accounts; 4, biographies; 5.3, Hoover administration policies and programs; 6.3, Roosevelt administration policies and programs; and 9.3, Midwest regional, state, and local affairs. For some agricultural topics, it could also be useful to peruse chapter 2, bibliography and historiography; 8, society; 10, thought and culture; 12.1, general foreign relations; and 12.7, trade and economic relations.

An author index provides a further means of access to the bibliography. The index designates topical categories in which one or more works by an author appear. It also indicates whether the work is a book, article, or dissertation.

The manner in which this bibliography was compiled deserves mention Using a Macintosh computer, I assembled a five hundred book bibliography on the 1930s in preparation for a 1986-87 graduate history seminar at the University of Akron. Seminar members were asked to look for additional titles in the course of their reading. The plan was to generate an expanded bibliography so that seminar members undertaking original research during the spring semester would have a useful tool at their disposal. Several students proved to be enthusiastic and sharp-eyed bibliographers. Within a semester they had added two thousand entries to the original list, expanding it to the point that publication began to seem worthwhile. During the subsequent semester, two students, Mary-Ann Blasio and Danny Moore, searched even further and more systematically. Summer support from the University of Akron Department of History allowed completion of the research. Dawn Corley, a graduate student not involved in the 1930s seminar, made a substantial contribution to the project in the latter stages. Mary-Ann Blasio very capably assumed principal responsibility for verifying citations as well as carrying out many of the small but necessary tasks involved in completing the manuscript, especially while I was serving as a Fulbright lecturer at the University of Tromsø in Norway.

In the course of the project, my collaborators and I have acquired several debts. At the University of Akron's Bierce Library, Ruth Clinefelter, the social sciences/humanities bibliographer and a former president of the Association for the Bibliography of History, provided valuable early assistance, while Sarah M. Lorenz graciously handled innumerable inter-library loan requests.   Gayle Seymour of the university's computer center patiently gave invaluable technical and moral support. The faculty and staff of the University of Akron Department of History encouraged and assisted the project in numerous ways from start to finish.   The Institute for Languages and Literature at the University of Tromsø facilitated final manuscript production.   All of these contributions are deeply appreciated.

The worth of any bibliography is measured by the use made of it.   It serves its purpose best if it stimulates new investigation and publication, in other words, if it renders itself obsolete.   My collaborators and I hope that this bibliography will do so, thereby requiring an updated edition.   In anticipation of such a development, we hope that users of the bibliography who find errors or omissions or who have suggestions for its improvement will send them to: New Day/New Deal Bibliography Project, Department of History, University of Akron, Akron, Ohio 44325.   In the meantime, we hope that this bibliography will encourage readers to explore the rich resources currently available for the study of this important period of modern American history.

David E. Kyvig

NEW DAY/NEW DEAL

1

Overviews & General Histories

Books

Allen, Donald R. French Views of America in the 1930s. New York: Garland, 1979.
Allen, Frederick Lewis. Since Yesterday: The Nineteen-Thirties in America, Sept. 3, 1929-1939. New York: Bantam, 1940.
Baskerville, Stephen W., and Ralph Willett, eds. Nothing Else to Fear: New Perspectives on America in the Thirties. Manchester: Manchester University Press, 1985.
Bendiner, Robert. Just Around the Corner: A Highly Selective History of the Thirties. New York: Harper and Row, 1967.
Bird, Caroline. The Invisible Scar. New York: David McKay, 1966.
Boardman, Fon W., Jr. The Thirties: America and the Great Depression. New York: Henry Z. Walck, 1967.
Braeman, John, Robert H. Bremner, and David Brody, eds. The New Deal; vol I. : The National Level; vol. II: The State and Local Levels. Columbus: Ohio State University Press, 1975.
Brandes, Stuart D. American Welfare Capitalism, 1880-1940. Chicago: University of Chicago Press, 1976.
[Bransten, Richard,] Bruce Minton [pseud.], and John Stuart. The Fat Years and the Lean. New York: Modern Age Press, 1940.
Brogan, Denis W. The Era of Franklin D. Roosevelt: A Chronicle of the New Deal and Global War. New Haven: Yale University Press, 1950.
Burner, David. The Politics of Provincialism: The Democratic Party in Transition, 1918-1932. New York: Knopf, 1968.
Chandler, Lester V. America's Greatest Depression, 1929-1941. New York: Harper & Row, 1970.
Clark, Norman H. Deliver Us From Evil: An Interpretation of American Prohibition. New York: W.W. Norton, 1976.
Cohen, Wilbur J., ed. The Roosevelt New Deal: A Program Assessment Fifty Years After. Austin: Lyndon B. Johnson School of Public Affairs, University of Texas, 1986.

Daniels, Jonathan. The Time Between the Wars: Armistice to Pearl Harbor. Garden City, N. Y.: Doubleday, 1966.

Dobyns, Fletcher. The Amazing Story of Repeal: An Exposé of the Power of Propaganda. Chicago: Willett, Clark, 1940.

Ellis, Edward Robb. A Nation in Torment: The Great American Depression, 1929-1939. New York: Capricorn, 1971.

Faulkner, Harold U. From Versailles to the New Deal: A Chronicle of the Harding Coolidge-Hoover Eras. New Haven: Yale University Press, 1950.

Garraty, John. The Great Depression: An Inquiry into the Causes, Course, and Consequences of the Worldwide Depression of the Nineteen-Thirties, as Seen by Contemporaries and in the Light of History. San Diego: Harcourt Brace Jovanovich, 1986.

Goldman, Eric. Rendezvous with Destiny: A History of Modern American Reform. New York: Knopf, 1952.

Goldston, Robert G. The Great Depression: The United States in the Thirties. Indianapolis: Bobbs-Merrill, 1968.

Graham, Otis L., Jr. An Encore for Reform: The Old Progressives and the New Deal. New York: Oxford University Press, 1967.

_____ and Meghan Robinson Wander, eds. Franklin D. Roosevelt: His Life and Times: An Encyclopedic View. Boston: G. K. Hall, 1985.

Grantham, Dewey W., Jr. The Democratic South. Athens: University of Georgia Press, 1963.

Hawley, Ellis W. The Great War and the Search for a Modern Order: A History of the American People and Their Institutions, 1917-1933. New York: St. Martin's, 1979.

Hicks, John D. Republican Ascendancy, 1921-1933. New York: Harper & Row, 1960.

Hofstadter, Richard. The Age of Reform: From Bryan to F.D.R. New York: Knopf, 1955.

Huthmacher, J. Joseph. Trial by War and Depression, 1917-1941. Boston: Allyn and Bacon, 1973.

Johnson, Walter. 1600 Pennsylvania Avenue: Presidents and the People. Boston: Little, Brown, 1960.

Karl, Barry D. The Uneasy State: The United States from 1915 to 1945. Chicago: University of Chicago Press, 1983.

Katz, Michael B. In the Shadow of the Poorhouse: A Social History of Welfare in America. New York: Basic, 1986.

Kirkendall, Richard S. The United States, 1929-1945: Years of Crisis and Change. New York: McGraw-Hill, 1973.

Kyvig, David E. Repealing National Prohibition. Chicago: University of Chicago Press, 1979.

_____, ed. Law, Alcohol, and Order: Perspectives on National Prohibition. Westport, Conn.: Greenwood, 1985.

Leighton, Isabel, ed. The Aspirin Age: 1919-1941. New York: Simon and Schuster, 1949.

Lerner, Max. Ideas for the Ice Age: Studies in a Revolutionary Era. New York: Viking, 1941.

Leuchtenburg, William E. The Perils of Prosperity, 1914-1932. Chicago: University of Chicago Press, 1958.

Lubell, Samuel. The Future of American Politics. New York: Harper, 1952.

McCoy, Donald R. Coming of Age: The United States During the 1920's and 1930's. Baltimore: Penguin Books, 1973.

McCraw, Thomas K. Prophets of Regulation: Charles Francis Adams, Louis D. Brandeis, James M. Landis, Alfred E. Kahn. Cambridge: Harvard University Press, 1984.

McElvaine, Robert S. The Great Depression: America, 1929-1941. New York: Times Books, 1984.

Meltzer, Milton. Brother, Can You Spare a Dime: The Great Depression, 1929-1933. New York: Knopf, 1969.

Mitchell, Broadus. Depression Decade: From New Era through New Deal, 1929-1941. New York: Holt, Rinehart & Winston, 1947.

Moley, Raymond. 27 Masters of Politics. New York: Funk & Wagnalls, 1949.

Nash, Gerald D. The Great Depression and World War II: Organizing America, 1933-1945. New York: St. Martin's, 1979.

Olsen, James S., ed. Historical Dictionary of the New Deal: From the Inauguration to Preparation for War. Westport, Conn.: Greenwood, 1985.

Ostrander, Gilman M. American Civilization in the First Machine Age, 1890-1940. New York: Harper & Row, 1970.

Patterson, James T. America's Struggle Against Poverty, 1900-1980. Cambridge: Harvard University Press, 1981.

_____. America's Struggle Against Poverty, 1900-1985. Revised edition; Cambridge: Harvard University Press, 1986.

Phillips, Cabell. From the Crash to the Blitz, 1929-1939. New York: Macmillan, 1969.

Piven, Frances, and Richard Cloward. Regulating the Poor: The Functions of Public Welfare. New York: Pantheon, 1971.

Schriftgeiser, Karl. This Was Normalcy: An Account of Party Politics during Twelve Republican Years, 1920-1932. Boston: Little, Brown, 1948.

Seldes, Gilbert. The Years of the Locust (America, 1929-1932). Boston: Little, Brown, 1933.

Shannon, David A. Between the Wars: America, 1919-1941. Boston: Houghton Mifflin, 1965.

_____. The Great Depression. Englewood Cliffs, N.J.: Prentice Hall, 1960.

Sinclair, Andrew. Prohibition: The Era of Excess. Boston: Little, Brown, 1962.

Smith, Page. Redeeming The Time: A People's History of the 1920s and the New Deal. New York: McGraw-Hill, 1986.

Stearns, Harold E. America: A Re-appraisal. New York: Hillman-Curl, 1937.

_____, ed. America Now: An Inquiry into Civilization in the United States by Thirty-Six Americans. New York: Scribner's, 1938.

Trattner, Walter. From Poor Law to Welfare State: A History of Social Welfare in America. New York: Free Press, 1974.

Wecter, Dixon. The Age of the Great Depression, 1929-1941. New York: Macmillan, 1948.

Wehle, Louis B. Hidden Threads of History: Wilson through Roosevelt. New York: Macmillan, 1953.

Wooddy, Carroll H. The Growth of the Federal Government, 1915-1932. New York: McGraw-Hill, 1934.

Articles

Aaron, Daniel. "The Thirties--Now and Then." American Scholar 35 (Summer 1966): 490-94.

Auerbach, Jerold S. "The Influence of the New Deal." Current History 48 (June 1965): 334-39, 365.

Baker, B. Kimball. "The Great Depression." Worklife 1 (Sept. 1976): 11-18.

Bennett, David H. "Could the New Deal Have Taken America to the Left?" In The Roosevelt New Deal: A Program Assessment Fifty Years After ed. by Wilbur J. Cohen (Austin: Lyndon B. Johnson School of Public Affairs, 1986), pp. 33-52.

Bernstein, Barton J. "The New Deal: The Conservative Achievements of Liberal Reform." In Towards A New Past: Dissenting Essays in American History ed. by Barton J. Bernstein (New York: Pantheon, 1968), pp. 263-88.

Black, Wilfred W. "America's Contribution of State Capitalism." Social Studies 64 (Nov. 1973): 266-70.

Commager, Henry Steele. "Twelve Years of Roosevelt." American Mercury 60 (April 1945): 391-401.

Dubofsky, Melvyn. "Not So 'Turbulent Years:' Another Look at the American 1930s." Amerikastudien 24 (1979): 5-20.

Ferguson, Thomas. "From Normalcy to New Deal: Industrial Structure, Party Competition, and American Public Policy in the Great Depression." International Organization 38 (Winter 1984): 41-94.

Freidel, Frank. "The New Deal: Conservative Reform Movement." In Conflict or Consensus in American History ed. by Allen F. Davis and Harold D. Woodman (Boston: D.C. Heath, 1966), pp. 344-59.

Garraty, John A. "The Big Picture of the Great Depression." American Heritage 37 (Aug./Sept. 1986): 90-97.

_____. "The New Deal, National Socialism, and the Great Depression." American Historical Review 78 (Oct. 1973): 907-44.

Keating, L. Clark. "The Future in Retrospect: A Frenchman's View of America Between Wars." Modern Language Journal 57 (Nov. 1973): 349-52.

Kesselman, Steven. "The Frontier Thesis and the Great Depression." Journal of the History of Ideas 29 (April-June 1968): 253-68.

Kirkendall, Richard S. "The Great Depression: Another Watershed in American History?" In Change and Continuity in Twentieth-Century America ed. by John Braeman, Robert H. Bremner, and Everett Walters (Columbus: Ohio State University Press, 1964), pp. 145-89.

Klein, Maury. "The New Deal: End of a Beginning." <u>American History Illustrated</u> 8 (Oct. 1973): 18-27, 30-32.

Ladenburg, Thomas. "Teaching the Prosperity and the Depression Decades." <u>Social Studies</u> 56 (Dec. 1965): 266-71.

Leuchtenburg, William E. "The Great Depression." In <u>The Comparative Approach to American History</u> ed. by C. Vann Woodward (New York: Basic Books, 1968), pp. 296-314.

_____. "The New Deal and the Analogue of War." In <u>Change and Continuity in Twentieth-Century America</u> ed. by John Braeman, Robert H. Bremner, and Everett Walters (Columbus: Ohio State University Press, 1964), pp. 81-143.

_____. "The United States: Prosperity and Depression." In <u>The Columbia History of the World</u> ed. by John A. Garraty and Peter Gay (New York: Harper and Row, 1972), pp. 1005-21.

Lichtman, Allan J. "Critical Election Theory and the Reality of American Presidential Politics, 1916-1940." <u>American Historical Review</u> 81 (April 1976): 317-51.

Maxwell, Robert S. "The Progressive Bridge: Reform Sentiment in the United States between the New Freedom and the New Deal." <u>Indiana Magazine of History</u> 63 (June 1967): 83-102.

Meltzer, Milton. "Brother, Can You Spare a Dime?" <u>Illinois History</u> 23 (April 1970): 147-50.

Naison, Mark. "Great Depression: The Threads of a Lost Tradition." <u>Journal of Ethnic Studies</u> 1 (Fall 1973): 31-52.

Patterson, James T. "Comparative Welfare History: Britain & the United States, 1930-1945." In <u>The Roosevelt New Deal: A Program Assessment Fifty Years After</u> ed. by Wilbur J. Cohen (Austin: Lyndon B. Johnson School of Public Affairs, 1986), pp. 125-43.

_____. "Federalism in Crisis: A Comparative Study of Canada and the United States in the Depression of the 1930s." In <u>The Great Depression: Essays and Memoirs from Canada and the United States</u> ed. by Victor Hoar (Vancouver: Capp Clark, 1969), pp. 1-30.

Paxson, Frederic L. "The Highway Movement, 1916-1935." <u>American Historical Review</u> 51 (Jan. 1946): 236-53.

Phillips, William. "What Happened in the 30s?" <u>Commentary</u> 34 (Sept. 1962): 204-12.

Radosh, Ronald. "The Myth of the New Deal." In <u>A New History of Leviathan: Essays on the Rise of the American Corporate State</u> ed. by Ronald Radosh and Murray Rothbard (New York: E. P. Dutton, 1972), pp. 146-87.

Schlesinger, Arthur M., Jr. "His Rendezvous with History." <u>New Republic</u> 114 (April 15, 1946): 550-54.

_____. "Sources of the New Deal: Reflections on the Temper of a Time." <u>Columbia University Forum</u> 2 (Fall 1959): 4-7.

Sivachev, Nikolai. "The Rise of Statism in 1930s America: A Soviet View of the Social and Political Effects of the New Deal." <u>Labor History</u> 24 (Fall 1983): 500-25.

Sternsher, Bernard. "Assessing Roosevelt and the New Deal: The Short Run and the Long Run." In The New Deal Viewed from Fifty Years ed. by Lawrence E. Gelfand and Robert J. Neymeyer (Iowa City: Center for the Study of Recent History of the United States, 1983), pp. 91-106.

_____. "The New Deal 'Revolution'." Social Studies 57 (April 1966): 157-62.

Strauss, David. "The Roosevelt Revolution: French Observers and the New Deal." American Studies 14 (Fall 1973): 25-42.

Susman, Warren I. "The Thirties." In The Development of an American Culture ed. by Stanley Cohen and Norman Ratner (Englewood Cliffs, N.J.: Prentice-Hall, 1970), pp. 179-218.

Tugwell, Rexford G. "The New Deal in Retrospect." Western Political Quarterly 1 (Dec. 1948): 373-85.

_____. "The Protagonists: Roosevelt and Hoover." Antioch Review 13 (Winter 1953-54): 419-42.

Viereck, Peter. "A Third View of the New Deal." New Mexico Quarterly 26 (Spring 1956): 44-52.

Wilson, William . "The Two New Deals: A Valid Concept?" Historian 28 (Feb. 1966): 268-88.

Wright, Esmond. "The Roosevelt Revolution of 1933-38." History Today 12 (Dec. 1962): 821-32.

Dissertations

Benedict, Arthur H. "Federal Centralization Through Congressional Legislation, 1924-39." Ph.D diss., Ohio State University, 1948.

Lester, Robert Leon. "Developments in Presidential-Congressional Relations: Franklin D. Roosevelt-John F. Kennedy." Ph.D diss., University of Virginia, 1969.

Markham, Sara H. "Elusive Prosperity: Images of the United States Conveyed in Selected German Travel Literature, 1923-1933." Ph.D diss., University of Wisconsin, 1983.

Shinkawa, Kensaburo. "The Emergence of American 'State Capitalism,' 1913-1940." Ph.D diss., University of Maryland, 1968.

2

Bibliography & Historiography

Books

Burke, Robert E., and Richard Lowitt, eds. The New Era and the New Deal, 1920-1940. Arlington Heights, Ill.: Harlan Davidson, 1981.

Dexter, Byron, ed. The Foreign Affairs 50-Year Bibliography: New Evaluations of Significant Books on International Relations, 1920-1970. New York: R. R. Bowker, 1972.

Doenecke, Justus D. The Literature of Isolationism: A Guide to Non-Interventionist Research, 1930-1972. Colorado Springs: Ralph Myles, 1972.

Herzberg, Donald G., ed. The Relevancy of Public Works History: The 1930's--A Case Study. Washington, D.C.: Georgetown University Department of History, 1975.

McDean, Harry C., comp. A Preliminary List of References for the History of American Agriculture during the New Deal Period, 1932-1940. Davis, Cal.: University of California, 1968.

Neufeld, Maurice F. A Representative Bibliography of American Labor History. Ithaca: Cornell University Press, 1964.

Ontiveros, Suzanne Robitaille, ed. The Great Depression: A Historical Bibliography. Santa Barbara, Cal.: ABC-Clio, 1984.

Stewart, William J., ed. The Era of Franklin D. Roosevelt: A Selected Bibliography of Periodical, Essay, and Dissertation Literature, 1945-1971. Hyde Park, N.Y.: Franklin D. Roosevelt Library, 1971.

Stroud, Gene S., and Gilbert E. Donahue. Labor History in the United States: A General Bibliography. Urbana: University of Illinois Press, 1961.

Woolbert, Robert Gale, ed. Foreign Affairs Bibliography: A Selected and Annotated List of Books on International Relations, 1932-1942. New York: Harper, 1945.

Articles

Auerbach, Jerold S. "New Deal, Old Deal, or Raw Deal: Some Thoughts on New
    Left Historiography." Journal of Southern History 35 (Feb. 1969): 18-30.
Bellush, Jewel. "Old and New Left Reappraisals of the New Deal and Roosevelt's
    Presidency." Presidential Studies Quarterly 9 (Summer 1979): 243-66.
Boles, John B. "Franklin D. Roosevelt and the New Deal: A Historiographical
    Survey." Southern Humanities Review 4 (Spring 1970): 163-77.
Bolt, Ernest C., Jr. "Isolation, Expansion, and Peace: American Foreign Policy
    Between the Wars." In American Foreign Relations: A Historiographical
    Review ed. by Gerald K. Haines and J. Samuel Walker (Westport, Conn.:
    Greenwood Press, 1981), pp. 133-157.
Bonner, Thomas, Jr. "A Bibliographical Introduction to the American Literature of the
    1930s and the Backgrounds." Bulletin of Bibliography and Magazine Notes 31
    (April-June 1974): 57-66.
Braeman, John. "The New Deal and the 'Broker State': A Review of the Recent
    Scholarly Literature." Business History Review 46 (Winter 1972): 409-2.
Chambers, Clarke A. "FDR, Pragmatist - Idealist: An Essay in Historiography."
    Pacific Northwest Quarterly 52 (April 1961): 50-55.
Cohen, Jacob. "Schlesinger and the New Deal." Dissent 8 (Autumn 1961): 461-72.
Cole, Wayne S. "American Entry into World War II: A Historiographical Appraisal."
    Mississippi Valley Historical Review 43 (March 1957): 595-617.
_____. "The United States in World Affairs, 1929-1941." In Interpreting and
    Teaching American History ed. by William H. Cartwright and Richard L.
    Watson, Jr. (Washington: National Council for the Social Studies, 1961), pp.
    282-95.
Dallek, Robert. "Franklin Roosevelt as World Leader: A Review Article." American
    Historical Review 76 (Dec. 1971): 1503-13.
Dodds, Gordon B. "Conservation and Reclamation in the Trans-Mississippi West: A
    Critical Bibliography." Arizona and the West 13 (Summer 1971): 143-71.
Doenecke, Justus D. "Beyond Polemics: An Historiographical Re-appraisal of
    American Entry into World War II." History Teacher 12 (Feb. 1979): 217-52.
_____. "Isolationists of the 1930's and 1940's: An Historiographical Essay." In
    American Diplomatic History: Issues and Methods ed. by R. Sellen and T.
    Bryson (Carrollton, Ga.: West Georgia College Studies in the Social Sciences,
    1974), pp. 5-40.
_____. "The Literature of Isolationism, 1972-1983: A Bibliogrpahical Guide."
    Journal of Libertarian Studies 7 (Spring 1983): 157-84.
Freidel, Frank. "The New Deal, 1929-1941." In Interpreting and Teaching American
    History ed. by William H. Cartwright and Richard L. Watson, Jr. (Washington:
    National Council for the Social Studies, 1961), pp. 264-81.
Graham, Hugh Davis. "The Enigma of Huey Long: An Essay Review." Journal of
    Southern History 36 (May 1970): 205-11.
Graham, Otis L., Jr. "Historians and the New Deal, 1944-1960." Social Studies 54
    (April 1963): 133-40.

_____. "New Deal Historiography: Retrospect and Prospect." In The New Deal: The Critical Issues ed by Otis L. Graham, Jr. (Boston: Little, Brown, 1971), pp. 171-79.

Isserman, Maurice. "Three Generations: Historians View American Communism." Labor History 26 (Fall 1985): 517-45.

Kirkendall, Richard S. "The New Deal as Watershed: The Recent Literature." Journal of American History 54 (March 1968): 839-52.

_____. "The New Deal for Agriculture: Recent Writings, 1971-76." In Farmers, Bureaucrats, and Middlemen: Historical Perspectives on American Agriculture ed. by Trudy Huskamp Peterson (Washington,D.C.: Howard University Press, 1980), pp. 296-308.

Lee, Bradford A. "The New Deal Reconsidered." Wilson Quarterly 6 (Spring 1982): 62-76.

Leuchtenburg, William E. "The Great Depression and the New Deal." In Interpreting American History: Conversations with Historians ed. by John A. Garraty (New York: Macmillan, 1970): II: 169-93.

Lowitt, Richard. "The New Deal: An Essay Review." Pacific Northwest Quarterly 68 (Jan. 1977): 25-30.

Lynn, Kenneth S. "Only Yesterday." American Scholar 49 (Autumn 1980): 513-18.

Malone, Michael P. "The New Deal and the West: A Review Essay." New Mexico Historical Review 59 (Oct. 1984): 415-18.

May, Ernest R. "Nazi Germany and the United States: A Review Essay." Journal of Modern History 41 (June 1969): 207-14.

McCoy, Donald R. "The Beginnings of the Franklin D. Roosevelt Library." Prologue 7 (Fall 1975): 137-50.

_____. "Trends in Viewing Herbert Hoover, Franklin D. Roosevelt, Harry S. Truman, and Dwight D. Eisenhower." Midwest Quarterly 20 (Winter 1979): 117-36.

McDean, Harry C. "Dust Bowl Historiography." Great Plains Quarterly 6 (Spring 1986): 117-26.

Mellon, Knox. "Historians' Perspectives on Depression-Time California." Pacific Historian 27 (Winter 1983): 48-49.

Melosh, Barbara. "Images of the 1930s." Reviews in American History 13 (Dec 1985): 494-99.

Moreau, John Adam. "Huey Long and His Chroniclers." Louisiana History 6 (Spring 1965): 121-39.

Morison, Samuel Eliot. "Did Roosevelt Start the War?: History Through a Beard." Atlantic Monthly 182 (Aug. 1948): 91-97.

Myers, Carol Fairbanks. "Supplement to 'A Bibliographical Introduction to the American Literature of the 1930's and the Backgrounds': Black American Literature." Bulletin of Bibliography and Magazine Notes 34 (April-June 1977): 68-72.

O'Brien, Patrick J., and Philip T. Rosen. "Hoover and the Historians: The Resurrection of a President, Part I." Annals of Iowa 46 (Summer 1981): 25-42.

_____. "Hoover and the Historians: The Resurrection of a President, Part II."
     Annals of Iowa 46 (Fall 1981): 83-99.
Peck, David R. "Salvaging the Art and Literature of the 1930's: A Bibliographic
     Essay." Centennial Review 20 (Spring 1976): 128-41.
_____. 'The Orgy of Apology': The Recent Reevaluation of Literature of the
     Thirties." Science and Society 32 (Fall 1968): 371-84.
Polenberg, Richard. "Historians and the Liberal Presidency: Recent Appraisals of
     Roosevelt and Truman." South Atlantic Quarterly 75 (Winter 1976): 20-35.
Pyron, Darden Asbury. "Making History: Gone with the Wind, A Bibliographical
     Essay." Atlanta Historical Journal 29 (Winter 1985-86): 226-35
Romasco, Albert U. "Hoover-Roosevelt and the Great Depression: A
     Historiographical Inquiry into a Perennial Comparison." In The New Deal: The
     National Level ed. by John Braeman, Robert H. Bremner, and David Brody
     (Columbus: Ohio State University Press, 1975): pp. 3-26.
Rosen, Elliot A. "Roosevelt and the Brains Trust: An Historiographical Overview."
     Political Science Quarterly 87 (Dec. 1972): 531-63.
Sternsher, Bernard. "Great Depression Labor Historiography since 1970: Middle-
     Range Questions, Ethnicultures, and Levels of Generalization." Reviews in
     American History 11 (June 1983): 300-19.
_____. "Tugwell's Appraisal of F.D.R." Western Political Quarterly 15 (March
     1962): 67-79.
Watson, Richard L., Jr. "Franklin Roosevelt in Historical Writing, 1950-57." South
     Atlantic Quarterly 57 (Winter 1958): 104-26.
Zieger, Robert H. "Toward the History of the CIO: A Bibliographical Report." Labor
     History 26 (Fall 1985): 487-516.

Dissertations

Hughes, Eloise A. Timmons. "The Great Depression: An Analysis of Selected High
     School Textbooks for United States History, 1939-1974." Ph.D. diss., University
     of Colorado, 1975.
Newell, William Dixon. "The Problem of American Entry into Twentieth Century
     World War: A Study in Conflicting Historiography." Ph.D. diss., University of
     Idaho, 1982.
Stoneman, William E. "A History of the Economic Analysis of the Great Depression
     in America." Ph.D. diss., Harvard University, 1970.

3

Participant Accounts

3.1 LETTERS AND DIARIES

Books

Asbell, Bernard, ed. Mother and Daughter: The Letters of Eleanor and Anna Roosevelt. New York: Coward, McCann, & Geoghegan, 1982.

Berle, Beatrice Bishop, and Travis Beal Jacobs, eds. Navigating the Rapids, 1918-1971: From the Papers of Adolph A. Berle. New York: Harcourt Brace Jovanovich, 1973.

Blum, John Morton. From the Morgenthau Diaries. 3 vols., Boston: Houghton Mifflin, 1959-67.

Bullitt, Orville H., ed. For the President, Personal and Secret: Correspondence between Franklin D. Roosevelt and William C. Bullitt. Boston: Houghton Mifflin, 1972.

Burke, Robert E., ed. The Diary Letters of Hiram Johnson, 1917-1945. New York: Garland, 1983.

Dodd, William E., Jr., and Martha. Ambassador Dodd's Diary, 1933-1938. New York: Harcourt, 1941.

Freedman, Max, ed. Roosevelt and Frankfurter: Their Correspondence, 1928-1945. Boston: Little, Brown, 1967.

Grant, H. Roger, and L. Edward Purcell, eds. Years of Struggle: The Farm Diary of Elmer G. Powers, 1931-1936. Ames: Iowa State University Press, 1976.

Hooker, Nancy Harvison, ed. The Moffat Papers: Selections from the Diplomatic Journals of Jay Pierrepont Moffat, 1919-1943. Cambridge: Harvard University Press, 1956.

Ickes, Harold L. The Secret Diary of Harold L. Ickes. 3 vols; New York: Simon & Shuster, 1953-54.

Johnson, Walter, ed. Selected Letters of William Allen White, 1899-1943. New York: H. Holt, 1947.

Kennan, George F. From Prague After Munich: Diplomatic Papers 1938-1940. Princeton: Princeton University Press, 1968.

Kimball, Warren F., ed. Churchill and Roosevelt: The Complete Correspondence. 3
    vols.; Princeton: Princeton University Press, 1984.
Kincaid, Diane D., ed. Silent Hattie Speaks: The Personal Journal of Senator Hattie
    Caraway. Westport, Conn.: Greenwood, 1979.
Lash, Joseph P., ed. From the Diaries of Felix Frankfurter. New York: W. W. Norton,
    1975.
Lawrence, David. Diary of a Washington Correspondent. New York: H. C. Kensey,
    1942.
Lilienthal, David E. The Journals of David E. Lilienthal: The TVA Years, 1939-1945.
    New York: Harper & Row, 1964.
Lindbergh, Charles A. The Wartime Journals of Charles A. Lindbergh, 1937-1945.
    New York: Harcourt, Brace, Jovanovich, 1970.
Low, Ann Marie. Dust Bowl Diary. Lincoln: University of Nebraska Press, 1984.
Lowitt, Richard, ed. Journal of a Tamed Bureaucrat: Nils A. Olsen and the BAE,
    1925-1935. Ames: Iowa State University Press, 1980.
_____ and Maurine Beasley, eds. One Third of a Nation: Lorena Hickok
    Reports on the Great Depression. Urbana: University of Illinois Press, 1981.
McElvaine, Robert S. Down and Out in the Great Depression: Letters from the
    "Forgotten" Man. Chapel Hill: University of North Carolina Press, 1983.
Roosevelt, Elliott, ed. F.D.R., His Personal Letters. 4 vols.; New York: Duell, Sloan &
    Pearce, 1947-50.
Sparks, George F., ed. A Many-Colored Toga: The Diary of Henry Fountain Ashurst.
    Tuscon: University of Arizona Press, 1962.

Articles

Bauman, John F., and Thomas H. Coode. "Depression Report: A New Dealer Tours
    Eastern Pennsylvania." Pennsylvania Magazine of History and Biography 104
    (Jan. 1980): 96-109.
Beasley, Maurine Hoffman. "Lorena Hickok to Harry Hopkins, 1933: A Woman
    Reporter Views Prairie Hard Times." Montana: The Magazine of Western
    History 32 (Spring 1982): 58-66.
Beddow, James B. "Depression and the New Deal: Letters from the Plains." Kansas
    Historical Quarterly 43 (Summer 1977): 140-53.
Blackwelder, Julia Kirk. "Letters from the Great Depression: A Tour through a
    Collection of Letters to an Atlanta Newspaperwoman." Southern Exposure 6
    (Fall 1978): 73-77.
Freidel, Frank. "Are There Too Many New Deal Diaries?" American Heritage 6
    (April 1955): 109-12.
Gallagher, Kevin J. "The President as Local Historian: The Letters of F.D.R. to Helen
    Wilkinson Reynolds." New York History 64 (April 1983): 137-70.
Gaydowski, J. D., ed. "Eight Letters to the Editor: The Genesis of the Townsend
    National Recovery Plan." Southern California Quarterly 52 (Dec. 1970): 365-
    82.

Grant, H. Roger, and L. Edward Purcell, eds. "A Year of Struggle: Excerpts from a Farmer's Diary, 1936." Palimpest 57 (Jan. 1976): 14-29.

_____ eds. "Implementing the AAA's Corn-Hog Program: An Iowa Farmer's Account." Annals of Iowa 43 (Fall 1976): 430-528.

Hurt, R. Douglas. "Letters From the Dust Bowl." Panhandle-Plains Historical Review 52 (1979): 1-13.

Morgenthau, Henry. "The Morganthau Diaries." Collier's 120 (Oct. 4, 1947): 20-21, 45, 48-49; (Oct. 11, 1947): 20-21, 72-79; (Oct. 18, 1947): 16-17, 71-75; (Oct. 25, 1947): 24-25, 83-86.

Phillips, Waite, and Clifford E. Trafzer. "Views from the Red River Valley: A 'Liberal' Republican's Philosophy." Red River Valley Historical Review 1 (Spring 1974): 70-77.

Schmidt, William T., ed. "Letters to their President: Mississippians to Franklin D. Roosevelt, 1932-1933." Journal of Mississippi History 40 (Aug. 1978): 231-52.

Shover, John L., ed. "Depression Letters from American Farmers." Agricultural History 36 (July 1962): 163-68.

Sletten, Harvey, ed. "'Having the Time of My Life': Letters from a Wanderer, 1930-1932." North Dakota History 46 (Spring 1979): 14-21.

3.2   PUBLIC STATEMENTS AND SPEECHES

Books

Beasley, Maurine, ed. The White House Press Conference of Eleanor Roosevelt. New York: Garland, 1983.

Dewey, Thomas E. The Case Against the New Deal. New York: Harper, 1940.

Douglas, Lewis W. The Liberal Tradition: A Free People and a Free Economy. New York: D. Van Nostrand, 1935.

Hoover, Herbert C. Addresses upon the American Road, 1933-1938. New York: Scribners, 1938.

_____. Addresses upon the American Road, 1940-1941. New York: Scribners, 1941.

_____. Further Addresses upon the American Road, 1938-1940. New York: Scribners, 1940.

_____. The Challenge to Liberty. New York: Scribners, 1934.

_____. The New Day: Campaign Speeches of Herbert Hoover, 1928. Stanford: Stanford University Press, 1928.

Landon, Alfred M. America at the Crossroads. New York: Dodge, 1971.

Lippmann, Walter. Interpretations, 1931-1932. New York: Macmillan, 1932.

_____. Interpretations, 1933-1935. New York: Macmillan, 1936.

Myers, William Starr, ed. The State Papers and Other Public Writings of Herbert Hoover. Garden City, N.Y.: Doubleday, Doran, 1934.

Nixon, Edgar B., ed. Franklin D. Roosevelt and Conservation, 1911-1945. 2 vols.;
    Hyde Park: National Archives, 1957.
_____, ed. Franklin D. Roosevelt and Foreign Affairs. Vols. 1-3; Cambridge:
    Harvard University Press, 1969.
Roosevelt, Franklin D. Complete Presidential Press Conferences of Franklin D.
    Roosevelt. 25 vols.; New York: DaCapo Press, 1972.
_____. The Public Papers of Franklin D. Roosevelt, Forty-Eighth Governor of
    the State of New York. Albany, N.Y.: J. B. Lyon, 1930-39.
Rosenman, Samuel I., ed. The Public Papers and Addresses of Franklin D. Roosevelt.
    13 vols.; New York: Random House and others, 1938-50.
Schewe, Donald B., ed. Franklin D. Roosevelt and Foreign Affairs. Vols. 4-16; New
    York: Clearwater, 1979.
Seligman, Lester G., and Elmer E. Cornwall, eds. New Deal Mosiac: Roosevelt
    Confers with his National Emergency Council, 1933- 1936. Eugene: University
    of Oregon Books, 1965.
Christman, Henry M., ed. Kingfish to America, Share Our Wealth: Selected Senatorial
    Papers of Huey P. Long. New York: Schocken, 1985.
Douglas, William O. Democracy and Finance: The Addresses and Public Statements
    of William O. Douglas as Member and Chairman of the Securities and Exhange
    Commission. New Haven: Yale University Press, 1940.

Article

Morrison, Allan. "The Secret Papers of FDR." Negro Digest 9 (Jan. 1951): 3-13.

3.3   MEMOIRS AND AUTOBIOGRAPHIES

Books

Aaron, Daniel, and Robert Bendiner, eds. The Strenuous Decade: A Social and
    Intellectual Record of the 1930s. Garden City, N.Y.: Doubleday, 1970.
Acheson, Dean. Morning and Noon. Boston: Houghton Mifflin, 1965.
Adamic, Louis. My America, 1928-1938. New York: Harper, 1938.
Arnold, Thurman. Fair Fights and Foul. New York: Harcourt, Brace and World, 1965.
Asbell, Bernard. The FDR Memoirs. Garden City, N. Y.: Doubleday, 1973.
Banks, Ann, ed. First-Person America. New York: Knopf, 1980.
Barkley, Alben W. That Reminds Me. Garden City, N.Y.: Doubleday, 1954.
Baruch, Bernard M. Baruch. 2 vols.; New York: Henry Holt, 1957-60.
Berle, Adolph A., Jr. Power. New York: Harcourt, Brace & World, 1969.
Biddle, Francis B. In Brief Authority. Garden City, N.Y.: Doubleday, 1962.
Bowers, Claude G. My Life: The Memoirs of Claude G. Bowers. New York: Simon
    and Schuster, 1962.

_____. My Mission to Spain: Watching the Rehearsal for World War II. London: Victor Gallancz, 1954.

Brownlow, Louis. A Passion for Anonymity: The Autobiography of Louis Brownlow. Chicago: University of Chicago Press, 1958.

_____. A Passion for Politics: The Autobiography of Louis Brownlow. Chicago: University of Chicago Press, 1955.

Byrnes, James F. All in One Lifetime. New York: Harper, 1958.

Churchill, Winston. The Grand Alliance. Boston: Houghton Mifflin, 1951.

Congdon, Don, ed. The Thirties: A Time to Remember. New York: Simon & Schuster, 1962.

Connally, Thomas T., as told to Alfred Steinberg. My Name is Tom Connally. New York: Crowell, 1954.

Cox, James M. Journey through My Years. New York: Simon & Schuster, 1946.

Creel, George. Rebel at Large: Recollections of Fifty Crowded Years. New York: G. P. Putnam's Sons, 1947.

Cross, Wilbur. Connecticut Yankee: An Autobiography. New Haven: Yale University Press, 1943.

Danelski, David J., and Joseph S. Tulchin, eds. The Autobiographical Notes of Charles Evans Hughes. Cambridge: Harvard University Press, 1973.

Daniels, Josephus. Shirt-Sleeve Diplomat. Chapel Hill: University of North Carolina Press, 1947.

Davies, Joseph E. Mission to Moscow. New York: Simon & Schuster, 1941.

Douglas, Helen Gahagan. A Full Life. Garden City, N. Y.: Doubleday, 1982.

Douglas, William O. Go East, Young Man: The Early Years. New York: Random House, 1974.

_____. The Court Years, 1939-1975: The Autobiography of William O. Douglas. New York: Random House, 1980.

Eccles, Marriner S. Beckoning Frontiers: Public and Personal Recollections. New York: Knopf, 1951.

Farley, James A. Behind the Ballots: The Personal History of a Politician. New York: Harcourt, Brace, 1938.

_____. Jim Farley's Story: The Roosevelt Years. New York: Whittlesey House, 1948.

Feis, Herbert. Seen from E.A.: Three International Episodes. New York: Knopf, 1947.

Filler, Louis, ed. The Anxious Years: America in the 1930s, A Collection of Contemporary Writings. New York: Putnam, 1963.

Flynn, Edward J. You're the Boss. New York: Viking, 1947.

Grew, Joseph C. Turbulent Era: A Diplomatic Record of Forty Years, 1904-1945. Boston: Houghton Mifflin, 1952.

Guffey, Joseph F. Seventy Years on the Red Fire Wagon: From Tilden to Truman through New Freedom and New Deal. Lebanon, Pa.: 1952.

Hastings, Robert J. A Nickel's Worth of Skim Milk: A Boy's View of the Great Depression. Carbondale: University Graphics and Publications, Southern Illinois University at Carbondale, 1972.

_____. A Penny's Worth of Minced Ham: Another Look at the Great Depression. Carbondale: Southern Illinois University Press, 1986.

Hoover, Herbert C. Memoirs. 3 vols.; New York: Macmillan, 1951-52.

Hopkins, Harry L. Spending to Save: The Complete Story of Relief Policy. New York: W.W. Norton, 1936.

Hull, Cordell. The Memoirs of Cordell Hull. 2 vols.; New York: Macmillan, 1948.

Ickes, Harold L. The Autobiography of a Curmudgeon. New York: Reynal & Hitchcock, 1943.

Johnson, Hugh S. The Blue Eagle, from Egg to Earth. Garden City, N.Y.: Doubleday, Doran, 1935.

Jones, Jesse H., with Edward Augly. Fifty Billion Dollars: My Thirteen Years with the R.F.C., 1932-1945. New York: Macmillan, 1951.

Josephson, Matthew. Infidel in the Temple: A Memoir of the Nineteen-Thirties. New York: Knopf, 1967.

Kazin, Alfred. Starting Out in the Thirties. Boston: Little, Brown, 1965.

Kennan, George F. Memoirs, 1925-1950. Boston: Little, Brown, 1967.

Kimmel, Husband E. Admiral Kimmel's Story. Chicago: Regnery, 1955.

Krock, Arthur. In the Nation: 1932-1966. New York: McGraw-Hill, 1966.

Lilienthal, David E. TVA: Democracy on the March. New York: Harper, 1944.

Louchheim, Katie, ed. The Making of the New Deal: The Insiders Speak. Cambridge: Harvard University Press, 1983.

Martin, Joseph. My First Fifty Years in Politics. New York: McGraw-Hill, 1960.

Mason, Lucy Randolph. To Win These Rights: A Personal Story of the CIO in the South. New York: Harper, 1952.

McIntire, Ross T. White House Physician. New York: G.P. Putnam's Sons, 1946.

Michelson, Charles. The Ghost Talks. New York: G. P. Putnam's Sons, 1944.

Moley, Raymond. After Seven Years. New York: Harper, 1939.

Norris, George W. Fighting Liberal: The Autobiography of George W. Norris. New York: Macmillan, 1945.

O'Connor, Francis V., ed. The New Deal Arts Projects: An Anthology of Memoirs. Washington, D.C.: Smithsonian Institution, 1972.

O'Connor, J.F.T. The Banking Crisis and Recovery under the Roosevelt Administration. Chicago: Callaghan, 1938.

Patterson, Haywood, and Earl Conrad. Scottsboro Boy. Garden City, N.Y.: Doubleday, 1950.

Perkins, Frances. The Roosevelt I Knew. New York: Viking, 1946.

Philips, Harlan B. Felix Frankfurter Reminisces. New York: Reynal, 1960.

Phillips, William. Ventures in Diplomacy. Boston: Beacon, 1953.

Reuther, Victor G. The Brothers Reuther and the Story of the UAW: A Memoir. Boston: Houghton Mifflin, 1976.

Richardson, James O. On the Treadmill to Pearl Harbor: The Memoirs of Admiral James O. Richardson as Told to George C. Dyer. Washington, D.C.: Navel History Division, Department of the Navy, 1973.

Richberg, Donald. The Rainbow: After the Sunshine of Prosperity, the Deluge of the Depression, the Rainbow of the NRA. What Have We Learned? Where Are We Going? Garden City: Doubleday, Doran, 1936.

_____. My Hero: The Indiscreet Memoirs of an Eventful but Unheroic Life. New York: Putnam, 1954.

Roosevelt, Eleanor. This I Remember. New York: Harper, 1949.

_____. This Is My Story. New York: Harper, 1937.

Roosevelt, Elliott. A Rendezvous with Destiny: The Roosevelts of the White House. New York: Putnam, 1975.

_____. As He Saw It. New York: Duell, Sloan & Pearce, 1946.

_____ and James Brough. An Untold Story: The Roosevelts of Hyde Park. New York: Putnam, 1973.

_____ and James Brough. Mother R.: Eleanor Roosevelt's Untold Story. New York: Putnam, 1977.

Roosevelt, James, and Sidney Shalett. Affectionately, F.D.R.: A Son's Story of a Lonely Man. New York: Harcourt Brace, 1959.

_____. My Parents: A Differing View. Chicago: Playboy Press, 1976.

Roper, Daniel C. Fifty Years of Public Life. Durham, N.C.: Duke University Press, 1941.

Rosenman, Samuel I. Working with Roosevelt. New York: Harper, 1952.

_____ and Dorothy R. Rosenman. Presidential Style: Some Giants and a Pygmy in the White House. New York: Harper & Row, 1976.

Simon, Rita J., ed. As We Saw the Thirties: Essays on Social and Political Movements of a Decade. Urbana: University of Illinois Press, 1967.

Sinclair, Upton. Autobiography. New York: Harcourt, Brace, & World, 1962.

_____. I, Candidate for Governor: And How I Got Licked. Pasadena, Cal.: By the author, 1935.

Stimson, Henry L. The Far Eastern Crisis: Recollections and Observations. New York: Harper, 1936.

Svobida, Lawrence. Farming the Dust Bowl: A First-Hand Account from Kansas. Lawrence: University Press of Kansas, 1986.

Terrill, Tom E., and Jerrold Hirsch. Such As Us: Southern Voices of the Thirties. Chapel Hill: University of North Carolina Press, 1978.

Townsend, Francis E. New Horizons: An Autobiography. Chicago: J. L. Stewart, 1943.

Tugwell, Rexford G. Roosevelt's Revolution: The First Year, A Personal Perspective. New York: Macmillan, 1977.

_____. The Battle for Democracy. New York: Columbia University Press, 1935.

_____. The Brains Trust. New York: Viking, 1968.

_____. The Industrial Discipline and the Governmental Arts. New York: Columbia University Press, 1933.

Tully, Grace G.. FDR: My Boss. New York: Charles Scribner's Sons, 1949.

Turkel, Studs. Hard Times: An Oral History of the Great Depression. New York: Pantheon, 1970.

Warburg, James P. The Long Road Home: The Autobiography of a Maverick.
    Garden City, N.Y.: Doubleday, 1964.
Watson, James E. As I Knew Them: Memoirs of James Watson, Former United
    States Senator from Indiana. New York: Bobbs-Merrill, 1936.
Welles, Sumner. Seven Decisions That Shaped History. New York: Harper, 1951.
    _____. The Time for Decision. New York: Harper, 1944.
Wheeler, Burton K., and Paul F. Healey. Yankee from the West: The Candid,
    Turbulent Life Story of the Yankee-Born U. S. Senator from Montana. Garden
    City, N. Y.: Doubleday, 1962.
White, William Allen. The Autobiography of William Allen White. New York:
    Macmillan, 1946.
Wilson, Edmund. The American Earthquake: A Documentary of the Twenties and
    Thirties. Garden City, N.Y.: Doubleday, 1958.
    _____. The American Jitters: A Year of the Slump. New York: Scribner's,
    1932.
Winant, John Gilbert. Letter from Grosvenor Square: An Account of a Stewardship.
    Boston: Houghton Mifflin, 1947.
Yezierska, Anzia. Red Ribbon on a White Horse. New York: Scribner's, 1950.
Zinn, Howard, ed. New Deal Thought. Indianapolis: Bobbs-Merrill, 1966.

Articles

Aaron, Daniel, Malcolm Cowley, Kenneth Burke, Granville Hicks, and William Phillips.
    "Thirty Years Later: Memories of the First American Writers' Congress."
    American Scholar 35 (Summer 1966): 495-516.
Ajay, Abe. "Working for the WPA." Art in America 60 (Sept.-Oct. 1972): 70-75.
Bellow, Saul. "Starting Out in Chicago." American Scholar 44 (Winter 1974/75): 71-
    77.
Bethune, Mary McLeod. "My Secret Talks with FDR." Ebony 4 (April 1949): 42-51.
Brennell, Helen E. "Depression Memories." Utah Historical Quarterly 54 (Summer
    1986): 265-67.
Browder, Earl. "The American Communist Party in the Thirties." In As We Saw the
    Thirties: Essays on Social and Political Movements of a Decade ed. by Rita
    James Simon (Urbana: University of Illinois Press, 1967), pp. 216-53.
Carstensen, Vernon. "The Good Old Days or the Bad Old Days?: History and Related
    Muses in the Northwest in the 1930s." Pacific Northwest Quarterly 68 (July
    1977): 105-11.
Cohen,Wilbur J. "FDR and the New Deal: A Personal Reminiscence." Milwaukee
    History 6 (Autumn 1983): 70-82.
Corcoran, Thomas G. "Political Leadership and the Roosevelt Presidency." In
    Portraits of American Presidents: The Roosevelt Presidency ed. by Kenneth W.
    Thompson (New York: University Press of America, 1982), pp. 21-42.
Currie, Lauchlin. "Comments and Observations." History of Political Economy 10
    (Winter 1978): 541-48.

Douglas, William O. "When Justice Douglas Taught at Yale." Yale Alumni Magazine 38 (1974): 321-33.

Draper, Hal. "The Student Movement of the Thirties: A Political History." In As We Saw the Thirties: Essays on Social and Political Movements of a Decade ed. by Rita James Simon (Urbana: University of Illinois Press, 1967), pp. 151-89.

Duram, James C. "Algernon Lee's Correspondence with Karl Kautsky: An Old Guard Perspective on the Failure of American Socialism." Labor History 20 (Summer 1979): 420-34.

Frankfurter, Felix. "Remarks at the Graveside of Franklin D. Roosevelt, Hyde Park, Memorial Day, 1956." Centennial Review 9 (Spring 1965): 156-59.

Gurewitsch, Edna P. "Remembering Mrs. Roosevelt: An Intimate Memoir." American Heritage 33 (Dec. 1981): 10-18.

Hearst, James. "We All Worked Together: A Memory of Drought and Depression." Palimpsest 59 (May/June 1978): 66-76.

Hicks, Granville. "Writers in the Thirties." In As We Saw the Thirties: Essays on Social and Political Movements of a Decade ed. by Rita James Simon (Urbana: University of Illinois Press, 1967), pp. 76-101.

Hoover, Herbert. "My White House Years: The Great Depression." Collier's 119 (May 17, 1952): 36.

Kazin, Alfred. "The Bitter 30's: From a Personal History." Atlantic Monthly 209 (May 1962): 82-99.

Kuhn, Cliff. "Reminiscences: Interviews with Atlanta New Deal Social Workers." Atlanta Historical Journal 30 (Spring 1986): 107-16.

Laning, Edward "Memoirs of a WPA Painter." American Heritage 21 (Oct. 1967): 38-57, 86-89.

McCloud, Emma Gudger. "'So I Sung to Myself.'" Southern Exposure 7 (Spring 1979): 18-26.

McLaughlin, Doris B. "Putting Michigan Back to Work: Bill Haber Remembers the 1930s." Michigan History 66 (Jan. 1982): 30-37.

Muste, A. J. "My Experiences in the Labor and Radical Struggles of the Thirties." In As We Saw the Thirties: Essays on Social and Political Movements of a Decade ed. by Rita James Simon (Urbana: University of Illinois Press, 1967), pp. 123-50.

Nass, David L., ed. "Recollections of Rural Revolt." Minnesota History 44 (Winter 1975): 304-8.

Purdy, Virginia C., ed. "'Dust to Eat': A Document from the Dust Bowl." Chronicles of Oklahoma 58 (Winter 1980-81): 440-54

Roosevelt, Franklin D., Jr. "The Roosevelt Legacy." In Portraits of American Presidents: The Roosevelt Presidency ed. by Kenneth W. Thompson (New York: University Press of America, 1982), pp. 43-63.

Roosevelt, James. "Staffing My Father's Presidency: A Personal Reminiscence." Presidential Studies Quarterly 12 (Winter 1982): 48-49.

Rowe, James H., Jr. "Presidents I Have Known." In Portraits of American Presidents: The Roosevelt Presidency ed. by Kenneth W. Thompson (New York: University Press of America, 1982), pp. 1-19.

Schlatter, Richard. "On Being a Communist at Harvard." Partisan Review 44 (No. 4, 1977): 605-15.

Sepmeier, Emma Jane McKee. "Reminiscences of Life in Sheffield, Alabama, 1931-1934." Journal of Muscle Shoals History 5 (1977): 112-19.

Schactman, Max. "Radicalism in the Thirties: The Trotskyist View." In As We Saw the Thirties: Essays on Social and Political Movements of a Decade ed. by Rita James Simon (Urbana: University of Illinois Press, 1967), pp. 8-45.

Shirer, William L. "To Bring You the Picture of Europe Tonight." American Heritage 35 (June 1984): 65-80.

Smith, Gerald L. K. "The Huey Long Movement." In As We Saw the Thirties: Essays on Social and Political Movements of a Decade ed. by Rita James Simon (Urbana: University of Illinois Press, 1967), pp. 46-75.

Smith, John I. "Reminiscences of Farming and Business in the Depression, 1929-1933." Arkansas Historical Quarterly 65 (Winter 1986): 321-29.

Sprunk, Larry J. "Al J. Vohs--Williston." North Dakota History 44 (Fall 1977): 41-44.

_____. "Charlie Juma, Sr.--Stanley." North Dakota History 44 (Fall 1977): 66-67.

_____. "Gilbert and Pearl Wick--Robinson." North Dakota History 44 (Fall 1977): 59-65.

_____. "Hugh O'Connor--New Rockford." North Dakota History 44 (Fall 1977): 46-50.

_____. "Rueben P. Taralseth--Metigoshe." North Dakota History 44 (Fall 1977): 55-57.

Taussig, Joseph K., Jr. "I Remember Pearl Harbor." U.S. Naval Institute Proceedings 98 (Dec. 1972): 18-24.

Thomas, Norman. "The Thirties in America as a Socialist Recalls Them." In As We Saw the Thirties: Essays on Social and Political Movements of a Decade ed. by Rita James Simon (Urbana: University of Illinois Press, 1967), pp. 102-22.

Trilling, Lionel. "Young in the Thirties." Commentary 41 (May 1966): 43-51.

Wheeler, Burton K. "My Years with Roosevelt." In As We Saw the Thirties: Essays on Social and Political Movements of a Decade ed. by Rita James Simon (Urbana: University of Illinois Press, 1967), pp. 190-215.

White, Mary. "Mary White: Autobiography of an Ohio First Lady." Ohio History 82 (Winter-Spring 1973): 63-87.

Wright, Richard. "With Black Radicals in Chicago." Dissent 24 (Spring 1977): 156-61.

4

Biographies

ALEXANDER, WILL

Dykeman, Wilma, and James Stokely. <u>Seeds of Southern Change: The Life of Will Alexander</u>. Chicago: Harvard University Press, 1962.

AMLIE, THOMAS

Weiss, Stuart L. "Thomas Amlie and the New Deal." <u>Mid-America</u> 59 (Jan. 1977): 19-38.

BAILEY, JOSIAH WILLIAM

Moore, John Robert. "Josiah W. Bailey of North Carolina and the New Deal, 1931-1941." Ph.D. diss., Duke University, 1962.
_____. <u>Senator Josiah William Bailey of North Carolina: A Political Biography</u>. Ann Arbor: Books on Demand UMI, 1968.

BAKER, NEWTON D.

Cramer, C. H. <u>Newton D. Baker: A Biography</u>. Cleveland: World, 1961.

BANKHEAD, WILLIAM B.

Heacock, Walter J. "William B. Bankhead and the New Deal." <u>Journal of Southern History</u> 21 (Aug. 1955): 347-59.

BARKLEY, ALBEN W.

Davis, Polly Ann. Alben W. Barkley: Senate Majority Leader and Vice President. New York: Garland, 1979.

BARUCH, BERNARD

Coit, Margaret L. Mr. Baruch. Boston: Houghton Mifflin, 1957.

Grant, James. Bernard M. Baruch: The Adventures of a Wall Street Legend. New York: Simon & Schuster, 1983.

Schwarz, Jordan A. "Bernard Baruch and the Vocation of Presidential Adviser." In The Roosevelt New Deal: A Program Assessment Fifty Years After ed. by Wilbur J. Cohen (Austin: Lyndon B. Johnson School of Public Affairs, 1986), pp. 269-80.

_____. The Speculator: Bernard Baruch in Washington, 1917-1965. Chapel Hill: University of North Carolina Press, 1981.

BECK, JAMES M.

Keller, Morton. In Defense of Yesterday: James M. Beck and the Politics of Conservatism, 1861-1936. New York: Coward-McCann, 1958.

BERLE, ADOLPH A., JR.

Kirkendall, Richard S. "A. A. Berle, Jr., Student of the Corporation, 1917-1932." Business History Review 35 (Spring 1961): 43-58.

BETHUNE, MARY MCLEOD

Holt, Rackham. Mary McLeod Bethune: A Biography. Garden City, N. Y.: Doubleday, 1964.

Leffall, Dolores D., and Janet L. Sims. "Mary McLeod Bethune--The Educator; Also including a Selected Annotated Bibliography." Journal of Negro Education 45 (Summer 1976): 342-59.

Smith, Elaine M. "Mary McLeod Bethune." In Notable American Women: The Modern Period ed. by Barbara Sicherman and Carol Hurd Green (Cambridge: Harvard University Press, 1980), pp. 76-80.

BILBO, THEODORE G.

Giroux, Vincent Arthur, Jr. "Theodore G. Bilbo: Progressive to Public Racist." Ph.D. diss., Indiana University, 1984.

Green, A. Wigfall. The Man Bilbo. Baton Rouge: Louisiana State University Press, 1963.

Morgan, Chester Monroe. "Demagogue or Democrat: Theodore G. Bilbo and the New Deal." Ph.D. diss., Memphis State University, 1982.

_____. Redneck Liberal: Theodore G. Bilbo and the New Deal. Baton Rouge: Louisiana State University Press, 1985.

BLACK, HUGO

Ball, Howard. The Vision and the Dream of Justice Hugo L. Black: An Examination of a Judicial Philosophy. University: University of Alabama Press, 1975.

Black, Hugo, Jr. My Father: A Remembrance. New York: Random House, 1975.

Dunne, Gerald T. Hugo Black and the Judicial Revolution. New York: Simon and Schuster, 1977.

Frank, John Paul. Mr. Justice Black: The Man and His Opinions. New York: Knopf, 1948.

Hamilton, Virginia Van Der Veer. Hugo Black: The Alabama Years. Baton Rouge: Louisiana State University Press, 1972.

Magee, James J. Mr. Justice Black: Absolutionist on the Court. Charlottesville: University of Virginia Press, 1980.

Van Der Veer, Virginia "Hugo Black and the KKK." American Heritage 19 (April 1968): 62-64, 108-11.

Williams, Charlotte. Hugo L. Black: A Study in the Judicial Process. Baltimore: Johns Hopkins University Press, 1950.

BORAH, WILLIAM

Cooper, John Milton, Jr. "William E. Borah, Political Thespian." Pacific Northwest Quarterly 56 (Oct. 1965): 145-58.

Johnson, Claudius O. Borah of Idaho. New York Longmans Green, 1936.

McKenna, Marian. Borah. Ann Arbor: University of Michigan Press, 1961.

Pinckney, Orde S. "William E. Borah and the Republican Party, 1932-1940." Ph.D. diss., University of California, Berkeley, 1957.

BRANDEIS, LOUIS

Lief, Alfred. Brandeis: The Personal History of an American Ideal. New York: Stackpole, 1936.

Mason, Alpheus T. Brandeis: A Free Man's Life. New York: Viking, 1946.
Paper, Lewis J. Brandeis. Englewood Cliffs, N. J.: Prentice-Hall, 1983.
Strum, Philippa. Louis D. Brandeis: Justice for the People. Cambridge: Harvard
     University Press, 1984.
Urofsky, Melvin I. A Mind of One Piece: Brandeis and American Reform. New
     York: Scribner's, 1971.
_____. Louis Brandeis and the Progressive Tradition. Boston: Little, Brown,
     1981.

BROWDER, EARL

Rosenberg, Roger E. "Guardian of the Fortress: A Biography of Earl Russell
     Browder, U.S. Communist Party General-Secretary from 1930-1944." Ph.D.
     diss., University of California, Santa Barbara, 1982.

BYRNS, JOSEPH W.

Galloway, J. M. "Speaker Joseph W. Byrns: Party Leader in the New Deal."
     Tennessee Historical Quarterly 25 (Spring 1966): 63-76.

CALLAHAN, PATRICK HENRY

Ellis, William E. "Patrick Henry Callahan: A Kentucky Democrat in National Politics."
     Filson Club History Quarterly 51 (Jan. 1977): 17-30.

CAPPER, ARTHUR

Socolofsky, Homer E. Arthur Capper: Publisher, Politican, and Philanthropist.
     Lawrence: University of Kansas Press, 1962.

CARDOZO, BENJAMIN N.

Hellman, George S. Benjamin N. Cardoza: American Judge. New York: McGraw-
     Hill, 1940.
Pollard, Joseph Percival. Mr. Justice Cardozo: A Liberal Mind in Action. Westport,
     Conn.: Greenwood, 1970.

CERMAK, ANTON

Gottfried, Alex. <u>Boss Cermak of Chicago: A Study of Political Leadership</u>. Seattle: University of Washington Press, 1962.

CHANDLER, WALTER

Coode, Thomas H. "Walter Chandler as Congressman." <u>West Tennessee Historical Society Papers</u> 29 (1975): 25-37.

CLARK, GRENVILLE

Dunne, Gerald T. <u>Grenville Clark: Public Citizen</u>. New York: Farrar, Straus & Giroux, 1985.

CONNALLY, TOM

Smyrl, Frank H. "Tom Connally and the New Deal." Ph.D. diss., University of Oklahoma, 1968.

CONWAY, MICHAEL P.

Dileva, Frank D. "Iowa's Biggest Politician." <u>Annals of Iowa</u> 41 (Spring 1973): 1258-72.

COOKE, MORRIS LLEWELLYN

Christie, Jean. <u>Morris Llewellyn Cooke, Progressive Engineer</u>. New York: Garland, 1983.

Trombley, Kenneth E. <u>The Life and Times of a Happy Liberal: A Biography of Morris Llewellyn Cooke</u>. New York: Harper, 1954.

CORCORAN, THOMAS G.

Niznik, Monica Lynne. "Thomas G. Corcoran: The Public Service of Franklin Roosevelt's 'Tommy The Cork'." Ph.D. diss., University of Notre Dame, 1981.

COUGLIN, CHARLES

Marcus, Sheldon. Father Coughlin: The Tumultuous Life of the Priest of the Little Flower. Boston: Little, Brown, 1973.

COUZENS, JAMES

Barnard, Harry. Independent Man: The Life of Senator James Couzens. New York: Scribner, 1958.

CROSS, WILBUR

Woodbury, Robert L. "Wilbur Cross: New Deal Ambassador to a Yankee Culture." New England Quarterly 41 (Sept. 1968): 323-40.

CROWLEY, LEO T.

Weiss, Stuart. "Leo T. Crowley: Pragmatic New Dealer." Mid-America 64 (Jan. 1982): 33-52.

CURLEY, JAMES MICHAEL

Dinneen, Joseph F. The Purple Shamrock: The Hon. James Michael Curley of Boston. New York: W. W. Norton, 1949.

CURTIS, CHARLES

Ewy, Marvin. "Charles Curtis of Kansas: Vice President of the United States, 1929-1933." Emporia State Research Studies 10 (1961): 5-58.

DANCY, JOHN C.

Pollock, Bradley H. "John C. Dancy, The Depression and the New Deal." UCLA History Journal 5 (1984): 5-23.

DANIELS, JOSEPHUS

Kilpatrick, Carroll, ed. Roosevelt and Daniels: A Friendship in Politics. Chapel Hill: University of North Carolina Press, 1952.

Morrison, Joseph L. Josephus Daniels: The Small-d Democrat. Chapel Hill: University of North Carolina Press, 1966.

DEWEY, THOMAS E.

Beyer, Barry K. Thomas E. Dewey, 1937-1947: A Study in Political Leadership. New York: Garland, 1979.

_____. "Thomas E. Dewey, 1937-1947: A Study in Political Leadership." Ph.D. diss., University of Rochester, 1962.

Moore, Stanley Joel. "Young Tom Dewey: The Prosecutor and the Politican." Ph.D. diss., University of Kansas, 1982.

Smith, Richard Norton. Thomas E. Dewey & His Times. New York: Simon & Schuster, 1984.

DEWSON, MARY WILLIAMS

Taylor, Paul C. "Mary Williams Dewson." In Notable American Women: The Modern Period ed. Barbara Sicherman and Carol Hurd Green (Cambridge: Harvard University Press, 1980), pp. 188-91.

DODD, WILLIAM E.

Dallek, Robert. Democrat and Diplomat: The Life of William E. Dodd. New York: Oxford University Press, 1968.

_____. "Roosevelt's Ambassador: The Public Career of William E. Dodd." Ph.D. diss., Columbia University, 1964.

Offner, Arnold A. "William E. Dodd: Romantic Historian and Diplomatic Cassandra." Historian 24 (Aug. 1962): 451-69.

DOUGLAS, HELEN GAHAGEN

Scobie, Ingrid Winther. "Helen Gahagan Douglas and the Roosevelt Connection." In Without Precedent: The Life and Career of Eleanor Roosevelt ed. by Joan Hoff Wilson and Marjorie Lightman (Bloomington: Indiana University Press, 1984), pp. 153-76.

DOUGLAS, LEWIS W.

Browder, Robert Paul, and Smith, Thomas G. Independent: A Biography of Lewis W. Douglas. New York: Knopf, 1986.
Cosulich, Bernice. "Mr. Douglas of Arizona: Friend of Cowboys and Kings." Arizona Highways 29 (Sept. 1953): 2-6.

DOUGLAS, WILLIAM O.

Duram, James. Justice William O. Douglas. Boston: Twayne, 1981.
Simon, James F. Independent Journey: The Life of William O. Douglas. New York: Harper & Row, 1980.

DULLES, JOHN FOSTER

Pruessen, Ronald W. "Toward the Threshold: John Foster Dulles, 1888-1939." Ph.D. diss., University of Pennsylvania, 1968.

EARHART, AMELIA

Salo, Mauno. "Amelia Earhart: A Short Biography." American Aviation Historical Society Journal 22 (Summer 1977): 82-86.

ECCLES, MARRINER S.

Hyman, Sidney. Marriner S. Eccles: Private Entrepreneur and Public Servant. Stanford: Graduate School of Business, 1976.

FLETCHER, DUNCAN UPSHAW

Flynt, J. Wayne. Duncan Upshaw Fletcher: Dixie's Reluctant Progressive. Tallahassee: Florida State University Press, 1971.

FOLKS, HOMER

Trattner, Walter I. Homer Folks: Pioneer in Social Welfare. New York: Columbia University Press, 1968.

FRANK, JEROME

Volkomer, Walter E. The Passionate Liberal: The Political and Legal Ideas of Jerome Frank. The Hague: Nijhoff, 1970.

FRANKFURTER, FELIX

Baker, Liva. Felix Frankfurter. New York: Coward-McCann, 1969.
Hirsch, H. N. The Enigma of Felix Frankfurter. New York: Basic, 1981.
Parrish, Michael E. Felix Frankfurter and His Times: The Reform Years. New York: Free Press, 1982.

GARDNER, O. MAX

Morrison, Joseph L. O. Max Gardner: A Power in North Carolina and New Deal Washington. Chapel Hill: University of North Carolina Press, 1971.

GARNER, JOHN NANCE

Fisher, Ovie C. Cactus Jack. Waco, Texas: Texian, 1978.
Timmons, Bascom Nolly. Garner of Texas: A Personal History. New York: Harper, 1948.

GLASS, CARTER

Beasley, Norman, and Rixey Smith. Carter Glass: A Biography. New York: Longmans Green, 1939.
Palmer, James E., Jr. Carter Glass: Unreconstructed Rebel: A Biography. Roanoke, Va.: Institute of American Biography, 1938.
Koeniger, Alfred Cash. "'Unreconstructed Rebel': The Political Thought and Senate Career of Carter Glass, 1929-1936." Ph.D. diss., Vanderbilt University, 1980.

GORE, THOMAS P.

Billington, Monroe. Thomas P. Gore: The Blind Senator from Oklahoma. Lawrence: University of Kansas Press, 1967.

GREEN, THEODORE FRANCIS

Levine, Erwin L. Theodore Francis Green. The Rhode Island Years. 1906-1936.
     Providence: Brown University Press, 1963.
_____   Theodore Francis Green. The Washington Years, 1937-1960.
     Providence: Brown University Press, 1971.

HAGUE, FRANK

Connors, Richard J. A Cycle of Power: The Career of Jersey City Mayor Frank
     Hague. Metuchen, N.J.: Scarecrow, 1971.
Foster, Mark S. "Frank Hague of Jersey City: 'The Boss' as Reformer." New Jersey
     History 86 (Summer 1968): 106-17.

HARRISON, PAT

Swain, Martha H. Pat Harrison: The New Deal Years. Jackson: University of
     Mississippi Press, 1978.
_____. "Pat Harrison and the New Deal." Ph.D. diss., Vanderbilt University,
     1975.

HICKOK, LORENA

Faber, Doris. The Life of Lorena Hickok: E.R.'s Friend. New York: Morrow, 1980.
Christie, Jean. "Lorena A. Hickok." In Notable American Women: The Modern
     Period ed. by Barbara Sicherman and Carol Hurd Green (Cambridge: Harvard
     University Press, 1980), pp. 338-40.

HILLMAN, SIDNEY

Josephson, Matthew. Sidney Hillman: Statesman of American Labor. Garden City,
     N.Y.: Doubleday, 1952.

HILLQUIT, MORRIS

Pratt, Norma Fain. Morris Hillquit: A Poltiical History of an American Jewish
     Socialist. Westport, Conn.: Greenwood, 1979.

HOLMES, OLIVER WENDELL, JR.

Biddle, Francis Beverly. Mr. Justice Holmes. New York: Scribner's, 1942.
Bowen, Catherine D. Yankee From Olympus: Justice Holmes and His Family.
    Boston: Little, Brown, 1944.
Howe, Mark. Justice Oliver W. Holmes. 2 vols.; Cambridge: Harvard University
    Press, 1957-63.

HOOVER, HERBERT C.

Books

Best, Gary Dean. Herbert Hoover: The Postpresidential Years, 1933-1964. Stanford,
    Cal.: Hoover Institution Press, 1983.
Burner, David. Herbert Hoover, A Public Life. New York: Knopf, 1979.
Irwin, Will. Herbert Hoover: A Reminiscent Biography. New York: Century, 1928.
Lyons, Eugene. Herbert Hoover: A Biography. Garden City, N. Y.: Doubleday, 1964.
Smith, Richard Norton. An Uncommon Man: The Triumph of Herbert Hoover. New
    York: Simon & Schuster, 1984.
Wilson, Joan Hoff. Herbert Hoover: Forgotten Progressive. Boston: Little, Brown,
    1974.

Articles

Best, Gary Dean. "An Evangelist among Skeptics: Hoover's Bid for Leadership of the
    GOP, 1937-1938." Proceedings of the American Philosophical Society 123
    (Feb. 1979): 1-14.
_____. "Herbert Hoover as Titular Leader of the GOP, 1933-35." Mid-America
    61 (April 1979): 81-97.
_____. "The Hoover-for-Presidency Boom." Mid-America 53 (Oct. 1971):
    227-44.
Blainey, Geoffrey. "Herbert Hoover's Forgotten Years." Business Archives and
    History 3 (Feb. 1963): 53-70.
Clements, Kendrick A. "Herbert Hoover and the Fish." Journal of Psychohistory 10
    (Winter 1983): 333-48.
Davis, Joseph. "Herbert Hoover, 1874-1964: Another Appraisal." South Atlantic
    Quarterly 68 (Summer 1969): 295-318.
Degler, Carl N. "The Ordeal of Herbert Hoover." Yale Review 52 (Summer 1963):
    563-83.
Hawley, Ellis W. "Herbert Hoover, the Commerce Secretariat, and the Vision of an
    'Associative State,' 1921-1928." Journal of American History 61 (June 1974):
    116-40.

Hoff-Wilson, Joan. "Herbert Hoover's Progressive Response to the New Deal." In Three Progressives from Iowa ed. by John N. Schact (Iowa City: University of Iowa Press, 1980), pp. 17-35.

Hofstadter, Richard. "Herbert Hoover and the Crisis of American Individualism." In The American Political Tradition (New York: Knopf, 1949), pp. 283-314.

Johnson, James P. "Herbert Hoover and David Copperfield: A Tale of Two Childhoods." Journal of Psychohistory 7 (Spring 1980): 467-75.

_____. "Herbert Hoover: The Orphan as Children's Friend." Prologue 12 (Winter 1980): 193-206.

Nash, George H. "The Social Philosophy of Herbert Hoover." Annals of Iowa 45 (Fall 1980): 478-96.

Nelsen, Clair E. "Herbert Hoover, Republican." Centennial Review 17 (Winter 1973): 41-63.

Olson, James S. "The Philosophy of Herbert Hoover: A Contemporary Perspective." Annals of Iowa 43 (Winter 1976): 181-91.

Rothbard, Murray N. "Herbert Clark Hoover: A Reconsideration." New Individualist Review 4 (Winter 1966): 3-12.

Shriver, Phillip R. "A Hoover Vignette." Ohio History 91 (1982): 74-82.

Wagner, William J. "A Philatelic History of Herbert Hoover." Annals of Iowa 38 (Winter 1966): 161-81.

Zieger, Robert H. "Herbert Hoover: A Reinterpretation." American Historical Review 81 (Oct. 1976): 800-10.

Dissertations

Brandes, Joseph. "Herbert Hoover as Secretary of Commerce: Economic Foreign Policy, 1921-1928." Ph.D. diss., New York University, 1958.

Chavez, Leo Eugene. "Herbert Hoover and Food Relief: An Application of American Ideology." Ph.D. diss., University of Michigan, 1976.

Koerselman, Gary Harlan. "Herbert Hoover and the Farm Crisis of the Twenties: A Study of the Commerce Department's Efforts to Solve the Agricultural Depression, 1921-1928." Ph.D. diss., Northern Illinois University, 1971.

Lohof, Bruce Alan. "Hoover and the Mississippi Valley Flood of 1927: A Case Study of the Political Thought of Herbert Hoover." D.S.S. diss., Syracuse University, 1968.

HOOVER, LOU HENRY

Pryor, Helen B. "Lou Henry Hoover." Palimpsest 52 (July 1971): 353-400.

HOPKINS, HARRY

Adams, Henry H. Harry Hopkins: A Biography. New York: Putnam, 1977.

Charles, Searle F. "Harry L. Hopkins: New Deal Administrator, 1933-38." Ph.D. diss., University of Illinois, 1953.

_____. Minister of Relief: Harry Hopkins and the Depression. Syracuse: Syracuse University Press, 1963.

Cotham, Perry Coleman. "Harry L. Hopkins: Spokesman for Franklin D. Roosevelt in Depression and War." Ph.D. diss., Wayne State University, 1970.

Kurzman, Paul A. Harry Hopkins and the New Deal. Fair Lawn, N.J.: R. E. Burdick, 1974.

McJimsey, George. Harry Hopkins: Ally of the Poor and Defender of Democracy. Cambridge: Harvard University Press, 1987.

Sherwood, Robert E. Roosevelt and Hopkins: An Intimate History. New York: Harper, 1948.

Rader, Frank J. "Harry L Hopkins, the Ambitious Crusader: An Historical Analysis of the Major Influences on His Career, 1912-1940." Annals of Iowa 44 (Fall 1977): 83-102.

HORNER, HENRY

Littlewood, Thomas B. Horner of Illinois. Evanston: Northwestern University Press, 1969.

HOWE, LEWIS MCHENRY

Rollins, Alfred B., Jr. Roosevelt and Howe. New York: Knopf, 1962.

Stiles, Lela. The Man behind Roosevelt: The Story of Louis McHenry Howe. Cleveland: World, 1954.

HUGHES, CHARLES EVANS

Pusey, Merlo J. Charles Evans Hughes. New York: Macmillan, 1951.

HULL, CORDELL

Drummond, Donald F. "Cordell Hull." In An Uncertain Tradition: American Secretaries of State in the Twentieth Century ed. by Norman Graebner (New York: McGraw-Hill, 1961), pp. 184-222.

Hinton, Harold B. Cordell Hull: A Biography. Garden City, N. Y.: Doubleday, 1942.

Pratt, Julius W. Cordell Hull, 1933-1944. New York: Cooper Square Publishers, 1964.

ICKES, HAROLD L.

Lear, Linda J. Harold L. Ickes: The Aggressive Progressive, 1874-1933. New York: Garland, 1981.

Maze, John, and Graham White. "Harold L. Ickes: A Psychohistorical Perspective." Journal of Psychohistory 8 (Spring 1981): 421-44.

White, Graham, and John Maze. Harold Ickes of the New Deal: His Private Life and Public Career. Cambridge: Harvard University Press, 1985.

JACKSON, GARDNER

Schlesinger, Arthur M., Jr. "Gardner Jackson, 1897-1965." New Republic 152 (May 1, 1965): 17.

JOHNSON, HIRAM

Greenbaum, Fred. "Hiram Johnson and the New Deal." Pacific Historian 18 (Fall 1974): 20-35.

JOHNSON, HUGH S.

Ohl, John Kennedy. Hugh S. Johnson and the New Deal. DeKalb: Northern Illinois University Press, 1985.

_____. "Tales Told By a New Dealer: General Hugh S. Johnson." Montana: The Magazine of Western History 25 (Oct. 1975): 66-77.

JOHNSON, OLIN D.

Huss, John E. Senator for the South: A Biography of Olin D. Johnson. Garden City, N.Y.: Doubleday, 1961.

JONES, JESSE H.

Timmons, Bascom N. Jesse H. Jones: The Man and the Statesman. New York: Henry Holt, 1956.

KELLER, KENT

Weiss, Stuart. "Kent Keller, the Liberal Bloc, and the New Deal." Journal of the Illinois State Historical Society 68 (April 1975): 143-58.

KENNEDY, JOSEPH P.

Beschloss, Michael R. Kennedy and Roosevelt: The Uneasy Alliance. New York: W.W. Norton, 1980.

Koskoff, David E. Joseph P. Kennedy: A Life and Times. Englewood Cliffs, N.J.: Prentice-Hall, 1974.

Whalen, Richard J. The Founding Father, The Story of Joseph P. Kennedy. New York: New American Library, 1964.

LA FOLLETTE, ROBERT M., JR.

Maney, Patrick J. "Young Bob" LaFollette: A Biography of Robert M. LaFollette, Jr., 1895-1953. Columbia: University of Missouri Press, 1978.

Rosenof, Theodore. "'Young Bob' LaFollette on American Capitalism." Wisconsin Magazine of History 55 (Winter 1971): 130-39.

LA GUARDIA, FIORELLO

Mann, Arthur. LaGuardia: A Fighter Against His Times, 1882-1933. Philadelphia: Lippincott, 1959.

_____. LaGuardia Comes to Power: 1933. Philadelphia: Lippincott, 1965.

Manners, William. Patience and Fortitude: Fiorello La Guardia: A Biography. New York: 1976.

Zinn, Howard. La Guardia in Congress. Ithaca: Cornell University Press, 1959.

LANDIS, JAMES M.

Ritchie, Donald A. James M. Landis, Dean of the Regulators. Cambridge: Harvard University Press, 1980.

LANDON, ALFRED

McCoy, Donald R. Landon of Kansas. Lincoln: University of Nebraska Press, 1966.

_____. "Alfred M. Landon and the Oil Troubles of 1930-32." Kansas Historical Quarterly 31 (Summer 1965): 113-37.

LANGE, DOROTHEA

Meltzer, Milton. Dorothea Lange: A Photographer's Life. New York: Farrar, Straus & Giroux, 1978.

Ohrn, Karin Becker. Dorothea Lange and the Documentary Tradition. Baton Rouge: Louisiana State University Press, 1980.

LEHMAN, HERBERT H.

Bellush, Jewel. "Roosevelt's Good Right Arm: Lieut. Governor Herbert H. Lehman." New York History 41 (Oct. 1960): 423-43.

_____. "Selected Case Studies of the Legislative Leadership of Governor Herbert H. Lehman." Ph.D. diss., Columbia University, 1959.

Nevins, Allan. Herbert H. Lehman and His Era. New York: Charles Scribner's Sons, 1963.

LEMKE, WILLIAM

Blackorby, Edward C. Prairie Rebel: The Public Life of William Lemke. Lincoln: University of Nebraska Press, 1963.

_____. "William Lemke: Agrarian Radical and Union Party Presidential Candidate." Mississippi Valley Historical Review 49 (June 1962): 67-84.

LEWIS, JOHN L.

Alinsky, Saul David. John L. Lewis: An Unauthorized Biography. New York: Putnam, 1949

Dubofsky, Melvyn, and Warren Van Tine. John L. Lewis: A Biography. New York: Quadrangle/New York Times Books, 1977.

Wechsler, James A. Labor Baron: A Portrait of John L. Lewis. New York: W. Morrow, 1944.

LINDBERGH, CHARLES A.

Davis, Kenneth S. The Hero: Charles A. Lindbergh and the American Dream. Garden City, N. Y.: Doubleday, 1959.

Ross, Walter S. The Last Hero: Charles A. Lindbergh. New York: Harper, 1968.

LIPPMANN, WALTER

Childs, Marquis William, and James Reston, eds. Walter Lippmann and His Times. New York: Harcourt, Brace, 1959.

Dam, Hari N. The Intellectual Odyssey of Walter Lippmann: A Study of His Protean Thought, 1910-1960. New York: Gordon, 1973.

Morrissette, Ashley L. "Walter Lippmann: Architect of Crisis." Ph.D. diss., Claremont Graduate School, 1984.

Schapsmeier, Edward L. and Frederick. Walter Lippman: Philosopher Journalist. Washington: Public Affairs Press, 1969.

Schapsmeier, Frederick H. "The Political Philosophy of Walter Lippmann: A Half Century of Thought and Commentary." Ph.D. diss., University of Southern California, 1965.

Steel, Ronald. Walter Lippmann and the American Century. Boston: Litle, Brown, 1980.

Weingast, David Elliott. Walter Lippmann: A Study in Personal Journalism. Westport, Conn: Greenwood, 1970.

Wellborn, Charles. Twentieth Century Pilgrimage: Walter Lippmann and the Public Philosophy. Baton Rouge: Louisiana State University Press, 1969.

LONG, HUEY P.

Books

Fields, Harvey G. A True History of the Life, Works, Assassination, and Death of Huey Pierce Long. Farmerville, La.: Fields Publishing Agency, 1945.

Opotowsky, Stan. The Longs of Louisiana. New York: Dutton, 1960.

Williams, T. Harry. Huey Long. New York: Knopf, 1969.

Articles

Badger, Anthony J. "Huey Long and the New Deal." In Nothing Else to Fear: New Perspectives on America in the Thirties ed. by Stephen W. Baskerville and Ralph Willett (Manchester: Manchester University Press, 1985), pp. 65-103.

Bates, J. Leonard. "Huey Long, the 'Kingfish' Seen through Oral History." Historian 34 (Nov. 1971): 116-20.

Carter, Hodding. "Huey Long: American Dictator." In The Aspirin Age, 1919-1941 ed. by Isabel Leighton (New York: Simon and Schuster, 1949), pp. 339-63.

Cassity, Michael J. "Huey Long: Barometer of Reform in the New Deal." South Atlantic Quarterly 72 (Spring 1973): 255-69.

Dethloff, Henry C. "Huey Pierce Long: Interpretations." Louisiana Studies 3 (Summer 1964): 219-32.

Gillette, Michael L. "Huey Long and the Chaco War." Louisiana History 1 (Fall 1970): 293-311.

Green, Joe L. "The Educational Significance of Huey P. Long." Louisiana Studies 13 (Fall 1974): 263-76.

King, Peter J. "Huey Long: The Louisiana Kingfish." History Today 14 (March 1964): 151-60.

Maddox, Robert J. "'The 'Kingfish.'" American History Illustrated 5 (May 1970): 12-24.

Snyder, Robert E. "Huey Long and the Cotton-Holiday of 1931." Louisiana History 18 (Spring 1977): 133-60.

_____. "Huey Long and the Presidential Election of 1936." Louisiana History 16 (Spring 1975): 117-43.

_____. "The Concept of Demagoguery: Huey Long and His Literary Critics." Louisiana Studies 15 (Spring 1976): 61-84.

Whisenhunt, Donald W. "Huey Long and the Texas Cotton Acreage Control Law of 1931." Louisiana Studies 13 (Summer 1974): 142-53.

Williams, T. Harry. "The Gentleman from Louisiana: Demagogue or Democrat." Journal of Southern History 26 (Feb. 1960): 3-21.

LUBIN, ISODOR

Lansky, Lewis. "Isodor Lubin: The Ideas and Career of a New Deal Labor Economist." Ph.D. diss., Case Western Reserve University, 1976.

MARCANTONIO, VITO

LaGumina, Salvatore J. Vito Marcantonio: The People's Politician. Dubuque, Iowa: Kendall/Hunt, 1969.

Schaffer, Alan L. "Caucus in a Phone Booth: The Congressional Career of Vito Marcantonio, 1934-1950." Ph.D. diss., University of Virginia, 1962.

_____. Vito Marcantonio, Radical in Congress. Syracuse: Syracuse University Press, 1966.

MAVERICK, MAURY

Henderson, Richard B. Maury Maverick: A Political Biography. Austin: University of Texas Press, 1970.

Weiss, Stuart L. "Maury Maverick and the Liberal Bloc." Journal of American History 57 (March 1971): 880-95.

MEYER, EUGENE

Pusey, Merlo J. Eugene Meyer. New York: Knopf, 1974.

MCCARRAN, PAT

Edwards, Jerome E. Pat McCarran: Political Boss of Nevada. Reno: University of Nevada Press, 1982.

MCGILL, RALPH

Martin, Harold. "About Ralph McGill." New South 28 (Spring 1973): 24-33.

MCKELLER, KENNETH DOUGLAS

Felsenthal, Edward. "Kenneth Douglas McKeller: The Rich Uncle of TVA." West Tennessee Historical Society Papers 20 (1966): 108-22.

MCNARY, CHARLES L.

Johnson, Roger T. "Charles L. McNary and the Republican Party during Prosperity and Depression." Ph.D. diss., University of Wisconsin, 1967.

MCNUTT, PAUL V.

Blake, I. George. Paul V. McNutt: Portrait of a Hoosier Statesman. Indianapolis: Central Publishing Co., 1966.

Neff, Robert R. "The Early Career and Governorship of Paul V. McNutt." Ph.D. diss., Indiana University, 1963.

Rosenberg, Edwin A. "Paul V. McNutt, Candidate." Connecticut Review 3 (Oct. 1969): 45-57.

MELLON, ANDREW W.

Murray, Lawrence L., III. "Andrew W. Mellon, Secretary of the Treasury, 1921-1932: A Study in Policy." Ph.D. diss., Michigan State University, 1970.

O'Connor, Harry. Mellon's Millions: The Biography of a Fortune: The Life and Times of Andrew Mellon. New York: John Day, 1933.

MILLER, EMMA GUFFEY

Melder, Keith "Emma Guffey Miller." In Notable American Women: The Modern
Period ed. by Barbara Sicherman and Carol Hurd Green (Cambridge: Harvard
University Press, 1980), pp. 476-88.

MILTON, GEORGE FORT

Hodges, James A. "George Fort Milton and the New Deal." Tennessee Historical
Quarterly 36 (Fall 1977): 383-409.

MINTON, SHERMAN

Corcoran, David Howard. "Sherman Minton: New Deal Senator." Ph.D. diss.,
University of Kentucky, 1977.

MOLEY, RAYMOND

Sargent, James E. "Raymond Moley and the New Deal: An Appraisal." Ball State
University Forum 18 (Summer 1977): 62-71.

MOLYNEAUX, PETER

May, Irvin M., Jr. "Peter Molyneaux and the New Deal." Southwestern Historical
Quarterly 73 (Jan. 1970): 309-25.

MORGAN, ARTHUR E.

Barde, Robert E. "Arthur E. Morgan, First Chairman of TVA." Tennessee Historical
Quarterly 30 (Fall 1971): 299-314.
Talbert, Roy, Jr. FDR's Utopian: Arthur Morgan of the TVA. Jackson: University
Press of Mississippi, 1987.

MORGENTHAU, HENRY

Blum, John Morton. Roosevelt and Morgenthau. Boston: Houghton Mifflin, 1970.

MURPHY, FRANK

Fine, Sidney. Frank Murphy: The Detroit Years. Ann Arbor: University of Michigan Press, 1975.

_____. Frank Murphy: The New Deal Years. Chicago: University of Chicago Press, 1979.

_____. Frank Murphy: The Washington Years. Ann Arbor: University of Michigan Press, 1984.

Howard, J. Woodford, Jr. Mr. Justice Murphy: A Political Biography. Princeton: Princeton University Press, 1968.

Lunt, Richard D. The High Ministry of Government: The Political Career of Frank Murphy. Detroit: Wayne State University Press, 1965.

MURRAY, WILLIAM HENRY DAVID ("ALFALFA BILL")

Bryant, Keith L., Jr. Alfalfa Bill Murray. Norman: University of Oklahoma Press, 1968.

MURRAY, JAMES E.

Spritzer, Donald E. New Dealer from Montana: The Senate Career of James E. Murray. New York: Garland, 1980.

_____. "New Dealer from Montana: The Senate Career of James E. Murray." Ph.D. diss., University of Montana, 1980.

NIEBUHR, REINHOLD

Becker, William H. "Reinhold Niebuhr: From Marx to Roosevelt." Historian 35 (Aug. 1973): 539-50.

Bingham, June. Courage to Change: An Introduction to the Life and Thought of Reinhold Niebuhr. New York: Scribner's, 1961.

Davies, David Richard. Reinhold Niebuhr: Prophet from America. New York: Macmillan, 1948.

NORBECK, PETER

Fite, Gilbert C. Peter Norbeck: Prairie Statesman. Columbia: University of Missouri Press, 1948.

NORRIS, GEORGE

Clancy, Manus J., III. "Senator George W. Norris: An Analysis and Evaluation of His
    Role of Insurgency during the Hoover Years." Ph.D. diss., St. John's University,
    1965.
Fellman, David. "The Liberalism of Senator Norris." American Political Science
    Review 40 (Feb. 1946): 27-51.
Lief, Alfred. Democracy's Norris: The Biography of a Lonely Crusade. New York:
    Stackpole, 1939.
Lowitt, Richard. George W. Norris: The Persistence of a Progressive, 1913-1933.
    Urbana: University of Illinois Press, 1971.
_____. George W. Norris: The Triumph of a Progressive, 1933-1944. Urbana:
    University of Illinois Press, 1978.
Zucker, Norman L. George W. Norris: Gentle Knight of American Democracy.
    Urbana: University of Illinois Press, 1966.
_____. "The Political Philosophy of George W. Norris." Ph.D. diss., Rutgers
    University, 1961

NYE, GERALD P.

Rylance, Daniel. "A Controversial Career: Gerald P. Nye, 1925-1946." North Dakota
    Quarterly 36 (Winter 1968): 5-19.

OLSON, FLOYD B.

Mayer, George H. The Political Career of Floyd B. Olson. Minneapolis: University of
    Minnesota Press, 1951.

O'MAHONEY, JOSEPH C.

Moore, Carl M. "Joseph Christopher O'Mahoney: A Brief Biography." Annals of
    Wyoming 41 (Oct. 1969): 159-86.
Ninneman, Thomas R. "Wyoming's Senator Joseph C. O'Mahoney." Annals of
    Wyoming 49 (Fall 1977): 193-222.

PERKINS, FRANCES

Martin, George. Madam Secretary: Frances Perkins. Boston: Houghton Mifflin, 1976.
Puckett, Patty L. "Yankee Reformer in a Man's World: Frances Perkins as Secretary
    of Labor." Ph.D. diss., Michigan State University, 1978.

Trout, Charles H. "Frances Perkins." In <u>Notable American Women: The Modern Period</u> ed. by Barbara Sicherman and Carol Hurd Green (Cambridge: Harvard University Press, 1980), pp. 535-39.

PINCHOT, GIFFORD

Olson, James S. "Gifford Pinchot and the Politics of Hunger, 1932-1933." <u>Pennsylvania Magazine of History and Biography</u> 96 (Oct. 1972): 508-20.

PITTMAN, KEY

Glad, Betty. <u>Key Pittman: The Tragedy of a Senate Insider</u>. New York: Columbia University Press, 1986.

Israel, Fred L. <u>Nevada's Key Pittman</u>. Lincoln: University of Nebraska Press, 1963.

_____. "Key Pittman and New Deal Politics." <u>Nevada Historical Society Quarterly</u> 14 (Fall 1971): 19-26.

_____. "The Fulfillment of Bryan's Dream: Key Pittman and Silver Politics, 1918-1933." <u>Pacific Historical Review</u> 30 (Nov. 1961): 359-80.

POPE, JAMES P.

Sims, Robert C. "James P. Pope, Senator from Idaho: Borah's New Deal Senator Colleague." <u>Idaho Yesterdays</u> 15 (Fall 1971): 9-15

PRENTIS, HENNING WEBB

Winpenny, Thomas R. "Henning Webb Prentis and the Challenge of the New Deal." <u>Journal of the Lancaster County Historical Society</u> 81 (1977): 1-24.

RAINEY, HENRY T.

Waller, Robert A. <u>Rainey of Illinois: A Political Biography, 1903-34</u>. Urbana: University of Illinois Press, 1977.

RANDOLPH, A. PHILIP

Anderson, Jervis. <u>A. Philip Randolph: A Biographical Portrait</u>. New York: Harcourt Brace Jovanovich, 1973.

Harris, William H. "A. Philip Randolph as a Charismatic Leader, 1925-1941." Journal of Negro History 64 (Fall 1979): 301-15.

RASKOB, JOHN J.

Lopata, Roy Haywood. "John J. Raskob: A Conservative Businessman in the Age of Roosevelt." Ph.D. diss., University of Delaware, 1975.

RAYBURN, SAM

Champagne, Anthony. Congressman Sam Rayburn. New Brunswick, N.J.: Rutgers University Press, 1984.
Hardeman, D. B., and Donald C Bacon. Rayburn: A Biography. Austin: Texas Monthly Press, 1987.
Shanks, Alexander G. "Sam Rayburn and the New Deal, 1933-1936." Ph.D. diss., University of North Carolina, 1965.
_____. "Sam Rayburn: The Texas Politician as New Dealer." East Texas Historical Journal 5 (March 1967): 51-59.
Steinberg, Alfred. Sam Rayburn: A Biography. New York: Hawthorn Books, 1975.

RENO, MILO

White, Roland A. Milo Reno, Farmers Union Pioneer. Iowa City: Athens Press, 1941.

REUTHER, WALTER

Barnard, John. Walter Reuther and the Rise of the Auto Workers. Boston: Little, Brown, 1983.

RICE, CHARLES OWEN

Betten, Neil. "Charles Owen Rice: Pittsburgh Labor Priest, 1936-1940." Pennsylvania Magazine of History and Biography 94 (Oct. 1970): 518-32.

RICHBERG, DONALD

Vadney, Thomas E. The Wayward Liberal: A Political Biography of Donald Richberg. Lexington: University Press of Kentucky, 1970.

_____. "Donald Richberg and American Liberalism." Ph.D. diss., University of Wisconsin, 1968.

ROCHE, JOSEPHINE

Hornbein, Marjorie. "Josephine Roche: Social Worker and Coal Operator." Colorado Magazine 53 (Summer 1976): 243-60.

RONALD, W. R.

Williams, Elizabeth E. "W.R. Ronald: Prairie Editor and an AAA Architect." South Dakota History 1 (Summer 1971): 272-92.

ROOSEVELT, ELEANOR

Books

Beasley, Maurine H. Eleanor Roosevelt and the Media: A Public Quest for Self Fulfillment. Urbana: University of Illinois Press, 1987.

Hareven, Tamara. Eleanor Roosevelt: An American Conscience. Chicago: Quadrangle, 1968.

Hoff-Wilson, Joan, and Marjorie Lightman. Without Precedent: The Life and Career of Eleanor Roosevelt. Bloomington: Indiana University Press, 1984.

Kearney, James R. Anna Eleanor Roosevelt: The Evolution of a Reformer. Boston: Houghton Mifflin, 1968.

Lash, Joseph. Eleanor and Franklin: The Story of Their Relationship based on Eleanor Roosevelt's Private Papers. New York: W. W. Norton, 1971.

_____. Love, Eleanor: Eleanor Roosevelt and Her Friends. Garden City, N.Y.: Doubleday, 1982.

Articles

Chafe, William. "Biographical Sketch." In Without Precedent: The Life and Career of Eleanor Roosevelt ed. by Joan Hoff-Wilson and Marjorie Lightman (Bloomington: Indiana University Press, 1984), pp. 3-27.

_____. "Anna Eleanor Roosevelt." In Notable American Women: The Modern Period ed. by Barbara Sicherman and Carol Hurd Green (Cambridge: Harvard University Press, 1980), pp. 595-601.

Erikson, Joan M. "Nothing to Fear: Notes on the Life of Eleanor Roosevelt." Daedalus 93 (Spring 1964): 781-801.

Hareven, Tamara K. "ER and Reform." In Without Precedent: The Life and Career
        of Eleanor Roosevelt ed. by Joan Hoff-Wilson and Marjorie Lightman
        (Bloomington: Indiana University Press, 1984), pp. 201-13.
Hoff-Wilson, Joan. "Did Eleanor Roosevelt Make a Difference?" Texas Humanist 7
        (Nov.-Dec. 1984): 33-37.
McCarthy, Abigall Q. "ER as First Lady." In Without Precedent: The Life and
        Career of Eleanor Roosevelt ed. by Joan Hoff-Wilson and Marjorie Lightman
        (Bloomington: Indiana University Press, 1984), pp. 214-25.
Perry, Elisabeth Israel. "Training for Public Life: ER and Women's Political Networks
        in the 1920s." In Without Precedent: The Life and Career of Eleanor Roosevelt
        ed. by Joan Hoff-Wilson and Marjorie Lightman (Bloomington: Indiana
        University Press, 1984), pp. 28-45.
Scharf, Lois. "ER and Feminism." In Without Precedent: The Life and Career of
        Eleanor Roosevelt ed. by Joan Hoff-Wilson and Marjorie Lightman
        (Bloomington: Indiana University Press, 1984), pp. 226-53.
Wandersee, Winifred D. "ER and American Youth: Politics and Personality in a
        Bureaucratic Age." In Without Precedent: The Life and Career of Eleanor
        Roosevelt ed. by Joan Hoff-Wilson and Marjorie Lightman (Bloomington:
        Indiana University Press, 1984), pp. 63-87.
Ware, Susan. "ER and Democratic Politics: Women in the Postsuffrage Era." In
        Without Precedent: The Life and Career of Eleanor Roosevelt ed. by Joan
        Hoff-Wilson and Marjorie Lightman (Bloomington: Indiana University Press,
        1984), pp. 46-60.

Dissertations

Hareven, Tamara K. "The Social Thought of Eleanor Roosevelt." Ph.D. diss., Ohio
        University, 1965.
Kearney, James R., III. "Anna Eleanor Roosevelt: Years of Experiment, 1884-1940."
        Ph.D. diss., University of Wisconsin, 1967.

ROOSEVELT, FRANKLIN DELANO

Books

Alsop, Joseph. FDR, 1882-1945: A Centenary Remembrance. New York: Viking,
        1982.
Bellush, Bernard. Franklin D. Roosevelt as Governor of New York. New York:
        Columbia University Press, 1955.
Burns, James MacGregor. Roosevelt: The Lion and the Fox. New York: Harcourt
        Brace, 1956.

_____. Roosevelt: The Soldier of Freedom. New York: Harcourt Brace
      Jovanovich, 1970.

Davis, Kenneth S. F.D.R.: The Beckoning of Destiny, 1882-1928. New York: Putnam,
      1972.

_____. F.D.R.: The New Deal Years, 1933-1937. New York: Random House,
      1986

_____. F.D.R.: The New York Years, 1928-1933. New York: Random House,
      1985.

Freidel, Frank. Franklin D. Roosevelt: The Apprenticeship. Boston: Little, Brown,
      1952.

_____. Franklin D. Roosevelt: The Ordeal. Boston: Little, Brown, 1954.

_____. Franklin D. Roosevelt: The Triumph. Boston: Little, Brown, 1956.

Gallagher, Hugh Gregory. FDR's Splendid Deception. New York: Dodd, Mead, 1985.

Geddes, Donald Porter, ed. Franklin Delano Roosevelt: A Memorial. New York:
      Pocket Books, 1945.

Goldberg, Richard T. The Making of Franklin D. Roosevelt: Triumph over Disability.
      Cambridge, Mass.: Abt Books, 1981.

Lindley, Ernest K. Franklin D. Roosevelt: A Career in Progressive Democracy.
      Indianapolis: Bobbs-Merrill, 1931.

Lippman, Theo. The Squire of Warm Springs: F.D.R. in Georgia, 1924-1945. New
      York: Playboy Press, 1977.

Miller, Nathan. The Roosevelt Chronicles. Garden City, N. Y.: Doubleday, 1979.

Morgan, Ted. FDR: A Biography. New York: Simon and Schuster, 1985.

Nash, Gerald D. Franklin D. Roosevelt. Englewood Cliffs, N.J.: Prentice-Hall, 1967.

Tugwell, Rexford G. The Democratic Roosevelt: A Biography of Franklin D.
      Roosevelt. Garden City, N. Y.: Doubleday, 1957.

Venkataramani, M.S., ed. The Sunny Side of FDR. Athens: Ohio University Press,
      1973.

Ward, Geoffrey C. Before the Trumpet: Young Franklin Roosevelt, 1882-1905. New
      York: Harper & Row, 1985.

Articles

Alsop, Joseph. "Roosevelt Remembered." Smithsonian 12 (Jan. 1982): 38-49.

Blum, John Morton. "'That Kind of a Liberal': Franklin D. Roosevelt after Twenty-
      Five Years." Yale Review 60 (Autumn 1970): 14-23.

Clark, Grenville. "FDR's Political Ambitions." Harvard Alumni Bulletin 97 (April 28,
      1945): 25.

Fabricant, Noah. "Franklin D. Roosevelt's Nose and Throat Ailments." Eye, Ear,
      Nose and Throat Monthly 36 (Feb. 1957): 103-6.

Helicher, Karl. "The Education of Franklin D. Roosevelt." Presidential Studies
      Quarterly 12 (Winter 1982): 50-53.

Henderson, F. P. "FDR at Warm Springs." Marine Corps Gazette 66 (July 1982):
      54-58.

Hofstadter, Richard. "Franklin D. Roosevelt: The Patrician as Opportunist." In The American Political Tradition (New York: Knopf, 1949), pp. 315-52.

_____ "The Roosevelt Reputation." Progressive 12 (Nov. 1948): 9-12.

McAvoy, Thomas. "Roosevelt: A Modern Jefferson." Review of Politics 7 (July 1945): 270-79.

Nevins, Allan. "The Place of Franklin D. Roosevelt in History." American Heritage 17 (June 1966): 12-15, 101-4.

Perkins, Frances. "Franklin Roosevelt's Apprenticeship." New Republic 132 (April 25, 1955): 19-21.

Potter, David M. "Sketches for the Roosevelt Portrait." Yale Review 39 (Autumn 1949): 39-53.

Rollins, Alfred B., Jr. "Young Franklin D. Roosevelt as the Farmers' Friend." New York History 43 (April 1962): 186-98.

Rossiter, Clinton J. "The Political Philosophy of F. D. Roosevelt: A Challenge to Scholarship." Review of Politics 11 (Jan. 1949): 87-95.

Slichter, Gertrude Almy. "Franklin D. Roosevelt's Policy as Governor of New York State, 1928-1932." Agricultural History 33 (Oct. 1959): 167-76.

Stewart, William J., and Cheryl C. Pollard. "Franklin D. Roosevelt, Collector." Prologue 1 (Winter 1969): 13-28.

Tugwell, Rexford G. "The Preparation of a President." Western Political Quarterly 1 (June 1948): 131-153.

_____. "The Progressive Orthodoxy of Franklin D. Roosevelt." Ethics 64 (1953): 1-21.

_____. "The Two Great Roosevelts." Western Political Quarterly 5 (March 1952): 84-93.

Ward, Geoffrey C. "The House at Hyde Park." American Heritage 38 (April 1987): 41-50.

Dissertations

Barron, Gloria Joan. "A Study in Presidential Leadership: Franklin D. Roosevelt in the Prewar Years, 1938-1941." Ph.D. diss., Tufts University, 1971.

Bellush, Bernard. "Apprenticeship for the Presidency: Franklin D. Roosevelt as Governor of New York." Ph.D. diss., Columbia University, 1951.

Brooks, George Edward. "A Rhetorical Comparison of Woodrow Wilson and Franklin D. Roosevelt, Based Upon Aristotelian Criteria." Ph.D. diss., Ohio State University, 1945.

Coady, Joseph William. "Franklin D. Roosevelt's Early Washington Years (1913-1920)." Ph.D. diss., St. John's University, 1968.

Ferdon, Nona Stinson. "Franklin D. Roosevelt: A Psychological Interpretation of His Childhood and Youth." Ph.D. diss., University of Hawaii, 1971.

Moody, Frank Kennon. "F.D.R. and His Neighbors: A Study of the Relationship between Franklin D. Roosevelt and the Residents of Dutchess County." Ph.D. diss., State University of New York at Albany, 1981.

Pennington, Paul Jordan. "A Rhetorical Study of the Gubernatorial Speaking of Franklin D. Roosevelt." Ph.D. diss., Louisiana State University, 1957.

Rollins, Alfred B., Jr. "The Political Education of Franklin Roosevelt: His Career in New York Politics, 1909-1928." Ph.D. diss., Harvard University, 1953.

ROSENMAN, SAMUEL I.

Hand, Samuel B. Counsel and Advise: A Political Biography of Samuel I. Rosenman. New York: Garland, 1979.

_____. "Rosenman, Thucydides, and the New Deal." Journal of American History 55 (Sept. 1968): 334-48.

_____. "Samuel I. Rosenman: His Public Career." Ph.D. diss., Syracuse University, 1960.

RYAN, JOHN A.

Broderick, Francis L. Right Reverend New Dealer, John A. Ryan. New York: Macmillan, 1963.

SEABURY, SAMUEL

Mitgang, Herbert. The Man Who Rode the Tiger: The Life and Times of Judge Samuel Seabury. Philadelphia: Lippincott, 1963.

SHIPSTEAD, HENRIK

Ross, Martin. Shipstead of Minnesota. Chicago: Packard, 1940.

SINCLAIR, UPTON

Bloodworth, William A., Jr. Upton Sinclair. Boston: Twayne, 1977.

Grenier, Judson. "Upton Sinclair: The Road to California." Southern California Quarterly 56 (Winter 1974): 325-36.

Harris, Leon. Upton Sinclair: American Rebel. New York: Crowell, 1975.

SMITH, ALFRED E.

Handlin, Oscar. Al Smith and His America. Boston: Little, Brown, 1958.

Josephson, Matthew and Hannah. Al Smith: Hero of the Cities: A Political Portrait Drawing on the Papers of Frances Perkins. Boston: Houghton Mifflin, 1969.

O'Conner, Richard. The First Hurrah: A Biography of Alfred E. Smith. New York: G.P. Putnam's Sons, 1970.

Schwarz, Jordan A. "Al Smith in the Thirties." New York History 45 (Oct. 1964): 316-30.

SNELL, BERTRAND H.

Barone, Louis A. "The Fighting Lumberjack: Bertrand H. Snell of New York and the New Deal, 1933-1939." In An American Historian: Essays to Honor Selig Adler ed. by Milton Plesur (Buffalo: State University of New York, 1980), pp. 159-66.

SPINGARN, J. E.

Ross, Barbara Joyce. J. E. Spingarn and the Rise of the NAACP, 1911-1939. New York: Atheneum, 1972.

STEAGALL, HENRY B.

Key, Jack Brien. "Henry B. Steagall: The Conservative as a Reformer." Alabama Review 17 (July 1964): 198-209.

STEINBECK, JOHN

Benson, Jackson J. The True Adventures of John Steinbeck, Writer: A Biography. New York: Viking, 1984.

French, Warren. John Steinbeck. Boston: Twayne, 1975.

Kiernan, Thomas. The Intricate Music: A Biography of John Steinbeck. Boston: Little, Brown, 1979.

Short, John D., Jr. "John Steinbeck: A 1930's Photo-Recollection." San Jose Studies 2 (May 1976): 75-81.

STIMSON, HENRY L.

Current, Richard N. "Henry L. Stimson." In An Uncertain Tradition: American Secretaries of State in the Twentieth Century ed. by Norman A. Graebner (New York: McGraw-Hill, 1961), pp. 168-83.

_____. Secretary Stimson: A Study in Statecraft. New Brunswick, N.J.: Rutgers University Press, 1954.

Ferrell, Robert H. Frank B. Kellogg and Henry L. Stimson. New York: Cooper Square, 1963.

Morrison, Elting E. Turmoil and Tradition: The Life and Times of Henry L. Stimson. Boston: Houghton Mifflin, 1960.

STONE, HARLAN FISKE

Mason, Alpheus T. Harlan Fiske Stone: Pillar of the Law. New York: Viking, 1956.

SULLIVAN, ANNA

O'Farrell, M. Brigid and Lydia Kleiner. "Anna Sullivan: Trade Union Organizer." Frontiers 2 (Summer 1977): 29-36.

SWANSON, CLAUDE A.

Ferrell, Henry C., Jr. Claude A. Swanson of Virginia: A Political Biography. Lexington: University Press of Kentucky, 1985.

SYKES, EUGENE OCTAVE

Meek, Edwin E. "Eugene Octave Sykes, Member and Chairman of Federal Communications Commission and Federal Radio Commission, 1927-1939." Journal of Mississippi History 36 (Nov. 1974): 377-86.

TAFT, ROBERT A.

Patterson, James T. Mr. Republican: A Biography of Robert A. Taft. Boston: Houghton Mifflin, 1972.

TALMADGE, EUGENE

Anderson, William. The Wild Man from Sugar Creek: The Political Career of Eugene Talmadge. Baton Rouge: Louisiana State University Press, 1975.

Lemmon, Sarah M. "The Public Career of Eugene Talmadge, 1926-1936." Ph.D. diss., University of North Carolina, 1952.

THOMAS, NORMAN

Duram, James C. Norman Thomas. New York: Twayne, 1974.
Fleischman, Harry. Norman Thomas: A Biography. New York: W. W. Norton, 1964.
Seidler, Murray Benjamin. Norman Thomas: Respectable Rebel. Syracuse: Syracuse University Press, 1967.
Swanberg, W. A. Norman Thomas: The Last Idealist. New York: Scribner's, 1976.

TRUMAN, HARRY S.

Dorsett, Lyle W. "Truman and the Pendergast Machine." American Studies 7 (Fall 1966): 16-27.
Fink, Gary M., and James W. Hilty. "Prologue: The Senate Voting Record of Harry S. Truman." Journal of Interdisciplinary History 4 (Autumn 1973): 207-35.
Kirkendall, Richard S. "Truman and the Pendergast Machine: A Comment." American Studies 7 (Fall 1966): 36-39.
Schmidtlein, Gene. "Harry S. Truman and the Pendergast Machine." American Studies 7 (Fall 1966): 28-35.
_____. "Truman's First Senatorial Election." Missouri Historical Review 57 (Jan. 1963): 128-55.

TUGWELL, REXFORD GUY

Sternsher, Bernard. Rexford Tugwell and the New Deal. New Brunswick, N.J.: Rutgers University Press, 1964.
_____. "Rexford Guy Tugwell and the New Deal." Ph.D. diss., Boston University, 1957.

VANDENBERG, ARTHUR H.

Tompkins, C. David. Senator Arthur H. Vandenberg: The Evolution of a Modern Republican, 1884-1945. East Lansing: Michigan State University Press, 1970.
_____. "Senator Arthur H. Vandenburg, 1884-1945." Ph.D. diss., University of Michigan, 1966.

VANN, ROBERT L.

Brewer, James H. "Robert Lee Vann, Democrat or Republican: An Exponent of Loose-Leaf Politics." Negro History Bulletin 21 (Feb. 1958): 100-3.
Buni, Andrew. Robert L. Vann of the Pittsburgh Courier: Politics and Black Journalism. Pittsburgh: University of Pittsburgh Press, 1974.

WADSWORTH, JAMES W., JR.

Fausold, Martin L. James W. Wadsworth, Jr.: The Gentleman from New York. Syracuse: Syracuse University Press, 1975.

WAGNER, ROBERT F.

Huthmacher, J. Joseph. Senator Robert F. Wagner and the Rise of Urban Liberalism. New York: Atheneum, 1971.

WALKER, FRANK

Simon, Paul L. "Frank Walker: New Dealer." Ph.D. diss., University of Notre Dame, 1965.

WALKER, JIMMY

Fowler, Gene. Beau James: The Life and Times of Jimmy Walker. New York: Viking, 1949.

WALLACE, HENRY A.

Kirkendall, Richard S. "Commentary on the Thought of Henry A. Wallace." Agricultural History 41 (April 1967): 139-42.
_____. "The Mind of a Farm Leader." Annals of Iowa 47 (Fall 1983): 138-53.
_____ and Glenda Riley. "Henry A. Wallace and the Mystique of the Farm Male, 1921-1933." Annals of Iowa 48 (Summer 1985): 32-55.
Kirschner, Don S. "Henry A. Wallace as Farm Editor." American Quarterly 17 (Summer 1965): 187-202.
Lord, Russell. The Wallaces of Iowa. Boston: Houghton Mifflin, 1947.
MacDonald, Dwight. Henry Wallace: The Man and the Myth. New York: Vanguard, 1948.
Rosenof, Theodore. "The Economic Ideas of Henry A. Wallace, 1933-1948." Agricultural History 41 (April 1967): 143-53.
Schapsmeier, Edward L. "Henry A. Wallace: The Origins and Development of His Political Philosophy, the Agrarian Years, 1920-1940." Ph.D. diss., University of Southern California, 1965.
Schapsmeier, Edward L. and Frederick H. "A Prophet in Politics: The Public Career of Henry A. Wallace." Annals of Iowa 39 (Summer 1967): 1-21.
_____. "Henry A. Wallace: Agrarian Idealist or Agricultural Realist?" Agricultural History 41 (April 1967): 127-37.

_____. "Henry A. Wallace as Agricultural Secretary and Agrarian Reformer." In The Roosevelt New Deal: A Program Assessment Fifty Years After ed. by Wilbur J. Cohen (Austin: Lyndon B. Johnson School of Public Affairs, 1986), pp. 221-33.

_____. "Henry A. Wallace: New Deal Philosopher." Historian 32 (Feb. 1970): 177-90.

_____. Henry A. Wallace of Iowa: The Agrarian Years, 1910-1940. Ames: Iowa State University Press, 1968.

_____. Prophet in Politics: Henry A. Wallace and the War Years, 1940-1965. Ames: Iowa State University Press, 1970.

Shideler, James H. "Henry C. Wallace and Persisting Progressivism: A Comment." Agricultural History 41 (April 1967): 121-25.

WALSH, THOMAS J.

O'Keane, Josephine. Thomas J. Walsh: A Senator from Montana. Francestown, N.H.: M. Jones, 1955.

WHEELER, BURTON K.

Burke, Robert E. "A Friendship in Adversity: Burton K. Wheeler [and] Hiram W. Johnson." Montana: The Magazine of Western History 36 (Winter 1986): 12-25.

Ruetten, Richard T. "Burton K. Wheeler of Montana: A Progressive between the Wars." Ph.D. diss., University of Oregon, 1961.

WICKARD, CLAUDE R.

Albertson, Dean. Roosevelt's Farmer: Claude R. Wickard in the New Deal. New York: Columbia University Press, 1961.

_____. "Roosevelt's Farmer: The Life of Claude R. Wickard." Ph.D. diss., Columbia University, 1955.

WILKIE, WENDELL

Barnard, Ellsworth. Wendell Wilkie, Fighter for Freedom. Marquette: Northern Michigan University Press, 1966.

Barnes, Joseph. Wilkie: The Events He Was Part Of, The Ideas He Fought For. New York: Simon & Schuster, 1952.

Dillon, Mary E. Wendell Wilkie, 1892-1944. Philadelphia: Lippincott, 1952.

Neal, Steve. <u>Dark Horse: A Biography of Wendell Wilkie</u>. Garden City, N. Y.:
Doubleday, 1984.

Drummon, Roscoe. "Wendell Wilkie: A Study in Courage." In <u>The Aspirin Age,
1919-1941</u> ed. by Isabel Leighton (New York: Simon and Schuster, 1949), pp.
444-75.

Thompson, Sarah Ann C. "Wendell Wilkie: A Hoosier Liberal." Ph.D. diss., Ball State
University, 1980.

WILLIAMS, AUBREY WILLIS

Salmond, John A. <u>A Southern Rebel, the Life and Times of Aubrey Willis Williams,
1890-1965</u>. Chapel Hill: University of North Carolina Press, 1983.

_____. "Aubrey Williams: Atypical New Dealer?" In <u>The New Deal: The
National Level</u> ed. by John Braeman, Robert H. Bremner, and David Brody.
(Columbus: Ohio State University Press, 1975): pp. 218-45.

WILSON, M. L.

Kirkendall, Richard S. "A Professor in Farm Politics." <u>Mid-America</u> 41 (Oct. 1959):
210-17.

WINANT, JOHN GILBERT

Bellush, Bernard. <u>He Walked Alone: A Biography of John Gilbert Winant</u>. The
Hague: Mouton, 1968.

WITTE, EDWIN E.

Schlabach, Theron F. <u>Edwin E. Witte: Cautious Reformer</u>. Madison: State Historical
Society of Wisconsin, 1969.

WOLFE, THOMAS

Donald, David H. <u>Look Homeward: A Life of Thomas Wolfe</u>. Boston: Little, Brown,
1987.

WOOD, ROBERT E.

Doenecke, Justus D. "General Robert E. Wood: The Evolution of a Conservative."
Journal of the Illinois State Historical Society 71 (Aug. 1978): 162-75.

WOODRING, HARRY H.

McFarland, Keith D. Harry H. Woodring: A Political Biography of FDR's
Controversial Secretary of War. Lawrence: University Press of Kansas, 1975.
_____. "Secretary of War Harry Woodring: Early Career in Kansas." Kansas
Historical Quarterly 39 (Summer 1973): 206-19.

WOODRUM, CLIFTON A.

Sargent, James E. "Clifton A. Woodrum of Virginia: A Southern Progressive in
Congress, 1923-1945." Virginia Magazine of History and Biography 89 (July
1981): 341-64.

WOODWARD, ELLEN S.

Swain, Martha H. "Ellen S. Woodward: The Gentlewoman as Federal Administrator."
Furman Studies 26 (Dec. 1980): 92-103.
_____. "Ellen Sullivan Woodward." In Notable American Women: The Modern
Period ed. by Barbara Sicherman and Carol Hurd Green (Cambridge: Harvard
University Press, 1980), pp. 747-49.

5

The Hoover Administration

5.1 GENERAL

Books

Bassett, Reginald. Nineteen Thirty-One Political Crisis. New York: St. Martin's, 1958.

Daniels, Roger. The Bonus March: An Episode of the Great Depression. Westport, Conn.: Greenwood, 1971.

Fausold, Martin L. The Presidency of Herbert C. Hoover. Lawrence: University Press of Kansas, 1985.

_____ and George T. Mazuzan. The Hoover Presidency: A Reappraisal. Albany: State University of New York Press, 1974.

Huthmacher, J. Joseph, and Warren Susman, eds. Herbert Hoover and the Crisis of American Capitalism. Cambridge: Harvard University Press, 1973.

Joslin, Theodore G. Hoover Off the Record. Garden City, N. Y.: Doubleday, Doran, 1934.

Krog, Carl E., and William R. Tanner, eds. Herbert Hoover and the Republican Era: A Reconsideration. Lanham, Md.: University Press of America, 1984.

Lisio, Donald J. Hoover, Blacks, & Lily-Whites: A Study of Southern Strategies. Chapel Hill: University of North Carolina Press, 1985.

_____. The President and Protest: Hoover, Conspiracy, and the Bonus Riot. Columbia: University of Missouri Press, 1974.

Lloyd, Craig. Aggressive Introvert: A Study of Herbert Hoover and Public Relations Management, 1912-1932. Columbus: Ohio State University Press, 1972.

Myers, William Starr, and Walter H. Newton. The Hoover Administration: A Documented Narrative. New York: Scribners, 1936.

Robinson, Edgar E., and Vaughn D. Bornet. Herbert Hoover: President of the United States. Stanford, Cal.: Hoover Institution Press, 1975.

Romasco, Albert U. The Poverty of Abundance: Hoover, the Nation, the Depression. New York: Oxford University Press, 1965.

Schwarz, Jordan A. The Interregnum of Dispair: Hoover, Congress, and the
    Depression. Urbana: University of Illinois Press, 1970.
Smith, Gene. The Shattered Dream: Herbert Hoover and the Great Depression. New
    York: Morrow, 1970.
Tugwell, Rexford G. Mr. Hoover's Economic Policy. New York: John Day, 1932.
Warren, Harris Gaylord. Herbert Hoover and the Great Depression. New York:
    Oxford University Press, 1959.

Articles

Albjerg, Victor L. "Hoover: The Presidency in Transition." Current History 39 (Oct
    1960): 213-19.
Arnold, Peri E. "Herbert Hoover and the Continuity of American Public Policy."
    Public Policy 20 (Fall 1972): 525-44.
Burner, David. "Before the Crash: Hoover's First Eight Months in the Presidency." In
    The Hoover Presidency: A Reappraisal ed. by Martin L. Fausold and George
    T. Mazuzan (Albany: State University of New York Press, 1974), pp. 50-65.
Freidel, Frank. "The Interregnum Struggle Between Hoover and Roosevelt." In The
    Hoover Presidency: A Reappraisal ed. by Martin L. Fausold and George T.
    Mazuzan (Albany: State University of New York Press, 1974), pp. 134-49.
Garcia, George F. "Herbert Hoover and the Issue of Race." Annals of Iowa 44
    (Winter 1979): 507-15.
Hamilton, David E. "Herbert Hoover and the Great Drought of 1930." Journal of
    American History 68 (March 1982): 850-75.
Karl, Barry D. "Presidential Planning and Social Science Research: Mr. Hoover's
    Experts." Perspectives in American History 3 (1969): 347-409.
Killigrew, John W. "The Army and the Bonus Incident." Military Affairs 26
    (Summer 1962): 59-65.
Kollock, Will. "The Story of a Friendship: Mark Sullivan and Herbert Hoover." Pacific
    Historian 18 (Spring 1974): 31-48.
Lambert, C. Roger. "Hoover and the Red Cross in the Arkansas Drought of 1930."
    Arkansas Historical Quarterly 29 (Spring 1970): 3-19.
_____. "Hoover, the Red Cross and Food for the Hungry." Annals of Iowa 44
    (Winter 1979): 530-40.
Lisio, Donald J. "A Blunder Becomes Catastrophe: Hoover, the Legion, and the
    Bonus Army." Wisconsin Magazine of History 51 (Autumn 1967): 37-50.
McGoff, Kevin. "The Bonus Army." American History Illustrated 12 (Feb. 1978):
    28-37.
McCoy, Donald R. "To the White House: Herbert Hoover, August 1927--March
    1929." In The Hoover Presidency: A Reappraisal ed. by Martin L. Fausold and
    George T. Mazuzan (Albany: State University of New York Press, 1974), pp.
    29-49.
O'Reilly, Kenneth. "Herbert Hoover and the FBI." Annals of Iowa 47 (Summer
    1983): 46-63.

Olsen, James S. "Herbert Hoover and the 'War' on the Depression." Palimpsest 54 (July 1973): 26-31.

Padelford, Norman J. "The Veterans' Bonus and the Constitution." American Political Science Review 27 (Dec. 1933): 923-29.

Parker, Robert V. "The Bonus March of 1932: A Unique Experience in North Carolina Political and Social Life." North Carolina Historical Review 51 (Jan. 1974): 64-89.

Rollins, Alfred B. "The View From the State House: FDR." In The Hoover Presidency: A Reappraisal ed. by Martin L. Fausold and George T. Mazuzan (Albany: State University of New York Press, 1974), pp. 132-33.

Rothbard, Murray N. "Herbert Hoover and the Myth of Laissez-Faire." In A New History of Leviathan: Essays on the Rise of the American Corporate State ed. by Ronald Radosh and Murrary N. Rothbard (New York: E. P. Dutton, 1972), 111-45.

Sizer, Rosanne. "Herbert Hoover and the Smear Book, 1930-1932." Annals of Iowa 47 (Spring 1984): 343-61.

Snyder, J. Richard. "Hoover and the Hawley-Smoot Tariff: A View of Executive Leadership." Annals of Iowa 41 (Winter 1973): 1173-89.

Stabile, Donald R. "Herbert Hoover, the FAES, and the AF of L." Technology and Culture 27 (Oct. 1986): 819-27.

Vivian, James F. and Jean H. "The Bonus March of 1932: The Role of General George Van Horn Moseley." Wisconsin Magazine of History 51 (Autumn 1967): 26-36.

Weaver, John D. "Bonus March" American Heritage 14 (June 1963): 18-23, 92-97.

Whisenhunt, Donald W. "Texas and the Bonus Expeditionary Army." East Texas Historical Journal 23 (Spring 1985): 27-32.

Dissertations

Edwards, Richard Earl. "Herbert Hoover and the Public Relations Approach to Economic Recovery, 1929-1932." Ph.D. diss., University of Iowa, 1976.

Nelsen, Clair Everet. "The Image of Herbert Hoover as Reflected in the American Press." Ph.D. diss., Stanford University, 1956.

Lloyd, Craig. "Aggressive Introvert: A Study of Herbert Hoover and Public Relations Management, 1912-1932." Ph.D. diss., University of Iowa, 1970.

Romasco, Albert U. "American Institutions in the Great Depression: The Hoover Years." Ph.D. diss., University of Chicago, 1961.

Shaw, William W. "The Political and Economic Thought of Herbert Hoover." Ph.D. diss., Princeton University, 1936.

Sneller, Maurice P., Jr. "The Bonus March of 1932: A Study of Depression Leadership and Its Legacy." Ph.D. diss., University of Virginia, 1960.

Westrate, J. Lee. "The Administrative Theory and Practice of Herbert Hoover." Ph.D. diss., University of Chicago, 1963.

Wilson, John Richard Meredith. "Herbert Hoover and the Armed Forces: A Study of Presidential Attitudes and Policy." Ph.D. diss., Northwestern University, 1971.

5.2 POLITICS

Books

Lichtman, Allan J. Prejudice and the Old Politics: The Presidential Election of 1928. Chapel Hill: University of North Carolina Press, 1979.

Moore, Edmund A. A Catholic Runs for President: The Campaign of 1928. New York: Ronald Press, 1956.

Peel, Roy Victor, and Thomas C. Donnelly. The 1928 Camapign: An Analysis. New York: New York University Bookstore, 1931.

Sherman, Richard B. The Republican Party and Black America: From McKinley to Hoover, 1896-1933. Charlottesville: University Press of Virginia, 1973.

Silva, Ruth C. Rum, Religion, and Votes: 1928 Re-examined. University Park: Pennsylvania State University Press, 1962.

Articles

Barclay, Thomas S. "The Publicity Division of the Democratic Party, 1929-30." American Political Science Review 25 (Feb. 1931): 68-72.

Carlson, Earland I. "Franklin D. Roosevelt's Post-Mortem of the 1928 Election." Midwest Journal of Political Science 8 (Aug. 1964): 298-308.

Carter, Paul A. "The Campaign of 1928 Re-examined: A Study in Political Folklore." Wisconsin Magazine of History 46 (Summer 1963): 263-72.

_____. "The Other Catholic Candidate: The 1928 Presidential Bid of Thomas J. Walsh." Pacific Northwest Quarterly 55 (Jan. 1966): 1-7.

Clubb, Jerome M., and Howard W. Allen. "The Cities and the Election of 1928: Partisan Realignment?" American Historical Review 74 (April 1969): 1205-20.

Day, David S. "Herbert Hoover and Racial Politics: The DePriest Incident." Journal of Negro History 65 (Winter 1980): 6-17.

Doherty, Herbert J., Jr. "Florida and the Presidential Election of 1928." Florida Historical Quarterly 26 (Oct. 1947): 174-86.

Fuchs, Lawrence H. "Election of 1928." In History of American Presidential Elections, 1789-1968 ed. by Arthur M. Schlesinger, Jr., and Fred L. Israel (New York: Chelsea House, 1971): III: 1789-1968.

Ginzl, David J. "Lily-Whites Versus Black-and-Tans: Mississippi Republicans during the Hoover Administration." Journal of Mississippi History 42 (Aug. 1980): 194-211.

_____. "Patronage, Race, and Politics: Georgia Republicans During the Hoover Administration." Georgia Historical Quarterly 64 (Fall 1980): 280-93.

_____. "The Politics of Patronage: Florida Republicans during the Hoover Administration." Florida Historical Quarterly 61 (July 1982): 1-19.

Harper, Glenn T. "'Cotton Tom' Heflin and the Election of 1930: The Price of Party Disloyalty." Historian 30 (May 1968): 389-411.

McCarthy, G. Michael. "The Brown Derby Campaign in West Tennessee: Smith, Hoover, and the Politics of Race." West Tennessee Historical Society Publications 27 (1973): 81-98.

Reagan, Hugh D. "Race as a Factor in the Presidential Election of 1928 in Alabama." Alabama Review 19 (Jan. 1966): 5-19.

Schmelzer, Janet. "Wright Patman and the Impeachment of Andrew Mellon." East Texas Historical Journal 23 (No. 2, 1985): 33-46.

Schofield, Kent. "The Public Image of Herbert Hoover in the 1928 Campaign." Mid-America 51 (Oct. 1969): 278-93.

Schwarz, Jordan A. "Hoover and Congress: Politics, Personality, and Perspective in the Presidency." In The Hoover Presidency: A Reappraisal ed. by Martin L. Fausold and George T. Mazuzan (Albany: State University of New York Press, 1974), pp. 87-100.

Stegh, Leslie J. "A Paradox of Prohibition: Election of Robert J. Bulkley as Senator from Ohio, 1930." Ohio History 83 (Summer 1974): 170-82.

Stevens, Susan. "The Congressional Elections of 1930: Politics of Avoidance." In An American Historian: Essays to Honor Selig Adler ed. by Milton Plesur (Buffalo: State University of New York, 1980), pp. 149-58.

Strange, Douglas C. "Al Smith and the Republican Party at Prayer: The Lutheran Vote--1928?" Review of Politics 32 (July 1970): 347-64.

Straton, Hillyer H., and Ferenc M. Szasz. "John Roach Straton and the Presidential Election of 1928." New York History 49 (April 1968): 200-17.

Watson, Richard L, Jr. "A Southern Democratic Primary: Simmons vs. Bailey in 1930." North Carolina Historical Review 42 (Winter 1965): 21-46.

Dissertations

Allan, Arnold A. "The Party Principles of the Hoover Administration." Ph.D. diss., University of Iowa, 1937.

Dollar, Charles M. "The Senate Progressive Movement, 1921-1933: A Roll Call Analysis." Ph.D. diss., University of Kentucky, 1966.

Ginzl, David James. "Herbert Hoover and Republican Patronage Politics in the South, 1928-1932." Ph.D. diss., Syracuse University, 1977.

Morrison, Glenda E. "Women's Participation in the 1928 Presidential Campaign." Ph.D. diss., University of Kansas, 1978.

Savage, Hugh J. "Political Independents of the Hoover Era: The Progressive Insurgents of the Senate." Ph.D. diss., University of Illinois, 1961.

Schofield, Kent Michael. "The Figure of Herbert Hoover in the 1928 Campaign." Ph.D. diss., University of California, Riverside, 1966.

Schwarz, Jordan Abraham. "The Politics of Fear: Congress and the Depression during the Hoover Administration." Ph.D. diss., Columbia University, 1967.

Stevens, Susan F. "Congressional Elections of 1930: Politics of Avoidance." Ph.D. diss., State University of New York at Buffalo, 1980.

5.3 POLICIES AND PROGRAMS

Books

Barber, William J. From New Era to New Deal: Herbert Hoover, The Economists, and American Economic Policy, 1921-1933. New York: Cambridge University Press, 1985.

Himmelberg, Robert. The Origins of the National Recovery Administration: Business, Government, and the Trade Association Issue, 1921-1933. New York: Fordham University Press, 1976.

Hubbard, Preston. Origins of the TVA: The Muscle Shoals Controversy, 1920-1932. Nashville: Vanderbilt University Press, 1961.

Olsen, James S. Herbert Hoover and the Reconstruction Finance Corporation, 1931-1933. Ames: Iowa State University Press, 1977.

Schattschneider, E. E. Politics, Pressures and the Tariff: A Study of Free Private Enterprise in Pressure Politics, as Shown in the 1929-1930 Revision of the Tariff. New York: Prentice-Hall, 1935.

Swain, Donald C. Federal Conservation Policy, 1921-1933. Berkeley: University of California Press, 1963.

Wilber, Ray Lyman , and Arthur Mastick Hyde. The Hoover Policies. New York: Scribner's, 1937.

Woodruff, Nan Elizabeth. As Rare as Rain: Federal Relief in the Great Southern Drought of 1930-31. Urbana: University of Illinois Press, 1985.

Articles

Clements, Kendrick A. "Herbert Hoover and Conservation, 1921-33." American Historical Review 89 (Feb. 1984): 67-88.

Edwards, John Carver. "Herbert Hoover's Public Lands Policy: A Struggle for Control of the Western Domain." Pacific Historian 20 (Spring 1976): 34-45.

Fausold, Martin L. "President Hoover's Farm Policies, 1929-1933." Agricultural History 51 (April 1977): 362-77.

Hawley, Ellis W. "Herbert Hoover and American Corporatism, 1929-1933." In The Hoover Presidency: A Reappraisal ed. by Martin L. Fausold and George T. Mazuzan (Albany: State University of New York Press, 1974), pp. 101-19.

Lambert, C. Roger. "Herbert Hoover and Federal Farm Board Wheat." Heritage of Kansas 10 (Winter 1977): 22-33.

_____. "Hoover and Congress Debate Food Relief: 1930-1931." Red River Valley Historical Review 7 (Fall 1982): 42-49.

Lowitt, Richard. "Progressive Farm Leaders and Hoover's Moratorium." Mid - America 50 (July 1968): 236-39.

Meyer, Eugene. "From Laissez-Faire with William Graham Sumner to the R.F.C." Public Policy 5 (1946): 3-27.

Nash, Gerald D. "Herbert Hoover and the Origins of the Reconstruction Finance Corporation." Mississippi Valley Historical Review 46 (Dec. 1959): 455-68.

Olson, James S. "Harvey C. Couch and the Reconstruction Finance Corporation." Arkansas Historical Quarterly 32 (Winter 1973): 217-25.

_____. "The End of Voluntarism: Herbert Hoover and the National Credit Corporation." Annals of Iowa 41 (Fall 1972): 104-13.

Romasco, Albert U. "Herbert Hoover's Policies for Dealing with the Great Depression: The End of the Old Order or the Beginning of the New?" In The Hoover Presidency: A Reappraisal ed. by Martin L. Fausold and George T. Mazuzan (Albany: State University of New York Press, 1974), pp. 69-86.

Schwarz, Jordan A. "John Nance Garner and the Sales Tax Rebellion of 1932." Journal of Southern History 30 (May 1964): 162-80.

Stein, Herbert. "Pre-Revolutionary Fiscal Policy: The Regime of Herbert Hoover." Journal of Law and Economics 11 (Oct. 1966): 189-223.

Dissertations

Caine, Philip David. "The American Periodical Press and Military Preparedness during the Hoover Administration." Ph.D. diss., Stanford University, 1966.

DelPapa, Eugene Michael. "Herbert Hoover and the Struggle for Relief, 1930-1933." Ph.D. diss., Miami University, 1974.

Hubbard, Preston J. "The Muscle Shoals Controversy, 1920-1932: Public Policy in the Making." Ph.D. diss., Vanderbilt University, 1955.

Muessig, Raymond Henry. "Herbert Hoover and Education." Ed.D. diss., Stanford University, 1959.

Vlaun, Joan Gloria. "Herbert Hoover's Economic Foreign Policies for Dealing with the Great Depression: 1929-1933." Ph.D. diss., New York University, 1977.

6

The Roosevelt Administration

6.1 GENERAL

Books

Alsop, Joseph, and Robert Kintner. Men Around the President. New York: Doubleday, Doran, 1939.

Beard, Charles A., and George H. E. Smith. The Old Deal and the New. New York: Macmillan, 1941.

[Carter, John Franklin] "The Unofficial Observer." The New Dealers. New York: Simon and Schuster, 1934.

Conkin, Paul. FDR and the Origins of the Welfare State. New York: Thomas Y. Crowell, 1967.

_____. The New Deal. Arlington Heights, Ill.: Harlan Davidson, 1975.

Editors of the Economist. The New Deal: An Analysis and Appraisal. New York: Knopf, 1937.

Einaudi, Mario. The Roosevelt Revolution. New York: Harcourt, Brace, 1959.

Fenno, Richard F., Jr. The President's Cabinet: An Analysis in the Period from Wilson to Eisenhower. Cambridge: Harvard University Press, 1959.

Flynn, John T. The Roosevelt Myth. New York: Devin-Adair, 1948.

Freidel, Frank. FDR and the South. Baton Rouge: Louisiana State University Press, 1965.

_____. Franklin D. Roosevelt: Launching the New Deal. Boston: Little, Brown, 1973.

Gelfand, Lawrence E., and Robert J. Neymeyer. The New Deal Viewed from Fifty Years: Papers Commemorating the Fiftieth Anniversary of the Launching of Franklin D. Roosevelt's New Deal in 1933. Iowa City: Center for the Study of Recent History of the United States, 1984.

Goodman, Walter. The Committee: The Extraordinary Career of the House Committee on Un-American Activities. New York: Farrar, Straus & Giroux, 1968.

Graham, Otis L., Jr. The New Deal: The Critical Issues. Boston: Little, Brown, 1971.

Greer, Thomas H. What Roosevelt Thought: The Social and Political Ideas of Franklin D. Roosevelt. East Lansing: Michigan State University Press, 1958.

Gunther, John. Roosevelt in Retrospect: A Profile in History. New York: Harper & Row, 1950.

Hacker, Louis M. A Short History of the New Deal. New York: F.S. Crofts, 1934.

Halasz, Nicholas. Roosevelt Through Foreign Eyes. Princeton: Van Nostrand, 1961.

Hallgren, Mauritz. The Gay Reformer: Profits before Plenty under Franklin D. Roosevelt. New York: Knopf, 1935.

Henry, Laurin. Presidential Transitions. Washington, D.C.: Brookings Institution, 1960.

High, Stanley. Roosevelt--And Then? New York: Harper, 1937.

Hollingsworth, Harold M. and William F. Holmes, eds. Essays on the New Deal. Arlington: University of Texas Press, 1969.

Humphrey, Hubert H. The Political Philosophy of the New Deal. Baton Rouge: Louisiana State University Press, 1970.

Jacob, Charles E. Leadership in the New Deal: The Administrative Challenge. Englewood Cliffs, N.J.: Prentice-Hall, 1967.

Johnson, Gerald. Roosevelt: Dictator or Democrat? New York: Harper, 1941.

Kemler, Edgar. The Deflation of American Ideals: An Ethical Guide for New Dealers. Washington, D.C.: American Council on Public Affairs, 1941.

Kirkendall, Richard S., ed. The New Deal: The Historical Debate. New York: John Wiley, 1973.

Kyvig, David E. FDR's America. St. Charles, Mo.: Forum Press, 1976.

Leuchtenburg, William E. Franklin D. Roosevelt and the New Deal, 1932-1940. New York: Harper & Row, 1963.

_____. New Deal and Global War. New York: Time, Inc., 1964.

_____, ed. Franklin D. Roosevelt: A Profile. New York: Hill and Wang, 1967.

_____, ed. The New Deal: A Documentary History. New York: Harper & Row, 1968.

Lindley, Ernest K. Half Way with Roosevelt. New York: Viking, 1936.

_____. The Roosevelt Revolution: First Phase. New York: Viking, 1933.

McFarland, C. K. Roosevelt, Lewis, and the New Deal, 1933-1940. Fort Worth: Texas Christian University Press, 1970.

Moley, Raymond, and Elliott A. Rosen. The First New Deal. New York: Harcourt Brace, 1966.

Ogden, August Raymond. The Dies Committee: A Study of the Special House Committee for the Investigation of Un-American Activities, 1938-1944. Washington: Catholic University of America Press, 1945.

Perkins, Dexter. The New Age of Franklin Roosevelt, 1932-1945. Chicago: University of Chicago Press, 1957.

Ramsay, Marion L. Pyramids of Power: The Story of Roosevelt, Insull and the Utility Wars. Indianapolis: Bobbs-Merrill, 1937.

Rauch, Basil. The History of the New Deal, 1933-1938. New York: Creative Age, 1944.

Robinson, Edgar E. The Roosevelt Leadership, 1933-1945. Philadelphia: Lippincott, 1955.

Romasco, Albert U. The Politics of Recovery: Roosevelt's New Deal. New York: Oxford University Press, 1983.

Rosen, Elliot A. Hoover, Roosevelt, and the Brains Trust: From Depression to New Deal. New York: Columbia University Press, 1977.

Sargent, James E. Roosevelt and the Hundred Days: Struggle for the Early New Deal. New York: Garland, 1981.

Schlesinger, Arthur M., Jr. The Coming of the New Deal. Boston: Houghton Mifflin, 1958.

_____. The Crisis of the Old Order. Boston: Houghton Mifflin, 1956.

_____. The Politics of Upheaval. Boston: Houghton Mifflin, 1960.

Sitkoff, Harvard, ed. Fifty Years Later: The New Deal Evaluated. Philadelphia: Temple University Press, 1985.

Sutton, Anthony C. Wall Street and FDR. New Rochelle, N.Y.: Arlington House, 1975.

Thompson, Kenneth W., ed. The Roosevelt Presidency: Four Intimate Perspectives on Franklin Delano Roosevelt. Lanham, Md.: University Press of America, 1982.

Tugwell, Rexford G. FDR: Architect of an Era. New York: Macmillan, 1967.

_____. In Search of Roosevelt. Cambridge: Harvard University Press, 1972.

_____. The Enlargement of the Presidency. Garden City, N. Y.: Doubleday, 1960.

Wann, A. J. The President as Chief Administrator: A Study of Franklin D. Roosevelt. Washington, D.C.: Public Affairs Press, 1968.

Warren, Frank A., and Michael Wreszin, eds. The New Deal: An Anthology. New York: Thomas Y. Crowell, 1968.

Wolfskill, George, and John A. Hudson. All But the People: Franklin D. Roosevelt and His Critics, 1933-1939. New York: Macmillan, 1969.

Woods, John A. Roosevelt and Modern America. London: English Universities Press, 1959.

Articles

Abramowitz, Mildred W. "Eleanor Roosevelt and the National Youth Administration, 1935-1943--An Extension of the Presidency." Presidential Studies Quarterly 14 (Fall 1984): 569-80.

Albright, Horace M. "A Ride with FDR." American History Illustrated 7 (May 1972): 23-25.

Alexander, Albert. "The President and the Investigator: Roosevelt and Dies." Antioch Review 15 (March 1955): 106-17.

Arnold, Thurman. "Roosevelt's Contribution to the American Competitive Ideal." Centennial Review 9 (Spring 1965): 192-208.

Ashby, LeRoy. "The Disappearing Dry: Raymond Robins and the Last Days of Prohibition." North Carolina Historical Review 51 (Oct. 1974): 401-19.

Berlin, Isaiah. "President Franklin D. Roosevelt." Political Quarterly 26 (Dec. 1955): 336-44.

_____. "Roosevelt through European Eyes." Atlantic Monthly 196 (July 1955): 67-71.

Blum, John Morton. "Franklin Roosevelt and the Problem of Priorities." In The Progressive Presidents: Roosevelt, Wilson, Roosevelt, Johnson (New York: W. W. Norton, 1980), pp. 107-62.

Brinkley, Alan. "The New Deal: Prelude." Wilson Quarterly 6 (Spring 1982): 50-61.

Brown, Richard C. "Mark Sullivan Views the New Deal from Avondale." Pennsylvania Magazine of History and Biography 99 (July 1975): 351-61.

Burke, Robert E. "The Roosevelt Administrations." Current History 39 (Oct. 1960): 220-24.

Butow, R. J. C. "The FDR Tapes." American Heritage 33 (Feb./March 1982): 8-24.

Davis, Kenneth S. "Incident in Miami." American Heritage 32 (Dec. 1980): 86-95.

Dawson, Nelson L. "Louis D. Brandeis, Felix Frankfurter, and Franklin D. Roosevelt: The Origins of a New Deal Relationship." American Jewish History 68 (Sept. 1978): 32-42.

Eulau, Heinz. "Neither Ideology Nor Utopia: The New Deal in Retrospect." Antioch Review 19 (Winter 1959-60): 523-37.

Finkelstein, Leo, Jr. "The Calendrical Rite of the Ascension to Power." Western Journal of Speech Communication 45 (Winter 1981): 51-59.

Fleming, Harold. "The New Deal in Retrospect." Challenge: The Magazine of Economic Affairs 8 (Oct. 1959): 64-68.

Frisch, Morton J. "Franklin D. Roosevelt and the Problem of Democratic Liberty." Ethics 72 (April 1962): 18-92.

_____. "Roosevelt the Conservator: A Rejoinder to Hofstadter." Journal of Politics 25 (May 1963): 361-72.

Galbraith, J. K. "On the Economics of F.D.R.: What a President Ought to Know." Commentary 22 (Aug. 1956): 172-73.

_____. "FDR: A Practical Magician." American Heritage 34 (Feb. 1983): 90-93.

Hand, Samuel B. "Al Smith, Franklin D. Roosevelt and the New Deal: Some Comments on Perspective." Historian 27 (May 1965): 366-81.

Hawley, Ellis W. "A Partnership Formed, Dissolved and in Renegotiation: Business and Government in the Franklin D. Roosevelt Era." In Business and Government: Essays in 20th Century Cooperation and Confrontation ed. by Joseph R. Freese, S. J., and Jacob Judd (Terrytown, N.Y.: Sleepy Hollow Restorations, 1985), pp. 187-219.

Holt, James. "The New Deal and the American Anti-Statist Tradition." In The New Deal: The National Level ed. by John Braeman, Robert H. Bremner, and David Brody (Columbus: Ohio State University Press, 1975): pp. 27-49.

Jaffe, Louis L. "Professors and Judges as Advisors to Government: Reflections on the Roosevelt-Frankfurter Relationship." Harvard Law Review 83 (Dec. 1969): 366-76.

Jones, Terry L. "An Adminstration Under Fire: The Long-Farley Affair of 1935." Louisiana History 28 (Winter 1987): 5-17.

Kehl, James A., and Samuel J. Astorino. "A Bull Moose Responds to the New Deal: Pennsylvania's Gifford Pinchot." Pennsylvania Magazine of History and Biography 88 (Jan. 1964): 37-51.

Kirkendall, Richard S. "Franklin D. Roosevelt and the Service Intellectual." Mississippi Valley Historical Review 49 (Dec. 1962): 456-71.

Kyvig, David E. "Objection Sustained: Prohibition Repeal and the New Deal." In Alcohol, Reform, and Society: The Liquor Issue in Social Context ed. by Jack S. Blocker (Westport, Conn.: Greenwood, 1979), pp. 211-33.

Larson, Bethene Wookey. "Franklin D. Roosevelt's Visit to Sidney During the Drouth of 1936." Nebraska History 65 (Spring 1984): 1-14.

Leiter, William M. "The Presidency and Non-federal Government: FDR and the Promotion of State Legislative Action." Presidential Studies Quarterly 9 (Spring 1979): 101-21.

Lepawsky, Albert. "The Planning Apparatus: A Vignette of the New Deal." Journal of the American Institute of Planners 42 (Jan. 1976): 16-32.

Leuchtenburg, William E. "FDR and the Kingfish." American Heritage 36 (Oct. 1985): 56-63.

Louchheim, Katie. "The Little Red House." Virginia Quarterly Review 56 (Winter 1980): 119-34.

Mason, Bruce. "The EPIC Movement." Arizona Quarterly 11 (1955): 320-31.

McFarland, C. K. "Coalition of Convenience: Lewis and Roosevelt, 1933-1940." Labor History 13 (Summer 1972): 400-14.

McIntosh, Clarence F. "The Significance of the End-Poverty-in-California Movement." Pacific Historian 27 (Winter 1983): 21-25.

Millis, Walter. "Roosevelt in Retrospect." Virginia Quarterly Review 21 (Summer 1945): 321-30.

Neustadt, Richard E. "Approaches to Staffing the Presidency: Notes on FDR and JFK." American Political Science Review 57 (Dec. 1961): 855-64.

O'Reilly, Kenneth. "A New Deal for the FBI: The Roosevelt Administration, Crime Control, and National Security." Journal of American History 69 (Dec. 1982): 638-58.

_____. "The Roosevelt Administration and Legislative-Executive Conflict: The FBI vs. the Dies Committee." Congress & The Presidency 10 (Spring 1983): 79-93.

Patenaude, Lionel. "Vice President John Nance Garner: A Study in the Use of Influence during the New Deal." Texana 11 (No. 2, 1973): 124-44.

Patterson, James T. "F.D.R. and the Democratic Triumph." Current History 47 (Oct. 1964): 216-20, 243-44.

Polenberg, Richard. "Franklin Roosevelt and Civil Liberties: The Case of the Dies Committee." Historian 30 (Feb. 1968): 165-78.

_____. "The Decline of the New Deal, 1937-1940." In The New Deal: The National Level ed. by John Braeman, Robert H. Bremner, and David Brody (Columbus: Ohio State University Press, 1975), pp. 246-66.

Pusateri, C. Joseph. "A Study in Misunderstanding: Franklin D. Roosevelt and the Business Community." Social Studies 60 (Oct. 1969), 204-11.

Roberts, Chalmers M. "FDR and the Presidential Press Conference." In Portraits of American Presidents: The Roosevelt Presidency ed. by Kenneth W. Thompson (New York: University Press of America, 1982), pp. 65-83.

Rollins, Alfred B., Jr. "'Was There Really a Man Named Roosevelt?'" In American History: Retrospect and Prospect ed. by George Athan Billias and Gerald N. Grob (New York: Free Press, 1971), pp. 232-70.

Rosen, Elliot A. "Intranationalism vs. Internationalism: The Interregnum Struggle for the Sanctity of the New Deal." Political Science Quarterly 81 (June 1966): 274-97.

Ross, Irwin. "Fifteen Seconds of Terror." American History Illustrated 10 (July 1975): 10-13.

Ryan, Halford Ross. "Roosevelt's First Inaugural: A Study of Technique." Quarterly Journal of Speech 65 (April 1979): 137-49.

Ryan, John A. "Roosevelt and Social Justice." Review of Politics 7 (July 1945): 297-305.

Schlesinger, Arthur M., Jr. "The First Hundred Days of the New Deal." In The Aspirin Age, 1919-1941 ed. by Isabel Leighton (New York: Simon and Schuster, 1949), pp. 275-96.

Schnell, J. Christopher. "New Deal Scandals: E. Y. Mitchell and F.D.R.'s Commerce Department." Missouri Historical Review 69 (July 1975): 357-75.

Seligman, Lester G. "Presidential Leadership: The Inner Circle and Institutionalization." Journal of Politics 18 (Aug. 1956): 410-26.

Sheffer, Martin S. "The Attorney General and Presidential Power: Robert H. Jackson, Franklin Roosevelt, and the Prerogative Presidency." Presidential Studies Quarterly 12 (Winter 1982): 54-65.

Sirevag, Torbjorn. "Franklin D. Roosevelt and the Uses of History." In Americana Norwegica: Norwegian Contributions to American Studies, vol. 2, ed. by Sigmund Skard (Philadelphia: University of Pennsylvania Press, 1968), pp. 299-342.

Skau, George H. "Franklin D. Roosevelt and the Expansion of Presidential Power." Current History 66 (June 1974): 246-48.

Snowiss, Sylvia. "Presidential Leadership of Congress: An Analysis of Roosevelt's First Hundred Days." Publius 1 (No. 1, 1971): 59-87.

Steele, Richard W. "The Pulse of the People: Franklin D. Roosevelt and the Gauging of American Public Opinion." Journal of Contemporary History 9 (Oct. 1974): 195-216.

Sussman, Leila A. "FDR and the White House Mail." Public Opinion Quarterly 20 (Spring 1956): 5-15.

Swain, Martha H. "The Lion and the Fox: The Relationship of President Franklin D. Roosevelt and Senator Pat Harrison." Journal of Mississippi History 38 (Nov. 1976): 333-59.

Theoharis, Athan G. "The FBI's Stretching of Presidential Directives, 1936-1953." Political Science Quarterly 91 (Winter 1976-77): 631-47.

Trani, Eugene P. "Conflict or Compromise: Harold Ickes and Franklin D. Roosevelt."
    North Dakota Quarterly 36 (Winter 1968): 20-29.
Tugwell, Rexford G. "Franklin D. Roosevelt on the Verge of the Presidency." Antioch
    Review 16 (Spring 1956): 46-79.
_____. "Roosevelt and Frankfurter: An Essay Review." Political Science
    Quarterly 85 (March 1970): 99-114.
_____. "Transition: Hoover to Roosevelt 1932-1933." Centennial Review 9
    (Spring 1965): 160-91.
_____. "Roosevelt and the Bonus Marchers of 1932." Political Science
    Quarterly 87 (Sept. 1972): 563-76.
_____. "The Compromising Roosevelt." Western Political Quarterly 6 (June
    1953): 320-41.
_____. "The New Deal: The Available Instruments of Governmental Power."
    Western Political Quarterly 2 (Dec. 1949): 545-80.
_____. "The New Deal: The Decline of Government, Part I." Western Political
    Quarterly 4 (June 1951): 295-312.
_____. "The New Deal: The Decline of Government, Part II." Western
    Political Quarterly 4 (Sept. 1951): 469-86.
_____. "The New Deal: The Progressive Tradition." Western Political
    Quarterly 3 (Sept. 1950): 390-427.
_____. "The Sources of New Deal Reformism." Ethics 64 (1954): 249-76.
Williams, David. "'They Never Stopped Watching Us': FBI Political Surveillance,
    1924-1936." UCLA Historical Journal 2 (1981): 5-28.
Winfield, Betty H. "Mrs. Roosevelt's Press Conference Association: The First Lady
    Shines a Light." Journalism History 8 (Summer 1981): 54-55, 63-70.
_____. "F.D.R.'s Pictorial Image, Rules and Boundaries." Journalism History 5
    (Winter 1978-79): 110-14, 136.
_____. "Franklin D. Roosevelt's Efforts to Influence the News during His First
    Term Press Conferences." Presidential Studies Quarterly 11 (Spring 1981):
    189-99.
Wolfskill, George. "New Deal Critics: Did They Miss the Point?" In Essays on the
    New Deal ed. by Harold M. Hollingsworth and William F. Holmes (Austin:
    University of Texas Press, 1969), pp. 49-68.

Dissertations

Bradley, Leslie L. "Certain Phases in the Inter-Relationship between Hugh S. Johnson
    and the New Deal, 1935-1942." Ph.D. diss., Northwestern University, 1944.
Bush, John M., III. "Disillusioned New Dealers." Ph.D. diss., Mississippi State
    University, 1964.
Curlee, Joan E. "Some Aspects of the New Deal Rationale: The Pre-1936 Writings of
    Six of Roosevelt's Advisers." Ph.D. diss., Vanderbilt University, 1957.
Fine, Robert S. "Roosevelt's Radio Chatting: Its Development and Impact During the
    Great Depression." Ph.D. diss., New York University, 1977.

Graham, Otis L., Jr. "The Old Progressive and the New Deal: A Study of the Modern Reform Tradition." Ph.D. diss., Columbia University, 1966.

Imler, Joseph Anthony. "The First One Hundred Days of the New Deal: The View from Capitol Hill." Ph.D. diss., Indiana University, 1975.

Ingram, Marvin Lee. "Franklin D. Roosevelt's Exercise of the Veto Power." Ph.D. diss., New York University, 1947.

McWilliams, John C. "The Protectors: Harry J. Anslinger and the Federal Bureau of Narcotics, 1930-1962." Ph.D. diss., Pennsylvania State University, 1986.

Milkis, Sidney M. "The New Deal, the Decline of Parties and the Administrative State." Ph.D. diss., University of Pennsylvania, 1981.

Namorato, Michael Vincent. "Donald Richberg and Rexford Tugwell: Capitalist Planning in the New Deal." Ph.D. diss., Michigan State University, 1975.

Ragland, James Franklin. "Franklin D. Roosevelt and Public Opinion, 1933-1940." Ph.D. diss., Stanford University, 1954.

Robinson, George W. "Right of Roosevelt: Negativism and the New Deal, 1933-1937." Ph.D. diss., University of Wisconsin, 1956.

Sargent, James Edward. "The Hundred Days: Franklin D. Roosevelt and the Early New Deal, 1933." Ph.D. diss., Michigan State University, 1972.

Schoenherr, Steven Edlo. "Selling the New Deal: Stephen T. Early's Role as Press Secretary to Franklin D. Roosevelt." Ph.D. diss., University of Delaware, 1976.

Silver, Paul L. "Wilsonians and the New Deal." Ph.D. diss., University of Pennsylvania, 1964.

Syron, Leslie W. "The New Deal and the Technicways: A Preliminary Study of the Innovations and Power Structure of the Early Roosevelt Administration." Ph.D. diss., University of North Carolina, 1952.

Tilman, Lee R. "The American Business Community and the Death of the New Deal." Ph.D. diss., University of Arizona, 1966.

Van Patten, Paul L., Jr. "B.O.B. and F.D.R.: A Stage in the Growth of the Institutional Presidency." Ph.D. diss., University of Notre Dame, 1983.

Wann, Andrew Jackson. "Franklin D. Roosevelt and the Administrative Organization of the Executive Branch." Ph.D. diss., University of Missouri, 1961.

Williams, Dorothy G. "The Treatment of the Second Roosevelt Administration in Three Popular Magazines." Ph.D. diss., University of Chicago, 1948.

Wilson, John Fletcher. "An Analysis of the Criticism of Selected Speeches by Franklin D. Roosevelt." Ph.D. diss., University of Wisconsin, 1955.

Zavin, Howard S. "Forward to the Land: Franklin D. Roosevelt and the City, 1882-1933." Ph.D. diss., New York University, 1972.

6.2   POLITICS

Books

Allswang, John M. The New Deal and American Politics: A Study in Political Change. New York: John Wiley, 1978.

Anderson, Kristi. The Creation of a Democratic Majority, 1928-1936. Chicago: University of Chicago Press, 1979.

Campbell, Persia C. Consumer Representation in the New Deal. New York: Columbia University Press, 1940.

Donahoe, Bernard F. Private Plans and Public Dangers: The Story of FDR's Third Nomination. South Bend, Ind.: University of Notre Dame Press, 1965.

Dorsett, Lyle. Franklin D. Roosevelt and the City Bosses. Port Washington, N.Y.: Kennikat, 1977.

_____. The Pendergast Machine. New York: Oxford University Press, 1968.

Feinman, Ronald L. Twilight of Progressivism: The Western Republican Senators and the New Deal. Baltimore: Johns Hopkins University Press, 1981.

Frisch, Morton J. Franklin D. Roosevelt: The Contribution of the New Deal to American Political Thought and Practice. New York: Twayne, 1975.

Gosnell, Harold F. Champion Campaigner: Franklin D. Roosevelt. New York: Macmillan, 1952.

Johnson, Donald Bruce. The Republican Party and Wendell Wilkie. Urbana: University of Illinois Press, 1960.

McCoy, Donald R. Angry Voices: Left-of-Center Politics in the New Deal. Lawrence: University of Kansas Press, 1958.

Mooney, Booth. Roosevelt and Rayburn: A Political Partnership. Philadelphia: Lippincott, 1971.

Moscow, Warren. Roosevelt and Wilkie. Englewood Cliffs, N. J.: Prentice-Hall, 1968.

Mulder, Ronald A. The Insurgent Progressives in the United States Senate and the New Deal, 1933-1939. New York: Garland, 1979.

Oulahan, Richard. The Man Who . . .The Story of the 1932 Democratic National Convention. New York: Dial, 1971.

Parmet, Herbert S., and Marie B. Hecht. Never Again: A President Runs for a Third Term. New York: Macmillan, 1968.

Patterson, James T. Congressional Conservatism and the New Deal: The Growth of the Conservative Coalition in Congress, 1933-1939. Lexington: University of Kentucky Press, 1967.

Peel, Roy Victor, and Thomas C. Donnelly. The 1932 Camaipgn: An Analysis. New York: Farrar Rinehart, 1935.

Robinson, Edgar E. They Voted for Roosevelt: The Presidential Vote, 1932-1944. Stanford: Stanford University Press, 1947.

Stein, Charles W. The Third-Term Tradition. New York: Columbia University Press, 1943.

Sussman, Leila A. Dear FDR: A Study of Political Letter-Writing. Totowa, N.J.:
  Bedminster Press, 1963.

Articles

Appleby, Paul H. "Roosevelt's Third-Term Decision." American Political Science
  Review 46 (Sept. 1952): 754-65.

Arthur, Thomas H. "An Actor in Politics: Melvyn Douglas and the New Deal."
  Journal of Popular Culture 14 (Fall 1980): 196-211.

Bailey, Robert J. "Theodore G. Bilbo and the Senatorial Election of 1934." Southern
  Quarterly 10 (Oct. 1971): 91-105.

Blayney, Michael Stewart. "Honor Among Gentlemen: Herbert Pell, Franklin
  Roosevelt, and the Campaign of 1936." Rhode Island History 39 (Aug. 1980):
  95-102.

Boorstin, Daniel J. "Selling the President to the People." Commentary 20 (Nov.
  1955): 421-24.

Brinkley, Alan. "Comparative Biography as Political History: Huey Long and Father
  Coughlin." History Teacher 18 (Nov. 1984): 9-16.

Burke, Robert E. "Election of 1940." In History of American Presidential Elections,
  1789-1968 ed. by Arthur M. Schlesinger, Jr., and Fred L. Israel (New York:
  Chelsea House, 1971), IV: 2917-3006.

Carlson, Paul H. and Steve Porter. "South Dakota Congressmen and the Hundred
  Days of the New Deal." South Dakota History 8 (Fall 1978): 327-39.

Casey, Ralph D. "Republican Propaganda in the 1936 Campaign." Public Opinion
  Quarterly 1 (April 1937): 27-44.

Cobb, James C. "Not Gone, But Forgotten: Eugene Talmadge and the 1938 Purge
  Campaign." Georgia Historical Quarterly 59 (Summer 1975): 197-209.

Coode, Thomas H. "Georgia Congressmen and the First Hundred Days of the New
  Deal." Georgia Historical Quarterly 53 (June 1969): 129-46.

_____. "Tennessee Congressmen and the New Deal, 1933-1938." West
  Tennessee Historical Society Papers 31 (1977): 132-58.

_____. "The Presidential Election of 1940 as Reflected in the Tennessee
  Metropolitan Press." East Tennessee Historical Society Publications 40 (1968):
  85-100.

Cummings, Tom. "An Examination of the Lubell Thesis: McIntosh County, North
  Dakota, 1936-1940." North Dakota Quarterly 42 (Autumn 1974): 26-41.

Dalfiume, Richard M. "Military Segregation and the 1940 Presidential Election."
  Phylon 30 (Spring 1969): 42-55.

Davies, Richard O. "The Politics of Desperation: Willliam A. Hirth and the
  Presidential Election of 1932." Agricultural History 38 (Oct. 1964): 226-34.

Davis, Polly. "Court Reform and Alben W. Barkley's Election as Majority Leader."
  Southern Quarterly 15 (Oct. 1976): 15-31.

Dewitt, Howard A. "Miracle in Philadelphia: The Nomination of Wendell Willkie, A Reappraisal." Western Pennsylvania Historical Magazine 55 (Oct. 1972): 295-309.

Dinnerstein, Leonard. "The Senate's Rejection of Aubrey Williams as Rural Electrification Administrator." Alabama Review 21 (April 1968): 133-43.

Dorsett, Lyle W. "Frank Hague, Franklin Roosevelt and the Politics of the New Deal." New Jersey History 94 (Spring 1976): 23-35.

Dubay, Robert W. "Pyrrhic Victory: The Election of 1936." Georgia Historical Quarterly 66 (Spring 1982): 69-72.

Erikson, Robert S., and Kent L. Tedin. "The 1928-1936 Partisan Realignment: The Case for the Conversion Hypothesis." American Political Science Review 75 (Dec. 1981): 951-62.

Evjen, Henry O. "The Wilkie Campaign: An Unfortunate Chapter in Republican Leadership." Journal of Politics 14 (May 1952): 241-56.

Feinman, Ronald L. "The Progressive Republican Senate Bloc and the Presidential Election of 1932." Mid-America 59 (April 1977): 73-91.

Fink, Gary M. "Northern Great Plains Senators in the New Deal Era." Capitol Studies 3 (Fall 1975): 129-52.

Freidel, Frank. "The Election of 1932." In History of American Presidential Elections, 1789-1968 ed. by Arthur M. Schlesinger, Jr., and Fred L. Israel (New York: Chelsea House, 1971), III: 2707-2806.

Gosnell, Harold F., and Norman Gill. "Analysis of the 1932 Presidential Vote in Chicago." American Political Science Review 29 (Dec. 1935): 967-84.

Gough, Paul A. "Economic Conditions and Congressional Elections: An Attempt to Control for the Depression." American Political Quarterly 12 (Jan. 1984): 71-85.

Gourwitch, Peter Alexis. "Breaking with Orthodoxy: The Politics of Economic Policy Responses to the Depression of the 1930s." International Organization 38 (Winter 1984): 95-129.

Graham, Jeanne. "Kenneth D. McKellar's 1934 Campaign: Issues and Events." West Tennessee Historical Society Papers 18 (1964): 107-29.

Graham, Otis L.. Jr. "The Democratic Party, 1932-1942." In History of U.S. Political Parties ed. by Arthur M. Schlesinger (New York: Chelsea House, 1973), 3: 1939-2066.

Grant, Philip A. "The Presidential Election of 1932 in Iowa." Annals of Iowa 44 (Winter 1979): 541-50.

_____. "The Presidential Election of 1932 in Western Massachusetts." Historical Journal of Western Massachusetts 8 (Jan. 1980): 3-13.

_____. "Appalachian Congressmen during the New Deal Era." Appalachian Journal 2 (Autumn 1974): 72-77.

_____. "Congressional Leaders from the Great Plains, 1921-1932." North Dakota History 46 (Winter 1979): 19-23.

_____. "East Texas Congressmen during the New Deal." East Texas Historical Journal 11 (Fall 1973): 53-58.

_____. "Editorial Reaction to the Harrison-Barkley Senate Leadership Contest, 1937." Journal of Mississippi History 36 (May 1974): 127-41.

_____. "Establishing a Two-Party System: The 1932 Presidential Election in South Dakota." Presidential Studies Quarterly 10 (Winter 1980): 73-79.

_____. "Great Plains Congressmen, 1933-36." Heritage of the Great Plains 11 (Winter 1978): 35-44.

_____. "Iowa Congressional Leaders, 1921-1932." Annals of Iowa 42 (Fall 1974): 430-42.

_____. "Ten Mississippians Who Served in Congress, 1931-1937." Journal of Mississippi History 39 (Aug. 1977): 205-12.

_____. "The Election of Harry S. Truman to the United States Senate." Missouri Historical Society Bulletin 36 (Jan. 1980): 103-9.

_____. "The Kansas Congressional Delegation and the Selective Service Act of 1940." Kansas History 2 (Aug. 1979): 196-205.

_____. "The Kentucky Press and the 1938 Democratic Senatorial Primary." Appalachian Notes 2 (No.4, 1974): 49-58.

_____. "The Pennsylvania Congressional Delegation and the Bituminous Coal Acts of 1935 and 1937." Pennsylvania History 49 (April 1982): 121-31.

_____. "The Presidential Election of 1932 in Michigan." Michigan Historical Review 12 (Spring 1986): 83-94.

_____. "The Presidential Election of 1932 in Missouri." Missouri Historical Society Bulletin 35 (April 1979): 164-70.

Hall, Alvin L. "Politics and Patronage: Virginia's Senators and the Roosevelt Purges of 1938." Virginia Magazine of History and Biography 82 (July 1974): 331-50.

Hamilton, Marty. "Bull Moose Plays an Encore: Hiram Johnson and the Presidential Campaign of 1932." California Historical Quarterly 16 (Sept. 1962): 212-21.

Harrington, Jerry. "Senator Guy Gillette Foils the Execution Committee." Palimpsest 62 (Nov.-Dec. 1981): 170-80.

Heinemann, Ronald L. "'Harry Byrd for President': The 1932 Campaign." Virginia Cavalcade 25 (Summer 1975): 28-37.

Herring, E. Pendleton. "First Session of the Seventy-third Congress, March 9, 1933, to June 16, 1933." American Political Science Review 28 (Jan. 1934): 65-70.

Hixon, Walter L. "The 1938 Kentucky Senate Election: Alben W. Barkley, 'Happy' Chandler, and the New Deal." Register of the Kentucky Historical Society 80 (Summer 1982): 304-29.

Jakoubek, Robert E. "A Jeffersonian's Dissent: John W. Davis and the Campaign of 1936." West Virginia History 35 (Jan. 1974): 145-53.

Jensen, Richard. "The Cities Reelect Roosevelt: Ethnicity, Religion, and Class in 1940." Ethnicity 8 (June 1981): 189-95.

Jones, Gene Delon. "The Origins of the Alliance between the New Deal and the Chicago Machine." Journal of the Illinois State Historical Society 67 (June 1974): 253-74.

Kirkendall, Richard. "The New Deal and American Politics." In Fifty Years Later: The New Deal Evaluated ed. by Harvard Sitkoff (New York: Knopf, 1985), pp. 11-36.

Koeniger, A. Cash. "The Politics of Independence: Carter Glass and the Elections of 1936." South Atlantic Quarterly 80 (Winter 1981): 95-106.

Kyvig, David E. "Raskob, Roosevelt, and Repeal." Historian 37 (May 1975): 469-87.

Lamb, Karl A. "John Hamilton and the Revitalization of the Republican Party, 1936-40." Papers of the Michigan Academy of Science, Arts and Letters 45 (1960): 233-50.

Leuchtenburg, William E. "Election of 1936." In History of American Presidential Elections, 1789-1968 ed. Arthur M. Schlesinger, Jr., and Fred L. Israel (New York: Chelsea House, 1971), 3: 2809-2914.

Levin, James. "Governor Albert C. Ritchie and the Democratic Convention of 1932." Maryland Historical Magazine 67 (Fall 1972): 278-93.

Ludwig, E. Jeffrey. "Pennsylvania: The National Election of 1932." Pennsylvania History 31 (July 1964): 334-51.

Marcello, Ronald E. "Senator Josiah Bailey, Harry Hopkins, and the WPA: A Prelude to the Conservative Coalition." Southern Studies 22 (Winter 1983): 321-39.

_____. "The Selection of North Carolina's WPA Chief, 1935: A Dispute over Political Patronage." North Carolina Historical Review 52 (Jan. 1975): 59-76.

Massey, Robert K., Jr. "The Democratic Laggard: Massachusetts in 1932." New England Quarterly 44 (Dec. 1971): 553-74.

Mayer, George H. "Alf M. Landon as Leader of the Republican Opposition, 1937-1940." Kansas Historical Quarterly 32 (Autumn 1966): 325-33.

McCoy, Donald R. "The New Deal Through Alf Landon's Eyes." Midwest Quarterly 6 (Oct. 1964): 59-74.

Mead, Howard N. "Russell vs. Talmadge: Southern Politics and the New Deal." Georgia Historical Quarterly 65 (Spring 1981): 28-45.

Meredith, Howard L. "Small Dam Politics: The Sandstone Creek Project." Great Plains Journal 6 (Spring 1967): 97-107.

Moore, John Robert. "Senator Josiah W. Bailey and the 'Conservative Manifesto' of 1937." Journal of Southern History 31 (Feb. 1965): 21-39.

Mulder, Ronald A. "Reluctant New Dealers: The Progressive Insurgents in the United States Senate, 1933-1934." Capitol Studies 2 (Winter 1974): 5-22.

_____. "The Progressive Insurgents in the United States Senate, 1935-1936: Was There a Second New Deal?" Mid-America 57 (April 1975): 106-25.

Nichols, Jeanette P. "Silver Inflation and the Senate in 1933." Social Studies 25 (Jan. 1934): 12-18.

O'Brien, Patrick J. "A Reexamination of the Senate Farm Bloc, 1921-1933." Agricultural History 47 (July 1973): 248-63.

Patenaude, Lionel V. "The Garner Vote Switch to Roosevelt: 1932 Democratic Convention." Southwestern Historical Quarterly 79 (1975): 189-204.

Patterson, James T. "A Conservative Coalition Forms in Congress, 1933-39." Journal of American History 52 (March 1966): 757-72.

Plambeck, Herb. "The National Drought Conference in Des Moines: When FDR and Alf Landon Met." Palimpsest 67 (Nov. 1986): 194-201.

Pleasants, Julian M. "'Buncombe Bob' and Red Russian Fish Eggs: The Senatorial Election of 1932 in North Carolina." Appalachian Journal 4 (Autumn 1976): 51-62.

Plesur, Milton. "The Republican Congressional Comeback of 1938." Review of Politics 24 (Oct. 1962): 525-62.

Polenberg, Richard. "Franklin Roosevelt and the Purge of John O'Connor." New York History 49 (July 1968): 306-26.

Porter, David L. "The Iowa Congressional Delegation and the Great Economic Issues, 1929-1933." Annals of Iowa 46 (Summer 1982): 337-54

Posner, Russell M. "California's Role in the Nomination of Franklin D. Roosevelt." California Historical Society Quarterly 39 (June 1960): 121-39.

Price, Charles M., and Joseph Boskin. "The Roosevelt 'Purge': A Reappraisal." Journal of Politics 28 (Aug. 1966): 660-70.

Prindle, David F. "Voter Turnout, Critical Elections, and the New Deal Realignment." Social Science History 3 (Winter 1979): 144-70.

Reiter, Howard L. "The Perils of Partisan Recall." Public Opinion Quarterly 44 (Fall 1980): 385-88.

Richardson, Elmo R. "Western Politics and New Deal Policies: A Study of T. A. Walters of Idaho." Pacific Northwest Quarterly 54 (Jan. 1963): 9-18.

Rosen, Elliot A. "Baker on the Fifth Ballot? The Democratic Alternative: 1932." Ohio History 75 (Autumn 1966): 226-46.

_____. "The Midwest Opposition to the New Deal." In The New Deal Viewed from Fifty Years ed. by Lawrence E. Gelfand and Robert J. Neymeyer (Iowa City: Center for the Study of Recent History of the United States, 1983), pp. 55-90.

Ross, Hugh. "John L. Lewis and the Election of 1940." Labor History 17 (Spring 1976): 133-59.

_____. "Roosevelt's Third-Term Nomination." Mid-America 44 (April 1962): 80-94.

_____. "Was the Nomination of Wendell Wilkie a Political Miracle?" Indiana Magazine of History 58 (June 1962): 79-100.

Ryan, Thomas G. "Ethnicity in the 1940 Presidential Election in Iowa: A Quantitiative Approach." Annals of Iowa 43 (Spring 1977): 615-35.

Sanford, Dudley Gregory. "You Can't Get There from Here: The Presidential Boomlet for Governor George D. Aiken, 1937-1939." Vermont History 49 (Fall 1981): 197-208.

Schnell, J. Christopher. "Missouri Progressives and the Nomination of F.D.R." Missouri Historical Review 68 (April 1974): 269-79.

Seligmann, G. L., Jr. "The Purge That Failed: The 1934 Senatorial Election in New Mexico: Yet Another View." New Mexico Historical Review 47 (Oct. 1972): 361-81.

Shanks, Alexander Graham. "Sam Rayburn and the Democratic Convention of 1932." Texana 3 (Winter 1965): 321-32.

Shannon, Jasper B. "Presidential Politics in the South: 1938." Journal of Politics 1 (1939): 146-170; 278-300.

Shively, W. Phillips. "A Reinterpretation of the New Deal Realignment." Public
     Opinion Quarterly 35 (Winter 1971-1972): 621-24.
Sinclair, Barbara Deckard. "Party Realignment and the Transformation of the Political
     Agenda: The House of Representatives, 1925-1938." American Political
     Science Review 71 (Sept. 1977): 940-53.
_____. "The Policy Consequences of Party Realignment: Social Welfare
     Legislation in the House of Representatives, 1933-1954." American Journal of
     Political Science 22 (Feb. 1978): 83-105.
Smith, Harold T. "Pittman, Creel, and New Deal Politics." Nevada Historical Society
     Quarterly 22 (Winter 1979): 254-70.
Spencer, Thomas T. "'As Goes Maine, So Goes Vermont': The 1936 Democratic
     Campaign in Vermont." Vermont History 46 (Fall 1978): 234-43.
_____. "Auxiliary and Non-Party Politics: The 1936 Democratic Presidential
     Campaign in Ohio." Ohio History 90 (Spring 1981): 114-28.
_____. "Bennett Champ Clark and the 1936 Presidential Campaign." Missouri
     Historical Review 75 (Jan. 1981): 197-213.
_____. "FDR's Forgotten Friend: Henry H. McPike and the 1932 Democratic
     Presidential Nomination." California History 63 (Summer 1984): 194-99.
_____. "'Labor is with Roosevelt': The Pennsylvania Non-partisan League and
     the Election of 1936." Pennsylvania History 46 (Jan. 1979): 3-16.
_____. "The Air Mail Controversy of 1934." Mid-America 62 (Oct. 1980):
     161-72.
_____. "The New Deal Comes To the 'Granite State': The 1936 Democratic
     Presidential Campaign in New Hampshire." Historical New Hampshire 35
     (Summer 1980): 186-201.
_____. "The Roosevelt All-Party Agricultural Committee and the 1936
     Election." Annals of Iowa 45 (Summer 1979): 44-57.
Sternsher, Bernard. "The Emergence of the New Deal Party System: A Problem in
     Historical Analysis of Voter Behavior." Journal of Interdisciplinary History 6
     (Summer 1975): 127-50.
_____. "The New Deal Party System: A Reappraisal." Journal of
     Interdisciplinary History 15 (Summer 1982): 85-105.
Stickle, Warren E. "The Republican Campaign of 1940." New Jersey History 93
     (Spring 1975): 43-59.
Syrett, John. "Jim Farley and Carter Glass: Allies against a Third Term." Prologue
     15 (Summer 1983): 89-102.
Tarter, Brent. "A Flier on the National Scene: Harry F. Byrd's Favorite-Son
     Presidential Candidacy of 1932." Virginia Magazine of History and Biography
     82 (July 1974): 282-305.
Wolf, T. Phillip. "Bronson Cutting and Franklin D. Roosevelt: Factors in Presidential
     Endorsement." New Mexico Historical Review 52 (Oct. 1977): 317-34.
_____. "Cutting vs. Chavez Re-Examined: A Commentary on Pickens'
     Analysis." New Mexico Historical Review 47 (Oct 1972): 317-36.
Zeigler, Luther Harmon, Jr. "Senator Walter George's 1938 Campaign." Georgia
     Historical Quarterly 43 (Dec. 1959): 333-52.

Dissertations

Boskin, Joseph. "Politics of an Opposition Party: The Republican Party in the New Deal Period, 1936-1940." Ph.D. diss., University of Minnesota, 1959.

Carlson, Earland Irving. "Franlkin D. Roosevelt's Fight for the Presidential Nomination, 1928-1932." Ph.D. diss., University of Illinois, 1955.

Coode, Thomas H. "Georgia Congressmen and the New Deal, 1933-1938." Ph.D. diss., University of Georgia, 1966.

Cowperthwaite, Lowery L. "A Criticism of the Speaking of Franklin D. Roosevelt in the Presidential Campaign of 1932." Ph.D. diss., University of Iowa, 1951.

Donahoe, Bernard F. "New Dealers, Conservatives and the Democratic Nominees of 1940." Ph.D. diss., University of Notre Dame, 1965.

Everman, Henry Esli. "Herbert Hoover and the New Deal, 1933-1940." Ph.D. diss. Louisiana State University, 1971.

Fagin, Vernon Allen. "Franklin D. Roosevelt, Liberalism in the Democratic Party, and the 1938 Congressional Elections: The Urge to Purge." Ph.D. diss., University of California, Los Angeles, 1979.

Heleniak, Roman J. "The Election of 1936." Ph.D. diss., Mississippi State University, 1964.

Hilty, James Walter. "Voting Alignments in the United States Senate, 1933-1944." Ph.D. diss., University of Missouri, 1973.

Hope, Ben Walter. "The Rhetoric of Defense: A Study of the Tactics and Techniques of Refutation in President Franklin D. Roosevelt's Speeches in His Three Campaigns for Reelection." Ph.D. diss., Ohio State University, 1960.

Hopper, John Edward. "The Purge: Franklin D. Roosevelt and the 1938 Democratic Nominations." Ph.D. diss., University of Chicago, 1967.

Malsberger, John William. "The Emergence of a Moderate Coalition: Senate Voting, 1938-1952." Ph.D. diss., Temple University, 1980.

Mihelich, Dennis N. "The Congressional Mavericks, 1935-1939." Ph.D. diss., Case Western Reserve University, 1972.

Morris, Harry W. "The Republicans in a Minority Role, 1933-1938." Ph.D. diss. University of Iowa, 1960.

Newquist, Gloria W. "James A. Farley and the Politics of Victory, 1928-1936." Ph.D. diss., University of Southern California, 1966.

Patterson, James T. "The Conservative Coalition in Congress, 1933-1939." Ph.D. diss., Harvard University, 1964.

Reeves, William D. "The Politics of Public Works, 1933-1935." Ph.D. diss., Tulane University, 1968.

Ross, Hugh. "The Third-Term Campaign of 1940." Ph.D. diss., Stanford University, 1960.

Schmidt, Lester F. "The Farmer-Labor Progressive Federation: The Study of a 'United Front' Movement among Wisconsin Liberals, 1934-1941." Ph.D. diss., University of Wisconsin, 1955.

Shuff, Stephen M. "Partisan Realignment in the New Deal Era." Ph.D. diss., Harvard University, 1983.

Sullivan, Patricia Ann. "Gideon's Southern Soldiers: New Deal Politics and Civil
    Rights Reform, 1933-1948." Ph.D. diss., Emory University, 1983.
Tull, Charles J. "Father Coughlin, the New Deal, and the Election of 1936." Ph.D.
    diss., University of Notre Dame, 1962.
Zebroski, Shirley. "Franklin D. Roosevelt and the 77th Congress: Domestic Issues."
    Ph.D. diss., Ohio University, 1983.

6.3 POLICIES AND PROGRAMS

Books

Abbott, Grace. From Relief to Social Security: The Development of the New Public
    Welfare Services and Their Administration. New York: Russell & Russell, 1941.
Altmeyer, Arthur J. The Formative Years of Social Security. Madison: University of
    Wisconsin Press, 1966.
Arnold, Joseph L. The New Deal in the Suburbs: A History of the Greenbelt Town
    Program, 1935-1954. Columbus: Ohio State University Press, 1971.
Aronovici, Carol. Housing the Masses. New York: J. Wiley & Sons, 1939.
Baldwin, Sidney. Poverty and Politics: The Rise and Decline of the Farm Security
    Administration. Chapel Hill: University of North Carolina Press, 1968.
Bellush, Bernard. The Failure of the NRA. New York: W. W. Norton, 1975.
Bernstein, Irving. The New Deal Collective Bargaining Policy. Berkeley: University
    of California Press, 1950.
Brown, D. Clayton. Electricity for Rural America: The Fight for the REA. Westport,
    Conn.: Greenwood, 1980.
Brown, Douglass V., Edward Chamberlin, Seymour Harris, et al. The Economics of
    the Recovery Program. New York: McGraw-Hill, 1934.
Brown, J. Douglas. An American Philosophy of Social Security: Evolution and Issues.
    Princeton: Princeton University Press, 1972.
Campbell, Christina M. The Farm Bureau and the New Deal: A Study of the Making
    of National Farm Policy, 1933-1940. Urbana: University of Illinois Press, 1962.
Carothers, Doris. Chronology of the Federal Emergency Relief Administration, May
    12, 1933, to December 31, 1935. Washington, D.C.: GPO, 1937.
Clapp, Gordon R. The TVA: An Approach to the Development of a Region. Chicago:
    University of Chicago Press, 1955.
Clawson, Marion. New Deal Planning: The National Resources Planning Board.
    Baltimore: Johns Hopkins University Press, 1981.
Colean, Miles L. A Backward Glance--An Oral History: The Growth of Government
    Housing Policy in the United States, 1934-1975. Washington: The Fund, 1975.
Conkin, Paul K. Tomorrow a New World: The New Deal Community Program.
    Ithaca: Cornell University Press, 1959.
DeBedts, Ralph E. The New Deal's S.E.C.: The Formative Years. New York:
    Columbia University Press, 1964.

Douglas, Paul H. Social Security in the United States: An Analysis and Appraisal of the Federal Social Security Act. New York: DaCapo, 1971.

Droze, Wilman H. High Dams and Slack Waters: TVA Rebuilds a River. Baton Rouge: Louisiana State University Press, 1965.

Emmerich, Herbert. Essays on Federal Reorganization. Birmingham: University of Alabama Press, 1950.

Epstein, Abraham. Insecurity, A Challenge to America: A Study of Social Insurance in the United States and Abroad. New York: Random House, 1938.

Funigiello, Philip. Toward a National Power Policy: The New Deal and the Electrical Utility Industry. Pittsburgh: University of Pittsburgh Press, 1973.

Fusfeld, Daniel. The Economic Thought of Franklin D. Roosevelt and the Origins of the New Deal. New York: Columbia University Press, 1956.

Gross, James A. The Making of the National Labor Relations Board: A Study in Economics, Politics and the Law, 1933-1937. Albany: State University of New York Press, 1974.

_____. The Reshaping of the National Labor Relations Board: National Labor Policy in Transition, 1937-1947. Albany: State University of New York Press, 1981.

Hargrove, Erwin, and Paul K. Conklin. TVA: Fifty Years of Grass-Roots Bureaucracy. Urbana: University of Illinois Press, 1983.

Hawley, Ellis W. The New Deal and the Problem of Monopoly: A Study in Economic Ambivalence. Princeton: Princeton University Press, 1966.

Hirshfield, David S. The Last Reform: The Campaign for Compulsory Health Insurance in the United States from 1932-1943. Cambridge: Harvard University Press, 1970.

Hobbs, Edward H. Executive Reorganization in the National Government. University: University of Mississippi Press, 1953.

Hodges, James A. New Deal Labor Policy and the Southern Cotton Textile Industry, 1933-1941. Knoxville: University of Tennessee Press, 1986.

Holland, Kenneth, and Frank Ernest Hill. Youth in the CCC. Washington, D. C.: American Council on Education, 1942.

Holley, Donald. Uncle Sam's Farmers: The New Deal Communities in the Lower Mississippi Valley. Urbana: University of Illinois Press, 1975.

Howard, Donald S. The WPA and Federal Relief Policy. New York: Russell Sage Foundation, 1943.

Isakoff, Jack Fein. The Public Works Administration. Urbana: University of Illinois Press, 1938.

Jackson, Charles. Food and Drug Legislation in the New Deal. Princeton: Princeton University Press, 1970.

Karl, Barry D. Executive Reorganization and Reform in the New Deal: The Genesis of Administrative Management, 1900-1939. Cambridge: Harvard University Press, 1963.

King, Judson. The Conservation Fight: From Theodore Roosevelt to the Tennessee Valley Authority. Washington, D.C.: Public Affairs Press, 1959.

Komons, Nick A. Bonfires to Beacons: Federal Civil Aviation Policy Under the Air Commerce Act, 1926-1938. Washington, D. C.: U. S. Department of Transportation, 1978.

Lacy, Leslie Alexander. Soil Soldiers: The Civilian Conservation Corps in the Great Depression. Radnor, Pa.: Chilton, 1976.

Latham, Earl. The Politics of Railroad Coordination, 1933-1936. Cambridge: Harvard University Press, 1959.

Leff, Mark H. The Limits of Symbolic Reform: The New Deal and Taxation, 1933-1939. New York: Cambridge University Press, 1984.

Lindley, Betty and Ernest K. A New Deal for Youth: The Story of the National Youth Administration. New York: Viking, 1938.

Lorwin, Lewis L. Youth Work Programs: Problems and Policies. Washington: American Council on Education, 1941.

Lubove, Roy. The Struggle for Social Security, 1900-1935. Cambridge: Harvard University Press, 1968.

Lyon, Leverett S., et al. Government and Economic Life: Development and Current Issues of American Public Policy. 2 vols.; Washington, D.C.: Brookings Institution, 1939-40..

_____. The National Recovery Administration: An Analysis and Appraisal. Washington, D.C.: Brookings Institution, 1935.

MacMahon, Arthur W., et al. The Administration of Federal Work Relief. Chicago: Public Administration Service, 1941.

May, Dean L. From New Deal to New Economics: The American Liberal Response to the Recession of 1937. New York: Garland, 1981.

McCraw, Thomas K. Morgan vs. Lilienthal: The Feud within the T.V.A. Chicago: Loyola University Press, 1970.

_____. TVA and the Power Fight, 1933-1939. Philadelphia: Lippincott, 1971.

McDonald, Michael J., and John Muldowny. TVA and the Dispossessed: The Resettlement of Population in the Norris Dam Area. Knoxville: University of Tennessee Press, 1982.

McDonell, Timothy. The Wagner Housing Act: A Case Study of the Legislative Process. Chicago: Loyola University Press, 1957.

McKinley, Charles, and Robert W. Frase. Launching Social Security: A Capture-and-Record Account, 1935-1937. Madision: University of Wisconsin Press, 1970.

Meriam, Lewis. Relief and Social Security. Washington, D.C.: Brookings Institution, 1946.

Mertz, Paul E. New Deal Policy and Southern Rural Poverty. Baton Rouge: Louisiana State University Press, 1978.

Millis, Harry A., and Emily C. Brown. From the Wagner Act to Taft-Hartley: A Study of National Labor Policy and Labor Relations. Chicago: University of Chicago Press, 1950.

Morgan, Arthur E. The Making of the TVA. Buffalo, N. Y.: Prometheus, 1974.

Muller, Frederick W. Public Rural Electrification. Washington, D.C.: American Council on Public Affairs, 1944.

Musto, David. The American Disease: Origins of Narcotic Control. New Haven: Yale University Press, 1973.

Nourse, Edwin G., Joseph S. Davis, and John D. Black. Three Years of the Agricultural Adjustment Administration. Washington: Brookings, 1937.

Otis, Alison T., William Honey, Thomas Hogg, and Kimberly Lakin. The Forest Service and the Civilian Conservation Corps: 1933-42. Washington, D. C.: United States Department of Agriculture, Forest Service, 1986.

Owen, A. L. Riesch. Conservation under FDR. New York: Praeger, 1983.

Owen, Marguerite. The Tennessee Valley Authority. New York: Praeger, 1973.

Parrish, Michael E. Securities Regulation and the New Deal. New Haven: Yale University Press, 1970.

Perkins, Van L. Crisis in Agriculture: The Agricultural Adjustment Administration and the New Deal, 1933. Berkeley: University of California Press, 1969.

Phelps, Orme W. The Legislative Background of the Fair Labor Standards Act: A Study of the Growth of National Sentiment in Favor of Government Regulation of Wages, Hours, and Child Labor. Chicago: University of Chicago Press, 1939.

Polenberg, Richard T. Reorganizing Roosevelt's Government: The Controversy over Executive Reorganization, 1936-1939. Cambridge: Harvard University Press, 1966.

Pritchett, C. Herman. The Tennessee Valley Authorty: A Study in Public Administration. Chapel Hill: University of North Carolina Press, 1943.

Roos, Charles Frederick. NRA Economic Planning. Bloomington, Ind.: Principia Press, 1937.

Rosenof, Theodore. Dogma, Depression, and the New Deal: The Debate of Political Leaders over Economic Recovery. Port Washington, N.Y.: Kennikat, 1975.

Rowley, William D. M.L. Wilson and the Campaign for the Domestic Allotment. Lincoln: University of Nebraska Press, 1970.

Salmond, John. The Civilian Conservation Corps, 1933-1942: A New Deal Case Study. Durham, N.C.: Duke University Press, 1967.

Sanders, Daniel S. The Impact of Reform Movements on Social Policy Change: The Case of Social Insurance. Fair Lawn, N. J.: R. E. Burdick, 1973.

Schwartz, Bonnie Fox. The Civil Works Administration, 1933-1934: The Business of Emergency Employment in the New Deal. Princeton: Princeton University Press, 1984.

Schwarz, Jordan A. 1933: Roosevelt's Decision: The United States Leaves the Gold Standard. New York: Chelsea House, 1969.

Selznick, Philip. TVA and the Grass Roots: A Study in the Sociology of Formal Organization. Berkeley: University of California Press, 1949.

Walker, Forrest A. The Civil Works Administration: An Experiment in Federal Work Relief, 1933-1934. New York: Garland, 1979.

Warken, Philip W. A History of the National Resources Planning Board, 1933-1943. New York: Garland, 1979.

Warner, George A. Greenbelt: The Cooperative Community: An Experience in Democratic Living. New York: Exposition Press, 1954.

Wengert, Norman I. Valley of Tomorrow: The TVA and Agriculture. Knoxville: Bureau of Public Administration, University of Tennessee, 1952.

Witte, Edwin. The Development of the Social Security Act: A Memorandum on the History of the Committtee on Economic Security and Drafting and Legislative History of the Social Security Act. Madison: University of Wisconsin Press, 1962.

Articles

Altmeyer, Arthur J. "The Wisconsin Idea and Social Security." Wisconsin Magazine of History 42 (Autumn 1958): 19-25.

Anderson, James E. "The New Deal, Capitalism, and the Regulatory State." In The Roosevelt New Deal: A Program Assessment Fifty Years After ed. by Wilbur J. Cohen (Austin: Lyndon B. Johnson School of Public Affairs, 1986), pp. 105-22.

Baldridge, Kenneth W. "Reclamation Work of the Civilian Conservation Corps, 1933-1942." Utah Historical Quarterly 39 (Summer 1971): 265-85.

Bartels, Andrew H. "The Office of Price Administration and the Legacy of the New Deal, 1939-1946." Public Historian 5 (Summer 1983): 5-29.

Baskerville, Stephen W. "Frankfurter, Keynes, and the Fight for Public Works, 1932-1935." Maryland Historian 9 (Spring 1978): 1-15.

Beezer, Bruce G. "Arthurdale: An Experiment in Community Education." West Virginia History 36 (Oct. 1974): 17-36.

Bellush, Jewell. "Milk Price Control: History of its Adoption, 1933." New York History 60 (June 1962): 79-104.

Bennett, James D. "Roosevelt, Wilkie, and the TVA." Tennessee Historical Quarterly 28 (Winter 1969): 388-96.

Benston, George J. "Required Disclosure and the Stock Market: An Evaluation of the Securities Exchange Act of 1934." American Economic Review 63 (March 1973): 132-55.

Birch, Eugenie Ladner. "Woman-Made America: The Case of Early Public Housing Policy." Journal of the American Institute of Planners 44 (April 1978): 130-44.

Berkowitz, Edward D. "The First Social Security Crisis." Prologue 15 (Fall 1983): 133-50.

Blakey, George T. "Ham That Never Was: The 1933 Emergency Hog Slaughter." Historian 30 (Nov. 1967): 41-57.

Brand, Donald R. "Corporatism, the NRA, and the Oil Industry." Political Science Quarterly 98 (Spring 1983): 99-118.

Branscome, James. "The TVA: It Ain't What It Used To Be." American Heritage 28 (Feb. 1977): 68-78.

Bremer, William W. "Along the 'American Way': The New Deal's Work Relief Programs for the Unemployed." Journal of American History 62 (Dec. 1975): 636-52.

Bremner, Robert H. "The New Deal and Social Welfare." In Fifty Years Later: The New Deal Evaluated ed. by Harvard Sitkoff (New York: Knopf, 1985), pp. 69-92.

Browning, Edgar K. "The Economics and Politics of the Emergence of Social Security: Comment." Cato Journal 3 (Fall 1983): 381-84.

Buttenwieser, Ann L. "Shelter for What and for Whom? On the Route toward Vladeck Houses, 1930-1940." Journal of Urban History 12 (Aug. 1986): 391-413.

Cart, Theodore W. "'New Deal' For Wildlife: A Perspective on Federal Conservation Policy, 1933-1940." Pacific Northwest Quarterly 63 (July 1972): 113-20.

Chambers, Clarke A. "Social Security: The Welfare Consensus of the New Deal." In The Roosevelt New Deal: A Program Assessment Fifty Years After ed. by Wilbur J. Cohen (Austin: Lyndon B. Johnson School of Public Affairs, 1986), pp. 145-59.

Christie, Jean. "New Deal Resources Planning: The Proposals of Morris L. Cooke." Agricultural History 53 (July 1979): 597-606.

_____. "The Mississippi Valley Committee: Conservation and Planning in the Early New Deal." Historian 32 (May 1970): 449-69.

Church, Verne V. "CCCs and Fire Fighting." Forest History 14 (Jan. 1971): 12-14.

Clawson, Marion. "Conserving the Soil." Proceedings of the Academy of Political Science 34 (No. 3, 1982): 89-98.

_____. "Resettlement Experience on Nine Selected Resettlement Projects." Agricultural History 52 (Jan. 1978): 1-92.

Coode, Thomas H., and John F. Bauman. "'Dear Mr. Hopkins': A New Dealer Reports from Eastern Kentucky." Register of the Kentucky Historical Society 78 (Winter 1980): 55-63.

Cooke, Morris Llewellyn. "The Early Days of the Rural Electrification Idea: 1914-1936." American Political Science Review 42 (June 1948): 431-47.

Cross, Whitney R. "Ideas in Politics: The Conservation Policies of the Two Roosevelts." Journal of the History of Ideas 14 (June 1953): 421-38.

Davis, Kenneth S. "The Birth of Social Security." American Heritage 30 (April/May 1979): 38-51.

DeBedts, Ralph F. "The First Chairman of the Securities and Exchange Commission: Successful Ambassador of the New Deal to Wall Street." American Journal of Economics and Sociology 23 (April 1964): 165-78.

Droze, Wilmon H. "TVA and the Ordinary Farmer." Agricultural History 53 (Jan. 1979): 188-202.

_____. "The New Deal's Shelterbelt Project, 1934-1942." In Essays on the New Deal ed. by Harold M. Hollingsworth and William F. Holmes (Austin: University of Texas Press, 1969), pp. 23-48.

Dubay, Robert W. "The Civilian Conservation Corps: A Study of Opposition, 1933-1935." Southern Quarterly 6 (April 1968): 341-58.

Eaton, Michael M. "The Robinson-Patman Act: Reconciling the Meeting Competition Defense with the Sherman Act." Antitrust Bulletin 18 (Fall 1973): 411-30.

Eliot, Thomas H. "The Social Security Bill: 25 Years After." Atlantic Monthly 206 (Aug. 1960): 72-75.

Erickson, Herman. "WPA Strike and Trials of 1939." Minnesota History 42 (Summer 1971): 483-510.

Felt, Jeremy P. "The Child Labor Provisions of the Fair Labor Standards Act." Labor History 11 (Fall 1970): 467-81.

Fickle, James E. "The S.P.A. and the N.R.A.: A Case Study of the Blue Eagle in the South." Southwestern Historical Quarterly 79 (Jan. 1976): 253-78.

Fine, Sidney. "Government and Labor Relations during the New Deal." Current History 37 (Sept. 1959): 139-45.

_____. "President Roosevelt and the Automobile Code." Mississippi Valley Historical Review 45 (June 1958): 23-50.

Finegold, Kenneth. "From Agrarianism to Adjustment: The Political Origins of New Deal Agricultural Policy." Politics and Society 11 (No. 1, 1982): 1-27.

Fleming, R. W. "The Significance of the Wagner Act." In Labor and the New Deal ed. by Milton Derber and Edwin Young (Madison: University of Wisconsin Press, 1957), pp. 121-56.

Fowler, Dorothy Ganfield. "Precursors of the Hatch Act." Mississippi Valley Historical Review 47 (Sept. 1960): 247-62.

Fulgham, Quida J. "Roosevelt Feeds the Hungry: The Federal Surplus Relief Corporation." Red River Valley Historical Review 7 (Fall 1982): 24-32.

Funigiello, Philip J. "Kilowatts for Defense: The New Deal and the Coming of the Second World War." Journal of American History 56 (Dec. 1969): 604-20.

_____. "The Bonneville Power Administration and the New Deal." Prologue 5 (Summer 1973): 89-97.

Galliher, John F., and Allyn Walker. "The Puzzle of the Social Origins of the Marihuana Tax Act of 1937." Social Problems 1977: 367-76.

Gatell, Frank Otto. "Independence Rejected: Puerto Rico and the Tydings Bill of 1936." Hispanic American Historical Review 38 (Feb. 1958): 25-44.

Gladwin, Lee A. "Arthurdale: Adventure into Utopia." West Virginia History 28 (July 1967): 305-17.

Goldberg, Joseph P. "Frances Perkins, Isador Lubin, and the Bureau of Labor Statistics." Monthly Labor Review 103 (April 1980): 22-30.

Golembe, Carter H. "The Deposit Insurance Legislation of 1933: An Examination of Its Antecedents and Its Purposes." Political Science Quarterly 75 (June 1960): 181-200.

Gower, Calvin W. "'Camp William James': A New Deal Blunder?" New England Quarterly 38 (Dec. 1965): 475-93.

_____. "Conservatism, Censorship, and Controversy in the CCC, 1930s." Journalism Quarterly 52 (Summer 1975): 277-84.

_____. "The C.C.C. Indian Division: Aid for Depressed Americans, 1932-1942." Minnesota History 43 (Spring 1972): 3-13.

Graham, Otis L., Jr. "The Planning Ideal and American Reality: The 1930s." In The Hofstadter Aegis: A Memorial ed. by Stanley Elkins and Eric McKitrick (New York: Knopf, 1974), pp. 257-99.

Greenbaum, Fred. "The Anti-Lynching Bill of 1935: The Irony of 'Equal Justice-- Under Law'." Journal of Human Relations 15 (Third Quarter, 1967): 72-85.

Greene, Nathan. "Civil Liberties and the NLRB." Guild Practioner 38 (1981): 101-9.

Gressley, Gene M. "Thurman Arnold, Antitrust, and the New Deal." Business History Review 38 (Summer 1964): 214-31.

Hacker, Louis M. "The Consequences of New Deal Legislation." In The United States and Its Place in World Affairs. 1918-1943 ed. by Allan Nevins and Louis M. Hacker (Boston: D.C. Heath, 1943), pp. 361-74.

Harpham, Edward J. "Social Security: Political History and Prospects for Reform." Cato Journal 3 (Fall 1983): 385-91.

Hatcher, John Henry. "Alben Barkley, Politics in Relief and the Hatch Act." Filson Club History Quarterly 40 (July 1966): 249-64.

Hawley, Ellis W. "The Corporate Ideal as Liberal Philosophy in the New Deal." In The Roosevelt New Deal: A Program Assessment Fifty Years After ed. by Wilbur J. Cohen (Austin: Lyndon B. Johnson School of Public Affairs, 1986), pp. 85-103.

Henningson, Berton E. "The Wealth of Nations and the Poverty of Producers: The Conflict Between Free Trade and the New Deal Farm Program." American Heritage 61 (Winter 1987): 74-93.

Huffman, Laurie. "The WPA Project as Humanistic Experience." Pacific Historian 27 (Winter 1983): 5-9.

Jackson, Charles O. "Muckraking and Consumer Protection: The Case of the 1938 Food, Drug and Cosmetic Act." Pharmacy in History 13 (No.3, 1971): 103-10.

Johnson, Charles W. "The Army and the Civilian Conservation Corps, 1933-42." Prologue 4 (Fall 1972): 139-56.

Johnson, Frederick K. "The Civilian Conservation Corps: A New Deal for Youth." Minnesota History 48 (Fall 1983): 295-302.

Johnson, James P. "Drafting the NRA Code of Fair Competition for the Bituminous Coal Industry." Journal of American History 53 (Dec. 1966): 521-41.

Jones, Byrd L. "A Plan for Planning in the New Deal." Social Science Quarterly 50 (Dec. 1969): 525-34.

Kern, Jean B. "WPA Project Ten Years Later." Palimpsest 30 (Jan. 1949): 15-22.

Keyserling, Leon H. "The Wagner Act: Its Origin and Current Significance." George Washington Law Review 29 (Dec. 1960): 199-233.

Knight, Oliver. "Correcting Nature's Error: The Colorado-Big Thompson Project." Agricultural History 30 (Oct. 1956): 169-75.

Koeniger, A. Cash. "Carter Glass and the National Recovery Administration." South Atlantic Quarterly 74 (Summer 1975): 349-64.

Koppes, Clayton, R. "Public Water, Privite Land: Origins of the Acreage Limitation Controversy, 1933-1953." Pacific Historical Review 47 (Nov. 1978): 607-36.

Kulsrud, Carl J. "The Archival Records of the Agricultural Adjustment Program." Agricultural History 22 (July 1948): 197-204.

Lambert, C. Roger. "Slaughter of the Innocents: The Public Protests AAA Killings of Little Pigs." Midwest Quarterly 14 (April 1973): 247-56.

_____. "The Illusion of Participatory Democracy: The AAA Organizes the Corn-Hog Farmers." Annals of Iowa 42 (Fall 1974): 468-77.

_____. "Want and Plenty: The Federal Surplus Relief Corporation and AAA." Agricultural History 46 (July 1972): 390-400.

Landis, James M. "The Legislative History of the Securities Act of 1933." George Washington Law Review 28 (Oct. 1959): 29-49.

Lear, Linda J. "Harold L. Ickes and the Oil Crises of the First Hundred Days." Mid-America 63 (Jan. 1981): 3-17.

Leff, Mark H. "Taxing the "Forgotten Man': The Politics of Social Security Finance in the New Deal." Journal of American History 70 (Sept. 1983): 359-81.

Leiserson, Avery. "Political Limitations on Executive Reorganization." American Political Science Review 41 (Feb 1947): 68-84.

Leotta, Louis. "Abraham Epstein and the Movement for Old Age Security." Labor History 16 (Summer 1975): 359-77.

Leuchtenburg, William E. "Roosevelt, Norris and the 'Seven Little TVA's'." Journal of Politics 14 (Aug. 1952): 418-41.

Loomis, Philip A., Jr. "The Securities Exchange Act of 1934 and the Investment Advisors Act of 1940." George Washington Law Review 28 (Oct. 1959): 214-49.

Lowitt, Richard. "Henry A. Wallace and the 1935 Purge in the Department of Agriculture." Agricultural History 53 (July 1979): 607-21.

Lowrie, Walter E. "Roosevelt and the Passamaquoddy Bay Tidal Project." Historian 31 (Nov. 1968): 64-89.

Lubove, Roy. "New Cities for Old: The Urban Reconstruction Program of the 1930's." Social Studies 53 (Nov. 1962): 203-13.

_____. "The New Deal and National Health." Current History 45 (Aug. 1963): 77-86.

Marten, James. "A 'Golden Opportunity': The South Dakota Agricultural Extension Service and the Agricultural Adjustment Administration, 1933-1935." South Dakota History 12 (Summer 1982): 163-81.

Martin, Robert E. "The Referendum Process in the Agricultural Adjustment Programs of the United States." Agricultural History 25 (Jan. 1951): 34-47.

McCoy, Donald R. "George S. McGill of Kansas and the Agricultural Adjustment Act of 1938." Historian 45 (Feb. 1983): 186-205.

Merriam, Charles E. "The National Resources Planning Board: A Chapter in American Planning Experience." American Political Science Review 38 (Dec. 1944): 1075-88.

Millett, John D., and Lindsay Rogers. "The Legislative Veto and the Reorganization Act of 1939." Public Administration Review 1 (Winter 1941): 176-89.

Miscamble, Wilson D. "Thurman Arnold Goes to Washington: A Look at Antitrust Policy in the Later New Deal." Business History Review 56 (Spring 1982): 1-15.

Mitchell, Virgil L. "Louisiana Health and the Civil Works Administration." Red River Valley Historical Review 7 (Winter 1982): 22-32.

_____. "The Louisiana Unemployed and the Civil Works Administration." Red River Valley Historical Review 5 (Summer 1980): 54-67.

Moore, James R. "Sources of New Deal Economic Policy: The International Dimension." Journal of American History 61 (Dec. 1974): 728-44.

Myhra, David. "Rexford Guy Tugwell: Initiator of America's Greenbelt New Towns, 1935 to 1936." Journal of the American Institute of Planners 40 (May 1974): 176-88.

Nash, Gerald D. "Experiments in Industrial Mobilization: WIB and NRA." Mid-America 45 (July 1963): 157-74.

_____. "F.D.R. and Labor: The World War I Origins of Early New Deal Labor Policy." Labor History 1 (Winter 1960): 39-52.

Nelson, Lawrence J. "The Art of the Possible: Another Look at the 'Purge' of the AAA Liberals in 1935." Agricultural History 57 (Oct. 1983): 416-35.

Norcross, Fred N. "Genesis of the Colorado-Big Thompson Project." Colorado Magazine 30 (Jan. 1953): 29-37.

Ober, Michael J. "The CCC Experience in Glacier National Park." Montana: The Magazine of Western History 26 (July 1976): 30-39.

Paulsen, George E. "Ghost of the NRA: Drafting National Wage and Hour Legislation in 1937." Social Science Quarterly 67 (June 1986): 241-54.

Perkins, Van L. "The AAA and the Politics of Agriculture: Agricultural Policy Formulation in the Fall of 1933." Agricultural History 39 (July 1965): 220-29.

Person, H. S. "The Rural Electrification Administration in Perspective." Agricultural History 24 (April 1950): 70-89.

Pinkett, Harold T. "Records of a Historic Thrust for Conservation." Prologue 8 (Summer 1976): 77-84.

Polenberg, Richard. "Conservation and Reorganization: The Forest Service Lobby, 1937-1938." Agricultural History 39 (Oct. 1965): 230-39.

_____. "The Great Conservation Contest." Journal of Forest History 10 (January 1967): 13-23.

Porter, David L. "The Battle of the Texas Giants: Hatton Sumners, Sam Rayburn, and the Logan-Walter Bill of 1939." Texana 12 (No. 4, 1974): 349-61.

_____. "Senator Carl Hatch and the Hatch Act of 1939." New Mexico Historical Review 48 (1973): 151-64.

Putnam, Carl M. "The CCC Experience." Military Review 53 (September 1973): 49-62.

Quadagno, Jill S. "Welfare Capitalism and the Social Security Act of 1935." American Sociological Review 49 (Oct. 1984): 632-47.

Reeves, William D. "PWA and Competitive Administration in the New Deal." Journal of American History 60 (Sept. 1973): 357-72.

Richardson, Elmo R. "Was There Politics in the Civilian Conservation Corps?" Forest History 16 (July 1972): 12-21.

Ritchie, Donald A. "The Legislative Impact of the Pecora Investigation." Capitol Studies 5 (Fall 1977): 87-101.

Robbins, William G. "The Great Experiment in Industrial Self-Government: The Lumber Industry and the National Recovery Administration." Journal of Forest History 25 (July 1981): 128-43.

Rogers, Lindsay. "Reorganization: Post-Mortem Notes." Political Science Quarterly 53 (June 1938): 161-72.

Rosentreter, Roger L. "Roosevelt's Tree Army: The Civilian Conservation Corps in Michigan." Michigan History 70 (May 1986): 14-23.

Salamon, Lester M. "The Time Dimension in Policy Evaluation: The Case of the New Deal Land Reform Experiments." Public Policy 27 (Spring 1979): 129-85.

Sargent, James E. "FDR and Lewis W. Douglas: Budget Balancing and the Early New Deal." Prologue 6 (Spring 1974): 33-43.

_____. "Roosevelt's Economy Act: Fiscal Conservatism and the Early New Deal." Congressional Studies 7 (Winter 1980): 33-51.

_____. "Woodrum's Economy Bloc: The Attack on Roosevelt's WPA, 1937-1939." Virginia Magazine of History and Biography 93 (April 1985): 175-207.

Schaffer, Daniel. "Environment and TVA: Toward a Regional Plan for the Tennessee Valley, 1930s." Tennessee Historical Quarterly 43 (Winter 1984): 333-54.

Schaller, Michael. "The Federal Prohibition of Marihuana." Journal of Social History 4 (Fall 1970): 61-74.

Schuyler, Michael W. "The Politics of Change: The Battle for the Agricultural Adjustment Act of 1938." Prologue 15 (Fall 1983): 164-78.

Shapiro, Edward S. "Donald Davidson and the Tennessee Valley Authority: The Response of a Southern Conservative." Tennessee Historical Quarterly 33 (Winter 1974): 436-51.

_____. "The Southern Agrarians and the Tennessee Valley Authority." American Quarterly 22 (Winter 1970): 791-806.

Shover, John L. "Populism in the Nineteen-Thirties: The Battle for the AAA." Agricultural History 39 (Jan. 1965): 17-24.

Skocpol, Theda, and Kenneth Finegold. "State Capacity and Economic Intervention in the Early New Deal." Political Science Quarterly 97 (Summer 1982): 255-78.

Smiley, David L. "A Slice of Life in Depression America: The Records of the Historical Records Survey." Prologue 3 (Winter 1971): 153-59.

_____. "The W.P.A. Historical Records Survey." In In Support of Clio: Essays in Memory of Herbert A. Kellar ed. by William B. Hesseltine and Donald R. McNeil (Madison: State Historical Society of Wisconsin, 1958), pp. 3-28.

Soffar, Allan J. "The Forest Shelterbelt Project, 1934-1944." Journal of the West 14 (July 1975): 95-107.

Spencer, Thomas T. "The Ocean Mail Controversy of 1934." American Neptune 41 (April 1981): 110-22.

_____. "The Air Mail Controversy of 1934." Mid-America 62 (Oct. 1980): 161-72.

Stetson, Frederick W. "The Civilian Conservation Corps in Vermont." Vermont History 46 (Winter 1978): 24-42.

Swain, Donald C. "Harold Ickes, Horace Albright, and the Hundred Days: A Study in Conservation Administration." Pacific Historical Review 34 (Nov. 1965): 455-65.

_____. "The Bureau of Reclamation and the New Deal, 1933-1940." Pacific Northwest Quarterly 61 (July 1970): 137-46.

_____. "The National Park Service and the New Deal, 1933-1940." Pacific Historical Review 41 (Aug. 1972): 312-32.

Swain, Martha H. "Pat Harrison and the Social Security Act of 1935." Southern Quarterly 15 (Oct. 1976): 1-14.

Sweets, John F. "The Civilian Conservation Corps in Florida." Apalachee 6 (1967): 77-86.

Talbert, Roy, Jr. "Arthur E. Morgan's Social Philosophy and the Tennessee Valley Authority." East Tennessee Historical Society Publications 41 (1969): 86-99.

Torodash, Martin. "The Blue Eagle: Government House Organ." Journalism Quarterly 46 (Spring 1969): 144-46.

Tugwell, Rexford G. "Some Aspects of New Deal Farm Policy: The Resettlement Idea." Agricultural History 33 (Oct. 1959): 159-64.

Urban, Raymond, and Richard Mancke. "Federal Regulation of Whisky Labelling: From the Repeal of Prohibition to the Present." Journal of Law and Economics 15 (Oct. 1972): 411-26.

Wade, Michael G. "'Farm Dorm Boys:' The Origins of the NYA Resident Training Program." Louisiana History 27 (Spring 1986): 117-32.

Walker, Forrest A. "Graft and the Civil Works Administration." Southwestern Social Science Quarterly 46 (Sept. 1965): 164-70.

Wallis, John Joseph. "The Birth of the Old Federalism: Financing the New Deal, 1932-1940." Journal of Economic History 44 (March 1984): 139-59.

Walsh, Margaret. "The Motor Carrier Act of 1935: The Origins and Establishment of Federal Regulation of the Interstate Bus Industry in the United States." Journal of Transport History 8 (March 1987): 66-80.

Weaver, Carolyn C. "The Economics and Politics of the Emergence of Social Security: Some Implications for Reform." Cato Journal 3 (Fall 1983): 361-79.

Wengert, Norman. "Antecedents of TVA: The Legislative History of Muscle Shoals." Agricultural History 26 (Oct. 1952): 141-47.

_____. "TVA--Symbol and Reality." Journal of Politics 13 (Aug. 1951): 369-92.

Whatley, Larry. "The Works Progress Administration in Mississippi." Journal of Mississippi History 30 (Feb. 1968): 35-50.

Wright, Gavin. "The Political Economy of New Deal Spending: An Economic Analysis." Review of Economics and Statistics 56 (Feb. 1974): 30-38.

Dissertations

Arnold, Joseph L. "The New Deal in the Suburbs: The Greenbelt Town Program, 1935-1952." Ph.D. diss., Ohio University, 1968.

Benincasa, Frederick A. "An Analysis of the Historical Development of the Tennessee Valley Authority from 1933 to 1961." Ph.D. diss., St. John's University, 1961.

Bennett, James D., II. "Struggle for Power: The Relationship between the Tennessee Valley Authority and the Private Power Industry." Ph.D. diss., Vanderbilt University, 1969.

Bernstein, Irving. "The New Deal Collective Bargaining Policy: A Legislative History." Ph.D. diss., Harvard University, 1948.

Bradford, David B. "Twentieth Century Pastoral: Epideictic Discourse in the Founding of the Tennessee Valley Authority." Ph.D. diss., Rensselaer Polytechnic Institute, 1982.

Colignon, Richard A. "TVA: Grass Roots or Power Fight." Ph.D. diss., University of Wisconsin, 1983.

Conkin, Paul K. "Tomorrow a New World: The New Deal Community Program." Ph.D. diss., Vanderbilt University, 1957.

DeBedts, Ralph F. "The New Deal's SEC." Ph.D. diss., University of Florida, 1960.

Egbert, Arch O. "Marriner S. Eccles and the Banking Act of 1935." Ph.D. diss., Brigham Young University, 1967.

Fusfeld, Daniel Roland. "Roots of the New Deal: The Economic Thought of Franklin D. Roosevelt to 1932." Ph.D. diss., Columbia University, 1953.

Hawley, Ellis W. "The New Deal and the Problem of Monopoly, 1934-1938: A Study in Economic Schizophrenia." Ph.D. diss., University of Wisconsin, 1959.

Jackson, Charles O. "Food and Drug Law Reform in the New Deal." Ph.D. diss., Emory University, 1967.

Johnson, Charles W. "The Civilian Conservation Corps: The Role of the Army." Ph.D. diss., University of Michigan, 1968.

Kalish, Richard J. "National Resource Planning, 1933-1939." Ph.D. diss., University of Colorado, 1963.

Kornbluh, Joyce Lewis. "A New Deal for Workers' Education: The Workers' Service Program under the Federal Emergency Relief Administration and the Works Progress Administration, 1933-1942." Ph.D. diss., University of Michigan, 1983.

Lambert, Walter K. "New Deal Revenue Acts: The Politics of Taxation." Ph.D. diss., University of Texas, 1970.

Leff, Mark Hugh. "The New Deal and Taxation, 1933-1938: The Limits of Symbolic Reform." Ph.D. diss., University of Chicago, 1978.

Leotta, Louis, Jr. "Abraham Epstein and the Movement for Social Security, 1920-1939." Ph.D. diss., Columbia University, 1965.

Levine, Rhonda Faye. "Class Struggle and the Capitalist State: The National Industrial Recovery Act and the New Deal." Ph.D. diss., State University of New York at Binghamton, 1980.

McCraw, Thomas K. "TVA and the Power Fight, 1933-1939." Ph.D. diss., University of Wisconsin, 1970.

McEvoy, Richard E. "State-Federal Public Assistance, 1935-1946." Ph.D. diss. University of Maryland, 1980.

Perkins, Van L. "Crisis in Agriculture: The Agriculutral Adjustment Administration from Its Inception to the Peek Resignation." Ph.D. diss., Harvard University, 1966.

Perna, Francis Michael. "The National Recovery Administration: The Interest Group Approach to Economic Planning." Ph.D. diss., Cornell University, 1981.

Phillips, Norma Kolko. "Social Work, Government, and Social Welfare: The Social Security Act." D.S.W. diss., Yeshiva University, 1981.

Pill, Michael. "Labor Law and Economics: Case Study of the National Labor Relations Act." Ph.D. diss., University of Massachusetts, 1983.

Polenberg, Richard. "Franklin D. Roosevelt and the Reorganization Controversy: 1936-1938." Ph.D. diss., Columbia University, 1964.

Rawick, George P. "The New Deal and Youth: The Civilian Conservation Corps, the National Youth Administration, and the American Youth Congress." Ph.D. diss., University of Wisconsin, 1957.

Reiman, Richard Andrew. "Planning the National Youth Administration: Citizenship and Community in New Deal Thought." Ph.D. diss., University of Cincinnati, 1984.

Riesch, Anna L. "Conservation Under Franklin D. Roosevelt." Ph.D. diss., University of Wisconsin, 1952.

Saalberg, John J. "Roosevelt, Fechner and the CCC: A Study in Executive Leadership." Ph.D. diss., Cornell University, 1962.

Salmond, John A. "'Roosevelt's Tree Army': A History of the Civilian Conservation Corps, 1933-1942." Ph.D. diss., Duke University, 1964.

Schaffer, Daniel. "Garden Cities for America: The Radburn Experience." Ph.D. diss., Rutgers University, 1981.

Schuyler, Michael W. "Agricultural Relief Activities of the Federal Government in the Middle West, 1933-1936." Ph.D. diss., University of Kansas, 1969.

Schwartz, Bonnie Fox. "The Civil Works Administration, 1933-34: The Business of Emergency Employment in the New Deal." Ph.D. diss., Columbia University, 1978.

Sipe, Daniel Albert. "A Moment of the State: The Enactment of the National Labor Relations Act, 1935." Ph.D. diss., University of Pennsylvania, 1981.

Smallwood, Johnny B., Jr. "George W. Norris and the Conception of a Planned Region." Ph.D. diss., University of North Carolina, 1963.

Walker, Forrest A. "The Civil Works Administration: An Experiment in Federal Work Relief, 1933-1934." Ph.D. diss., University of Oklahoma, 1962.

Wallis, John J. "Work Relief and Unemployment in the 1930's." Ph.D. diss., University of Washington, 1981.

Warken, Phillip W. "A History of the National Resources Planning Board, 1933-1943." Ph.D. diss., Ohio University, 1969.

Winger, Sarah E. B. "The Genesis of TVA." Ph.D. diss., University of Wisconsin, 1959.

Wolvin, Andrew Davis. "The 1933 Blue Eagle Campaign: A Study in Persuasion and Coercion." Ph.D. diss., Purdue University, 1968.

Woods, James Russell. "The Legend and the Legacy of Franklin D. Roosevelt and the Civilian Conservation Corps." D.S.S. diss., Syracuse University, 1964.
Woodyatt, Lyle J. "The Origins and Evolution of the New Deal Public Housing Program." Ph.D. diss., Washington University, St. Louis, 1968.

7

The Economy

7.1 GENERAL

Books

Abbott, Edith. Public Assistance. Chicago: University of Chicago Press, 1940.

Adams, Grace. Workers on Relief. New Haven: Yale University Press, 1939.

Arndt, H. W. The Economic Lessons of the 1930s. London: Oxford University Press, 1944.

Arnold, Thurman W. The Folklore of Capitalism. New Haven: Yale University Press, 1937.

Barger, Harold. Outlay and Income in the United States, 1921-1938. New York: National Bureau of Economic Research, 1942.

Bell, Spurgeon. Productivity, Wages, and National Income. Washington, D.C.: Brookings Institution, 1940.

Beney, M. Ada. Wages, Hours, and Employment in the United States, 1914-1936. New York: National Industrial Conference Board, 1936.

Berle, Adolf A., Jr., and Gardiner C. Means. The Modern Corporation and Private Property. New York: Macmillan, 1932.

Brooks, John. Once in Golconda: A True Drama of Wall Street, 1920-1938. New York: Harper & Row, 1969.

Brown, Josephine C. Public Relief, 1929-1939. New York: Henry Holt, 1940.

Burns, Arthur E., and Donald Watson. Government Spending and Economic Expansion. Washington, D.C.: American Council on Public Affairs, 1940.

Burns, Arthur E., and Edward A. Williams. Federal Work, Security and Relief Programs. Washington, D.C.: GPO, 1941.

Charnow, John. Work Relief Experience in the United States. Washington, D.C.: Committee on Social Security, Social Science Reserch Council, 1943.

Chase, Stuart. Idle Money, Idle Men. New York: Harcourt, Brace, 1940.

Colcord, Joanna C. Cash Relief. New York: Russell Sage Foundation, 1936.

Collins, Robert M. The Business Response to Keynes, 1929-1964. New York: Columbia University Press, 1981.

Davis, Joseph S. The World Between the Wars, 1919-1939: An Economist's View. Baltimore: Johns Hopkins University Press, 1975.

Dillingham, William Pyrle. Federal Aid to Veterans, 1917-1941. Gainesville: University of Florida Press, 1952.

Friedman, Milton, and Anna Schwartz. The Great Contraction, 1929-1933. Princeton: Princeton University Press, 1965.

Galbraith, John K. The Great Crash, 1929. Boston: Houghton Mifflin, 1955.

_____ and Gove G. Johnson, Jr. The Economic Effects of the Federal Public Works Expenditures, 1933-1938. Washington: GPO, 1940.

Hansen, Alvin. America's Role in the World Economy. New York: W.W. Norton, 1945.

Harris, Seymour E. Exchange Depreciation: Its Theory and History, 1931-1935, with some Consideration of Related Domestic Policies. Cambridge: Harvard University Press, 1936.

_____, ed. The New Economics: Keynes' Influence on Theory and Public Policy. New York: Knopf, 1948.

Keynes, John Maynard. The General Theory of Employment, Interest and Money. New York: Harcourt, Brace, 1936.

Kindleberger, Charles P. The World in Depression, 1929-1939. London: Allen Lane, 1973.

Klein, Lawrence R. Economic Fluctuations in the United States, 1921-1941. New York: Wiley, 1950.

Kuznets, Simon Smith. National Income and Its Composition, 1919-1938. 2 vols.; New York: National Bureau of Eonomic Research, 1941.

Lekachman, Robert. The Age of Keynes. New York: Random House, 1966.

Lent, George E. The Impact of the Undistributed Profits Tax, 1936-1937. New York: Columbia University Press, 1948.

Lynch, David. The Concentration of Economic Power. New York: Columbia University Press, 1946.

Nelson, Daniel. Unemployment Insurance: The American Experience, 1915-1935. Madison: University of Wisconsin Press, 1969.

Nordhauser, Norman. The Quest for Stability: Domestic Oil Regulation, 1917-1935. New York: Garland, 1979.

Nutter, G. Warren. The Extent of Enterprise Monopoly in the United States, 1899-1939: A Quantitative Study of Some Aspects of Monopoly. Chicago: University of Chicago Press, 1951.

Potter, Jim. The American Economy Between the World Wars. New York: Wiley, 1974.

Roose, Kenneth D. The Economics of Recession and Revival, An Interpretation of 1937-38. New Haven: Yale University Press, 1954.

Rothbard, Murray N. America's Great Depression. Princeton: Van Nostrand, 1963.

Stein, Herbert. The Fiscal Revolution in America. Chicago: University of Chicago Press, 1969.

Stolberg, Benjamin, and Warren Jay Vinton. The Economic Consequences of the New Deal. New York: Harcourt Brace, 1935.

Stoneman, William E. A History of the Economic Analysis of the Great Depression in America. New York: Garland, 1979.

Thomas, Gordon, and Max Morgan-Witts. The Day the Bubble Burst: A Social History of the Wall Street Crash of 1929. Garden City, N. Y.: Doubleday, 1979.

Wigmore, Barrie A. The Crash and its Aftermath: A History of Securities Markets in the United States, 1929-1933. Westport, Conn.: Greenwood, 1985.

Williams, Edward A. Federal Aid for Relief. New York: Columbia University Press, 1939.

Willoughby, W. F. Financial Condition and Operations of the National Government, 1921-1930. Washington, D.C.: Brookings, 1931.

Articles

Allen, William R. "Irving Fisher, F.D.R., and the Great Depression." History of Political Economy 9 (Winter 1977): 560-87.

Anderson, Barry L., and James L. Butkiewicz. "Money, Spending, and the Great Depression." Southern Economic Journal 47 (Oct. 1980): 388-403.

Arnold, Thurman. "The Crash--and What It Meant." In The Aspirin Age, 1919-1941 ed. by Isabel Leighton (New York: Simon and Schuster, 1949), pp. 214-31.

Ayres, Clarence E. "The Impact of the Great Depression on Economic Thinking." American Economic Review 36 (May 1946): 112-25.

Barber, Clarence L. "On the Origins of the Great Depression." Southern Economic Journal 44 (Jan. 1978): 432-56.

Baskerville, Stephen W. "Cutting Loose from Prejudice: Economists and the Great Depression." In Nothing Else to Fear: New Perspectives on America in the Thirties ed. by Stephen W. Baskerville and Ralph Willett (Manchester: Manchester University Press, 1985), pp. 259-84.

Baskin, Alex. "The Ford Hunger March--1932." Labor History 13 (Summer 1972): 331-60.

Berle, Adolf A. "Reshaping the American Economy." Centennial Review 9 (Spring 1965): 209-21.

Brockie, Melvin D. "Theories of the 1937-38 Crisis and Depression." Economic Journal 60 (June 1950): 292-310.

Brown, E. Cary. "Fiscal Policy in the Thirties: A Reappraisal." American Economic Review 46 (Dec. 1956): 857-79.

Carosso, Vincent. "Washington and Wall Street: The New Deal and Investment Bankers, 1933-1940." Business History Review 44 (Winter 1970): 425-45.

Chandler, Alfred E., and Galambos, Louis. "The Development of Large-Scale Economic Organizations in Modern America." Journal of Economic History 30 (March 1970): 201-17

Coppe, A. "International Consequences of the Great Crisis." In The Great
    Depression Revisited: Essays on the Economics of the Thirties ed. by Herman
    Van Der Wee (The Hague: Martinus Nijhoff, 1972), pp. 13-23.
Critchlow, Donald L. "The Political Control of the Economy: Deficit Spending as a
    Political Belief, 1932-1952." Public Historian 3 (Spring 1981): 5-22.
Currie, Lauchlin. "Causes of the Recession [1938]." History of Political Economy 12
    (Fall 1980): 316-35.
_____. "Comments on Pump Priming." History of Political Economy 10
    (Winter 1978): 525-33.
_____ and Martin Krost. "Federal Income-Increasing Expenditures, 1932-
    1935." History of Political Economy 10 (Winter 1978): 534-54.
Darby, Michael R. "Three-and-a-Half Million U.S. Employees have been Mislaid: or,
    an Explanation of Unemployment, 1934-1941." Journal of Political Economy 84
    (Feb. 1976): 1-16.
Devine, James N. "Under-consumption, Over-investment, and the Origins of the
    Great Depression." Review of Radical Political Economics 15 (Summer 1983):
    1-27.
Eichengreen, Barry, and Jeffrey Sachs. "Exchange Rates and Economic Recovery in
    the 1930s." Journal of Economic History 45 (Dec. 1985): 925-46.
Erickson, Erling A. "The Great Crash of October, 1929." In The Great Depression
    Revisited: Essays on the Economics of the Thirties ed. by Herman Van Der
    Wee (The Hague: Martinus Nijhoff, 1972), pp. 3-12.
Eyskens, Mark. "The Influence of the Great Depression on Economic Theory." In
    The Great Depression Revisited: Essays on the Economics of the Thirties ed.
    by Herman Van Der Wee (The Hague: Martinus Nijhoff, 1972), pp. 24-42.
Field, Alexander J. "A New Interpretation of the Onset of the Great Depression."
    Journal of Economic History 44 (June 1984): 489-98.
Fleisig, Heywood. "War-Related Debts and the Great Depression." American
    Economic Review 66 (May 1976): 52-58.
Galbraith, John Kenneth. "The Days of Boom and Bust." American Heritage 9 (Aug.
    1958): 28-33, 101-2.
Garraty, John A. "Unemployment during the Great Depression." Labor History 17
    (Spring 1976): 133-59.
Ginzburg, Benjamin. "Wall Street Under the New Deal." North American Review
    245 (July 1938): 58-81.
Gramm, William P. "The Real-Balance Effect in the Great Depression." Journal of
    Economic History 32 (June 1972): 499-519.
Hacker, Louis M. "Economic Policies under Roosevelt." In The United States and Its
    Place in World Affairs, 1918-1943 ed. by Allan Nevins and Louis M. Hacker
    (Boston: D.C. Heath, 1943), pp. 347-60.
Hunter, Helen M. "The Role of Business Liquidity during the Great Depression and
    Afterwards: Differences between Large and Small Firms." Journal of
    Economic History 42 (Dec. 1982): 883-902.
Johnson, James P. "The Apple Sellers of the Great Depression." American History
    Illustrated 14 (Jan. 1980): 22-24.

Jones, Byrd L. "Lauchlin Currie and the Causes of the 1937 Recession." History of Political Economy 12 (Fall 1980): 303-15.

_____. "Lauchlin Currie, Pump Priming and New Deal Fiscal Policy, 1934-1936." History of Political Economy 10 (Winter 1978): 509-24.

Kidd, Stuart. "Collectivist Intellectuals and the Idea of National Economic Planning, 1929-33." In Nothing Else to Fear: New Perspectives on America in the Thirties ed. by Stephen W. Baskerville and Ralph Willett (Manchester: Manchester University Press, 1985), pp. 15-33.

Kirkendall, Richard S. "Four Economists in the Political Process." Journal of Farm Economics 41 (May, 1959): 194-210.

Leab, Daniel J. "'United We Eat': The Creation and Organization of the Unemployed Councils in 1930." Labor History 8 (Fall 1967): 300-15.

Lewis, Ben W. "State Regulation in Depression and War." American Economic Review 36 (May 1946): 384-404.

Lively, Robert A. "The South and Freight Rates: Political Settlement of an Economic Argument." Journal of Southern History 14 (Aug. 1948): 357-84.

Lucas, Robert E., Jr., and Leonard A. Rapping. "Unemployment in the Great Depression: Is There a Full Explanation?" Journal of Political Economy 80 (Jan./Feb. 1972): 186-91.

Mayer, Thomas. "Consumption in the Great Depression." Journal of Political Economy 86 (Feb. 1978): 139-45.

_____. "Money and the Great Depression: A Critique of Professor Temin's Thesis." Explorations in Economic History 15 (April 1978): 127-45.

McCraw, Thomas K. "The New Deal and the Mixed Economy." In Fifty Years Later: The New Deal Evaluated ed. by Harvard Sitkoff (New York: Knopf, 1985), pp. 37-67.

Nye, Ronald L. "The Challenge to Philanthropy: Unemployment Relief in Santa Barbara, 1930-1932." California Historical Quarterly 56 (Winter 1977-78): 310-27.

Parrish, John B. "Nation's Labor Supply, 1930-1937." American Economic Review 29 (June 1939): 325-336.

Patinkin, Don. "Keynes and Chicago." Journal of Law and Economics 22 (Oct. 1979): 213-32.

Patterson, James T. "Mary Dewson and the American Minimum Wage Movement." Labor History 5 (Spring 1964): 134-52.

Peppers, Larry C. "Full-Employment Surplus Analysis and Structural Change: The 1930s." Explorations in Economic History 10 (Winter 1973): 197-210.

Renaghan, Thomas M. "Distributional Effects of Federal Tax Policy, 1929-1939." Explorations in Economic History 21 (Jan. 1984): 40-63.

Richardson, H. W. "The Basis of Economic Recovery in the Nineteen-Thirties: A Review and a New Interpretation." Economic History Review 15 (Dec. 1962): 344-63.

Scheinman, Daniel. "Financing Unemployment Relief, 1930-1938." In State-Local Fiscal Relations in Illinois ed. by Simon E. Leland (Chicago: University of Chicago Press, 1941), pp. 180-93.

Schmitz, Mark, and Price V. Fishback. "The Distribution of Income in the Great Depression: Preliminary State Estimates." Journal of Economic History 43 (March 1983): 217-30.

Scriabine, Christine Brendel. "The Frayed White Collar: Professional Unemployment in the Early Depression." Pennsylvania History 49 (Jan. 1982): 3-24.

Shankman, Arnold. "The Five-Day Plan and the Depression." Historian 43 (May 1981): 393-409.

Sirkin, Gerald. "The Stock Market of 1929 Revisited: A Note." Business History Review 49 (Summer 1975): 223-31.

Smithies, Arthur. "The American Economy in the Thirties." American Economic Review 36 (May 1946): 11-27.

Taylor, Arthur R. "Losses to the Public in the Insull Collapse, 1932-1946." Business History Review 36 (Summer 1962): 188-204.

Wallis, John Joseph, and Daniel K. Benjamin. "Public Relief and Private Employment in the Great Depression." Journal of Economic History 41 (March 1981): 97-102.

Webbink, Paul. "Unemployment in the United States, 1930-1940." American Economic Review 30 (Feb. 1941): 248-72.

Wilkins, Mira. "Foreign Direct Investment in the United States in the Interwar Years: The Role of the U.S. Federal Government, 1918-1941." In Business and Government: Essays in 20th Century Cooperation and Confrontation ed. by Joseph R. Frese, S. J., and Jacob Judd (Terrytown, N.Y.: Sleepy Hollow Restorations, 1985), pp. 85-118.

Dissertations

Agee, Steven Craig. "An Emperical Examination of the Roles that Consumption, Investment and Money Played during the Great Depression." Ph.D. diss., University of Kansas, 1982.

Alchom, Guy. "Technocratic Social Science and the Rise of Managed Capitalism, 1910-1933." Ph.D. diss., University of Iowa, 1982.

Bartels, Andrew Hudson. "The Politics of Price Control: The Office of Price Administration and the Dilemmas of Economic Stabilization, 1940-1946." Ph.D. diss., Johns Hopkins University, 1980.

Chow, Chee W. "An Investigation of the Wealth Impacts of the 1933 and 1934 Securities Acts' Financial Disclosure Requirements." Ph.D. diss., University of Oregon, 1981.

Davis, James Ronnie. "Pre-Keynesian Economic Policy Proposals in the United States during the Great Depression." Ph.D. diss., University of Virginia, 1967.

Hanson, Richard X. "Antecedents of the 1929 Recession." Ph.D. diss., University of California, Los Angeles, 1986.

Kidd, S. S. "Alternative Strategies for National Industrial Planning in the United States, 1929-22." Ph.D. diss., University of Keele, 1979.

Nelson, Daniel M. "The Development of Unemployment Insurance in the United States, 1915-1935." Ph.D. diss., University of Wisconsin, 1967.

Nordhauser, Norman E. "The Quest for Stability: Domestic Oil Policy, 1919-1935." Ph.D. diss., Stanford University, 1970.

Renaghan, Thomas M. "A New Look at Fiscal Policy in the 1930s." Ph.D. diss., University of California, Davis, 1985.

Weber, Ernst Juerg. "The Great Depression in Switzerland, Sweden and the United States: The Money Hypothesis versus the Spending Hypothesis." Ph.D. diss., University of Rochester, 1984.

7.2 AGRICULTURE

Books

Barger, Harold, and Hans H. Landsberg. American Agriculture, 1899-1939: A Study of Output, Employment and Productivity. New York: National Bureau of Economic Research, 1942.

Black, John D. Parity, Parity, Parity. Cambridge: Harvard Committee on Research in the Social Sciences, 1942.

Blaisdell, Donald C. Government and Agriculture: The Growth of Federal Farm Aid. New York: Farrar and Rinehart, 1940.

Brunner, Edmund, and Irving, Lorge. Rural Trends in Depression Years: A Survey of Village Centered Agricultural Communities, 1930-1936. New York: Columbia University Press, 1937.

Calef, Wesley Carr. Private Grazing and Public Lands: Studies of the Local Management of the Taylor Grazing Act. Chicago: University of Chicago Press, 1960.

Cantor, Louis. A Prologue to the Protest Movement: The Missouri Sharecropper Roadside Demonstration of 1939. Durham: Duke University Press, 1969.

Chambers, Clarke A. California Farm Organizations: A Historical Study of the Grange, the Farm Bureau, and the Associated Farmers, 1929-1941. Berkeley: University of California Press, 1952.

Childs, Marquis W. The Farmer Takes a Hand: The Electric Power Revolution in Rural America. Garden City, N. Y.: Doubleday, 1952.

Conrad, David E. The Forgotten Farmers: The Story of the Sharecroppers in the New Deal. Urbana: University of Illinois Press, 1965.

Daniel, Cletus E. Bitter Harvest: A History of California Farmworkers, 1870-1941. Ithaca: Cornell University Press, 1981.

Davis, Joseph S. On Agricultural Policy, 1926-1938. Stanford: Stanford University, 1939.

_____. Wheat and the AAA. Washington, D.C.: Brookings Institution, 1935.

Fite, Gilbert C. George N. Peek and the Fight for Farm Parity. Norman: University of Oklahoma Press, 1954.

Fitzgerald, Dennis A. Corn and Hogs under the Agricultural Adjustment Act: Developments up to March, 1934. Washington, D.C.: Brookings Institution, 1934.

_____. Livestock under the AAA. Washington, D.C.: Brookings Institution, 1935.

Foss, Philip O. Politics and Grass: The Administration of Grazing on the Public Domain. Seattle: University of Washington Press, 1960.

Genung, Albert B. The Agricultural Depression Following World War I and Its Political Consequences: An Account of the Deflation Episode, 1921-1934. Ithaca: Northeast Farm Foundation, 1954.

Grubbs, Donald H. Cry from the Cotton: The Southern Tenant Farmers' Union and the New Deal. Chapel Hill: University of North Carolina Press, 1971.

Hoag, W. Gifford. The Farm Credit System: A History of Financial Self-Help. Danville, Ill.: Interstate, 1976.

Kirkendall, Richard S. Social Scientists and Farm Politics in the Age of Roosevelt. Columbia: University of Missouri Press, 1966.

Kramer, Dale. The Wild Jackasses: The American Farmer in Revolt. New York: Hastings House, 1956.

McCune, Wesley. The Farm Bloc. Garden City, N. Y.: Doubleday, 1943.

Richards, Henry Irving. Cotton and the AAA. Washington, D.C.: Brookings, 1936.

Rowe, Harold B. Tobacco under the AAA. Washington, D.C.: Brookings, 1935.

Saloutos, Theodore. The American Farmer and the New Deal. Ames: Iowa State University Press, 1982.

Schmidt, Carl T. American Farmers in the World Crisis. New York: Oxford University Press, 1941.

Shover, John L. Cornbelt Rebellion: The Farmers' Holiday Association. Urbana: University of Illinois Press, 1965.

Steichen, Edward, ed. The Bitter Years, 1935-1941: Rural America as Seen by the Photographers of the Farm Security Administration. New York: Museum of Modern Art, 1962.

Stokes, W. N., Jr. Credit to Farmers: The Story of the Federal Intermediate Credit Banks and Production Credit Associations. Washington, D. C.: Farm Credit Administration, 1973.

Taylor, Paul. On the Ground in the Thirties. Salt Lake City: G. M. Smith, 1983.

Articles

Abrahams, Paul. "Agricultural Adjustment During the New Deal Period: The New York Milk Industry: A Case Study." Agricultural History 39 (April 1965): 92-101.

Anderson, Clifford B. "Agrarian Attitudes Toward the City, Business and Labor in the 1920's and 1930's." Mississippi Quarterly 14 (Fall 1961): 183-89.

_____. "The Metamorphosis of American Agrarian Idealism in the 1920's and 1930's." Agricultural History 35 (Oct. 1961): 182-88.

Anhalt, Walter C., and Glen H. Smith. "He Saved the Farm? Governor Langer and the Mortgage Moratoria." North Dakota Quarterly 44 (Autumn 1976): 5-17.

Ankli, Robert E. "Farm Income on the Great Plains and Canadian Praries, 1920-1940." Agricultural History 51 (Jan. 1977): 92-103.

Arrington, Leonard J. "Western Agriculture and the New Deal." Agricultural History 44 (Oct. 1970): 337-53.

Auerbach, Jerold S. "Southern Tenant Farmers: Socialist Critics of the New Deal." Labor History 7 (Winter 1966): 3-18.

Baker, Gladys L. "'And to Act for the Secretary': Paul H. Appleby and the Department of Agriculture, 1933-1940." Agricultural History 45 (Oct. 1971): 235-58.

Banks, Ann. "Tobacco Talk." Southern Exposure 8 (Winter 1980): 34-45.

Berck, Peter. "A Note on the Real Cost of Tractors in the 1920s and 1930s." American Heritage 59 (Jan. 1985): 66-71.

Brown, William L. "H. A. Wallace and the Development of Hybrid Corn." Annals of Iowa 47 (Fall 1983): 167-79.

Bulkley, Peter B. "Agrarian Crisis in Western New York: New Deal Reinforcement of the Farm Depression." New York History 59 (Oct. 1978): 391-407.

Cantor, Louis. "A Prologue to the Protest Movement: The Missouri Sharecropper Roadside Demonstration of 1939." Journal of American History 55 (March 1969): 804-22.

Carey, James C. "The Farmers' Independence Council of America, 1935-1938." Agricultural History 35 (April 1961): 70-77.

Case, H. C. M. "Farm Debt Adjustment During the Early 1930s." Agricultural History 34 (Oct. 1960): 173-81.

Daniel, James C. "The North Carolina Tobacco Marketing Crisis of 1933." North Carolina Historical Review 41 (Winter 1964): 370-82.

Dethloff, Henry C. "Missouri Farmers and the New Deal: A Case Study of Farm Policy Formulations on the Local Level." Agricultural History 39 (July 1965): 141-46.

Dileva, Frank D. "Frantic Farmers Fight Law." Annals of Iowa 32 (Oct. 1953): 81-109.

_____. "Iowa Farm Price Revolt." Annals of Iowa 32 (Jan 1954): 171-202.

Dodd, James W. "Resolutions, Programs and Policies of the North Dakota Farmers' Holiday Association, 1932-1937." North Dakota History 28 (April 1961): 107-17.

Dyson, Lowell K. "The Southern Tenant Farmers Union and Depression Politics." Political Science Quarterly 88 (June 1973): 230-52.

_____. "Was Agricultural Distress in the 1930s A Result of Land Speculation During World War I?: The Case of Iowa." Annals of Iowa 40 (Spring 1971): 577-84.

Eon, Joseph W. "Marketing Problems of Northwestern Apples, 1929-1940." Agricultural History 16 (April 1942): 103-15.

Feder, Ernest. "Farm Debt Adjustments During the Depression--The Other Side of the Coin." Agricultural History 35 (April 1961): 78-81.

Fite, Gilbert C. "Farmer Opinion and the Agricultural Adjustment Act, 1933."
    Mississippi Valley Historical Review 48 (March 1962): 656-73.
    _____. "The McNary-Haugen Episode and the Triple-A." Journal of Farm
    Economics 42 (Dec. 1960): 1084-93.
    _____. "Voluntary Attempts to Reduce Cotton Acreage in the South, 1914-
    1933." Journal of Southern History 14 (Nov. 1948): 481-99.
Giebelhaus, August W. "Farming for Fuel: The Alcohol Motor Fuel Movement of the
    1930s." American Heritage 54 (Jan. 1980): 173-84.
Gilbert, Jess, and Steve Brown. "Alternative Land Reform Proposals in the 1930s:
    The Nashville Agrarians and the Southern Tenant Farmers' Union."
    Agricultural History 55 (Oct. 1981): 351-69.
Grant, Philip A., Jr. "Northern Great Plains Congressmen and Farm Legislation,
    1933-1938." Heritage of the Great Plains 15 (Summer 1982): 37-46.
    _____. "Southern Congressmen and Agriculture, 1921-1932." Agricultural
    History 53 (Jan. 1979): 338-51.
Grubbs, Donald H. "Gardner Jackson, That 'Socialist' Tenant Farmers' Union, and the
    New Deal." Agricultural History 42 (April 1968): 125-37.
Guth, James L. "The National Cooperative Council and Farm Relief, 1929-1942."
    Agricultural History 51 (April 1977): 441-58.
Hargreaves, Mary W. M. "Land-Use Planning in Response to Drought: The
    Experience of the Thirties" Agricultural History 50 (Oct. 1976): 561-82.
Hoglund, A. William. "A Comment on the Farm Strikes of 1932 and 1962."
    Agricultural History 39 (Oct. 1965): 213-16.
    _____. "Wisconsin Dairy Farmers on Strike." Agricultural History 35 (Jan.
    1961): 24-34.
Hurt, R. Douglas. "Agricultural Technology in the Dust Bowl, 1932-1940." In The
    Great Plains: Environment and Culture ed. by Brian W. Blouet and Frederick C.
    Luebke (Lincoln: University of Nebraska Press, 1979), pp. 139-56.
    _____. "REA: A New Deal for Farmers." Timeline 2 (Dec. 1985): 32-47.
    _____. "The National Grasslands: Origins and Development." Agricultural
    History 59 (April 1985): 246-59.
Jacklin, Thomas M. "Mission to the Sharecroppers: Neo-Orthodox Radicalism and
    the Delta Farm Venture, 1936-40." South Atlantic Quarterly 78 (Summer
    1979): 302-16.
Johnson, William R. "National Farm Organizations and the Reshaping of Agricultural
    Policy in 1932." Agricultural History 37 (Jan. 1963): 35-42.
Jones, C. Clyde. "The Burlington Railroad's Swine Sanitation Trains of 1929: A Case
    Study in Agricultural Development." Iowa Journal of History 57 (Jan. 1959):
    23-33.
Karr, Rodney D. "Farmer Rebels in Plymouth County, Iowa, 1932-1933." Annals of
    Iowa 47 (Winter 1985): 637-45.
Kirkendall, Richard S. "Corn Huskers and Master Farmers: Henry A. Wallace and
    the Merchandising of Iowa Agriculture." Palimpsest 65 (May 1984): 82-93.
    _____. "Howard Tolley and Agricultural Planning in the 1930's." Agricultural
    History 39 (Jan. 1965): 25-33.

_____. "L. C. Gray and the Supply of Agricultural Land." Agricultural History 37 (Oct. 1963): 205-16.

_____. "The New Deal and Agriculture." In The New Deal: The National Level ed. by John Braeman, Robert H. Bremner, and David Brody (Columbus: Ohio State University Press, 1975), pp. 83-109.

Kollmorgen, Walter M. "Kollmorgen as a [Department of Agriculture] Bureaucrat." Annals of the Association of American Geographers 69 (March 1979): 77-89.

Kramer, Randall A. "Federal Crop Insurance, 1938-1982." Agricultural History 57 (April 1983): 181-200.

Lambert, C. Roger. "Drought Relief for Cattlemen: The Emergency Purchase Program of 1933-1935." Panhandle-Plains Historical Review 45 (1972): 21-35.

_____. "Texas Cattlemen and the AAA, 1933-1935." Arizona and the West 14 (Summer 1972): 137-54.

_____. "The Drought Cattle Purchase, 1934-1936: Problems and Complaints." Agricultural History 45 (April 1971): 85-93.

Lemmon, Sarah McCulloh. "The Agricultural Policies of Eugene Talmadge." Agricultural History 28 (Jan. 1954): 21-30.

Lopez, Ron W. "The El Monte Berry Strike of 1933." Aztlan 1 (Spring 1970): 101-14.

Lovin, Hugh T. "Agrarian Radicalism at Ebb Tide: The Michigan Farmer-Labor Party, 1933-1937." Old Northwest 5 (Summer 1979): 149-66.

Lowitt, Richard, ed. "Shelterbelts in Nebraska." Nebraska History 57 (Fall 1976): 405-22.

Mathews, Allan. "Agrarian Radicals: The United Farmers League of South Dakota." South Dakota History 3 (Fall 1973): 408-21.

Matthews, Glenna. "The Apricot War: A Study of the Changing Fruit Industry During the 1930s." American Heritage 59 (Jan. 1985): 25-39.

May, Irvin, Jr. "Marvin Jones: Agrarian and Politician." Agricultural History 51 (April 1977): 421-40.

_____. "Cotton and Cattle: The FSRC and Emergency Work Relief." Agricultural History 46 (July 1972): 401-13.

_____. "Southwestern Agricultural Experiment Stations during the New Deal." Journal of the West 18 (Oct. 1979): 75-84.

_____. "Welfare and Ranchers: The Emergency Cattle Purchase Program and Emergency Work Relief Program in Texas, 1934-1935." West Texas Historical Association Yearbook 47 (1970): 3-19.

McCorkle, James L., Jr. "Problems of a Southern Agrarian Industry: Cooperation and Self-Interest." Southern Studies 17 (Fall 1978): 241-54.

McDean, Harry C. "Federal Farm Policy and the Dust Bowl: The Half-Right Solution." North Dakota History 47 (Summer 1980): 21-31.

_____. "Social Scientists and Farm Poverty on the North American Plains, 1933-1940." Great Plains Quarterly 3 (Winter 1983): 17-29.

Miller, John E. "Restrained, Respectable Radicals: The South Dakota Farm Holiday." American Heritage 59 (July 1985): 429-47.

Mitchell, H. L. "The Founding and Early History of the Southern Tenant Farmers Union." Arkansas Historical Quarterly 32 (Winter 1973): 342-69.

Nall, Garry L. "Dust Bowl Days: Panhandle Farming in the 1930's." Panhandle Plains Historical Review 48 (1975): 42-63.

Nelson, Lawrence J. "New Deal and Free Market: The Memphis Meeting of the Southern Commissioners of Agriculture, 1937." Tennessee Historical Quarterly 40 (Fall 1981): 225-38.

_____. "Oscar Johnson, the New Deal, and the Cotton Subsidy Payments Controversy, 1936-1937." Journal of Southern History 40 (Aug. 1974): 399-416.

Peterson, Tarla Rai. "The Will to Conservation: A Burkean Analysis of Dust Bowl Rhetoric and American Farming Motives." Southern Speech Communication Journal 52 (Fall 1986): 1-21.

Pinkett, Harold T. "The Soil Conservation Service and Farm Woodland Management, 1938-1945." American Heritage 59 (April 1985): 280-89.

Rasmussen, Wayne D., and Jane M. Porter. "Agriculture in the Industrial Economies of the West during the Great Depression, with Special Reference to the United States." In The Great Depression Revisited: Essays on the Economics of the Thirties ed. by Herman Van Der Wee (The Hague: Martinus Nijhoff, 1972), pp. 120-33.

Remele, Larry. "Public Industries to Save the Farm: Arthur C. Townley's 1933 Plan for Diversifying the Rural Economy." Heritage of the Great Plains 14 (Spring 1981): 29-40.

Riley, Glenda, and Richard S. Kirkendall. "Henry A. Wallace and the Mystique of the Farm Male, 1929-1933." Annals of Iowa 48 (Summer 1985): 32-55.

Saloutos, Theodore. "Edward A. O'Neal: The Farm Bureau and the New Deal." Current History 28 (June 1955): 356-61.

_____. "Land Policy and Its Relation to Agricuitural Production, 1862 to 1933." Journal of Economic History 22 (Dec. 1962): 445-60.

_____. "New Deal Agricultural Policy: An Evaluation." Journal of American History 61 (Sept. 1974): 394-416.

_____. "The New Deal and Farm Policy in the Great Plains." Agricultural History 43 (July 1969): 345-55.

_____. "William A. Hirth: Middle Western Agrarian." Mississippi Valley Historical Review 38 (Sept. 1951): 215-32.

Schapsmeier, Edward L. and Frederick H. "Farm Policy from FDR to Eisenhower: Southern Democrats and the Politics of Agriculture." Agricultural History 53 (Jan. 1979): 352-71.

_____. "The Wallaces and Their Farm Paper: A Story of Agrarian Leadership." Journalism Quarterly 44 (Summer 1967): 289-96.

Schulyer, Michael W. "The Hair-Splitters: Reno and Wallace, 1932-1933." Annals of Iowa 43 (Fall 1976): 403-29.

Schwieder, Dorothy. "The Granger Homestead Project." Palimpsest 58 (Sept.-Oct. 1977): 149-61.

Sears, Paul. "The Black Blizzards." In America in Crisis ed. by Daniel Aaron (New York: Knopf, 1952), pp. 287-302.

Shover, John L. "The Communist Party and the Midwest Farm Crisis of 1933." Journal of American History 51 (Sept. 1964): 248-66.

_____. "The Farmers' Holiday Association Strike, August 1932." Agricultural History 39 (Oct. 1965): 196-203.

Skaggs, Richard H. "Drought in the United States, 1931-40." Annals of the Association of American Geographers 65 (Sept. 1975): 391-402.

Slichter, Gertrude Almy. "Franklin D. Roosevelt and the Farm Problem, 1929-1932." Mississippi Valley Historical Review 43 (Sept. 1956): 238-58.

Smith, Henry Nash. "Rain Follows the Plow." Huntington Library Quarterly 10 (Feb. 1947): 187-88.

Snyder, Robert E. "The Cotton Holiday Movement in Mississippi, 1931." Journal of Mississippi History 40 (Feb. 1978): 1-32.

Soth, Lauren. "Henry Wallace and the Farm Crisis of the 1920s and 1930s." Annals of Iowa 47 (Fall 1983): 195-214.

Starch, Elmer. "A Better Life on the Plains." Yearbook of Agriculture 1979: 197-204.

Stein, Walter J. "The 'Okie' as Farm Laborer." Agricultural History 49 (Jan. 1975): 202-15.

Stout, Joe A., Jr. "Cattlemen, Conservationists, and the Taylor Grazing Act." New Mexico Historical Review 45 (Oct. 1970): 311-32.

Thrasher, Sue, and Leah Wise. "The Southern Tenant Farmers' Union." Southern Exposure 1 (Winter 1974): 5-32.

Tontz, Robert L. "Legal Parity: Implementation of the Policy of Equality for Agriculture, 1929-1954." Agricultural History 29 (Oct. 1955): 171-81.

_____. "Origin of the Base Period Concept of Parity: A Significant Value Judgment in Agricultural Policy." Agricultural History 32 (Jan. 1958): 3-13.

Venkataramani, M. S. "Norman Thomas, Arkansas Sharecroppers, and the Roosevelt Agricultural Policies, 1933-39." Mississippi Valley Historical Review 47 (Sept. 1960): 225-46.

_____. "Norman Thomas, Arkansas Sharecroppers, and the Roosevelt Agricultural Policies, 1933-1937." Arkansas Historical Quarterly 24 (Spring 1965): 3-28.

Wall, Joseph F. "The Iowa Farmer in Crisis, 1920-1936." Annals of Iowa 47 (Fall 1983): 116-27.

Wessel, Thomas. "Roosevelt and the Great Plains Shelterbelt." Great Plains Journal 8 (Spring 1969): 57-74.

Winters, Donald L. "The Persistence of Progressivism: Henry Cantwell Wallace and the Movement for Agricultural Economics." Agricultural History 41 (April 1967): 109-20.

Worster, Donald. "Grass to Dust: The Great Plains in the 1930's." Environmental Review 3 (1977): 2-13.

_____. "The Dirty Thirties: A Study in Agricultural Capitalism." Great Plains Quarterly 6 (Spring 1986): 107-16.

Dissertations

Adams, John Clifford. "Franklin D. Roosevelt's Gold Policies in a Farm Sector Strategy, 1933." Ph.D. diss., Indiana University, 1976.

Aeschbacher, William D. "Political Activity of Agricultural Organizations, 1929-1939." Ph.D. diss., University of Nebraska, 1948.

Babcock, John Gilbert Chittenden. "The Role of Public Discourse in the Soil Conservation Movement, 1865-1935." Ph.D. diss., University of Michigan, 1985.

Baldwin, Sidney. "The Farm Security Administration: A Study in Politics and Administration." Ph.D. diss., Syracuse University, 1956.

Berberet, William G. "The Evolution of a New Deal Agricultural Program: Soil Conservation Districts and Comprehensive Land and Water Development in Nebraska." Ph.D. diss., University of Nebraska, 1970.

Campbell, Christiana M. "The Farm Bureau and the New Deal, 1933-40: A Study in Agricultural Sectionalism." Ph.D. diss., University of Chicago, 1960.

Clarke-Hazlett, Christopher. "The Road to Dependency: Policy, Planning, and the Rationalization of American Agriculture, 1920-1945." Ph.D. diss., University of Rochester, 1986.

Conrad, David E. "The Forgotten Farmers: The AAA and the Southerns Tenants, 1933-1936." Ph.D. diss., University of Oklahoma, 1962.

Graham, Robert C. "Diffusion during Depression: The Adoption of the Tractor by Illinois Farmers." Ph.D. diss., University of Illinois, 1985.

Grubbs, Donald H. "The Southern Tenant Farmer's Union and the New Deal." Ph.D. diss., University of Florida, 1963.

Hamilton, David E. "From New Day to New Deal: American Agricultural in the Hoover Years, 1928-1933." Ph.D. diss., University of Iowa, 1985.

Holley, James Donald. "The New Deal and Farm Tenancy: Rural Resettlement in Arkansas, Louisiana, and Mississippi." Ph.D. diss., Louisiana State University, 1969.

Johnson, William Rudolph. "Farm Policy in Transition: 1932, Year of Crisis." Ph.D. diss., University of Oklahoma, 1963.

Kirkendall, Richard S. "The New Deal Professors and the Politics of Agriculture." Ph.D. diss., University of Wisconsin, 1958.

Klass, Bernard. "John D. Black: Agricultural Economist and Policy Adviser 1920-1942." Ph.D. diss., University of California, Los Angeles, 1969.

Korgan, Julius. "Farmers Picket the Depression." Ph.D. diss., American University, 1961.

Lambert, C. Roger. "New Deal Experiments in Production Control: The Livestock Program, 1933-1935." Ph.D. diss., University of Oklahoma, 1962.

McCann, John B. "The New Deal Farm Production Controls, 1933-1936." Ph.D. diss., University of Illinois, 1950.

Smith, Wilda M. "Reactions of Kansas Farmers to the New Deal Farm Program." Ph.D. diss., University of Illinois, 1969.

Snyder, Robert Edward. "The Cotton Holiday Movement in the South." Ph.D. diss., Syracuse University, 1980.

Webb, David D. "Farmers, Professors and Money: Agriculture and the Battle for
   Managed Money, 1920-1941." Ph.D. diss., University of Oklahoma, 1978.

7.3 BANKING, FINANCE, AND MONETARY AFFAIRS

Books

Beyen, J. W. Money in a Maelstrom. New York: Macmillan, 1949.

Brennan, John A. Silver and the First New Deal. Reno: University of Nevada Press,
   1969.

Brown, William Adams, Jr. The International Gold Standard Reinterpreted, 1914-1938.
   New York: National Bureau of Economic Research, 1940.

Burns, Helen M. The American Banking Community and New Deal Banking Reforms
   1933-1935. Westport, Conn.: Greenwood, 1974.

Chandler, Lester V. American Monetary Policy, 1929-1941. New York: Harper & Row,
   1971.

Clarke, Stephen V. O. Central Bank Cooperation, 1924-1931. New York: Federal
   Reserve Bank of New York, 1967.

Crawford, Arthur Whipple. Monetary Management Under the New Deal: The Evolution
   of a Managed Currency System - Its Problems and Results. Washington, D.C.:
   American Council on Public Affairs, 1940.

Everest, Allan S. Morganthau, the New Deal, and Silver: A Story of Pressure Politics.
   New York: Kings Crown Press, 1950.

Fleisig, Heywood W. Long Term Capital Flows and the Great Depression: The Role of
   the United States, 1927-1933. New York: Arno Press, 1975.

Johnson, Gove G., Jr. The Treasury and Monetary Policy, 1933-1938. Cambridge:
   Harvard University Press, 1939.

Kennedy, Susan Estabrook. The Banking Crisis of 1933. Lexington: University Press of
   Kentucky, 1973.

Neville, Howard R. The Detroit Banking Collapse of 1933. East Lansing: Bureau of
   Business and Economic Research, College of Business and Public Service, Michigan
   State University, 1960.

Paris, James Daniel. Monetary Policies of the United States, 1932-1938. New York:
   Columbia University Press, 1938.

Sullivan, Lawrence. Prelude to Panic: The Story of the Bank Holiday. Washington, D.C.:
   Statesman Press, 1936.

Temin, Peter. Did Monetary Forces Cause the Great Depression? New York: W.W.
   Norton, 1976.

Wicker, Elmus R. Federal Reserve Monetary Policy, 1917-1933. New York: Random
   House, 1966.

Articles

Angel, James W. "Gold, Banks and the New Deal." Political Science Quarterly 49 (Dec. 1934): 481-505.

Arrington, Leonard J., and Gwynn W. Barrett. "Stopping a Run on a Bank: The First Security Bank of Idaho and the Great Depression." Idaho Yesterdays 14 (Winter 1970): 2-11.

Awalt, Francis G. "Recollections of the Banking Crisis in 1933." Business History Review 43 (Autumn 1969): 347-71.

Ballantine, Arthur. "When All the Banks Closed." Harvard Business Review 26 (March 1948): 129-43.

Bird, Caroline. "The Day the Money Stopped." Look 27 (March 12, 1963): 84-91.

Brennan, John A. "The Politics of Silver in the New Deal." Nevada Historical Society Quarterly 14 (Fall 1971): 5-18.

Esbitt, Milton. "Bank Portfolios and Bank Failures during the Great Depression: Chicago." Journal of Economic History 46 (June 1986): 455-62.

Fahey, John. "Beating A Depression: The Portland Home Loan Bank." Pacific Northwest Quarterly 75 (Jan. 1984): 34-40.

Frost, Peter A. "Banks' Demand for Excess Reserves." Journal of Political Economy 79 (July/Aug. 1971): 805-25.

Gandolfi, Arthur E., and James R. Lothian. "The Demand for Money from the Great Depression to the Present." American Economic Review 66 (May 1976): 46-51.

Hamilton, David E. "The Causes of the Banking Panic of 1930: Another View." Journal of Southern History 51 (Nov. 1985): 581-608.

Hamilton, Walton H. "When the Banks Closed." In America in Crisis ed. by Daniel Aaron (New York: Knopf, 1952), pp. 267-84.

Holch, Arthur. "When Rubber Checks Didn't Bounce." American Heritage 12 (June 1961): 58-59.

Howson, Susan. "The Management of Sterling, 1932-1939." Journal of Economic History 40 (March 1980): 53-60.

Jervey, William H., Jr. "When the Banks Closed: Arizona's Bank Holiday of 1933." Arizona and the West 10 (Summer 1968): 127-52.

Kennedy, Susan Estabrook. "Nevada's Banking Holiday: 1932." Nevada Historical Society Quarterly 17 (Fall 1974): 125-30.

_____. "The Michigan Banking Crisis of 1933." Michigan History 57 (Fall 1973): 237-64.

Macdonald, Henry. "The 1933 Banking Crisis in Erie." Journal of Erie Studies 12 (Fall 1983): 18-27.

Miranti, Paul J., Jr. "Associationalism, Statism, and Professional Regulation: Public Accountants and the Reform of the Financial Markets, 1896-1940." Business History Review 60 (Autumn 1986): 438-68.

Muchmore, Lynn. "The Banking Crisis of 1933: Some Iowa Evidence." Journal of Economic History 30 (Sept. 1970): 627-39.

O'Hara, Maureen, and David Easley. "The Postal Savings System in the Depression." Journal of Economic History 39 (Sept. 1979): 741-53.

Olson, James S. "Rehearsal for Disaster: Hoover, the R.F.C., and the Banking Crisis in Nevada, 1932-1933." Western Historical Quarterly 6 (April 1975): 149-61.

_____. "The Boise Bank Panic of 1932." Idaho Yesterdays 18 (Winter 1974-1975): 25-28.

Porter, David L. "Key Pittman and the Monetary Act of 1939." Nevada Historical Society Quarterly 21 (Fall 1978): 205-13.

Redman, J. H. "Restored Confidence in Iowa Banks." Annals of Iowa 30 (July 1949): 56-61.

Rothbard, Murray N. "The New Deal and the International Monetary System." In Watershed of Empire: Essays on New Deal Foreign Policy ed. by Leonard P. Liggio and James J. Martin (Colorado Springs: Ralph Myles, 1976), pp. 19-64.

Smart, Eynon. "Bank Holidays--And Much Else." History Today 21 (Dec. 1971): 870-76.

Trescott, Paul B. "Federal Reserve Policy in the Great Contraction: A Counter-factual Assessment." Explorations in Economic History 19 (July 1982): 211-20.

Webb, Pamela. "Business as Usual: The Bank Holiday in Arkansas." Arkansas Historical Quarterly 39 (Autumn 1980): 247-61.

White, Eugene Nelson. "A Reinterpretation of the Bank Crisis of 1930." Journal of Economic History 44 (March 1984): 119-38.

Wicker, Elmus. "A Reconsideration of the Causes of the Banking Panic of 1930." Journal of Economic History 40 (Sept. 1980): 571-83.

_____. "Roosevelt's 1933 Monetary Experiment." Journal of American History 57 (March 1970): 864-79.

Dissertations

Burns, Helen M. "The American Banking Community and New Deal Banking Reform, 1933-1935." Ph.D. diss., New York University, 1965.

Everest, Allan S. "Morganthau, The New Deal, and Silver." Ph.D. diss., Columbia University, 1948.

Ferguson, Albert Thomas, Jr. "Critical Realignment: The Fall of the House of Morgan and the Origins of the New Deal." Ph.D. diss., Princeton University, 1981.

Fleisig, Heywood William. "Long Term Capital Flows and the Great Depression: The Role of the United States, 1927-1933." Ph.D. diss., Yale University, 1969.

Graham, Fred C. "Free Reserve Adjustment by Commercial Banks: The 1933-1942 Experience." Ph.D. diss., University of Virginia, 1985.

Reeve, Joseph Edwin. "Monetary Proposals for Curing the Depression in the United States, 1929-35." Ph.D. diss., University of Chicago, 1940.

Roe, Alfred L. "Banking and Politics in the New Era." Ph.D. diss., University of Minnesota, 1968.

Sessions, William L. "California's Innovative Banker: A.P. Giannini and the Banking Crisis of 1933." Ph.D. diss., University of Southern California, 1979.

7.4   BUSINESS AND INDUSTRY

Books

Burns, Arthur. The Decline of Competition: A Study of the Evolution of American Industry. New York: McGraw-Hill, 1936.

Childs, William R. Trucking and the Public Interest: The Emergence of Federal Regulation, 1914-1940. Knoxville: University of Tennessee Press, 1985.

Cochran, Thomas C. The American Business System: A Historical Perspective, 1900-1955. Cambridge: Harvard University Press, 1957.

Fine, Sidney. The Automobile Under the Blue Eagle: Labor, Management, and the Automobile Manufacturing Code. Ann Arbor: University of Michigan Press, 1963.

Galambos, Louis. Competition and Cooperation: The Emergence of a National Trade Association. Baltimore: Johns Hopkins University Press, 1966.

Johnson, James P. The Politics of Soft Coal: The Bituminous Industry from World War I through the New Deal. Urbana: University of Illinois Press, 1979.

Koch, Albert R. The Financing of Large Corporations, 1920-1939. New York: National Bureau of Economic Research, 1943.

Temin, Peter. Taking Your Medicine: Drug Regulation in the United States. Cambridge: Harvard University Press, 1980.

Warner, W. Lloyd, and James C. Abegglen. Occupational Mobility in American Business and Industry, 1928-1952. Minneapolis: University of Minnesota Press, 1955.

Articles

Alford, B. W. E., and C. E. Harvey. "Copperbelt Merger: The Formation of the Rhokana Corporation, 1930-1932." Business History Review 54 (Autumn 1980): 331-58.

Barrett, Glen. "Reclamation's New Deal for Heavy Construction: M-K in the Great Depression." Idaho Yesterdays 22 (Fall 1978): 21-27

Bernanke, Ben S. "Employment, Hours, and Earnings in the Depression: An Analysis of Eight Manufacturing Industries." American Economic Review 76 (March 1986): 82-109.

Collins, Robert M. "Positive Business Responses to the New Deal: The Roots of the Committee for Economic Development, 1933-1942." Business History Review 52 (Autumn 1978): 369-91.

Ellsworth, Catherine C. "Integration Into Crude Oil Transportation in the 1930's--A Case Study: The Standard Oil Co. (Ohio)." Business History Review 35 (Summer 1961): 180-210.

French, M.J. "The Emergence of a U. S. Multinational Enterprise: The Goodyear Tire and Rubber Company, 1910-39." Economic History Review 40 (Feb. 1987): 64-79.

Fricke, Ernest B. "The New Deal and the Modernization of Small Business: The McCreary Tire & Rubber Company, 1930-1940." Business History Review 56 (Winter 1982): 559-76.

Harper, F. J. "'A New Battle of Evolution': The Anti-Chain Store Trade-at-Home Agitation of 1929-1930." Journal of American Studies 16 (Dec. 1982): 407-26.

Hawley, Ellis W. "The New Deal and Business." In The New Deal: The National Level ed. by John Braeman, Robert H. Bremner, and David Brody (Columbus: Ohio State University Press, 1975), pp. 50-82.

Heath, Jim F. "American War Mobilization and the Use of Small Manufacturers, 1939-1943." Business History Review 46 (Autumn 1972): 295-319.

Hewins, Dana C. "Regulation without Historical Justification: The Case of Household Moving." Research in Economic History 1982 (Supplement 2): 91-92.

Himmelberg, Robert F. "Government and Business, 1917-1932: The Triumph of 'Corporate Liberalism'?" In Business and Government: Essays in 20th Century Cooperation and Confrontation ed. by Joseph R. Frese, S. J., and Jacob Judd (Tarrytown, N.Y.: Sleepy Hollow Restorations, 1985), pp. 1-23.

Johnson, Arthur M. "The Federal Trade Commission: The Early Years, 1915-1935." In Business and Government: Essays in 20th Century Cooperation and Confrontation ed. by Joseph R. Frese, S. J., and Jacob Judd (Tarrytown, N.Y.: Sleepy Hollow Restorations, 1985), pp. 157-86.

Longin, Thomas C. "Coal, Congress, and the Courts: The Bituminous Coal Industry and the New Deal." West Virginia Magazine 35 (Jan. 1974): 101-30.

McQuaid, Kim. "Competition, Cartellization and the Corporate Ethic: General Electric's Leadership during the New Deal Era, 1933-40." American Journal of Economics and Sociology 36 (Oct. 1977): 417-28.

_____. "Corporate Liberalism in the American Business Community, 1920-1940." Business History Review 52 (Autumn 1978): 342-68.

_____. "Industry and the Co-operative Commonwealth: William P. Hapgood and the Columbia Conserve Company, 1917-1943." Labor History 17 (Fall 1976): 510-29.

_____. "The Frustration of Corporate Revival during the Early New Deal." Historian 41 (Aug. 1979): 682-704.

_____. "Young, Swope and General Electric's 'New Capitalism': A Study in Corporate Liberalism, 1920-33." American Journal of Economics and Sociology 36 (July 1977): 323-34.

Ryant, Carl G. "The South and the Movement Against Chain Stores." Journal of Southern History 39 (May 1973): 207-22.

Tedlow, Richard S. "The National Association of Manufacturers and Public Relations during the New Deal." Business History Review 50 (Spring 1976): 25-45.

Tugwell, Rexford G. "The New Deal: The Rise of Business, Part I." Western Political Quarterly 5 (June 1952): 274-89.

_____. "The New Deal: The Rise of Business, Part II." Western Political
  Quarterly 5 (Sept. 1952): 483-503.
Warren, Wilson J. "The Welfare Capitalism of John Morrell and Company, 1922-
  1937." Annals of Iowa 47 (Fall 1984): 497-517.
Wilson, William H. "How the Chamber of Commerce Viewed the NRA: A Re-
  examination." Mid-America 44 (April 1962): 95-108.

Dissertations

Andrews, Pauline. "Manufacturing Fixed Investment and the Great Depression."
  Ph.D. diss., University of California, Berkeley, 1982.
Bernstein, Michael A. "Long-Term Economic Growth and the Problem of Recovery
  in American Manufacturing: A Study of the Great Depression in the United
  States, 1929-1939." Ph.D. diss., Yale University, 1982.
Brown, Linda K. "Challenge and Response: The American Business Community and
  the New Deal, 1932-1939." Ph.D. diss., University of Pennsylvania, 1972.
Childs, William Ralph. "Trucking and the Emergence of Federal Regulation, 1890-
  1940: A History of the Interactions of Technology, Business, Law, and Politics."
  Ph.D. diss., University of Texas, 1982.
Gable, Richard W. "A Political Analysis of an Employers' Association: The National
  Association of Manufacturers." Ph.D. diss., University of Chicago, 1950.
Hobor, Nancy Allen. "The United States vs. Montgomery Ward: A Case Study in
  Business Opposition to the New Deal, 1933-1945." Ph.D. diss., University of
  Chicago, 1973.
Johnson, James P. "A 'New Deal' for Soft Coal: The Attempted Revitalization of the
  Soft Coal Industry under the New Deal." Ph.D. diss., Columbia University,
  1968.
Longin, Thomas Charles. "The Search for Security: American Business Thought in
  the 1930s." Ph.D. diss., University of Nebraska, 1970.
Trommald, Elliott Corbett. "Business Responses to Crisis: The Depression 1929-
  1932." Ph.D. diss., State University of New York at Buffalo, 1977.
Volyn, Robert P. "The Broad Silk Industry in Paterson, New Jersey: A Troubled
  Industry in Microcosm, 1920 through 1935." Ph.D. diss., New York University,
  1980.

7.5 LABOR

Books

Ahearn, Daniel J., Jr. The Wages of Farm and Factory Laborers, 1914-1944. New
  York: Columbia University Press, 1945.

Allen, Ruth A. Chapters in the History of Organized Labor in Texas. Austin: The University, 1941.

Auerbach, Jerold S. Labor and Liberty: The La Follette Committee and the New Deal. Indianapolis: Bobbs-Merrill, 1966.

Bernstein, Irving. The Lean Years: A History of the American Worker, 1920-1933. Boston: Houghton Mifflin, 1960.

_____. The Turbulent Years: A History of the American Worker, 1933-1941. Boston: Houghton Mifflin, 1970.

_____. A Caring Society: The New Deal, the Worker, and the Great Depression. Boston: Houghton Mifflin, 1985.

Brody, David. The Butcher Workmen: A Study of Unionization. Cambridge: Harvard University Press, 1964.

Brooks, Robert R. R. Unions of Their Own Choosing: An Account of the National Labor Relations Board and Its Work. New Haven: Yale University Press, 1939.

Cochran, Bert. Labor and Communism: The Conflict That Shaped American Unions. Princeton: Princeton University Press, 1977.

Cohen, Sanford. State Labor Legislation, 1937-1947: A Study of State Laws Affecting the Conduct and Organization of Labor Unions. Columbus: Bureau of Business Research, College of Commerce and Administration, Ohio State University, 1948.

Derber, Milton, and Edwin Young, eds. Labor and the New Deal. Madison: University of Wisconsin Press, 1957.

DeWitt, Howard. Violence in the Fields: California Filipino Farm Labor Unionization During the Great Depression. Saratoga, Cal.: Century Twenty One Publishing, 1980.

Fine, Sidney. Sit Down: The General Motors Strike of 1936-1937. Ann Arbor: University of Michigan Press, 1969.

Friedlander, Peter. The Emergence of a UAW Local, 1936-1939: A Study in Class and Culture. Pittsburgh: University of Pittsburgh Press, 1975.

Galenson, Walter. The CIO Challenge to the AFL: A History of the American Labor Movement: 1935-1941. Cambridge: Harvard University Press, 1960.

Higgins, George G. Voluntarism in Organized Labor in the United States, 1930-1940. Washington, D.C.: Catholic University of America, 1944.

Kampelman, Max M. The Communist Party vs. the C.I.O.: A Study in Power Politics. New York: Praeger, 1957.

Keeran, Roger. The Communist Party and the Auto Workers Unions. Bloomington: Indiana University Press, 1980.

Kruchko, John G. The Birth of a Union Local: The History of UAW Local 674, Norwood, Ohio, 1933-1940. Ithaca: New York State School of Industrial and Labor Relations, Cornell University, 1972.

Leab, Daniel J. A Union of Individuals: The Formation of the American Newpaper Guild, 1933-1936. New York: Columbia University Press, 1970.

Levenstein, Harvey. Communism, Anticommunism, and the CIO. Westport, Conn.: Greenwood, 1981.

Meier, August, and Elliott Rudwick. Black Detroit and the Rise of the UAW. New York: Oxford University Press, 1979.

Milton, David. The Politics of U.S. Labor: From the Great Depression to the New Deal. New York: Monthly Review Press, 1982.

Morris, James O. Conflict within the AFL: A Study of Craft Versus Industrial Unionism, 1901-1938. Ithaca: Cornell University Press, 1958.

Newell, Barbara W. Chicago and the Labor Movement: Metropolitan Unionism in the 1930's. Urbana: University of Illinois Press, 1961.

Perry, Louis B. and Richard S. A History of the Los Angeles Labor Movement, 1911-1941. Berkeley: University of California Press, 1963.

Roberts, Harold S. The Rubber Workers: Labor Organization and Collective Bargaining in the Rubber Industry. New York: Harper, 1944.

Schacht, John N. The Making of Telephone Unionism, 1920-1947. New Brunswick, N.J.: Rutgers University Press, 1985.

Schatz, Ronald W. The Electrical Workers: A History of Labor at General Electric and Westinghouse, 1923-60. Urbana: University of Illinois Press, 1983.

Schwartz, Harvey. The March Inland: Origins of the ILWU Warehouse Division, 1934-1938. Los Angeles: Institute of Industrial Relations, 1978.

Suggs, George G., Jr. Union Busting in the Tri-State: The Oklahoma, Kansas, and Missouri Metal Workers Strike of 1935. Norman: University of Oklahoma Press, 1986.

Vittoz, Stanley. New Deal Labor Policy and the American Industrial Economy. Chapel Hill: University of North Carolina Press, 1987.

Zieger, Robert H. Madison's Battery Workers, 1934-1952: A History of Federal Labor Union 19587. Ithaca: New York State School of Industrial and Labor Relations, 1977.

_____. Rebuilding the Pulp and Paper Workers' Union, 1933-1941. Knoxville: University of Tennessee Press, 1984.

Articles

Allen, John E. "Eugene Talmadge and the Great Textile Strike in Georgia, September 1934." In Essays in Southern Labor History: Selected Papers, Southern Labor History Conference, 1976 ed. by Gary M. Fink and Merl E. Reed (Westport, Conn.: Greenwood Press, 1977), pp. 224-43.

Ansley, Fran, and Brenda Bell. "Davidson-Wilder 1932: Strikes in the Coal Camp." Southern Exposure 1 (Winter 1974): 113-36.

Argersinger, Jo Ann E. "'The Right to Strike': Labor Organization and the New Deal in Baltimore." Maryland History Magazine 78 (Winter 1983): 299-318.

Asher, Robert. "Jewish Unions and the American Federation of Labor Power Structure, 1903-1935." American Jewish Historical Quarterly 65 (March 1976): 215-27.

Auerbach, Jerold S. "The La Follette Committee: Labor and Civil Liberties in the New Deal." Journal of American History 51 (Dec. 1964): 435-59.

Bailey, Gary L. "The Terre Haute, Indiana, General Strike, 1935." Indiana Magazine of History 80 (Sept. 1984): 193-226.

Bain, Trevor. "Internal Union Conflict: The Flat Glass Workers, 1936-1937." Labor History 9 (Winter 1968): 106-9.

Barley, Gary L. "The Terre Haute, Indiana, General Strike, 1935." Indiana Magazine of History 80 (Sept. 1984): 193-226.

Barnard, John. "Rebirth of the United Automobile Workers: The General Motors Tool and Die-makers' Strike of 1939." Labor History 27 (Spring 1986): 165-87.

Bernhardt, Debra. "Ballad of a Lumber Strike." Michigan History 66 (Jan. 1982): 38-43.

Bernstein, Irving. "John L. Lewis and the Voting Behavior of the C.I.O." Public Opinion Quarterly 5 (June 1941): 233-49.

_____. "Public Policy and the American Worker, 1933-45." Monthly Labor Review 99 (Oct. 1976): 11-17.

_____. "The Growth of American Unions." American Economic Review 44 (June 1954): 301-18.

Blackwood, George D. "The Sit-Down Strike in the Thirties." South Atlantic Quarterly 55 (Oct. 1956): 438-48.

Blantz, Thomas E. "Father Haas and the Minneapolis Truckers Strike of 1934." Minnesota History 42 (Spring 1970-71): 5-15.

Boles, Frank. "Walter Reuther and the Kelsey Hayes Strike of 1936." Detroit in Perspective 4 (Winter 1980): 74-90.

Bonthius, Andrew. "Origins of the International Longshoremen's and Warehousemen's Union." Southern California Quarterly 59 (Winter 1977): 379-426.

Boryczka, Ray. "Militancy and Factionalism in the United Auto Workers, 1937-1941." Maryland Historian 8 (Fall 1977): 13-25.

_____. "Seasons of Discontent: Auto Union Factionalism and the Motor Products Strike of 1935-1936." Michigan History 61 (Spring 1977): 3-32.

Boyle, Kevin. "Rite of Passage: The 1939 General Motors Tool and Die Strike." Labor History 27 (Spring 1986): 188-203.

Brandeis, Elizabeth. "Organized Labor and Protective Labor Legislation." In Labor and the New Deal ed. by Milton Derber and Edwin Young (Madison: University of Wisconsin Press, 1957), pp. 193-230.

Brody, David. "Labor and the Great Depression: The Interpretive Prospects." Labor History 13 (Spring 1972): 231-44.

_____. "Radical Labor History and Rank and File Militancy." Labor History 16 (Winter 1975): 117-26.

_____. "The Emergence of Mass-Production Unionism." In Change and Continuity in Twentieth-Century America ed. by. John Braeman, Robert H. Bremner, and Everett Walters (Columbus: Ohio State University Press, 1964), pp. 221-62.

Brune, Lester H. "'Union Holiday--Closed Till Further Notice': The 1936 General Strike at Pekin, Illinois." Journal of the Illinois State Historical Society 75 (Spring 1982): 29-38.

Bubka, Tony. "The Harlan County Coal Strike of 1931." Labor History 11 (Winter 1970): 41-57.

Carpenter, Gerald. "Public Opinion in the New Orleans Street Railway Strike of 1929-1930." In Essays in Southern Labor History: Selected Papers, Southern Labor History Conference, 1976 ed. by Gary M. Fink and Merl E. Reed (Westport, Conn.,: Greenwood Press, 1977), pp. 191-207.

Cary, Lorin Lee. "The Reorganized United Mine Workers of America, 1930-1931." Journal of the Illinois State Historical Society 46 (Autumn 1973): 244-70.

Condon, Richard H. "Bayonets at the North Bridge: The Lewiston-Auburn Shoe Strike, 1937." Maine Historical Society Quarterly 21 (Fall 1981): 75-98.

Daniel, Cletus E. "Agricultural Unionism and the Early New Deal: The California Experience." Southern California Quarterly 59 (Summer 1977): 185-215.

Davin, Eric Leif, and Staughton Lynd. "Picket Line and Ballot Box: The Forgotten Legacy of the Local Labor Party Movement, 1932-1936." Radical History Review 22 (Winter 1979-80): 43-63.

Dembo, Jonathan. "John Danz and the Seattle Amusement Trades Strike, 1921-1935." Pacific Northwest Quarterly 71 (Oct. 1980): 182.

Derber, Milton. "Growth and Expansion." In Labor and the New Deal ed. by Milton Derber and Edwin Young (Madison: University of Wisconsin Press, 1957), pp. 1-44.

_____. "The Idea of Industrial Democracy in America: 1915-1935." Labor History 8 (Winter 1967): 3-29.

_____. "The New Deal and Labor." In The New Deal: The National Level ed. by John Braeman, Robert H. Bremner, and David Brody (Columbus: Ohio State University Press, 1975), pp. 110-32.

DeWitt, Howard A. "The Filipino Labor Union: The Salinas Lettuce Strike of 1934." Amerasia Journal 5 (Fall 1978): 1-21.

Draper, Theodore. "Communists and Miners 1928-1933." Dissent 19 (Spring 1972): 371-92.

Dubofsky, Melvyn. "The New Deal and the American Labor Movement." In The Roosevelt New Deal: A Program Assessment Fifty Years After ed. by Wilbur J. Cohen (Austin: Lyndon B. Johnson School of Public Affairs, 1986), pp. 73-82.

Dyson, Lowell K. "The Milk Strike of 1939 and the Destruction of the Dairy Farmers Union." New York History 51 (Oct. 1970): 523-45.

Edelman, Murray. "New Deal Sensitivity to Labor Interests." In Labor and the New Deal ed. by Milton Derber and Edwin Young (Madison: University of Wisconsin Press, 1957), pp. 157-92.

Engelmann, Larry D. "'We Were the Poor People': The Hormel Strike of 1933." Labor History 15 (Fall 1974): 483-510.

Fano, Ester. "The Problem of 'Technological Unemplyment' in the Industrial Research of the 1930s in the United States." History and Technology 1 (1984): 277-306.

Fast, Howard. "An Occurance at Republic Steel." In The Aspirin Age, 1919-1941 ed. by Isabel Leighton (New York: Simon and Schuster, 1949), pp. 383-402.

Filippelli, Ronald L. "UE: The Formative Years, 1933-1937." Labor History 17 (Summer 1976): 351-71.

Findlay, James F. "The Great Textile Strike of 1934: Illuminating Rhode Island History in the Thirties." Rhode Island History 42 (Feb. 1983): 17-29.

Fine, Sidney. "Frank Murphy, Law and Order, and Labor Relations in Michigan, 1937." In Union Power and Public Policy ed. by David B. Lipsky (Ithaca: (New York State School of Industrial and Labor Relations, 1975), pp. 1-23.

_____. "Proportional Representation of Workers in the Auto Industry, 1934-1935." Industrial and Labor Relations Review 12 (Jan. 1959): 182-205.

_____. "The General Motors Sit-Down Strike: A Re-examination." American Historical Review 70 (April 1965): 691-713.

_____. "The History of the American Labor Movement with Special Reference to Developments in the 1930's." In Labor in a Changing America ed. by William Haber (New York: Bantam, 1966), pp. 105-20.

_____. "The Origins of the United Automobile Workers, 1933-1935." Journal of Economic History 18 (Sept. 1958): 249-82.

_____. "The Toledo Chevrolet Strike of 1935." Ohio Historical Quarterly 67 (Jan. 1958): 326-56.

_____. "The Tool and Die Makers Strike of 1933." Michigan History 42 (Sept. 1958): 297-323.

_____, ed. "John L. Lewis Discusses the General Motors Sit-Down Strike: A Document." Labor History 15 (Fall 1974): 563-70.

Fishbein, Leslie. "A Lost Legacy of Labor Films." Film and History 9 (May 1979): 33-40.

Flanagan, Barney L. "A Labor Inspector During the Great Depression." Utah Historical Quarterly 54 (Summer 1986): 218-44.

Flynt, Wayne. "A Vignette of Southern Labor Politics--The 1936 Mississippi Senatorial Primary." Mississippi Quarterly 26 (Winter 1972-73): 89-99.

Fraser, Steve. "From the 'New Unionism' to the New Deal." Labor History 25 (Summer 1984): 405-30.

Fry, Joseph A. "Rayon, Riot, and Repression: The Covington Sit Down Strike of 1937." Virginia Magazine of History and Biography 84 (Jan. 1976): 3-18.

Gall, Gilbert J. "Heber Blankenhorn, The LaFollette Committee, and the Irony of Industrial Repression." Labor History 23 (Spring 1982): 246-53.

Gordon, Max. "The Communists and the Drive to Organize Steel, 1936." Labor History 23 (Spring 1982): 254-65.

Gottlieb, Peter. "The Complicated Equation: Worker Rebellion and Unionization." Appalachian Journal 6 (Summer 1979): 321-25.

Green, James. "Labor and the New Deal." In Working for Democracy ed. by Paul Buhle and Alan Dawley (Urbana: University of Illinois Press, 1985), pp. 83-91.

_____. "Working Class Militancy in the Depression." Radical America 6 (Nov.-Dec. 1972): 1-35.

Haynes, John E. "Communists and Anti-Communists in the Northern Minnesota CIO, 1936-1949." Upper Midwest History 1 (1981): 55-73.

Herring, Neill, and Sue Thrasher. "UAW Sitdown Strike: Atlanta, 1936." Southern Exposure 1 (Winter 1974): 63-83.

Hodges, James A. "Challenge to the New South: The Great Textile Strike in Elizabethton, Tennessee, 1929." Tennessee Historical Quarterly 23 (Dec. 1964): 343-57.

Hoffman, Abraham. "The El Monte Berry Pickers' Strike: International Involvement in a Local Labor Dispute, 1933." Journal of the West 12 (Jan. 1973): 71-84.

Holter, Darryl. "Sit-down Strikes in Milwaukee, 1937-1938." Milwaukee History 9 (Summer 1986): 58-64.

Hudson, James J. "The Role of the California National Guard during the San Francisco General Strike of 1934." Military Affairs 46 (April 1982): 76-83.

Hurd, Rick. "New Deal Labor Policy and the Containment of Radical Union Activity." Review of Radical Political Economics 8 (Fall 1976): 32-43.

Ingalls, Robert P. "Anti-Labor Vigilantes--The South in the 1930's." Southern Exposure 12 (Nov. 1984): 72-78.

Johnson, James P. "Reorganizing the United Mine Workers of America in Pennsylvania During the New Deal." Pennsylvania History 37 (April 1970): 117-32.

_____. "Theories of Labor Union Development and the United Mine Workers, 1932-1933." Register of the Kentucky Historical Society 73 (April 1975): 150-70.

Kahn, Lawrence M. "Unions and Internal Labor Markets: The Case of the San Francisco Longshoremen." Labor History 21 (Summer 1980): 369-91.

Keeran, Roger R. "Communist Influence in the Automobile Industry, 1920-1933: Paving the Way for an Industrial Union." Labor History 20 (Spring 1979): 189-226.

_____. "The Communists and UAW Factionalism, 1937-39." Michigan History 60 (Summer 1976): 115-35.

Kennedy, Donald. "Corporate Structure, Technology, and Unionism in the Full-Fashioned Hoisery Industry: The Berkshire Knitting Mills Strike of 1936-1937." Labor Studies Journal 3 (Winter 1979): 257-80.

Kritzberg, Barry. "An Unfinished Chapter in White-Collar Unionism: The Formative Years of the Chicago Newspaper Guild, Local 71, American Newspaper Guild, A.F.L.,-C.I.O." Labor History 14 (Summer 1973): 397-413.

Larrowe, Charles P. "The Great Maritime Strike of '34." Labor History 11 (Fall 1970): 403-51; 12 (Winter 1971): 3-37.

Leab, Daniel J. "Toward Unionization: The American Newspaper Guild and the Newark Ledger Strike of 1934-35." Labor History 11 (Winter 1970): 3-22.

Licht, Walter, and Hal Seth Barron. "Labor's Men: A Collective Biography of Union Officialdom during the New Deal Years." Labor History 19 (Fall 1978): 532-45.

Lovin, Hugh T. "CIO Innovators, Labor Party Ideologues, and Organized Labor's Muddles in the 1937 Detroit Elections." Old Northwest 8 (Fall 1982): 223-43.

_____. "The Automobile Workers Unions and the Fight for Labor Parties in the 1930s." Indiana Magazine of History 77 (June 1981): 123-49.

_____. "The CIO and that 'Damnable Bickering" in the Pacific Northwest, 1937-1971." Pacific Historian 23 (Spring 1979): 66-79.

_____. "The Persistence of Third Party Dreams in the American Labor Movement, 1930-1938." Mid-America 58 (Oct. 1976): 141-57.

Lynd, Staughton. "The United Front in America: A Note." Radical America 8 (July-Aug. 1974): 29-37.

Marquart, Frank. "From a Labor Journal: Unions and Radicals in the Depression Years." Dissent 21 (Summer 1974): 421-30.

Matthews, Glenna. "The Fruit Workers of the Santa Clara Valley: Alternative Paths to Union Organization during the 1930s." Pacific Historical Review 54 (Feb. 1985): 51-70.

McPherson, Donald S. "The 'Little Steel' Strike of 1937 in Johnstown, Pennsylvania." Pennsylvania History 39 (July 1972): 219-38.

Montgomery, David, and Ronald Schatz. "Facing Layoffs." Radical America 10 (March-April 1976): 15-27.

Nelson, Daniel. "Origins of the Sit Down Era: Worker Militancy and Innovation in the Rubber Industry, 1934-38." Labor History 23 (Spring 1982): 198-225.

_____. "The CIO at Bay: Labor Militancy and Politics in Akron, 1936-1938." Journal of American History 71 (Dec. 1984): 565-86.

_____. "The Great Goodyear Strike of 1936." Ohio History 92 (1983): 6-36.

_____. 'The Rubber Workers' Southern Strategy: Labor Organizing in the New Deal South, 1933-1943." Historian 46 (May 1984): 319-38.

Nyden, Linda. "Black Miners in Western Pennsylvania 1925-1931:The National Miners Union and the United Mine Workers of America." Science and Society 41 (Spring 1977): 69-101.

O'Brien, Larry D. "The Ohio National Guard in the Coal Strike of 1932." Ohio History 84 (Summer 1975): 127-44.

Papanikolas, Helen Z. "Unionism, Communism, and the Great Depression: The Carbon County Coal Strike of 1933." Utah Historical Quarterly 41 (Summer 1973): 254-300.

Perlman, Selig. "Labor and the New Deal in Historical Perspective." In Labor and the New Deal ed. by Milton Derber and Edwin Young (Madison: University of Wisconsin Press, 1957), pp. 361-72.

Pivar, David J. "The Hosiery Workers and the Philadelphia Third Party Impulse, 1929-1935." Labor History 5 (Winter 1964): 18-28.

Prickett, James R. "Communism and Factionalism in the United Automobile Workers, 1939-1945." Science and Society 32 (Summer 1968): 257-77.

_____. "Communist Conspiracy or Wage Dispute?: The 1941 Strike at North American Aviation." Pacific Historical Review 50 (May 1981): 215-33.

_____. "Communists and the Automobile Industry in Detroit Before 1935." Michigan History 57 (Fall 1973): 185-208.

Pullman, Doris E., and L. Reed Tripp. "Collective Bargaining Developments." In Labor and the New Deal ed. by Milton Derber and Edwin Young (Madison: University of Wisconsin Press, 1957), pp. 317-60.

Radosh, Ronald. "The Corporate Ideology of American Labor Leaders From Gompers to Hillman." Studies on the Left 6 (Nov.-Dec. 1966): 66-88.

Renshaw, Patrick. "Organized Labour and the Keynesian Revolution." In Nothing
    Else to Fear: New Perspectives on America in the Thirties ed. by. Stephen W.
    Baskerville and Ralph Willett (Manchester: Manchester University Press,
    1985), pp. 216-35.
————. "Organized Labour and the United States War Economy, 1939-1945."
    Journal of Contemporary History 21 (Jan. 1986): 3-22
Rischin, Moses. "From Gompers to Hillman: Labor Goes Middle Class." Antioch
    Review 13 (Summer 1953): 191-201.
Robinson, Jo Ann O. "The Pharos of the East Side, 1937-1940: Labor Temple Under
    the Director of A. J. Muste." Journal of Presbyterian History 48 (Spring 1970):
    18-37.
Rocha, Guy Louis. "The IWW and the Boulder Canyon Project: The Final Death
    Throes of American Syndicalism." Nevada Historical Society Quarterly 21
    (Spring 1978): 2-24.
Rollins, Alfred B., Jr. "Franklin Roosevelt's Introduction to Labor." Labor History 3
    (Winter 1962): 3-18.
Rose, Gerald A. "The March Inland: The Stockton Cannery Strike of 1937." Southern
    California Quarterly 54 (Spring, Summer, Fall 1972): 67-82, 155-75, 255-76.
Rosenzweig, Roy. "Organizing the Unemployed: The Early Years of the Great
    Depression, 1929-1933." Radical America 10 (July 1976): 37-60.
Rubenstein, Harry R. "The Great Gallup Coal Strike of 1933." New Mexico
    Historical Review 52 (July 1977): 173-92.
Schacht, John N. "Toward Industrial Unionism: Bell Telephone Workers and
    Company Unions, 1919-1937." Labor History 16 (Winter 1975): 5-36.
Schatz, Ronald. "Union Pioneers: The Founders of Local Unions at General Electric
    and Westinghouse, 1933-1937." Journal of American History 66 (Dec. 1979):
    586-602.
Schrode, Georg. "Mark Zuk and the Detroit Meat Strike of 1935." Polish American
    Studies 48 (Autumn 1986): 5-39.
Schwantes, Carlos A. "'We've Got 'Em on the Run, Brothers': The 1937 Non-
    Automotive Sit Down Strikes in Detroit." Michigan History 56 (Fall 1972): 179-
    200.
Schwartz, Bonnie Fox. "New Deal Work Relief and Organized Labor: The CWA and
    the AFL Building Trades." Labor History 17 (Winter 1976): 38-57.
Schwartz, Stephen. "Holdings on the 1934 West Coast Maritime Strike in the San
    Francisco Headquarters Archives, Sailors' Union of the Pacific: A Descriptive
    Summary." Labor History 27 (Summer 1986): 427-30.
Sears, Stephen W. "'Shut the Goddam Plant!" American Heritage 33 (April/May
    1982): 49-64.
Selby, John G. "Better to Starve in the Shade than in the Factory: Labor Protest in
    High Point, North Carolina, in the Early 1930s." North Carolina Historical
    Review 64 (Jan. 1987); 43-64.
Shiner, John F. "The 1937 Steel Labor Dispute and the Ohio National Guard." Ohio
    History 84 (Autumn 1975): 182-95.
Sills, Marion Brown. "Organizing in the 30's." Guild Practioner 39 (1982): 90-93.

Sofchalk, Donald G. "The Chicago Memorial Day Incident: An Episode in Mass Action." Labor History 6 (Winter 1965): 3-43.

Speer, Michael "The 'Little Steel' Strike Conflict for Control." Ohio History 78 (Autumn 1969): 275-87.

Sternsher, Bernard. "Scioto Marsh Onion Workers Strike, Hardin County, Ohio, 1934." Northwest Ohio Quarterly 58 (Spring/Summer 1986): 39-92.

Street, Richard Steven. "The 'Battle of Salinas': San Francisco Bay Area Press Photographers and the Salinas Valley Lettuce Strike of 1936." Journal of the West 26 (April 1987): 41-51.

Supina, Philip D. "Herndon J. Evans and the Harlan County Coal Strike." Filson Club History Quarterly 56 (July 1982): 318-35.

Sweeney, Eugene T. "The A.F.L.'s Good Citizen, 1920-1940." Labor History 13 (Spring 1972): 200-16.

Tomlins, Christopher L. "AFL Unions in the 1930s: Their Performance in Historical Perspective." Journal of American History 65 (March 1979): 1021-42.

Toy, Eckard V., Jr. "The Oxford Group and the Strike of the Seattle Longshoremen in 1934." Pacific Northwest Quarterly 69 (Oct. 1978): 174-84.

Tselos, George. "Self-Help and Sauerkraut: The Organized Unemployed, Inc., of Minneapolis." Minnesota History 45 (Winter 1977): 306-20.

Weir, Stan. "American Labor on the Defensive: A 1940 Odyssey." Radical America 9 (July 1975): 163-85.

Weisbord, Vera Buch. "Gastonia 1929: Strike at the Loray Mill." Southern Exposure 1 (Winter 1974): 185-203.

West, Kenneth B. "'On the Line': Rank and File Reminiscences of Working Conditions and the General Motors Sit-Down Strike of 1936-1937." Michigan Historical Review 12 (Spring 1986): 57-82.

Wilcock, Richard C. "Industrial Management's Policies Toward Unionism." In Labor and the New Deal ed. by Milton Derber and Edwin Young (Madison: University of Wisconsin Press, 1957), pp. 273-316.

Witte, Edwin E. "Organized Labor and Social Security." In Labor and the New Deal ed. by Milton Derber and Edwin Young (Madison: University of Wisconsin Press, 1957), pp. 239-74.

Wollenberg, Charles. "Race and Class in Rural California: The El Monte Berry Strike of 1933." California Historical Quarterly 51 (Summer 1972): 155-64.

Young, Edwin. "The Split in the Labor Movement." In Labor and the New Deal ed. by Milton Derber and Edwin Young (Madison: University of Wisconsin Press, 1957), pp. 45-76.

Zieger, Robert H. "Oldtimers & Newcomers: Change and Continuity in the Pulp, Sulphite Union in the 1930's." Journal of Forest History 21 (Oct. 1977): 188-201.

_____. "The Limits of Militancy: Organizing Paper Workers, 1933-1935." Journal of American History 63 (Dec. 1976): 638-57.

_____. "The Union Comes to Covington: Virginia Paperworkers Organize, 1933-1952." Proceedings of the American Philosophical Society 126 (Feb. 1982): 51-89.

Dissertations

Anderson, James R. "The New Deal Career of Frances Perkins, Secretary of Labor, 1933-1939." Ph.D. diss., Case Western Reserve University, 1968.

Asher, Nina Lynn. "Dorothy Jacobs Bellanca: Feminist Trade Unionist, 1894-1946." Ph.D. diss., State University of New York at Binghamton, 1982.

Auerbach, Jerold S. "The La Follette Committee: Labor and Civil Liberties in the New Deal." Ph.D. diss., Columbia University, 1965.

Blackwood, George D. "The United Automobile Workers of America, 1935-51." Ph.D. diss., University of Chicago, 1951.

Clepper, Irene F. "Minnesota's Definition of the Sit-Down Strike: An Analysis of Union Activities in Austin Minnesota, 1933-37, and their Coverage by Local, State, and National Media." Ph.D. diss., University of Minnesota, 1979.

Dzierba, Timothy Roger. "Organized Labor and the Coming of World War II, 1937-1941." Ph.D. diss., State University of New York at Buffalo, 1983.

Farber, Milton L, Jr. "Changing Attitudes of the American Federation of Labor toward Business and Government, 1929-1933." Ph.D. diss., Ohio University, 1959.

Filippelli, Ronald L. "The United Electrical, Radio and Machine Workers of America, 1939-1949: The Struggle for Control." Ph.D. diss., Pennsylvania State University, 1970.

Fraser, Steven Clark. "Sidney Hillman and the Origins of the 'New Unionism', 1890-1933." Ph.D. diss., Rutgers University, 1983.

Freeman, Joshua Benjamin. "The Transport Workers Union in New York City, 1933-1948." Ph.D. diss., Rutgers University, 1983.

Friedlander, Peter J. "The Emergence of a UAW Local, 1936-1939: A Study in Class and Culture." Ph.D. diss., State University of New York at Binghamton, 1976.

Gerstle, Gary L. "The Rise of Industrial Unionism: Class, Ethnicity and Labor Organization in Woonsocket, Rhode Island, 1931-1941." Ph.D. diss., Harvard University, 1982.

Gilbert, Hilda Kessler. "The United States Department of Labor in the New Deal Period." Ph.D. diss., University of Wisconsin, 1943.

Gordon, Gerald R. "The AFL, the CIO, and the Quest for a Peaceful World, 1914-1946." Ph.D. diss., University of Maine, 1967.

Gorin, Stephen Harry. "Labor-Management Relations and Democracy: The Wagner and Taft-Hartley Acts." Ph.D. diss., Brandeis University, 1983.

Haskett, William. "Ideological Radicals: The American Federation of Labor and Federal Labor Policy in the Strikes of 1934." Ph.D. diss., University of California, Los Angeles, 1957.

Hodges, James A. "The New Deal Labor Policy and the Southern Cotton Textile Industry, 1933-1941." Ph.D. diss., Vanderbilt University, 1963.

LaGumina, Salvatore J. "Vito Marcantonio, Labor and the New Deal (1935-1940)." Ph.D. diss., St. John's University, 1966.

Leab, Daniel. "A Union of Individuals: The Formation of the American Newspaper Guild, 1933-1936." Ph.D. diss., Columbia University, 1969.

Mabon, David W. "The West Coast Waterfront and Sympathy Strikes of 1934." Ph.D. diss., University of California, Berkeley, 1966.

McDonnell, James R. "The Rise of the CIO in Buffalo, New York, 1936-1942." Ph.D. diss., University of Wisconsin, 1970.

McFarland, Charles K. "Coalition of Convenience: The Roosevelt-Lewis Courtship, 1933-1941." Ph.D. diss., University of Arizona, 1965.

Milton, David Hepburn. "The Politics of Economism: Organized Labor Fights its Way into the American System under the New Deal." Ph.D. diss., University of California, Berkeley, 1980.

Monroe, Douglas K. "A Decade of Turmoil: John L. Lewis and the Anthracite Miners, 1926-1936." Ph.D. diss., Georgetown University, 1977.

Morris, James O. "The Origins of the C.I.O.: A Study of Conflict within the Labor Movement, 1921-1938." Ph.D. diss., University of Michigan, 1954.

Nelson, Joseph B. "Maritime Unionism and Working-Class Consciousness in the 1930s." Ph.D. diss., University of California, Berkeley, 1982.

Radosh, Ronald. "The Development of the Corporate Ideology of American Labor Leaders, 1914-1933." Ph.D. diss., University of Wisconsin, 1967.

Richards, Paul D. "The History of the Textile Workers Union of American, CIO, in the South, 1937 to 1945." Ph.D. diss., University of Wisconsin, 1978.

Schacht, John N. "The Rise of the Communications Workers of America: Union Organization and Centralization in the Telephone Industry, 1935-1947." Ph.D. diss., University of Iowa, 1977.

Shapiro, William. "Public Educational Interests and Positions of the CIO during the Era of the New Deal: An Historical Overview." Ed.D. diss., Columbia University, 1979.

Sperry, James R. "Organized Labor and Its Fight against Military and Industrial Conscription, 1917-1945." Ph.D. diss., University of Arizona, 1968.

Taylor, Paul F. "Coal and Conflict: The UMWA in Harlan County, 1931-1939." Ph.D. diss., University of Kentucky, 1969.

Tomlins, Christopher Lawrence. "The State and the Unions: Federal Labor Relations Policy and the Organized Labor Movement in America, 1935-55." Ph.D. diss., Johns Hopkins University, 1980.

Wakstein, Allen M. "The Open-Shop Movement, 1919-1933." Ph.D. diss., University of Illinois, 1961.

Weisstuch, Mark W. "The Theatre Union, 1933-1937: A History." Ph.D. diss., City University of New York, 1982.

Willett, Donald E. "Joe Curran and the National Maritime Union, 1936-1945." Ph.D. diss., Texas A & M University, 1985.

Wyche, Billy H. "Southern Attitudes toward Industrial Unions, 1933-1941." Ph.D. diss., University of Georgia, 1970.

Young, Dallas M. "A History of the Progressive Miners of America, 1932-1940." Ph.D. diss., University of Illinois, 1941.

8

Society

8.1 GENERAL

Books

Agee, James, and Walker Evans. Let Us Now Praise Famous Men: Three Tenant Families. Boston: Houghton Mifflin, 1941.

Angell, Robert Cooley. The Family Encounters the Depression. New York: Scribner's, 1936.

Bakke, E. Wight. Citizens without Work: A Study of the Effects of Unemployment upon the Workers' Social Relations and Practices. New Haven: Yale University Press, 1940.

Cavan, Ruth Shonle, and Katherine Howland Ranck. The Family and the Depression: A Study of One Hundred Chicago Families. Chicago: University of Chicago Press, 1938.

Chambers, Clarke A. Paul U. Kellogg and the Survey: Voices for Social Welfare and Social Justice. Minneapolis: University of Minnesota Press, 1971.

_____. Seedtime of Reform: American Social Service and Social Action, 1918-1933. Minneapolis: University of Minnesota Press, 1963.

Elder, Glen H., Jr. Children of the Great Depression: Social Change in Life Experience. Chicago: University of Chicago Press, 1974.

Enzler, Clarence J. Some Social Aspects of the Depression, 1930-1935. Washington: Catholic University of America Press, 1939.

Fisher, Jacob. The Response of Social Work to the Depression. Boston: G. K. Hall, 1980.

Hallgren, Mauritz A. Seeds of Revolt: A Study of American Life and the Temper of the American People During the Depression. New York: Knopf, 1933.

Janiewski, Dolores E. Sisterhood Denied: Race, Gender, and Class in a New South Community. Philadelphia: Temple University Press, 1985.

Jones, John F., and John M. Herrick. Citizens in Service: Volunteers in Social Welfare During the Depression, 1929-1941. East Lansing: Michigan State University Press, 1976.

Komarovsky, Mirra. The Unemployed Man and His Family: The Effect of Unemployment upon the Status of the Man in Fifty-Nine Families. New York: Dryden, 1940.

Lane, Marie D., and Francis Steegmuller. America on Relief. New York: Harcourt, Brace, 1938.

Lange, Dorothea, and Paul Schuster Taylor. An American Exodus: A Record of Human Erosion. New York: Reynal, 1939.

O'Neal, Hank. A Vision Shared: A Classic Portrait of America and Its People, 1935-1943. New York: St. Martin's, 1976.

Ogburn, William, ed. Social Changes During Depression and Recovery: (Social Changes in 1934). Chicago: University of Chicago Press, 1935.

Stryker, Roy Emerson, and Nancy Wood. In This Proud Land: America 1935-1943 as Seen in the FSA Photographs. Greenwich: New York Graphic Society, 1973.

Trolander, Judith Ann. Settlement Houses and the Great Depression. Detroit: Wayne State University Press, 1975.

Articles

Bennett, David H. "The Year of the Old Folks' Revolt." American Heritage 16 (Dec. 1964): 48-51, 99-107.

Brandes, Stuart D. "America's Super Rich, 1941." Historian 45 (May 1983): 307-23.

Brunner, Edmund deS. "Internal Migration in the United States, 1935-40." Rural Sociology 13 (March 1948): 9-22.

Bruns, Roger. "Hobo." American History Illustrated 16 (Jan. 1982): 9-15.

Centers, Richard. "Children of the New Deal: Social Stratification and Adolescent Attitudes." In Class, Status, and Power ed. by Reinhard Bendix and Seymour Martin Lipset (New York: Free Press, 1953), pp. 359-70.

Crouse, Joan M. "Precedents from the Past: The Evolution of Laws and Attitudes Pertinent to the 'Welcome' Accorded to the Indigent Transient during the Great Depression." In An American Historian: Essays to Honor Selig Adler ed. by Milton Plesur (Buffalo: State University of New York, 1980), pp. 191-203.

Dinwoodie, David H. "Indians, Hispanos, and Land Reform: A New Deal Struggle in New Mexico." Western Historical Quarterly 17 (July 1986): 291-325.

Harvey, Charles E. "Robert S. Lynd, John D. Rockefeller, Jr. and Middletown." Indiana Magazine of History 79 (Dec. 1983): 330-54.

Keller, Allan. "'The Baby is Found---Dead!': The Lindbergh Kidnapping.'" American History Illustrated 10 (May 1975): 10-21.

LaForte, Robert S., and Richard Himmel, eds. "'Middletown Looks at the Lynds': A Contemporary Critique by the Reverend Dr. Hillyer H. Straton of Muncie, Indiana, 1937." Indiana Magazine of History 79 (Sept. 1983): 248-64.

Leab, Daniel J. "Barter and Self-Help Groups, 1932-33." Midcontinent American Studies Journal 7 (Spring 1966): 15-24.

Liker, Jeffrey K., and Glen H. Elder, Jr. "Economic Hardship and Marital Relations in the 1930s." American Sociological Review 48 (June 1983): 343-59.

Maurer, D. W. "Language and the Sex Revolution: World War I through World War II." American Speech 51 (Spring-Summer 1976): 5-24.

Minton, Henry L. "Feminity in Men and Masculinity in Women: American Psychiatry and Psychology Portray Homosexuality in the 1930's." Journal of Homosexuality 13 (Fall 1986): 1-21.

Mishkin, Frederic S. "The Household Balance Sheet and the Great Depression." Journal of Economic History 38 (Dec. 1978): 918-37.

Peeler, David P. "Unlonesome Highways: The Quest for Fact and Fellowship in Depression America." Journal of American Studies 18 (Aug. 1984): 185-206.

Seretan, L. Glen. "The 'New' Working Class and Social Banditry in Depression America." Mid-America 63 (April-July 1981): 107-17.

Smith, Mark C. "Robert Lynd and Consumerism in the 1930's." Journal of the History of Sociology 2 (Fall-Winter 1979-80): 99-119.

Sternsher, Bernard. "Victims of the Great Depression: Self-Blame/Non-Self-Blame, Radicalism, and Pre-1929 Experiences." Social Science History 1 (Winter 1977): 137-77.

Verba, Sidney, and Kay Lehman Schlozman. "Unemployment, Class Consciousness, and Radical Politics: What Didn't Happen in the Thirties." Journal of Politics 39 (May 1977): 291-323.

Whisenhunt, Donald W. "The Transient in the Depression." Red River Valley Historical Review 1 (Spring 1974): 7-20.

_____. "Utopians, Communalism & the Great Depression." Communal Societies 3 (Fall 1983): 101-10.

Dissertations

Boxer, Andrea S. "The American Father and the Great Depression." Ph.D. diss., Bryn Mawr College, 1976.

Flood, Marilyn Esther. "The Troubling Expedient: General Staff Nursing in United States Hospitals in the 1930's: A Means to Institutional, Educational, and Personal Ends." Ph.D. diss., University of California, Berkeley, 1981.

Little, Maude Clay. "Effect of the Depression on the Conditions, Attitudes and Behavior of Young People in the United States." Ph.D. diss., University of Virginia, 1940.

Reynolds, Thomas H. "American Red Cross Disaster Services, 1930-1947." Ph.D. diss., Columbia University, 1954.

Rosenthal, Marguerite G. "Social Policy for Delinquent Children: Delinquency Activities of the U.S. Children's Bureau, 1912-1940." Ph.D. diss., Rutgers University, 1983.

Simmons, Christina C. "Marriage in the Modern Manner: Sexual Radicalism and
    Reform in America, 1914-1941." Ph.D. diss., Brown University, 1982.
Watson, Elizabeth J. "The Rationalization of Childhood: A Sociology of Knowledge
    Analysis of Popular Childrearing Literature, 1930-1940." Ph.D. diss., Rutgers
    University, 1986.

8.2 BLACKS

Books

Bunche, Ralph J. The Political Status of the Negro in the Age of FDR. Chicago:
    University of Chicago Press, 1973.
Carter, Dan T. Scottsboro: A Tragedy of the American South. Baton Rouge:
    Louisiana State University Press, 1969.
Cayton, Horace R., and George S. Mitchell. Black Workers and the New Unions.
    Chapel Hill: University of North Carolina Press, 1939.
Harris, William H. Keeping the Faith: A. Philip Randolph, Milton P. Webster, and the
    Brotherhood of Sleeping Car Porters, 1925-1937. Urbana: University of Illinois
    Press, 1977.
Homel, Michael W. Down From Equality: Black Chicagoans and the Public Schools,
    1920-41. Urbana: University of Illinois Press, 1984.
Kirby, John B. Black Americans in the Roosevelt Era: Liberalism and Race.
    Knoxville: University of Tennessee Press, 1980.
Myrdal, Gunnar. An American Dilemma: The Negro Problem and Modern
    Democracy. New York: Harper, 1944.
Nelson, Bernard H. The Fourteenth Amendment and the Negro since 1920.
    Washington, D.C.: Catholic University of America Press, 1946.
Patton, Gerald Wilson. War and Race: The Black Officer in the American Military,
    1915-1941. Westport, Conn.: Greenwood, 1981.
Record, Wilson. Race and Radicalism: The NAACP and the Communist Party in
    Conflict. Ithaca: Cornell University Press, 1964.
_____. The Negro and the Communist Party. Chapel Hill: University of North
    Carolina Press, 1951.
Sitkoff, Harvard. A New Deal for Blacks: The Emergence of Civil Rights as a
    National Issue: The Depression Decade. New York: Oxford University Press,
    1978.
Sternsher, Bernard. The Negro in Depression and War: Prelude to Revolution, 1930-
    1945. Chicago: Quadrangle, 1969.
Tatum, Elbert Lee. The Changed Political Thought of the Negro, 1915-1940. New
    York: Exposition Press, 1951.
Trotter, Joe William, Jr. Black Milwaukee: The Making of an Industrial Proletariat,
    1915-45. Urbana: University of Illinois Press, 1985.

Weiss, Nancy J. Farewell to the Party of Lincoln: Black Politics in the Age of FDR.
    Princeton: Princeton University Press, 1983.
_____. The National Urban League, 1910-1940. New York: Oxford University
    Press, 1974.
Wolters, Raymond. Negroes and the Great Depression: The Problem of Economic
    Recovery. Westport, Conn.: Greenwood, 1970.
Young, James O. Black Writers of the Thirties. Baton Rouge: Louisiana State
    University Press, 1973.
Zangrando, Robert L. The NAACP Crusade Against Lynching, 1909-1950.
    Philadelphia: Temple University Press, 1980.

Articles

Allswang, John M. "The Chicago Negro Voter and the Democratic Consensus: A
    Case Study, 1918-1936." Journal of the Illinois State Historical Society 60
    (Summer 1967): 145-75.
Bailer, Lloyd H. "The Automobile Unions and Negro Labor." Political Science
    Quarterly 59 (Dec. 1944): 548-77.
Bain, George W. "How Negro Editors Viewed the New Deal." Journalism Quarterly
    44 (Autumn 1967): 552-54.
Bauman, John F. "Black Slums/Black Projects: The New Deal and Negro Housing in
    Philadelphia." Pennsylvania History 41 (July 1974): 311-38.
Biles, Roger. "Robert R. Church, Jr. of Memphis: Black Republican Leader in the Age
    of Democratic Ascendancy, 1928-1940." Tennessee Historical Quarterly 42
    (Winter 1983): 362-82.
Broussard, Albert S. "Oral Recollection and the Historical Reconstruction of Black
    San Francisco, 1915-1940." Oral History Review 12 (1984): 63-80.
Carter, Dan T. "A Reasonable Doubt." American Heritage 19 (Oct. 1968): 40-43,
    95-101.
Collins, Ernest M. "Cincinnati Negroes and Presidential Politics." Journal of Negro
    History 61 (April 1956): 131-37.
Dailey, Maceo C., Jr., and Earnest D. Washington. "The Evolution of Doxey A.
    Wilkerson, 1935-1945." Freedomways 25 (Summer 1985): 101-15.
Dales, David G. "North Platte Racial Incident: Black-White Confrontation, 1929."
    Nebraska History 60 (Fall 1979): 424-46.
Daoust, Norma Lasalle. "Building the Democratic Party: Black Voting in Providence
    in the 1930's." Rhode Island History 44 (Aug. 1985): 81-88.
Day, David S. "Herbert Hoover and Racial Politics: The DePriest Incident." Journal
    of Negro History 65 (Winter 1980): 6-17.
Dent, Tom. "Octave Lilly, Jr.: In Memoriam." Crisis 83 (Aug.-Sept. 1976): 243-44.
DuBois, W.E.B. "Race Relations in the United States, 1917-1947." Phylon 9 (3rd qtr.
    1948): 234-47.
Dunn, Larry W. "Knoxville Negro Voting and the Roosevelt Revolution, 1928-1936."
    East Tennessee Historical Society Publications 43 (1971): 71-93.

Fishel, Leslie H., Jr. "The Negro in the New Deal Era." Wisconsin Magazine of History 48 (Winter 1964): 111-26.

Foreman, Clark. "The Decade of Hope." Phylon 12 (2nd qtr. 1951): 137-50.

Garcia, George F. "Black Disaffection from the Republican Party during the Presidency of Herbert Hoover, 1928-1932." Annals of Iowa 45 (Fall 1980): 462-97.

Gavins, Raymond. "Hancock, Jackson, and Young: Virginia's Black Triumvirate, 1930-1945." Virginia Magazine of History and Biography 85 (Oct. 1977): 470-86.

Genizi, Haim. "V. F. Calverton, A Radical Magazinist for Black Intellectuals, 1920-1940." Journal of Negro History 57 (July 1972): 241-53.

Giffin, William. "Black Insurgency in the Republican Party of Ohio, 1920-1932." Ohio History 82 (Winter-Spring 1973): 25-45.

Goodenow, Ronald K. "Paradox in Progressive Educational Reform: The South and the Education of Blacks in the Depression Years." Phylon 39 (March 1978): 49-65.

Gordon, Lawrence. "A Brief Look at Blacks in Depression Mississippi, 1929-1934; Eyewitness Accounts." Journal of Negro History 64 (Fall 1979): 377-90.

Gordon, Rita Werner. "The Change in the Political Alignment of Chicago Negroes During the New Deal." Journal of American History 56 (Dec. 1969): 584-603.

Gower, Calvin W. "The Struggle of Blacks for Leadership Positions in the Civilian Conservation Corps: 1933-1942." Journal of Negro History 61 (April 1976): 123-35.

Hamilton, Dona Cooper. "The National Urban League and New Deal Programs." Social Service Review 58 (June 1984): 227-43.

Harrell, James A. "Negro Leadership in the Election Year 1936." Journal of Southern History 34 (Nov. 1968): 545-64.

Hine, Darlene Clark. "Blacks and the Destruction of the Democratic White Primary 1935-1944." Journal of Negro History 62 (Jan. 1977): 43-59.

Hixson, William B., Jr. "Moorfield Storey and the Defense of the Dyer Anti-Lynching Bill." New England Quarterly 42 (March 1969): 65-81.

Hoffman, Edwin D. "The Genesis of the Modern Movement for Equal Rights in South Carolina, 1930-1939." Journal of Negro History 44 (Oct. 1959): 346-69.

Holley, Donald. "The Negro in the New Deal Resettlement Program." Agricultural History 45 (July 1971): 179-93.

Holmes, Michael S. "The Blue Eagle as 'Jim Crow Bird': The NRA and Georgia's Black Workers." Journal of Negro History 57 (July 1972): 276-83.

_____. "The New Deal and Georgia's Black Youth." Journal of Southern History 38 (August 1972): 443-60.

Homel, Michael W. "The Lilydale School Campaign of 1936: Direct Action in the Verbal Protest Era." Journal of Negro History 59 (July 1974): 228-41.

Howe, Irving, and B. J. Widick "The U.A.W. Fights Race Prejudice." Commentary 8 (Sept. 1949): 261-68.

Janowitz, Morris. "Black Legions on the March." In America in Crisis ed. by Daniel Aaron (New York: Knopf, 1952): 305-25.

Johnson, Charles W. "The Army, the Negro, and the Civilian Conservation Corps: 1933-1942." Military Affairs 36 (Oct. 1972): 82-88.

Kalmar, Karen L. "Southern Black Elites and the New Deal: A Case Study of Savannah, Georgia." Georgia Historical Quarterly 65 (Winter 1981): 341-55.

Karger, Howard Jacob. "Phyllis Wheatley House: A History of the Minneapolis Black Settlement House, 1924 to 1940." Phylon 47 (March 1986): 79-90.

Kirby, John B. "Ralph J. Bunche and Black Radical Thought in the 1930s." Phylon 35 (Summer 1974): 129-41.

Kruman, Marie W. "Quotas for Blacks: The Public Works Administration and the Black Construction Worker." Labor History 16 (Winter 1975): 37-51.

Lewis, David Levering. "The Politics of Art: The New Negro, 1920-1935." Prospects 3 (1977): 237-61.

Martin, Charles H. "Communists and Blacks: The ILD and the Angelo Herndon Case." Journal of Negro History 64 (Spring 1979): 131-41.

_____. "Negro Leaders, the Republican Party, and the Election of 1932." Phylon 32 (Spring 1971): 85-93.

_____. "Oklahoma's 'Scottsboro' Affair: The Jess Hollins Rape Case, 1931-1936." South Atlantic Quarterly 79 (Spring 1980): 175-88.

_____. "White Supremacy and Black Workers: Georgia's 'Black Shirts' Combat the Great Depression." Labor History 18 (Summer 1977): 366-81.

McBride, David, and Monroe H. Little. "The Afro-American Elite, 1930-1940: A Historical and Statistical Profile." Phylon 42 (June 1981): 105-19.

McGovern, James R., and Walter T. Howard. "Private Justice and National Concern: The Lynching of Claude Neal." Historian 43 (Aug. 1981): 546-59.

Meier, August, and Elliott M. Rudwick. "Negro Protest at the Chicago World's Fair, 1933- 1934." Journal of the Illinois State Historical Society 59 (Summer 1966): 161-71.

_____. "Communist Unions and the Black Community: The Case of the Transport Workers Union, 1934-1944." Labor History 23 (Spring 1982): 165-97.

Moore, John Hammond. "The Angelo Herndon Case, 1932-1937." Phylon 32 (Spring 1971): 60-71.

Muraskin, William. "The Harlem Boycott of 1934: Black Nationalism and the Rise of Labor-Union Consciousness." Labor History 13 (Summer 1972): 361-73.

Murray, Hugh T., Jr. "Aspects of the Scottsboro Campaign." Science and Society 35 (Summer 1971): 177-92.

_____. "The NAACP versus the Communist Party: The Scottsboro Rape Cases, 1931-32." Phylon 28 (Fall 1967): 276-87.

Naison, Mark. "Communism and Harlem Intellectuals in the Popular Front: Anti-Fascism and the Politics of Black Culture." Journal of Ethnic Studies 9 (Spring 1981): 1-25.

_____. "Historical Notes on Blacks and American Communism: The Harlem Experience." Science and Society 42 (Fall 1978): 324-43.

_____. "Communism and Black Nationalism in the Depression: The Case of Harlem." Journal of Ethnic Studies 2 (Summer 1974): 24-36.

Nelson, H. Viscount. "The Philadelphia NAACP: Race Versus Class Consciousness During the Thirties." Journal of Black Studies 5 (March 1975): 255-76.

Nipp, Robert E. "The Negro in the New Deal Resettlement Program: A Comment." Agricultural History 45 (July 1971): 195-200.

Northrup, Herbert R. "Organized Labor and Negro Workers." Journal of Political Economy 51 (June 1943): 206-21.

Oblinger, Carl D. "Southern-Born Blacks in Harrisburg, 1920-1950." Pennsylvania Heritage 4 (Dec. 1977): 64-68.

Oliver, Paul. "'Sales Tax On It': Race Records in the New Deal Years." In Nothing Else to Fear: New Perspectives on America in the Thirties ed. by. Stephen W. Baskerville and Ralph Willett (Manchester: Manchester University Press, 1985), pp. 197-213.

Olson, James S. "Organized Black Leadership and Industrial Unionism: The Racial Response, 1936-1945." Labor History 10 (Summer 1969): 475-86.

Painter, Nell, and Hosea Hudson. "Hosea Hudson: A Negro Communist in the Deep South." Radical America 11 (Aug. 1977): 7-23.

Parker, Russell D. "The Black Community in a Company Town: Alcoa, Tennessee, 1919-1939." Tennessee Historical Quarterly 37 (Summer 1978): 203-21.

Perry, Thelma D. "Melvin J. Chisum, Pioneer Newsman." Negro History Bulletin 36 (Dec. 1973): 176-80.

Potter, Barrett G. "The Civilian Conservation Corps and New York's 'Negro Question': A Case Study in Federal-State Race Relations During the Great Depression." Afro-Americans in New York Life and History 1 (1977): 183-200.

Raper, Arthur F. "The Southern Negro and the NRA." Georgia Historical Quarterly 64 (Summer 1980): 128-45.

Record, Wilson. "Negro Intellectual Leadership in the National Association for the Advancement of Colored People, 1910-1940." Phylon 27 (3rd qtr. 1956): 375-89.

Reed, Christopher Robert. "Black Chicago Political Realignment during the Great Depression and the New Deal." Illinois History Journal 78 (Winter 1985): 242-56.

Reed, John Shelton. "An Evaluation of an Anti-Lynching Organization." Social Problems 16 (Fall 1968): 172-81.

Romero, Patricia. "The Early Organization of Red Caps--1937-38." Negro History Bulletin 29 (Feb. 1966): 101-2.

Rosengarten, Theodore. "Reading the Hops: Recollections of Lorenzo Piper Davis and the Negro Baseball League." Southern Exposure 5 (No.2, 1977): 62-79.

Ross, B. Joyce. "Mary McLeod Bethune and the National Youth Administration: A Case Study of Power Relationships in the Black Cabinet of Franklin D. Roosevelt." Journal of Negro History 60 (Jan. 1975): 1-28.

Ryon, Roderick M. "An Ambiguous Legacy: Baltimore Blacks and the CIO, 1936-1941." Journal of Negro History 65 (Winter 1980): 18-33.

Salmond, John. "'Aubrey Williams Remembers': A Note on Franklin D. Roosevelt's Attitude Toward Negro Rights." Alabama Review 25 (Jan. 1972): 62-77.

_____. "The Civilian Conservation Corps and the Negro." Journal of American
History 52 (June 1965): 75-88.

Scott, William R. "Black Nationalism and the Italio-Ethiopian Conflict, 1934-1936."
Journal of Negro History 63 (April 1978): 118-34.

Sears, James M. "Black Americans and the New Deal." History Teacher 10 (Nov.
1976): 89-105.

Seawright, Sally. "Desegregation at Maryland: The NAACP and the Murray Case in
the 1930's." Maryland Historian 1 (Spring 1970): 59-73.

Shankman, Arnold. "Black Pride and Protest: The Amos 'n' Andy Crusade of 1931."
Journal of Popular Culture 12 (Fall 1979): 236-52.

Sitkoff, Harvard. "The New Deal and Race Relations." In Fifty Years Later: The
New Deal Evaluated ed. by Harvard Sitkoff (New York: Knopf, 1985), pp. 93-
112

Smith, Elaine M. "Mary McCleod Bethune and the National Youth Administration." In
Clio Was a Woman: Studies in the History of American Women ed. by Mabel
E. Deutrich and Virginia C. Purdy (Washington, D.C.: Howard University Press,
1980), pp. 149-77.

Spencer, Thomas T. "The Good Neighbor League Colored Committee and the 1936
Democratic Presidential Campaign." Journal of Negro History 63 (Fall 1978):
307-16.

Twining, Mary. "Harvesting and Heritage: A Comparison of Afro-American and
African Basketry." Southern Folklore Quarterly 42 (nos. 2-3, 1978): 159-74.

Walters, Ronald G. "The Negro Press and the Image of Success: 1920-1939."
Midcontinent American Studies Journal 11 (1970): 36-55.

Weaver, Robert C. "Negro Labor since 1929." Journal of Negro History 35 (Jan.
1950): 20-38.

Wennersten, John R. "The Black School Teacher in Maryland, 1930's." Negro
History Bulletin 38 (April/May 1975): 370-73.

Williams, Lillian S., ed. "Attica Prisoners Seek Aid from NAACP (1932)." Afro-
Americans in New York Life and History 1 (1977): 211-12.

Wolters, Raymond. "Section 7a and the Black Worker." Labor History 10 (Summer
1969): 459-74.

_____. "The New Deal and the Negro." In The New Deal: The National Level
ed. by John Braeman, Robert H. Bremner, and David Brody (Columbus: Ohio
State University Press, 1975), pp. 170-217.

Wright, George C. "The Faith Plan: A Black Institution Grows during the
Depression." Filson Club History Quarterly 51 (Oct. 1977): 336-49.

Wye, Christopher G. "The New Deal and the Negro Community: Toward a Broader
Conceptualization." Journal of American History 59 (Dec. 1972): 621-39.

Zangrando, Joanna Schneider and Robert L. "ER and Black Civil Rights." In Without
Precedent: The Life and Career of Eleanor Roosevelt ed. by Joan Hoff-Wilson
and Marjorie Lightman (Bloomington: Indiana University Press, 1984), pp. 88-
107.

Zangrando, Robert L. "The NAACP and a Federal Antilynching Bill, 1934-1940."
Journal of Negro History 50 (April 1965): 106-17.

Dissertations

Adubato, Robert A. "A History of the WPA's Negro Theater Project in New York City, 1935-1939." Ph.D. diss., New York University, 1978.

Blackwell, Barbara G. "The Advocacies and Ideological Commitments of a Black Educator: Mary McLeod Bethune 1875-1955." Ph.D. diss., University of Connecticut, 1979.

Charles, Cleophus. "Roy Wilkins, The NAACP and the Early Struggle for Civil Rights: Towards the Biography of a Man and a Movement in Microcosm, 1901-1939." Ph.D. diss., Cornell University, 1981.

Clegg, Brenda F. "Black Female Domestics during the Great Depression in New York City, 1930-1940." Ph.D. diss., University of Michigan, 1983.

Eisenberg, Bernard. "James Weldon Johnson and the National Association for the Advancement of Colored People, 1916-1934." Ph.D. diss., Columbia University, 1968.

Giffin, William W. "The Negro in Ohio, 1914-1939." Ph.D. diss., Ohio University, 1968.

Gill, Glenda E. "Six Black Performers in Relation to the Federal Theatre." Ph.D. diss., University of Iowa, 1981.

Grant, Nancy L. "Blacks, Regional Planning, and the TVA." Ph.D. diss., University of Chicago, 1978.

Green, Thomas Lee. "Black Cabinet Members in the Franklin Delano Roosevelt Administration." Ph.D. diss., University of Colorado, 1981.

Greene, Larry A. "Harlem in the Great Depression: 1928-1936." Ph.D. diss., Columbia University, 1979.

Gunther, Lenworth Alburn, III. "Flamin' Tongue: The Rise of Adam Clayton Powell, Jr., 1908-1941." Ph.D. diss., Columbia University, 1985.

Hadley, Worth J. "Roscoe Dunjee on Education: The Improvement of Black Education in Oklahoma, 1930-1955." Ph.D. diss., University of Oklahoma, 1981.

Haley, Charles T. "To Do Good and Do Well: Middle Class Blacks and the Depression, Philadelphia, 1929-1941." Ph.D. diss., State University of New York at Binghamton, 1980.

Hamilton, Dona C. "The National Urban League during the Depression, 1930-1939: The Quest for Jobs for Black Workers." Ph.D. diss., Columbia University, 1982.

Harris, Michael W. "The Advent of Gospel Blues in Black Old-Line Churches in Chicago, 1932-33 as Seen thorugh the Life and Mind of Thomas Andrew Dorsey." Ph.D. diss., Harvard University, 1982.

Harrison, William Jefferson. "The New Deal in Black St. Louis, 1932-1940." Ph.D. diss., Saint Louis University, 1976.

Hatfield, Eugene Adair. "The Impact of the New Deal on Black Politics in Pennsylvania, 1928-1938." Ph.D. diss., University of North Carolina, 1979.

Hunter, Gary Jerome. "'Don't Buy From Where You Can't Work': Black Urban Boycott Movements during the Depression." Ph.D. diss., University of Michigan, 1977.

Kifer, Allen F. "The Negro under the New Deal, 1933-1941." Ph.D diss., University of Wisconsin, 1961.

Pfeffer, Paula F. "A. Philip Randolph: A Case Study in Black Leadership." Ph.D. diss., Northwestern University, 1980.

Reed, Christopher R. "A Study of Black Politics and Protest in Depression-Decade Chicago: 1930-1939." Ph.D. diss., Kent State University, 1982.

Ross, Barbara J. "J.E. Spingarn and the Rise of the National Association for the Advancement of Colored People, 1911-1939." Ph.D. diss., American University, 1969.

Royster-Horn, Juana R. "The Academic and Extracurricular Undergraduate Experiences of Three Black Women at the University of Washington, 1935 to 1941." Ph.D. diss., University of Washington, 1980.

Sitkoff, Harvard Ira. "The Emergence of Civil Rights as a National Issue: The New Deal Era." Ph.D. diss., Columbia University, 1975.

Smith, Alonzo N. "Black Employment in the Los Angeles Area, 1938-1948." Ph.D. diss., University of California, Los Angeles, 1978.

Streater, John Baxter, Jr. "The National Negro Congress, 1936-1947." Ph.D. diss., University of Cincinnati, 1981.

Tatum, Elbert L. "The Changed Political Thought of the Negroes of the United States, 1915-1940." Ph.D. diss., Loyola University, 1946.

Weiss, Nancy J. "'Not Alms, but Opportunity': A History of the National Urban League, 1910-1940." Ph.D. diss., Harvard University, 1970.

Wolters, Raymond R. "The Negro and the New Deal Economic Recovery Program." Ph.D. diss., University of California, Berkeley, 1967.

Zangrando, Robert L. "The Efforts of the National Association for the Advancement of Colored People to Secure Passage of a Federal Anti-Lynching Law, 1920-1940." Ph.D. diss., University of Pennsylvania, 1963.

8.3   IMMIGRANTS AND ETHNICS

Books

Allswang, John M. A House for All Peoples: Ethnic Politics in Chicago, 1890-1936. Lexington: University Press of Kentucky, 1971.

Bayor, Ronald H. Neighbors in Conflict: The Irish, Germans, Jews, and Italians of New York City, 1929-1941. Baltimore: Johns Hopkins University Press, 1978.

Diner, Hasia R. In the Almost Promised Land: American Jews and Blacks, 1915-1935. Westport, Conn.: Greenwood, 1977.

Hoffman, Abraham. Unwanted Mexican Americans in the Great Depression: Repatriation Pressures, 1929-1939. Tucson: University of Arizona Press, 1974.

Modell, John. The Economics and Politics of Racial Accomodation: The Japanese of Los Angeles, 1900-1942. Urbana: University of Illinois Press, 1977.

Reisler Mark. By the Sweat of Their Brow: Mexican Immigrant Labor in the United States, 1900-1940. Westport, Conn.: Greenwood, 1976.

Articles

Allen, Howard W. "Studies of Political Loyalties of Two Nationality Groups: Isolationism and German-Americans." Journal of the Illinois State Historical Society 57 (Summer 1964): 143-49.

August, Jack. "The Anti-Japanese Crusade in Arizona's Salt River Valley, 1934-35." Arizona and the West 21 (Summer 1979): 113-36.

Berman, Hyman. "Political Antisemitism in Minnesota during the Great Depression." Jewish Social Studies 38 (Summer-Fall 1976): 247-64.

Betten, Neil, and Raymond A. Mohl. "From Discrimination to Repatriation: Mexican Life in Gary, Indiana, During the Great Depression." Pacific Historical Review 42 (Aug. 1973): 370-88.

Cannistraro, Philip V. "Facism and Italian Americans in Detroit, 1933-1935." International Migration Review 9 (Spring 1975): 29-40.

Christiansen, John B. "The Split Labor Market Theory and Filipino Exclusion: 1927-1934." Phylon 40 (March 1979): 66-74.

Dinnerstein, Leonard. "Franklin D. Roosevelt, American Jewry, and the New Deal." In The Roosevelt New Deal: A Program Assessment Fifty Years After ed. by Wilbur J. Cohen (Austin: Lyndon B. Johnson School of Public Affairs, 1986), pp. 21-30.

_____. "Jews and the New Deal." American Jewish History 72 (June 1983): 461-76.

Dinwoodie, D. H. "Deportation: The Immigration Service and the Chicano Labor Movement in the 1930s." New Mexico Historical Review 52 (July 1977): 193-206.

Gonzales, Phillip B. "Spanish Heritage and Ethnic Protest in New Mexico: The Anti-Fraternity Bill of 1933." New Mexico Historical Review 61 (Oct. 1986), 281-99.

Gonzalez, Rosalinda M. "Chicanas and Mexican Immigrant Families, 1920-1940: Women's Subordination and Family Exploitation." In Decades of Discontent: The Women's Movement, 1920-1940 ed. by Lois Scharf and Joan M. Jensen (Westport: Greenwood, 1983), pp. 59-84.

Hemminger, Carol. "Little Manila: The Filipino in Stockton Prior to World War II." Pacific Historian 24 (Summer 1980): 207-20.

Hess, Gary R. "The 'Hindu' in America: Immigration and Naturalization Policies and India, 1917-1946." Pacific Historical Review 38 (Feb. 1969): 59-79.

Hoffman, Abraham. "A Note on the Field Research Interviews of Paul S. Taylor for Mexican Labor in the United States Monographs." Pacific Historian 20 (Summer 1976): 123-31.

_____. "Stimulus to Repatriation: The 1931 Federal Deportation Drive and the Los Angeles Mexican Community." Pacific Historical Review 42 (May 1973): 205-19.

Kirczewski, Andre. "From Political Expediency to Moral Neglect: The United States and the Religo-Ethnic Experience, 1933-1945." American Jewish Archives 37 (Nov. 1985): 309-21.

Kiser, George, and David Silverman. "Mexican Repatriation during the Great Depression." Journal of Mexican American History 3 (1973): 139-64.

Kiser, George. "Mexican American Labor Before World War II." Journal of Mexican American History 2 (Spring 1972): 122-146.

Kumamoto, Bob. "The Search for Spies: American Counterintelligence and the Japanese American Community, 1931-1942." Amerasia Journal 6 (Fall 1979): 45-75.

LaGumina, Salvatore John. "The New Deal, the Immigrants and Congressman Vito Marcantonio." International Migration Review 4 (Spring 1970): 57-75.

Lazin, Fredrick A. "The Response of the American Jewish Committee on the Crisis of German Jewry, 1933-1939." American Jewish History 68 (March 1979): 283-394.

Lindmark, Sture. "End of the Great Migration: Decline, Restriction, and Press Reaction, 1929-1932." Swedish Pioneer Historical Quarterly 20 (Jan. 1969): 25-41.

_____. "Re-immigration to Sweden from the United States, 1929-1932." Swedish Pioneer Historical Journal 17 (July 1966): 146-53.

_____. "The Census of 1930 and the Swedes in the United States." Swedish Pioneer Historical Quarterly 16 (Oct. 1965): 216-32.

_____. "The Swedish-Americans and the Depression Years, 1929-1932." Swedish Pioneer Historical Quarterly 19 (Jan. 1968): 3-31.

Lothrop, Gloria Ricci. "Uno Sguardo Al Passato: A Backward Look at an Italian Household During Depression Days." Pacific Historian 27 (Winter 1983): 38-47.

Miller, James E. "A Question of Loyalty: American Liberals, Propaganda, and the Italian-American Community, 1939-1943." Maryland Historian 9 (Spring 1978): 49-71.

Mohl, Raymond A. "Cultural Pluralism in Immigrant Education: The International Institutes of Boston, Philadelphia, and San Francisco, 1920-1940." Journal of American Ethnic History 1 (Spring 1982): 35-58.

Monroy, Douglas. "La Costura En Los Angeles, 1933-1939: The ILGWU and the Politics of Domination." In Mexican Women in the United States: Struggles Past and Present ed. by Magdalena Mora and Adelaida R. DelCastillo (Los Angeles: University of California Chicano Studies Research Center, 1980), pp. 171-78.

Servin, Manuel P. "The Pre-World War II Mexican-American: An Interpretation." California Historical Society Quarterly 45 (Dec. 1966): 325-38.

Shafir, Shlomo. "American Jewish Leaders and the Emerging Nazi Threat (1928-January 1933)." American Jewish Archives 31 (Nov. 1979): 150-83.

Simon, Daniel T. "Mexican Repatriation in East Chicago, Indiana." Journal of Ethnic Studies 2 (Summer 1974): 11-23.

Szajkowski, Zosa. "A Note on the American Jewish Sruggle Against Nazism and Communism in the 1930's." American Jewish Historical Quarterly 59 (March 1970): 272-89.

_____. "Disunity in the Distribution of American Jewish Overseas Relief, 1919-1939." American Jewish Historical Quarterly 58 (March 1969): 376-407; (June 1969): 484-506.

_____. "Private American Jewish Overseas Relief (1919-1938): Problems and Attempted Solutions." American Jewish Historical Quarterly 57 (March 1968): 285-352.

_____. "Private and Organized American Jewish Overseas Relief (1914-1938)." American Jewish Historical Quarterly 57 (Sept. 1967): 52-106.

_____. "Private and Organized American Jewish Overseas Relief and Immigration (1914-1938)." American Jewish Historical Quarterly 57 (Dec. 1967): 191-253.

_____. "'Reconstruction' vs. 'Palliative Relief' in American Jewish Overseas Work (1919-1938)." Journal of Jewish Social Studies 32 (Jan. 1970): 14-42.

_____. "The Attitude of American Jews to Refugees from Germany in the 1930s," American Jewish Historical Quarterly 61 (Dec 1971): 101-43.

Wagner, Jonathan F. "Nazi Propaganda Among North Dakota's Germans, 1934-1941." North Dakota History 54 (Winter 1987): 15-24.

Weiss, Richard. "Ethnicity and Reform: Minorities and the Ambience of the Depression Years." Journal of American History 66 (Dec. 1979): 566-85.

Zelman, Donald L. "Alazan-Apache Courts: A New Deal Response to Mexican Housing Conditions in San Antonio." Southwestern Historical Quarterly 87 (Oct 1983): 123-50.

Dissertations

Balderrama, Francisco Enrique. "En Defensa de La Raza: The Los Angeles Mexican Consulate and Colonia Meicana during the Great Depression." Ph.D. diss., University of California, Los Angeles, 1978.

Bayor, Ronald H. "Ethnic Conflict in New York City, 1929-1941." Ph.D. diss., University of Pennsylvania, 1970.

Bell, Leland V. "Anatomy of a Hate Movement: The German American Bund, 1936-1941." Ph.D. diss., West Virginia University, 1968.

Cutter, Charles "The American Yiddish Daily Press Reaction to the Rise of Nazism, 1930-1933." Ph.D. diss., Ohio State University, 1979.

Garcia, Richard Amado. "The Making of the Mexican-American Mind, San Antonio, Texas, 1929-1941: A Social and Intellectual History of an Ethnic Community." Ph.D. diss., University of California, Irvine, 1980.

Guerin-Gonzales, Camille. "Cycles of Immigration and Repatriation: Mexican Farm Workers in California Industrial Agriculture, 1900-1940." Ph.D. diss., University of California, Riverside, 1985.

Hoffman, Abraham. "The Repatriation of Mexican Nationals from the United States during the Great Depression." Ph.D. diss., University of California, Los Angeles, 1970.

McKay, R. Reynolds. "Texas Mexican Repatriation during the Great Depression." Ph.D. diss., University of Oklahoma, 1982.

Monroy, Douglas G. "Mexicanos in Los Angeles, 1930-1941: An Ethnic Group in Relation to Class Forces." Ph.D. diss., University of California, Los Angeles, 1978.

Murillo, Louis Christopher. "The Detroit Mexican 'Colonia' from 1920 to 1932: Implication for Social and Education Policy." Ph.D. diss., Michigan State University, 1981.

Pinsky, Edward D. "Cooperation among American Jewish Organizations in Their Efforts to Rescue European Jewry during the Holocaust, 1939-1945." Ph.D. diss., New York University, 1980.

Tischauser, Leslie V. "The Burden of Ethnicity: The German Question in Chicago, 1914-1941." Ph.D. diss., University of Illinois at Chicago Circle, 1981.

8.4 NATIVE AMERICANS

Books

Hauptman, Laurence M. The Iroquois and the New Deal. Syracuse: Syracuse University Press, 1981.

Kelly, Lawrence C. The Assault on Assimilation: John Collier and the Origins of Indian Policy Reform. Albuquerque: University of New Mexico Press, 1983.
_____. The Navajo Indians and Federal Indian Policy, 1900-1935. Tucson: University of Arizona Press, 1968.

Nash, Jay B., ed. The New Day for the Indians: A Survey of the Working of the Indian Reorganization Act of 1934. New York: Academy, 1938.

Parman, Donald L. The Navajos and the New Deal. New Haven: Yale University Press, 1976.

Philip, Kenneth R. John Collier's Crusade for Indian Reform, 1920-1954. Tucson: University of Arizona Press, 1977.

Schrader, Robert Fay. The Indian Arts and Crafts Board: An Aspect of New Deal Indian Policy. Albuquerque: University of New Mexico Press, 1983.

Taylor, Graham D. The New Deal and American Indian Tribalism: The Administration of the Indian Reorganization Act, 1934-45. Lincoln: University of Nebraska Press, 1980.

Articles

Bernstein, Alison. "A Mixed Record: The Political Enfranchisement of American Indian Women during the Indian New Deal." Journal of the West 23 (July 1984): 13-20.

Bromert, Roger. "The Sioux and the Indian CCC." South Dakota History 8 (Fall 1978): 340-56.

Buffalohead, W. Roger. "The Indian New Deal: A Review Essay." Minnesota History 48 (Winter 1983): 339-41.

Downes, Randolph C. "A Crusade for Indian Reform, 1922-1934." Mississippi Valley Historical Review 32 (Dec. 1945): 331-54.

Fisch, Dov. "The Libel Trial of Robert Edward Edmondson: 1936-1938." American Jewish History 71 (Sept. 1981): 79-102.

Hauptman, Laurence M. "Alice Jamison: Seneca Political Activist, 1901-1964." Indian Historian 12 (Summer 1979): 15-22, 60-62.

_____. "The American Indian Federation and the Indian New Deal: A Reinterpretation." Pacific Historical Review 52 (Nov. 1983): 378-402.

_____. "Africa View: John Collier, the British Colonial Service, and American Indian Policy, 1933-1945." Historian 48 (May 1986): 359-74.

Hecht, Robert A. "Oliver LaFarge, John Collier, and the Hopi Constitution of 1936." Journal of Arizona History 26 (Summer 1985): 145-62.

Kelly, Lawrence C. "Choosing the New Deal Indian Commissioner: Ickes vs. Collier." New Mexico Historical Review 49 (Oct. 1974): 269-84.

_____. "The Indian Reorganization Act: The Dream and the Reality." Pacific Historical Review 44 (Aug. 1975): 291-312.

Kersey, Harry A., Jr. "Florida Seminoles in the Depression and New Deal, 1933-1942: An Indian Perspective." Florida Historical Quarterly 65 (Oct. 1986): 175-95.

Koppes, Clayton R. "From New Deal to Termination: Liberalism and Indian Policy, 1933-1953." Pacific Historical Review 46 (Nov. 1977): 543-66.

Parman, Donald L. "Inconstant Advocacy: The Erosion of Indian Fishing Rights in the Pacific Northwest, 1933-1956." Pacific Historical Review 53 (May 1984): 163-89.

_____. "The Indian and the Civilian Conservation Corps." Pacific Historical Review 40 (Feb. 1971): 39-56.

Philp, Kenneth. "Herbert Hoover's New Era: A False Dawn for the American Indian, 1929-1932." Rocky Mountain Social Science Journal 9 (April 1972): 53-60.

_____. "The New Deal and Alaskan Natives, 1936-1945." Pacific Historical Review 50 (Aug. 1981): 309-27.

Quinten, B. T. "Oklahoma Tribes, the Great Depression, and the Indian Bureau." Mid-America 49 (Jan. 1967): 29-43.

Stefon, Frederick J. "The Indians' Zarathustra: An Investigation into the Philosophical Roots of John Collier's Indian New Deal Educational and Administrative Programs." Journal of Ethnic Studies 11 (Fall 1983): 1-28.

Taylor, Graham D. "Anthropologists, Reformers, and the Indian New Deal."
    Prologue 7 (Fall 1975): 151-62.
    _____. "The Tribal Alternative to Bureaucracy: The Indian's New Deal, 1933-
    1945." Journal of the West 13 (Jan. 1974): 128-42.
Vlasich, James A. "Transitions in Pueblo Agriculture, 1938-1948." New Mexico
    Historical Review 55 (Jan. 1980): 25-46.
Weeks, Charles J. "The Eastern Cherokee and the New Deal." North Carolina
    Historical Review 53 (July 1976): 303-19.
Wright, Peter M. "John Collier and the Oklahoma Indian Welfare Act of 1936."
    Chronicles of Oklahoma 50 (Autumn 1972): 347-71.

Dissertations

Bromert, Roger. "The Sioux and the Indian New Deal, 1933-1944." Ph.D. diss.,
    University of Toledo, 1980.
Crum, Steven James. "The Western Shoshone of Nevada and the Indian New Deal."
    Ph.D. diss., University of Utah, 1983.
Foley, Rudolph X. "The Origins of the Indian Reorganization Act of 1934." Ph.D.
    diss., Fordham University, 1937.
Holm, Thomas Mark. "Indians and Progressives: From Vanishing Policy to the Indian
    New Deal." Ph.D. diss., University of Oklahoma, 1978.
Parman, Donald L. "The Indian Civilian Conservation Corps." Ph.D. diss., University
    of Oklahoma, 1967.
Schrader, Robert Fay. "The Indian Arts and Crafts Board: An Aspect of New Deal
    Indian Policy." Ph.D. diss., Marquette University, 1981.
Stefon, Frederick J. "Native American Education and the New Deal." Ph.D. diss.,
    Pennsylvania State University, 1983.

8.5 WOMEN

Books

Becker, Susan D. The Origins of the Equal Rights Amendment: American Feminism
    Between the Wars. Westport, Conn.: Greenwood, 1981.
Blackwelder, Julia Kirk. Women of the Depression: Caste and Culture in San Antonio,
    1929-1939. College Station: Texas A & M University Press, 1984.
Chafe, William. The American Woman: Her Changing Social, Economic, and Political
    Roles, 1920-1970. New York: Oxford University Press, 1972.
Gordon, Felice D. After Winning: The Legacy of the New Jersey Suffragists, 1920-
    1947. New Brunswick, N.J.: Rutgers University Press, 1986.

Pruette, Lorine, ed. Women Workers Through the Depression: A Study of White
    Collar Employment Made by the American Woman's Association. New York:
    Macmillan, 1934.
Scharf, Lois. To Work and to Wed: Female Employment, Feminism and the Great
    Depression. Westport, Conn.: Greenwood, 1980.
_____ and Joan M. Jensen, eds. Decades of Discontent: The Women's
    Movement, 1920-1940. Westport, Conn.: Greenwood, 1983.
Sealander, Judith. As Minority Becomes Majority: Federal Reaction to the
    Phenomenon of Women in the Work Force, 1920-1963. Westport, Conn.:
    Greenwood, 1983.
Wandersee, Winifred D. Women's Work and Family Values, 1920-1940. Cambridge:
    Harvard University Press, 1981.
Ware, Susan. Beyond Suffrage: Women in the New Deal. Cambridge: Harvard
    University Press, 1981.
_____. Holding Their Own: American Women in the 1930s. Boston: Twayne,
    1982.
Westin, Jeane. Making Do: How Women Survived the '30s. Chicago: Follett, 1976.

Articles

Anderson, M. Christine. "Home and Community for a Generation of Women: A Case
    Study of the Cincinnati Y.W.C.A. Residence, 1920-1940." Queen City Heritage
    43 (Winter 1985): 34-41.
Barber, Henry E. "The Association of Southern Women for the Prevention of
    Lynching, 1930-1942." Phylon 34 (Dec. 1973): 378-89.
Becker, Susan. "International Feminism between the Wars: The National Woman's
    Party Versus the League of Women Voters." In Decades of Discontent: The
    Women's Movement, 1930-1983 ed. by Lois Scharf and Joan M. Jensen
    (Westport: Greenwood, 1983), pp. 223-42.
Bennett, Sheila Kishler, and Glen H. Elder, Jr. "Women's Work in the Family
    Economy: A Study of Depression Hardship in Women's Lives." Journal of
    Family History 4 (Summer 1979): 153-76.
Blackwelder, Julia Kirk. "Quiet Suffering: Atlanta Women in the 1930s." Georgia
    Historical Quarterly 61 (Summer 1977): 112-24.
_____. "Women in the Work Force: Atlanta, New Orleans, and San Antonio,
    1930 to 1940." Journal of Urban History 4 (May 1978): 331-58.
Bolin, Winifred D. Wandersee. "The Economics of Middle-Income Family Life:
    Working Women During the Great Depression." Journal of American History
    65 (June 1978): 60-74.
Boddy, Julia. "Photographing Women: The Farm Security Administration Work of
    Marion Post Wolcott." In Decades of Discontent: The Women's Movement,
    1920-1940 ed. by Lois Scharf and Joan M. Jensen (Westport: Greenwood,
    1983), pp. 153-66.

Bullough, Vern, and Bonnie Bullough. "Lesbianism in the 1920s and 1930s: A New Found Study." Signs: Journal of Women in Culture and Society 2 (Summer 1977): 895-904.

Cowan, Ruth Schwartz. "Two Washes in the Morning and a Bridge Party at Night: The American Housewife Between the Wars." Women's Studies 3 (No. 2, 1976): 147-72.

Gerber, Ellen. "The Controlled Development of Collegiate Sports for Women, 1923-1936." Journal of Sport History 2 (Spring 1975): 1-28.

Gluck, Sherna. "Socialist Feminism between the Two World Wars: Insights from Oral History." In Decades of Discontent: The Women's Movement, 1920-1940 ed. by Lois Scharf and Joan M. Jensen (Westport: Greenwood, 1983), pp. 279-97.

Hargreaves, Mary W. M. "Darkness Before the Dawn: The Status of Women in the Depression Years." In Clio Was a Woman: Studies in the History of American Women ed. by Mabel E. Deutrich and Virginia C. Purdy (Washington: Howard University Press, 1980), pp. 178-88.

Honey, Maureen. "Images of Women in The Saturday Evening Post, 1931-1936." Journal of Popular Culture 10 (Fall 1976): 352-58.

Humphries, Jane. "Women: Scapegoats and Safety Valves in the Great Depression." Review of Radical Political Economics 8 (Spring 1971): 98-121.

Janiewski, Dolores. "Flawed Victories: The Experiences of Black and White Women Workers in Durham During the 1930s." In Decades of Discontent: The Women's Movement, 1920-1940 ed. by Lois Scharf and Joan M. Jensen (Westport: Greenwood, 1983), pp. 85-109.

Jensen, Joan M. "'I've Worked, I'm Not Afraid of Work': Farm Women in New Mexico, 1920-1940." New Mexico Historical Review 61 (Jan. 1986): 27-52.

Jones, Beverly W. "Race, Sex, and Class: Black Female Tobacco Workers in Durham, North Carolina, 1920-1940, and the Development of Female Consciousness." Feminist Studies 10 (Fall 1984): 441-51.

Kyvig, David E. "Women Against Prohibiton." American Quarterly 28 (Fall 1976): 465-82.

Levering, Patricia W. and Ralph B. "Women in Relief: The Carroll County Children's Aid Society in the Great Depression." Maryland Historical Magazine 72 (Winter 1977): 534-46.

McGovern, James R. "Helen Hunt West: Florida's Pioneer for ERA." Florida Historical Quarterly 57 (July 1978): 39-53.

Milkman, Ruth. "Women's Work and the Economic Crisis: Some Lessons from the Great Depression." Review of Radical Political Economics 8 (Spring 1976): 73-97.

_____. "The New Deal, the CIO, and Women in Industry." In The Roosevelt New Deal: A Program Assessment Fifty Years After ed. by Wilbur J. Cohen (Austin: Lyndon B. Johnson School of Public Affairs, 1986), pp. 167-83.

Pratt, Norma Fain. "Transitions in Judaism: The Jewish American Women through the 1930s." American Quarterly 30 (Winter 1978): 681-702.

Rosenfelt, Deborah. "From the Thirties: Tillie Olson and the Radical Tradition." Feminist Studies 7 (Fall 1981): 371-406.

Shaffer, Robert. "Women and the Communist Party, USA, 1930-1940." Socialist Review 45 (May-June 1979): 73-118.

Sholes, Elizabeth. "Women in the Media: A Report on Female Professionalism during the American Depression." Modernist Studies 1 (No. 3, 1974-75): 27-38.

Strom, Sharon Hartman. "Challenging 'Woman's Place': Feminism, the Left, and Industrial Unionism in the 1930s." Feminist Studies 9 (Summer 1983): 359-86.

Swain, Martha H. "A New Deal for Mississippi Women, 1933-1943." Journal of Mississippi History 46 (Aug. 1984): 191-212.

_____. "Ellen Woodward and Women's Economic Security, 1933-1953." Organization of American Historians Newsletter 11 (Nov. 1983): 13-15.

_____. "'The Forgotten Woman': Ellen S. Woodward and Woman's Relief in the New Deal." Prologue 15 (Dec. 1983): 201-13.

_____. "ER and Ellen Woodward: A Partnership for Women's Work, Relief and Security." In Without Precedent: The Life and Career of Eleanor Roosevelt ed. by Joan Hoff-Wilson and Marjorie Lightman (Bloomington: Indiana University Press, 1984), pp. 135-52.

Wandersee, Winnifred D. "A New Deal for Women: Government Programs, 1933-1940." In The Roosevelt New Deal: A Program Assessment Fifty Years After ed. by Wilbur J. Cohen (Austin: Lyndon B. Johnson School of Public Affairs, 1986), pp. 185-97.

Ware, Susan. "Women and the New Deal." In Fifty Years Later: The New Deal Evaluated ed. by Harvard Sitkoff (New York: Knopf, 1985), pp. 113-32.

Dissertations

Anderson, Mary C. "Gender, Class, and Culture: Women Secretarial and Clerical Workers in the United States, 1925-1955." Ph.D. diss., Ohio State University, 1986.

Carlson, Julia L. "American Women of the Thirties: Images of Women in American Fiction of the 1930s." Ph.D. diss., University of North Carolina, 1985.

Dudley, Julius W. "A History of the Association of Southern Women for the Prevention of Lynching, 1930-1942." Ph.D. diss., University of Cincinnati, 1979.

Gabin, Nancy F. "Women Auto Workers and the United Automobile Workers' Union (UAW-CIO), 1935-1955." Ph.D. diss., University of Michigan, 1984.

Heller, Rita R. "The Women of Summer: The Bryn Mawr Summer School for Woemn Workers: 1921-1938." Ph.D. diss., Rutgers University, 1986.

Helmold, Lois Rita. "Making Choices, Making Do: Black and White Working Class Women's Lives and Work during the Great Depression." Ph.D. diss., Stanford University, 1983.

Kleinegger, Christine C. "Out of the Barns and into the Kitchens: Farm Women's Domestic Labor, World War I to World War II." Ph.D. diss., State University of New York at Binghamton, 1986.

McDonald, Susan S. W. "Writing and Identity: Autobiographies of American Women Novelists, 1930-1955." Ph.D. diss., Saint Louis University, 1981.

Michel, Sonya A. "Children's Interests/Mothers' Rights: Women, Professionals, and the American Family, 1920-1945." Ph.D. diss., Brown University, 1986.

Scharf, Lois. "The Employment of Married Women during the Depression, 1929-1941." Ph.D. diss., Case Western Reserve University, 1977.

Schott, Linda K. "Women against War: Pacifism, Feminism, and Social Justice in the United States, 1915-1941." Ph.D. diss., Stanford University, 1985.

Taylor, Frances Sanders. "'On the Edge of Tomorrow': Southern Women, the Student YWCA, and Race, 1920-1944." Ph.D. diss., Stanford University, 1984.

Ware, Susan Wolfe. "Political Sisterhood in the New Deal: Women in Politics and Government, 1933-1940." Ph.D. diss., Harvard University, 1978.

Wladaver-Morgan, Susan. "Young Women and the New Deal: Camps and Resident Centers, 1933-1943." Ph.D. diss., Indiana University, 1982.

9

Regional, State & Local Affairs

9.1 GENERAL

Books

Anderson, Sherwood. Home Town: The Face of America. New York: Alliance,
    1940.
Foster, Mark S. From Streetcar to Superhighway: American City Planners and Urban
    Transportation, 1900-1940. Philadelphia: Temple University Press, 1981.
Gelfand, Mark I. A Nation of Cities: The Federal Government and Urban America,
    1933-1965. New York: Oxford University Press, 1975.
Kirschner, Don S. City and Country: Rural Responses to Urbanization in the 1920s.
    Westport, Conn.: Greenwood, 1970.
Patterson, James T. The New Deal and the States: Federalism in Transition.
    Princeton: Princeton University Press, 1969.
Sternsher, Bernard. Hitting Home: The Great Depression in Town and Country.
    Chicago: Quadrangle, 1970.

Articles

Patterson, James T. "The New Deal and the States." American Historical Review
    73 (Oct. 1967): 70-84.
Reading, Don C. "New Deal Activity in the States, 1932 to 1939." Journal of
    Economic History 33 (Dec. 1973): 792-807.
Trout, Charles H. "The New Deal and the Cities." In Fifty Years Later: The New
    Deal Evaluated ed. by Harvard Sitkoff (New York: Knopf, 1985), pp. 133-53.

Dissertations

Fairfield, John D. "Neighborhood and Metropolis: The Origins of Modern Urban Planning, 1877-1935." Ph.D. diss., University of Rochester, 1985.

Hannah, James Joseph. "Urban Reaction to the Great Depression in the United States, 1929-1933." Ph.D. diss., University of California, Berkeley, 1957.

Reiser, Mindy C. "The Arts and the Community: An Exploratory Study of Community Arts Councils in their American Cultural Context." Ph.D. diss., Brandeis University, 1981.

Steiner, Michael C. "The Regional Impulse in the United States, 1923-1941." Ph.D. diss., University of Minnesota, 1978.

Sullivan, Cornelius Henry, Jr. "Regionalism in American Thought: Provincial Ideals from the Gilded Age to the Great Depression." Ph.D diss., University of Chicago, 1977.

9.2   EAST: Connecticut, Delaware, District of Columbia, Maine, Massachusetts, Maryland, New Hampshire, New Jersey, New York, Pennsylvania, Rhode Island, Vermont, West Virginia

Books

Alderfer, Harold F. Presidential Elections by Pennsylvania Counties, 1920-1940. State College, Pa.: Pennsylvania State College, 1941.

Alderfer, Harold F., and Fannette H. Luhrs. Gubernatorial Elections in Pennsylvania, 1922-42. State College, Pa.: Pennsylvania Municipal Publications, 1946.

Blumberg, Barbara. The New Deal and the Unemployed: The View from New York City. Lewisberg, Pa.: Bucknell University Press, 1979.

Brandt, Lillian. An Impressionistic View of the Winter of 1930-31 in New York City: Based on Statements from some 900 Social Workers and Public-Health Nurses. New York: Welfare Council of New York City, 1932.

Bremer, William W. Depression Winters: New York Social Workers and the New Deal. Philadelphia: Temple University Press, 1984.

Cosnell, William A. The Political Career of John S. Fisher, Governor of Pennsylvania, 1927-1931. Pittsburgh: University of Pittsburgh Press, 1949.

Garrett, Charles. The La Guardia Years: Machine and Reform Politics in New York City. New Brunswick, N.J.: Rutgers University Press, 1961.

Heckscher, August. When LaGuardia Was Mayor: New York's Legendary Years. New York: W.W. Norton, 1978.

Huthmacher, J. Joseph. Massachusetts People and Politics, 1919-1933. Cambridge: Harvard University Press, 1959.

Ingalls, Robert P. Herbert H. Lehman and New York's Little New Deal. New York: New York University Press, 1975.

Judd, Richard M. The New Deal in Vermont: Its Impact and Aftermath. New York: Garland, 1979.

Keller, Richard C. Pennsylvania's Little New Deal. New York: Garland, 1982.

Leuchtenburg, William E. Flood Control Politics: The Connecticut River Valley Problem, 1927-1950. Cambridge: Harvard University Press, 1953.

McKean, Dayton D. The Boss: The Hague Machine In Action. Boston: Houghton Mifflin, 1940.

Millett, John D. The Works Progress Administration in New York City. Chicago: Public Administration Council, 1938.

Radomski, Alexander L. Work Relief in New York State, 1931-1935. New York: King's Crown Press, 1947.

Stave, Bruce M. The New Deal and the Last Hurrah: Pittsburgh Machine Politics. Pittsburgh: University of Pittsburgh Press, 1970.

Stern, Robert A. M., Gregory Gilmartin, and Thomas Mellins. New York 1930: Architecture and Urbanism Between the Two World Wars. New York: Rizzoli, 1987.

Trout, Charles H. Boston, The Great Depression, and the New Deal. New York: Oxford University Press, 1977.

Articles

Argersinger, Jo Ann E. "Assisting the 'Loafers': Transient Relief in Baltimore, 1933-1937." Labor History 23 (Spring 1982): 226-45.

Bauman, John F. "Safe and Sanitary Without the Costly Frills: The Evaluation of Public Housing in Philadelphia, 1929-1941." Pennsylvania Magazine of History and Biography 101 (Jan. 1977): 114-28.

Bronner, Edwin B. "The New Deal Comes to Pennsylvania: The Gubernatorial Election of 1934." Pennsylvania History 27 (Jan. 1960): 44-68.

Brown, Dorothy. "The Election of 1934: The 'New Deal' in Maryland." Maryland Historical Magazine 68 (Winter 1973): 405-22.

Bryan, Frank M. and Kenneth Bruno. "Black-Topping the Green Mountains: Socio-Economic and Political Correlates of Ecological Decision-Making." Vermont History 41 (Autumn 1973): 224-35.

Buhle, Paul M., ed. "Depression Rhode Island, 1929-1940." Rhode Island History 46 (Feb. 1987): 27-38.

Capeci, Dominic J., Jr. "Fiorello H. LaGuardia and the Harlem 'Crime Wave' of 1941." New York Historical Society Quarterly 64 (Jan. 1980): 7-29.

Chalmers, Leonard. "The Crucial Test of La Guardia's First Hundred Days: The Emergency Economy Bill." New York Historical Society Quarterly 57 (July 1973): 237-53.

Clement, Priscila Ferguson. "The Works Progress Administration in Pennsylvania, 1935 to 1940." Pennsylvania Magazine of History and Biography 95 (April 1971): 244-60.

Conwill, Joseph D. "Back to the Land: Pennsylvania's New Deal Era Communities." Pennsylvania Heritage 10 (Summer 1984): 12-17.

Coode, Thomas H., and Dennis Farbin. "The New Deal's Arthurdale Project in West Virginia." West Virginia History 36 (July 1975): 291-308.

David, David L. "Impoverished Politics: The New Deal's Impact on City Government in Providence, Rhode Island." Rhode Island History 42 (Aug. 1983): 86-100.

Fox, Bonnie R. "Unemployment Relief in Philadelphia, 1930-1932: A Study of the Depression's Impact on Voluntarism." Pennsylvania Magazine of History and Biography 93 (Jan. 1969): 86-108.

Genevro, Rosalie. "Site Selection and the New York City Housing Authority, 1934-1939." Journal of Urban History 12 (Aug. 1986): 334-52.

Gorvine, Harold. "The New Deal in Massachusetts." In The New Deal: The State and Local Levels ed. by John Braeman, Robert H. Bremner, and David Brody (Columbus: Ohio State University Press, 1975), pp. 3-44.

Grant, Philip A., Jr. "Maryland Reaction to the Roosevelt-Tydings Confrontation." Maryland Historical Magazine 68 (Winter 1974): 422-37.

Greenberg, Irwin F. "Philadelphia Democrats Get a New Deal: The Election of 1933." Pennsylvania Magazine of History and Biography 97 (April 1973): 210-32.

Greenberg, Irwin F. "Pinchot, Prohibition and Public Utilities: The Pennsylvania Election of 1930." Pennsylvania History 40 (Jan. 1973): 21-36.

Hand, Samuel B., and D. Gregory Sanford. "Carrying Water on Both Shoulders: George D. Aiken's 1936 Gubernatorial Campaign in Vermont." Vermont History 43 (Fall 1975): 292-306.

Hendrickson, Kenneth E., Jr. "The Civilian Conservation Corps in Pennsylvania: A Case Study of a New Deal Relief Agency in Operation." Pennsylvania Magazine of History and Biography 100 (Jan. 1976): 66-96.

_____. "The Socialist Administration in Reading, Pennsylvania, Part I, 1927-1931." Pennsylvania History 39 (Oct. 1972): 417-42.

_____. "Triumph and Disaster: The Reading Socialists in Power and Decline, 1932-1939-- Part II." Pennsylvania History 40 (Oct. 1973): 381-412.

Henwood, James N. J. "Experiment in Relief: The Civil Works Administration in Pennsylvania, 1933-1934." Pennsylvania History 39 (Jan. 1972): 50-71.

Hunter, Leslie Gene. "Greenbelt, Maryland: A City on a Hill." Maryland Historical Magazine 63 (June 1968): 105-36.

Ingalls, Robert P. "New York and the Minimum-Wage Movement, 1933-1937." Labor History 15 (Spring 1974): 179-98.

Jenkins, Philip. "The Ku Klux Klan in Pennsylvania, 1920-1940." Western Pennsylvania Historical Magazine 69 (April 1986): 121-37.

Johnson, Clark. "Burlington Since the 1930's: Change and Continuity in Vermont's Largest City." Vermont History 27 (Winter 1969): 52-62.

Keller, Richard C. "Pennsylvania's Little New Deal." In The New Deal: The State and Local Levels ed. by John Braeman, Robert H. Bremner, and David Brody (Columbus: Ohio State University Press, 1975), pp. 45-76.

Kenneally, James. "Prelude to the Last Hurrah: The Massachusetts Senatorial Election of 1936." Mid-America 62 (Jan. 1980): 3-20.

Kimberly, Charles M. "The Depression in Maryland: The Failure of Voluntaryism." Maryland Historical Magazine 70 (Summer 1975): 189-202.

Lamoreaux, David, and Gerson Eisenberg. "Baltimore Views the Great Depression, 1929-33." Maryland Historical Magazine 71 (Fall 1976): 428-42.

Lansky, Lewis. "Buffalo and the Great Depression, 1929-1933." In An American Historian: Essays to Honor Selig Adler ed. by Milton Plesur (Buffalo: State University of New York, 1980), pp. 204-13.

Lapomarda, Vincent A. "A New Deal Democrat in Boston: Maurice J. Tobin and the Policies of Franklin D. Roosevelt." Essex Institute Historical Collections 108 (1972): 135-52.

Mazuzan, George T. "Vermont's Traditional Republicanism vs. The New Deal: Warren R. Austin and the Election of 1934." Vermont History 39 (Spring 1971): 128-41.

McCarthy, Joe. "The '38 Hurricane." American Heritage 20 (Aug. 1969): 10-15, 102-4.

Morgan, Alfred L. "The Significance of Pennsylvania's 1938 Gubernatorial Election." Pennsylvania Magazine of History and Biography 102 (April 1978): 184-211.

Morton, Charles W. "Lean Times in Boston: Depression and the Drys." Atlantic Monthly 211 (Feb. 1963): 47-54.

Murray, Mary. "Connecticut's Depression Governor: Wilbur L. Cross." Connecticut History 16 (Aug. 1975): 44-64.

Noble, Richard A. "Patterson's Response to the Great Depression." New Jersey History 96 (Autumn 1978): 87-98.

Olson, James S. "The Depths of the Great Depression: Economic Collapse in West Virginia, 1932-1933." West Virginia History 38 (April 1977): 214-25.

Patterson, James T., ed. "Life on Relief in Rhode Island, 1934: A Contemporary View from the Field." Rhode Island History 39 (Aug. 1980): 79-91.

Pessen, Edward. "Those Marvelous Depression Years: Reminiscences of the Big Apple." New York History 62 (April 1981): 188-200.

Sanderlin, Walter S. "The Indictment of Joseph F. Guffey." Pennsylvania History 30 (Oct. 1963): 465-82.

Schwartz, Bonnie Fox. "Unemployment Relief in Philadelphia, 1930-1932: A Study of the Depression's Impact on Voluntarism." Pennsylvania Magazine of History and Biography 92 (Jan. 1969): 86-108.

Schwartz, Joel "Tenant Unions in New York City's Low Rent Housing, 1933-1949." Journal of Urban History 12 (Aug. 1986): 414-43.

Shover, John L. "The Emergence of a Two-Party System in Republican Philadelphia, 1924-1936." Journal of American History 60 (March 1974): 985-1002.

Smith, W. Wayne. "The Depression Strikes Indiana County." Pennsylvania Heritage 3 (Sept. 1977): 18-20.

Stave, Bruce M. "Pittsburgh and the New Deal." In The New Deal: The State and Local Levels ed. by John Braeman, Robert H. Bremner, and David Brody (Columbus: Ohio State University Press, 1975), pp. 376-406.

_____. "The 'La Follette Revolution' and the Pittsburgh Vote, 1932." Mid-America 49 (Oct. 1967): 244-51.

_____. "The New Deal, the Last Hurrah, and the Building of an Urban Political Machine: Pittsburgh Committeemen, A Case Study." Pennsylvania History 33 (Oct. 1966): 460-83.

Stein, Judith. "The Impact of the New Deal on New York Politics: Kenneth Simpson and the Republican Party." New York Historical Society Quarterly 56 (Jan. 1972): 29-53.

Stickle, Warren E. "Edison, 'Hagueism,' and the Split Ticket of 1940." New Jersey History 97 (Summer 1979): 69-86.

Thomas, Edmund B., Jr. "The Emergency Relief Commission of Fitchburg, 1931-1934." Historical Journal of Massachusetts 12 (June 1984): 132-43.

Dissertations

Argersinger, Jo Ann Eady. "Baltimore: The Depression Years." Ph.D. diss., George Washington University, 1980.

Astorino, Samuel J. "The Decline of the Republican Dynasty in Pennsylvania, 1929-1934." Ph.D. diss., University of Pittsburgh, 1962.

Bauman, John F. "The City, the Depression, and Relief: The Philadelphia Experience, 1929-1939." Ph.D. diss., Rutgers University, 1969.

Crews, Raymond M. "The Perils of Providence: Rhode Island's Capital City during the Depression and New Deal." Ph.D. diss., University of Connecticut, 1982.

Crouse, Joan Marie. "Transiency in New York State: The Impact of the Depression Decade, 1929-1940." Ph.D. diss., State University of New York at Buffalo, 1981.

Davidson, Judith Anne. "The Federal Government and the Democratization of Public Recreational Sport: New York City, 1933-43." Ph.D. diss., University of Massachusetts, 1983.

Gillette, Frieda A. "The New York State Constitutional Convention of 1938." Ph.D. diss., Cornell University, 1944.

Gorvine, Harold. "The New Deal in Massachusetts." Ph.D. diss., Harvard University, 1962.

Hodess, Annette M. "A Study of the History of the WPA Nursery Schools of Boston." Ph.D. diss., Boston University, 1983.

Judd, Richard M. "A History of the New Deal in Vermont." Ph.D. diss., Harvard University, 1959.

Keller, Richard C. "Pennsylvania's Little New Deal." Ph.D. diss., Columbia University, 1960.

Kimberly, Charles Michael. "The Depression and New Deal in Maryland." Ph.D. diss., American University, 1974.

Lashbrook, Lawrence G. "Work Relief in Maine: The Administration and Programs of the WPA." Ph.D. diss., University of Maine, 1977.

Leuchtenburg, William E. "Flood Control Politics: The Connecticut River Valley, 1927-1950." Ph.D. diss., Columbia University, 1951.

Lockard, Walter D. "The Role of Party in the Connecticut General Assembly, 1931-51." Ph.D. diss., Yale University, 1952.

Lombardo, Peter Joseph, Jr. "Connecticut in the Great Depression, 1929-1933." Ph.D. diss., University of Notre Dame, 1979.

Massey, Robert K., Jr. "The State Politics of Massachusetts Democracy, 1928-1938." Ph.D. diss., Duke University, 1968.

Mitchell, Rowland L, Jr. "Social Legislation in Connecticut, 1919-1939." Ph.D. diss., Yale University, 1954.

Munley, Kathleen Purcell. "From Minority to Majority: A Study of the Democratic Party in Lackawanna County 1920-1950." Ph.D. diss., Lehigh University, 1981.

Papaleo, Ralph J. "The Democratic Party in Urban Politics in New York State: 1933-1938." Ph.D. diss., St. John's University, 1978.

Stellhorn, Paul Anthony. "Depression and Decline: Newark, New Jersey: 1929-1941." Ph.D. diss., Rutgers University, 1982.

Taylor, John Craft. "Depression and New Deal in Pendleton: A History of a West Virginia County from the Great Crash to Pearl Harbor, 1929-1941." Ph.D. diss., Pennsylvania State University, 1980.

Verdicchio, Joseph J. "New Deal Work Relief and New York City: 1933-1938." Ph.D. diss., New York University, 1980.

9.3   MIDWEST: Illinois, Indiana, Iowa, Kansas, Michigan, Minnesota, Missouri, Nebraska, North Dakota, Ohio, South Dakota, Wisconsin

Books

Biles, Roger. Big City Boss in Depression and War: Mayor Edward J. Kelly of Chicago. DeKalb: Northern Illinois University Press, 1984.

Bonnifield, Mathew Paul. The Dust Bowl: Men, Dirt, and Depression. Albuquerque: University of New Mexico Press, 1979.

Brown, Andrew Theodore. The Politics of Reform: Kansas City's Municipal Government, 1925-1950. Kansas City, Mo.: Community Studies, 1958.

Campbell, William J. History of the Republican Party in Wisconsin Under the Convention Plan, 1924 to 1940. Oshkosh: n.p., 1942.

Carr, Carolyn Kinder. Ohio: A Photographic Portrait 1935-1941: Farm Security Administration Photographs. Akron, Ohio: Akron Art Institute, distributed by Kent State University Press, 1980.

Clark, James I. Wisconsin Meets the Great Depression. Madison: State Historical Society of Wisconsin, 1956.

Frost, Dayton H. Emergency Relief in Ohio, 1931-1935. Columbus: Federal Relief Administration in Ohio, 1942.

Glick, Frank Z. The Illinois Emergency Relief Commission. Chicago: University of Chicago Press, 1940.

Hawley, Amos H. Intrastate Migration in Michigan: 1935-1940. Ann Arbor: University of Michigan Press, 1953.

Hurt, R. Douglas. The Dust Bowl: An Agricultural and Social History. Chicago: Nelson-Hall, 1981.

Johnson, Roger T. Robert M. LaFollette, Jr., and the Decline of the Progressive Party in Wisconsin. Madison: University of Wisconsin Press, 1964.

Johnson, Vance. Heaven's Tableland: The Dust Bowl Story. New York: Farrar and Straus, 1947.

Lynd, Robert S. and Helen M. Middletown in Transition: A Study in Cultural Conflicts. New York: Harcourt Brace, 1937.

McKenney, Ruth. Industrial Valley. New York: Harcourt, 1939.

Miller, John E. Governor Philip F. LaFollette, The Wisconsin Progressives, and the New Deal. Columbia: University of Missouri Press, 1982.

Mitchell, Franklin D. Embattled Democracy: Missouri Democratic Politics, 1919-1932. Columbia: University of Missouri Press, 1968.

Ortquist, Richard T. Depression Politics in Michigan, 1929-1933. New York: Garland, 1982.

Reddig, William M. Tom's Town: Kansas City and the Pendergast Legend. Philadelphia: Lippincott, 1947.

Richardson, Lemont Kingsford. Wisconsin REA: The Struggle to Extend Electricity to Rural Wisconsin, 1935-1955. Madison: University of Wisconsin Experiment Station, College of Agriculture, 1961.

Saloutos, Theodore, and John D. Hicks. Twentieth Century Populism: Agricultural Discontent in the Middle West, 1900-1939. Lincoln: University of Nebraska Press, 1951.

Schruben, Francis W. Kansas in Turmoil, 1930-1936. Columbia: University of Missouri Press, 1969.

Walker, Harvey. Constructive Government in Ohio: The Story of the Administration of Governor Myers Y. Cooper, 1929-1930. Columbus: Ohio History Press, 1948.

Worster, Donald. Dust Bowl: The Southern Plains in the 1930s. New York: Oxford University Press, 1979.

Articles

Avery, Inda. "Some South Dakotans' Opinions about the New Deal." South Dakota History 7 (Summer 1977): 309-24.

Bader, Robert E. "The Curtailment of Railroad Service in Nebraska, 1920-1941." Nebraska History 36 (March 1955): 27-42.

Barrett, Paul "Public Policy and Private Choice: Mass Transit and the Automobile in Chicago Between the Wars." Business History Review 49 (Winter 1975): 473-97.

Booth, Douglas E. "Municipal Socialism and City Government Reform: The Milwaukee Experience, 1910-1940." Journal of Urban History 12 (Nov. 1985): 51-74.

Brown, Sharon A. "Creating the Dream: Jefferson National Expansion Memorial, 1933-1935." Missouri Historical Review 76 (April 1982): 302-26.

Cahan, Cathy and Richard. "The Lost City of the Depression." Chicago History 5 (Winter 1976-1977): 233-42.

Carlson, Robert. "O. Leonard Orvedal--Bismark." North Dakota History 44 (Fall 1977): 69-72.

Chafe, William H. "Flint and the Great Depression." Michigan History 53 (Fall 1969): 225-40.

Clapp, Tom. "Toledo Industrial Peace Board 1935-1943: Part I: The Depression Comes to Toledo." Northwest Ohio Historical Quarterly 40 (Spring 1968): 50-67.

_____. "Toledo Industrial Peace Board 1935-1943: Part II: The Organization of the Peace Board." Northwest Ohio Historical Quarterly 40 (Summer 1968): 97-110.

_____. "Toledo Industrial Peace Board 1935-1943: Part III: A Fair Trial-- Operation of the Board 1935-1937." Northwest Ohio Historical Quarterly 41 (Winter 1969): 25-41.

_____. "Toledo Industrial Peace Board 1935-1943: Part IV." Northwest Ohio Historical Quarterly 42 (Winter 1970): 19-28.

Clive, Alan. "The Reluctant Arsenal: Metropolitan Detroit from Peace to War, 1939-1941." Detroit in Perspective 5 (Spring 1981): 53-71.

Dileva, Frank D. "Attempt to Hang an Iowa Judge." Annals of Iowa 32 (July 1954): 337-64.

Dorn, Jacob H. "Subsistence Homesteading in Dayton, Ohio, 1933-1935." Ohio History 78 (June 1969): 75-93.

Dorsett, Lyle W. "Kansas City and the New Deal." In The New Deal: The State and Local Levels ed. by John Braeman, Robert H. Bremner, and David Brody (Columbus: Ohio State University Press, 1975), pp. 407-19.

Erickson, Erling A. "A North Dakota Farm Auction in the Great Depression." North Dakota Quarterly 39 (Winter 1971): 37-49.

Evans, Timothy K. "'This Certainly is Relief!': Matthew S. Murray and Missouri Politics During the Depression." Bulletin of the Missouri Historical Society 28 (July 1972): 219-33.

Fairbanks, Robert B. "Cincinnati and Greenhills: The Response to a Federal Community, 1935-1939." Cincinnati Historical Society Quarterly 36 (Winter 1978): 223-242.

Frank, Carrolyle M. "Who Governed Middletown? Community Power in Muncie, Indiana, in the 1930s." Indiana Magazine of History 75 (Dec. 1979): 320-43.

Frederich, John T. "Town and City in Iowa Fiction: The Nineteen Thirties." Palimpsest 35 (Feb. 1954): 75-84.

Friske, Leo J. "Roosevelt and Depression Days in Milwaukee." Milwaukee History 8 (Summer 1985): 85-92.

Garvey, Timothy. "The Duluth Homesteads: A Successful Experiment in Community Housing." Minnesota History 46 (Spring 1978): 2-16.

Garwood, Darrell D. "Gerald Burton Winrod and the Politics of Kansas During the Depression." Heritage of the Great Plains 17 (Winter 1984): 27-34.

Hendrickson, Kenneth E., Jr. "The Civilian Conservation Corps in South Dakota." South Dakota History 11 (Winter 1980): 1-20.

_____. "The National Youth Administration in South Dakota: Youth and the New Deal, 1935-1943." South Dakota History 9 (Spring 1979): 130-51.

_____. "Relief for Youth: The Civilian Conservation Corps and the National Youth Administration in North Dakota." North Dakota History 48 (Fall 1981): 17-27.

_____. "The Sugar-Beet Laborer and the Federal Government: An Episode in the History of the Plains in the 1930's." Great Plains Journal 3 (Spring 1964): 44-59.

Herman, Alan. "Dust, Depression and Demagogues: Political Radicals of the Great Plains, 1930-1936." Journal of the West 16 (Jan. 1977): 57-62.

Hofsommer, Donovan L. "Steel Plows and Iron Men: The Illinois Central Railroad and Iowa's Winter of 1936." Annals of Iowa 43 (Spring 1976): 292-98.

Hope, Clifford R. "Kansas in the 1930's." Kansas Historical Quarterly 36 (Spring 1970): 1-12.

Hurt, R. Douglas. "Dust." American Heritage 28 (Aug. 1977): 34-35.

_____. "Dust Bowl: Drought, Erosion, and Dispair on the Southern Great Plains." American West 14 (July-Aug. 1977): 22-27, 56-57.

_____. "Federal Land Reclamation in the Dust Bowl." Great Plains Quarterly 6 (Spring 1986): 94-106.

_____. "Irrigation on the Kansas Plains Since 1930." Red River Valley Historical Review 4 (Summer 1979): 64-72.

Jones, Alan. "The New Deal Comes to Iowa." In The New Deal Viewed from Fifty Years ed. by Lawrence E. Gelfand and Robert J. Neymeyer (Iowa City: Center for the Study of Recent History of the United States, 1983), pp. 21-53.

Katzman, David M. "Ann Arbor: Depression City." Michigan History 50 (Dec. 1966): 306-17.

Ketchum, Richard. "Faces from the Past--XI [Dust Bowl]." American Heritage 14 (Aug. 1963): 32-33.

Knauth, Otto. "The Winter of 1935-36." Annals of Iowa 35 (Spring 1960): 288-93.

Koch, Raymond L. "Politics and Relief in Minneapolis During the 1930s." Minnesota History 41 (Winter 1968): 153-70.

Kohn, Walter S. G. "Illinois Ratifies the Twenty-First Amendment." Journal of the Illinois State Historical Society 56 (Spring 1963): 692-712.

Koprowski-Kraut, Gayle. "The Depression's Effects on a Milwaukee Family." Milwaukee History 3 (Autumn 1980): 84-92.

Latta, Maurice C. "The Economic Effects of Drouth and Depression upon Custer County, 1929-1942." Nebraska History 33 (Dec. 1952): 220-36.

Logsden, Guy. "The Dust Bowl and the Migrant." American Scene 12 (1971): unnumbered.

Lovin, Hugh T. "The Ohio 'Farmer-Labor' Movement in the 1930's." Ohio History 87 (Autumn 1978): 419-37.

Lowitt, Richard. "George W. Norris and the New Deal in Nebraska, 1933-1936." Agricultural History 51 (April 1977): 396-405.

Maurer, David J. "Relief Problems and Politics in Ohio." In The New Deal: The State and Local Levels ed. by John Braeman, Robert H. Bremner, and David Brody (Columbus: Ohio State University Press, 1975), pp. 77-102.

_____. "Unemployment in Illinois during the Great Depression." In Essays in Illinois History in Honor of Glenn Huron Seymour ed. by Donald F. Tingley (Carbondale, Ill.: Southern Illinois University Press, 1968), pp. 120-32.

McCoy, Donald R. "Senator George S. McGill and the Election of 1938." Kansas History 4 (Spring 1981): 2-19.

McSeveney, Samuel T. "The Michigan Gubernatorial Campaign of 1938." Michigan History 45 (June 1961): 97-127.

Miller, John E. "Governor Philip F. La Follette's Shifting Priorities from Redistribution to Expansion." Mid-America 58 (April-July 1976): 119-26.

_____. "McCarthyism Before McCarthy: The 1938 Election in South Dakota." Heritage of the Great Plains 15 (Summer 1982): 1-21.

_____. "Progressivism and the New Deal: The Wisconsin Works Bill of 1935." Wisconsin Magazine of History 62 (Autumn 1978): 25-40.

Mills, George. "Iowa's Planning Programs of the Past and Present." Annals of Iowa 42 (Spring 1975): 583-96.

Mitchell, Franklin D. "'Who is Judge Truman?': The Truman-for-Governor Movement of 1931." American Studies 7 (Fall 1966): 3-15.

Morgan, Iwan. "Factional Conflict in Indiana Politics during the Later New Deal Years, 1936-1940." Indiana Magazine of History 79 (March 1983): 29-60.

_____. "Fort Wayne and the Great Depression: The Early Years, 1929-1933." Indiana Magazine of History 80 (June 1984): 122-45.

_____. "Fort Wayne and the Great Depression: The New Deal Years, 1933-1940." Indiana Magazine of History 80 (Dec. 1984): 348-78.

_____. "The Fort Wayne Plan: The FHA and Prefabricated Municipal Housing in the 1930s." Historian 47 (Aug. 1985): 538-59.

Nash, Gerald D. "History of the Great Plains During the Great Depression." In The Great Plains ed. by Sara Rosenberg (Lincoln: University of Mid-America, 1975), pp. 9.27.

O'Neill, Robert K. The Federal Writers' Project Files for Indiana." Indiana Magazine of History 76 (June 1980): 85-96.

O'Rourke, Paul A. "South Dakota Politics During the New Deal Years." South Dakota History 1 (Summer 1971): 231-71.

Ortquist, Richard T. "Depression Politics in Michigan: The Election of 1932." Michigan Academician 2 (Spring 1970): 3-12.

_____. "Tax Crisis and Politics in Early Depression Michigan." Michigan History 59 (Spring 1975): 91-119.

_____. "Unemployment and Relief: Michigan's Response to the Depression During the Hoover Years." Michigan History 57 (Fall 1973): 209-36.

Peterson, Charles. "Drama in the Dustbowl." Kansas Magazine 1952: 94-97.

Pickett, William B. "The Capehart Cornfield Conference and the Election of 1938: Homer E. Capehart's Entry into Politics." Indiana Magazine of History 73 (Dec. 1977): 251-75.

Reiman, Richard A. "The New Deal for Youth: A Cincinnati Connection." Queen City Heritage 44 (Fall 1986): 36-48.

Reiner, Milton K. "William Lemke and the Election of 1936 in North Dakota." North Dakota History 38 (Summer 1971): 351-60.

Remele, Larry. "The North Dakota Farm Strike of 1932." North Dakota History 41 (Fall 1974): 4-19.

Riebsame, William E. "The Dust Bowl: Historical Image, Psychological Anchor, and Ecological Taboo." Great Plains Quarterly 6 (Spring 1986): 127-36.

Ring, Daniel F. "The Cleveland Public Library and the WPA: A Case Study in Creative Partnership." Ohio History 84 (Summer 1975): 158-64.

Rogers, Ruby. "Michigan's CCC Museum." Michigan History 69 (July 1985): 12-15.

Rowley, William D. "The Loup City Riot of 1934: Main Street vs. the 'Far-Out' Left." Nebraska History 47 (Sept. 1966): 295-328.

Rynder, Constance B. "Progressive into New Dealer: Amy Maher and the Public Works Administration in Toledo." Northwest Ohio Quarterly 58 (Winter 1986): 3-19.

Sage, Leland L. "Rural Iowa in the 1920s and 1930s: Roots of the Farm Depression." Annals of Iowa 47 (Fall 1983): 91-103.

Salyers, James Ernest. "The Politics of the Depression: The Emergence and Eclipse of the Democratic Party in Missouri: A County-State Continuum, 1928-1944." Bulletin of the Missouri Historical Society 25 (Oct. 1968): 50-64.

Saults, Dan. "Search for a Lost Eden." Gateway Heritage 1 (Fall 1980): 12-17.

Schottenhamel, George C. "The Richardson County Oil Boom, 1938-1942." Nebraska History 60 (Fall 1979): 357-71.

Schuyler, Michael. "Drought and Politics, 1936: Kansas as a Test Case." Great Plains Journal 14 (Fall 1975): 3-27.

_____. "Federal Drought Relief Activities in Kansas, 1934." Kansas Historical Quarterly 42 (Winter 1976): 403-24.

Shaver, James H. "Drouth, Dust, & The Good Times." Kansas Quarterly 12 (Spring 1980): 17-22.

Simmons, Jerold. "Dawson County Responds to the New Deal, 1933-1940." Nebraska History 62 (Spring 1981): 47-72.

Soapes, Thomas F. "The Fragility of the Roosevelt Coaltion: The Case of Missouri." Missouri Historical Review 72 (Oct. 1972): 38-58.

Sobczak, John N. "The Politics of Relief: Public Aid in Toledo, 1933-1937." Northwest Ohio Quarterly 48 (Fall 1976): 134-42.

Sorden, L. D. "The Northern Wisconsin Settler Relocation Project, 1934-1940." Wisconsin Academy of Science, Arts, and Letters: Transactions 53 (1964): 135-38.

Sternsher, Bernard "Depression and New Deal in Ohio: Lorena A. Hickok's Reports to Harry Hopkins, 1934-1936." Ohio History 86 (Autumn 1977): 258-77.

Stimson, George P. "River on a Rampage: An Account of the Ohio River Flood of 1937." Cincinnati Historical Society Bulletin 22 (April 1964): 91-109.

Strickland, Arvah E. "The New Deal Comes to Illinois." Journal of the Illinois State Historical Society 63 (Spring 1970): 55-68.

Tingley, Ralph R. "The South Dakota Rendezvous of Franklin Roosevelt and Thomas Jefferson, 1936." Midwest Review 7 (Spring 1985): 31-39.

Towey, Martin G. "Hooverville: St. Louis Had the Largest." Gateway Heritage 1 (Fall 1980): 4-11.

Van Sickle, Frederick Mercer. "A Special Place: Lake Forest and the Great Depression, 1929-1940." Illinois Historical Journal 79 (Summer 1986): 113-26.

Webb, Bernice Larson. "I Remember Sappa Valley." Kansas Quarterly 12 (Spring 1980): 25-34.

Zeidel, Robert F. "Beer Returns to Cream City." Milwaukee History 4 (Spring 1981): 20-32.

Dissertations

Allswang, John M. "The Political Behavior of Chicago's Ethnic Groups, 1918-1932." Ph.D. diss., University of Pittsburgh, 1967.

Backstrom, Charles H. "The Progressive Party of Wisconsin, 1934-48." Ph.D. diss., University of Wisconsin, 1956.

Bader, Robert E. "The Curtailment of Railroad Service in Nebraska, 1920-1941." Ph.D. diss., University of Nebraska, 1952.

Baker, Samuel B. "The Cleveland Chamber of Commerce in the Great Depression." Ph.D. diss., Case Western Reserve University, 1984.

Bean, Philip Garth. "Illinois Politics during the New Deal." Ph.D. diss., University of Illinois, 1976.

Biles, William Roger. "Mayor Edward J. Kelly of Chicago: Big City Boss in Depression and War." Ph.D. diss., University of Illinois at Chicago Circle, 1981.

Floyd, Fred. "A History of the Dust Bowl." Ph.D. diss., University of Oklahoma, 1950.

Hamel, April Lee. "The Jefferson National Expansion Memorial: A Depression Relief Project in Missouri." Ph.D. diss., Saint Louis University, 1983.

Hamilton, Donald Eugene. "A History of FERA and WPA Workers' Education: The Indiana Experience 1933-1943." Ph.D. diss., Ball State University, 1984.

Hinderaker, Ivan H. "Harold Stassen and Developments in the Republican Party in Minnesota, 1937-43." Ph.D. diss., University of Minnesota, 1950.

Jones, Gene D. "The Local Political Significance of New Deal Relief Legislation in Chicago, 1932-1940." Ph.D. diss., Northwestern University, 1970.

Keiffer, William A. "Development of Family Social Work: A Case Study of the St. Louis Provident Association, 1920-1940." Ph.D. diss., Saint Louis University, 1984.

Maurer, David J. "Public Relief Programs and Policies in Ohio, 1929-1939." Ph.D. diss., Ohio University, 1962.

Meister, Richard J. "A History of Gary, Indiana, 1930-1940." Ph.D. diss., University of Notre Dame, 1967.

Mirel, Jeffrey E. "Politics and Public Education in the Great Depression: Detroit, 1929-1940." Ph.D. diss., University of Michigan, 1984.

Mitchell, Franklin D. "Embattled Democracy: Missouri Democratic Politics, 1918-1932." Ph.D. diss., University of Missouri, 1964.

Ortquist, Richard T. "Depression Politics in Michigan, 1929-1933." Ph.D. diss., University of Michigan, 1968.

Schruben, Francis W. "Kansas During the Great Depression, 1930-36." Ph.D. diss., University of California, Los Angeles, 1961.

Van Winkle, Mary L. "Education and Ethnicity in the 1930's in a Minnesota Mining Community." Ph.D. diss., Harvard University, 1982.

Ware, James W. "Black Blizzard: The Dust Bowl of the 1930's." Ph.D. diss., Oklahoma State University, 1977.

9.4   SOUTH: Alabama, Arkansas, Florida, Georgia, Kentucky, Louisiana, Mississippi, North Carolina, South Carolina, Tennessee, Virginia

Books

Akins, Bill, and Genevieve Wiggins, eds. Hard Times Remembered: A Study of the Depression in McMinn County. Athens, Tennessee: McMinn County Historical Society, 1983.

Alexander, Donald Crichton. The Arkansas Plantation, 1920-1942. New Haven: Yale University Press, 1943.

Badger, Anthony J. North Carolina and the New Deal. Raleigh: North Carolina Department of Cultural Resources, 1981.

_____. Prosperity Road: The New Deal, Tobacco, and North Carolina. Chapel Hill: University of North Carolina Press, 1980.

Biles, Roger . Memphis in the Great Depression. Knoxville: University of Tennessee Press, 1986.

Blakey, George T. Hard Times and New Deal in Kentucky, 1929-1939. Lexington: University Press of Kentucky, 1986.

Brannan, Beverly W., and David Horvath, eds. A Kentucky Album: Farm Security Administration Photographs, 1935-1943. Lexington: University Press of Kentucky, 1986.

Brown, James Seay, Jr. Up Before Daylight: Life Histories from the Alabama Writers Project, 1938-1939. University: University of Alabama Press, 1982.

Cobb, James C., and Michael V. Namorato, eds. The New Deal and the South. Jackson: University Press of Mississippi, 1984.

Dollard, John. Caste and Class in a Southern Town. New Haven: Yale University Press, 1937.

Duffus, Robert L. The Valley and Its People: A Portrait of TVA. New York: Knopf, 1944.

Heinemann, Ronald L. Depression and New Deal in Virginia: The Enduring Dominion. Charlottesville: University Press of Virginia, 1983.

Holmes, Michael S. The New Deal in Georgia: An Administrative History. Westport, Conn.: Greenwood, 1974.

Johnson, Brooks. Mountaineers to Main Streets: The Old Dominion as seen through the Farm Security Administration Photographs. Norfolk: Chrysler Museum, 1985.

Kane, Harnett T. Louisiana Hayride: The American Rehearsal for Dictatorship, 1928-1940. New York: B. W. Morrow, 1941.

Kirby, Jack Temple. Rural Worlds Lost: The American South, 1920-1960. Baton Rouge: Louisiana State University Press, 1987.

Krueger, Thomas A. And Promises to Keep: The Southern Conference for Human Welfare, 1938-1948. Nashville: Vanderbilt University Press, 1967.

Minton, John Dean. The New Deal in Tennessee, 1932-1938. New York: Garland, 1979.

Mitchell, Virgil L. The Civil Works Administration in Louisiana: A Study in New Deal Relief, 1933-1934. Lafayette: University of Southwestern Louisiana, 1976.

Noblin, Stuart. The Grange in North Carolina, 1929-1954: A Story of Agricultural Progress. Greensboro, N.C.: North Carolina State Grange, 1954.

Puryear, Elmer L. Democratic Party Dissension in North Carolina, 1928-1936. Chapel Hill: University of North Carolina Press, 1962.

Robinson, John L. Living Hard: Southern Americans in the Great Depression. Washington: University Press of America, 1981.

Saloutos, Theodore. Farmer Movements in the South, 1865-1933. Berkeley: University of California Press, 1960.

Sellers, James B. The Prohibition Movement in Alabama, 1702-1943. Chapel Hill: University of North Carolina Press, 1943.

Sindler, Allen P. Huey Long's Louisiana: State Politics, 1920-1952. Baltimore: Johns Hopkins University Press, 1956.

Snell, William R., ed. Hard Times Remembered: Bradley County and the Great Depression: Selected Essays and Recollections. Cleveland, Tenn.: Bradley County Historical Society, 1983.

Sosna, Morton. In Search of the Silent South: Southern Liberals and the Race Issue. New York: Columbia University Press, 1977.

Tharpe, William G., and Norman L. Collins, eds. From Hearth and Hoe: Union County, Tennessee, 1910-1940. Maynardville, Tenn.: Union County Historical Society, 1985.

Thomason, Michael V. R. Trying Times: Alabama Photographs, 1917-1945. University: University of Alabama Press, 1985.

Tindall, George B. The Disruption of the Solid South. Athens: University of Georgia Press, 1972.

_____. The Emergence of the New South, 1913-1945. Baton Rouge: Louisiana State University Press, 1967.

Vance, Rupert B. How the Other Half Is Housed: A Pictorial Record of Sub-minimum
    Farm Housing in the South. Chapel Hill: University of North Carolina Press,
    1936.
_____ and Gordon W. Blackwell. New Farm Homes for Old: A Study of Rural
    Public Housing in the South. University, Ala.: University of Alabama Press,
    1946.
Whitener, Daniel J. Prohibition in North Carolina, 1715-1946. Chapel Hill: University
    of North Carolina Press, 1946.
Whitman, Willson. God's Valley: People and Power Along the Tennessee River. New
    York: Viking, 1939.

Articles

Adams, J. W. "Governor Gordon Browning, Campaigner Extraordinary--The 1936
    Election for Governor." West Tennessee Historical Society Papers 30 (1976):
    5-23.
Armbrester, Margaret E. "John Temple Graves II: A Southern Liberal Views the
    New Deal." Alabama Review 32 (July 1979): 203-13.
Bentley, H. Blair. "Pedagogy in Peril: Education in the Volunteer State During the
    Depression." Tennessee Historical Quarterly 43 (Summer 1984): 173-88.
Biles, Roger. "The Persistence of the Past: Memphis in the Great Depression."
    Journal of Southern History 52 (May 1986); 183-212.
Black, Henry. "A Spear of Hell: The Tupelo Tornedo of 1936." Journal of Mississippi
    History 38 (Aug. 1976): 263-78.
Blakey, George T. "Kentucky Youth and the New Deal." Filson Club History
    Quarterly 60 (Jan. 1986): 37-68.
_____. "The New Deal and Rural Kentucky, 1933-1941." Register of the
    Kentucky Historical Society 84 (Spring 1986): 146-91.
Brown, D. Clayton. "Hen Eggs to Kilowatts: Arkansas Rural Electrification." Red
    River Valley Historical Review 3 (Winter 1978): 119-25.
_____. "North Carolina Rural Electrification: Precedent of the REA." North
    Carolina Historical Review 59 (April 1982): 109-24.
Burran, James A. "The WPA in Nashville, 1935-43." Tennessee Historical Quarterly
    34 (Fall 1975): 293-306.
Caldwell, Mary French. "Another Breakfast at the Hermitage: Part II, 1934."
    Tennessee Historical Quarterly 26 (Fall 1967): 249-54.
Cann, Marvin L. "The End of a Political Myth: The South Carolina Gubernatorial
    Campaign of 1938." South Carolina Historical Magazine 72 (July 1971): 139-
    49.
Cobb, William H. "The State Legislature and the 'Reds': Arkansas's General
    Assembly v. Commonwealth College, 1935-1937." Arkansas Historical
    Quarterly 45 (Spring 1986): 3-18.
Cofer, Richard. "Bootleggers in the Backwoods: Prohibition and the Depression in
    Hernando County." Tampa Bay History 1 (Spring-Summer 1979): 17-23.

Cox, Merlin G. "David Scholtz: New Deal Governor of Florida." Florida Historical Quarterly 46 (Oct. 1964): 142-52.

Cronon, E. David. "A Southern Progressive Looks at the New Deal." Journal of Southern History 24 (May 1958): 151-76.

Culbert, David H. "The Infinite Variety of Mass Experience: The Great Depression, W.P.A. Interviews, and Student Family History Projects." Louisiana History 19 (Winter 1978): 43-63.

Daniel, Pete. "The Transformation of the Rural South: 1930 to the Present." Agricultural History 55 (July 1981): 231-248.

Davis, Steve. "The South as 'the Nation's No. 1 Economic Problem': The NEC Report of 1938." Georgia Historical Quarterly 62 (Summer 1978): 119-32.

Dubay, Robert W. "Mississippi and the Proposed Federal Anti-Lynching Bills of 1937-1938." Southern Quarterly 7 (Oct. 1968): 73-89.

Ellis, William E. "'The Harvest Moon Was Shinin' on the Streets of Shelbyville': Southern Honor and the Death of General Henry H. Denhardt, 1937." Register of the Kentucky Historical Society 84 (Autumn 1986): 361-96.

Emerson, Thomas I. "Southern Justice in the Thirties." Civil Liberties Review 4 (May/June 1977): 70-74.

Fleming, Douglas L. "The New Deal in Atlanta: A Review of the Major Programs." Atlanta Historical Journal 30 (Spring 1986): 23-45.

Green, Fletcher. "Resurgent Southern Sectionalism, 1933-1955." North Carolina Historical Review 33 (April 1956): 222-40.

Hass, Edward F. "New Orleans on the Half Shell: The Maestri Era, 1936-1946." Louisiana History 13 (Summer 1972): 283-310.

Heinemann, Ronald L. "Blue Eagle or Black Buzzard?: The National Recovery Administration in Virginia." Virginia Magazine of History and Biography 89 (Jan. 1981): 90-100.

Heleniak, Roman. "Local Reaction to the Great Depression in New Orleans, 1929-1933." Louisiana History 10 (Fall 1969): 289-306.

Herndon, Jane Walker. "Ed Rivers and Georgia's 'Little New Deal.'" Atlanta Historical Journal 30 (Spring 1986): 97-105..

Hicks, Floyd W., and C. Roger Lambert. "Food for the Hungry: Federal Food Programs in Arkansas, 1933-1942." Arkansas Historical Quarterly 37 (Spring 1978): 23-43.

Hines, Tom S., Jr. "Mississippi and the Repeal of Prohibition: A Study of the Controversy over the Twenty-First Amendment." Journal of Mississippi History 24 (Jan. 1962): 1-39.

Hirsch, Jerrold, and Tom E. Terill. "Conceptualization and Implementation: Some Thoughts on Reading the Federal Writers' Project Southern Life Histories." Southern Studies 18 (Fall 1979): 351-62.

Holley, Donald. "Old and New Worlds in the New Deal Resettlement Program: Two Louisiana Projects." Louisiana History 11 (Spring 1970): 137-66.

Humphreys, Hubert. "In a Sense Experimental: The Civilian Conservation Corps in Louisiana." Louisiana History 4 (Fall 1964): 345-67; 6 (Winter 1965): 27-52.

Hunter, Robert F. "The AAA Between Neighbors: Virginia, North Carolina, and the New Deal Farm Program." Journal of Southern History 44 (Nov. 1978): 537-70.

_____. "Virginia and the New Deal." In The New Deal: The State and Local Levels ed. by John Braeman, Robert H. Bremner, and David Brody (Columbus: Ohio State University Press, 1975), pp. 103-36.

Ingalls, Robert P. "The Tampa Flogging Case: Urban Vigilantism." Florida Historical Quarterly 56 (July 1977): 13-27.

Ingram, Earl. "The Federal Emergency Relief Administration in Louisiana." Louisiana History 14 (Spring 1973): 194-202.

Klingman, Peter D. "Ernest Graham and the Hialeah Charter Fight of 1937." Tequesta 34 (1974): 37-43.

Klotter, James C., and John W. Muir. "Boss Ben Johnson, the Highway Commission, and Kentucky Politics, 1927-1937." Register of the Kentucky Historical Society 84 (Winter 1986): 18-50.

Koeniger, A. Cash. "The New Deal and the States: Roosevelt versus the Byrd Organization in Virginia." Journal of American History 68 (March 1982): 876-96.

Laird, William E., and James R. Rinehart. "Post-Civil War South and the Great Depression: A Suggested Parallel." Mid-America 48 (July 1966): 206-10.

Lambert, C. Roger. "The 1930 Drought in Northeast Arkansas." Craighead County Historical Quarterly 15 (Feb. 1977): 1-7

_____ and Floyd W. Hicks. "Food for the Hungry: Federal Food Programs in Arkansas, 1933-1942." Arkansas Historical Quarterly 37 (Spring 1978): 23-43.

Lee, David D. "The Triumph of Boss Crump: The Tennessee Gubernatorial Election of 1932." Tennessee Historical Quarterly 35 (Winter 1976): 393-413.

_____. "The Attempt to Impeach Governor Horton." Tennessee Historical Quarterly 34 (Summer 1975): 188-201.

Leopold, Robert J. "The Kentucky WPA Relief and Politics, May-November 1935." Filson Club History Quarterly 49 (April 1975): 152-68.

_____. "The Kentucky WPA: Relief and Politics, May-November, 1935." Filson Club History Quarterly 49 (April 1979): 152-68.

Lewis, John E. "Repeal in Alabama." Alabama Review 20 (Oct. 1967): 263-71.

Long, Durward. "Key West and the New Deal, 1934-1936." Florida Historical Quarterly 46 (Jan. 1968): 209-18.

Lowry, Charles B. "The PWA in Tampa: A Case Study." Florida Historical Quarterly 52 (April 1974): 363-80.

Majors, William R. "Gordon Browning and Tennessee Politics, 1937-1939." Tennessee Historical Quarterly 28 (Spring 1969): 57-69.

Miller, Kathleen Atkinson. "The Ladies and the Lynchers: A Look at the Association of Southern Women for the Prevention of Lynching." Southern Studies 17 (Fall 1978): 221-40.

Moore, John Robert. "The New Deal in Louisiana." In The New Deal: The State and Local Levels ed. by John Braeman, Robert H. Bremner, and David Brody (Columbus: Ohio State University Press, 1975): pp. 137-165.

Moran, Robert E., Sr. "Public Relief in Louisiana from 1928 to 1960." Louisiana History 14 (Fall 1973): 369-85.

Morgan, Chester M. "Senator G. Bilbo, the New Deal, and Mississippi Politics (1934-1940)." Journal of Mississippi History 47 (Aug. 1985): 147-64.

Morgan, Thomas S., Jr. "A 'Folly . . . Manifest to Everyone': The Movement to Enact Unemployment Insurance Legislation in North Carolina, 1935-1936." North Carolina Historical Review 52 (July 1975): 283-302.

Mugleston, William F. "Cornpone and Potlikker: A Moment of Relief in the Great Depression." Louisiana History 16 (Summer 1975): 279-288.

Murray, Gail S. "Forty Years Ago: The Great Depression Comes to Arkansas." Arkansas Historical Quarterly 29 (Winter 1970): 291-312.

Nelson, Lawrence J. "Welfare Capitalism on a Mississippi Plantation in the Great Depression." Journal of Southern History 50 (May 1984): 225-50.

Nixon, H. Clarence. "The New Deal and the South." Virginia Quarterly Review 19 (Summer 1943): 321-33.

Patterson, James T. "The Failure of Party Realignment in the South, 1937-1939." Journal of Politics 27 (Aug. 1965): 602-17.

Pleasant, John R., Jr. "Ruffin G. Pleasant and Huey P. Long on the Prisoner-Stripe Controversy." Louisiana History 15 (Fall 1975): 357-66.

Price, Michael E. "The New Deal in Tennessee: The Highlander Folk School and Worker Response in Grundy County." Tennessee Historical Quarterly 43 (Summer 1984): 99-120.

Rable, George C. "The South and the Politics of Antilynching Legislation, 1920-1940." Journal of Southern History 51 (May 1985): 201-20.

Rainard, R. Lyn. "Ready Cash on Easy Terms: Local Responses to the Depression in Lee County." Florida Historical Quarterly 64 (Jan. 1986): 284-300.

Ray, Joseph M. "The Influence of the Tennessee Valley Authority on Government in the South." American Political Science Review 43 (Oct. 1949): 922-32.

Reed, Merl E. "FEPC and the Federal Agencies in the South." Journal of Negro History 65 (Winter 1980): 43-56.

Renegar, Judy. "The History of Wilson Dam and Muscle Shoals Properties." Journal of Muscle Shoals History 3 (1975): 58-64.

Robison, Daniel M. "From Tillman to Huey Long: Some Striking Leaders of the Rural South." Journal of Southern History 3 (No. 3, 1937): 288-310.

Simmons, Dennis E. "Conservation, Cooperation, and Controversy: The Establishment of Shenandoah National Park, 1924-1936." Virginia Magazine of History and Biography 89 (Oct. 1981): 387-404.

Smathers, Mike. "The Search for the Garden: Planned Communities." Southern Exposure 8 (Spring 1980): 57-63.

Smith, Douglas L. "Continuity and Change in the Urban South: The New Deal Experience." Atlanta Historical Journal 30 (Spring 1986): 7-22.

Smith, Mary Kay. "Dark Days of the Depression: Lonoke County, Arkansas, 1930-1933." Red River Valley Historical Review 7 (Fall 1982): 14-23.

Snell, William R. "Masked Men in the Magic City: Activities of the Revised Klan in Birmingham, 1916-1940." Alabama Historical Quarterly 34 (Fall-Winter 1972): 206-27.

Spears, James E. "Where Have All the Peddlers Gone?" Kentucky Folklore Record 21 (July-Sept. 1975): 77-81.

Stoesen, Alexander R. "Claude Pepper and the Florida Canal Controversy, 1939-1943." Florida Historical Quarterly 50 (Jan. 1972): 235-51.

Swint, Henry L. "Northern Interest in the Shoeless Southerner." Journal of Southern History 16 (Nov. 1950): 457-71.

Taylor, Paul F. "London: Focal Point of Kentucky Turbulence." Filson Club History Quarterly 49 (July 1975): 256-65.

Terrill, Tom, and Jerrold Hirsch. "Such As Us." Southern Exposure 6 (No.1, 1978): 67-72.

Thorton, J. Mills, III. "Alabama Politics, J. Thomas Heflin, and the Expulsion Movement of 1929." Alabama Review 21 (April 1968): 83-112.

Tindall, George B. "The 'Colonial Economy' and the Growth Psychology: The South in the 1930's." South Atlantic Quarterly 64 (Autumn 1965): 465-77.

Tobin, Sidney. "The Early New Deal in Baton Rouge as Viewed by the Daily Press." Louisiana History 10 (Fall 1969): 307-37.

Towns, Stuart. "A Louisiana Medicine Show: The Kingfish Elects an Arkansas Senator." Arkansas Historical Quarterly 25 (Summer 1966): 117-27.

Webb, Pamela. "By the Sweat of the Brow: The Back-to-the-Land Movement in Depression Arkansas." Arkansas Historical Quarterly 42 (Winter 1983): 332-45.

Whatley, Warren C. "Labor for the Picking: The New Deal in the South." Journal of Economic History 43 (Dec. 1983): 905-29.

Whisenhunt, Donald W. "The Great Depression in Kentucky: The Early Years." Register of the Kentucky Historical Society 67 (Jan. 1969): 55-62.

Williams, Bobby Joe. "Let There Be Light: Tennessee Valley Authority Comes to Memphis." West Tennessee Historical Society Papers. 30 (1976): 43-66.

Williams, John. "Struggles of the Thirties in the South." Political Affairs 44 (Feb. 1965): 15-25.

Winter, William. "Governor Mike Conner and the Sales Tax, 1932." Journal of Mississippi History 41 (Aug. 1979): 213-30.

Woodruff, Nan E. "The Failure of Relief During the Arkansas Drought of 1930-31." Arkansas Historical Quarterly 39 (Winter 1980): 301-13.

Wyche, Billy H. "Southern Industrialists View Organized Labor in the New Deal Years, 1933-1941." Southern Studies 19 (Summer 1980): 157-71.

Dissertations

Abrams, Douglas Carl. "North Carolina and the New Deal, 1932-1940." Ph.D. diss., University of Maryland, 1981.

Beckham, Sue Bridwell. "A Gentle Reconstruction: Depression Post Office Murals and Southern Culture." Ph.D. diss., University of Minnesota, 1984.

Cann, Marvin L. "Burnet Rhett Maybank and the New Deal in South Carolina, 1931-1941." Ph.D. diss., University of North Carolina, 1967.

Donaldson, Gary Alan. "A History of Louisiana's Rural Electric Cooperatives, 1937-1983." Ph.D. diss., Louisiana State University, 1983.

Fleming, Douglas Lee. "Atlanta, the Depression, and the New Deal." Ph.D. diss., Emory University, 1984.

Fossett, Roy E. "The Impact of the New Deal on Georgia Politics, 1933-1941." Ph.D. diss., University of Florida, 1960.

Heinemann, Ronald L. "Depression and New Deal in Virginia." Ph.D. diss., University of Virginia, 1968.

Holmes, Michael S. "The New Deal in Georgia: An Administrative History." Ph.D. diss., University of Wisconsin, 1969.

Lofton, Paul Stroman, Jr. "A Social and Economic History of Columbia, South Carolina, during the Great Depression, 1929-1940." Ph.D. diss., University of Texas, 1977.

Lyon, Edwin Austin, II. "New Deal Archaeology in the Southeast: WPA, TVA, NPS, 1934-1942." Ph.D. diss., Louisiana State University, 1982.

Minton, John D. "The New Deal in Tennessee, 1932-1938." Ph.D. diss., Vanderbilt University, 1959.

Morgan, Thomas S., Jr. "A Step toward Altruism: Relief and Welfare in North Carolina, 1930-1938." Ph.D. diss., University of North Carolina, 1969.

Smith, Douglas Lloyd. "The New Deal and the Urban South: The Advancement of a Southern Urban Consciousness during the Depression Decade." Ph.D. diss., University of Southern Mississippi, 1978.

Sudheendran, Kesavan. "Community Power Structure in Atlanta: A Study in Decision Making, 1920-1939." Ph.D. diss., Georgia State University, 1983.

Tate, Roger D., Jr. "Easing the Burden: The Era of Depression and New Deal in Mississippi." Ph.D. diss., University of Tennessee, 1978.

Tenfarelli, Ronda C. "The Southern Review: An Episode in Southern Intellectual History, 1935-1942." Ph.D diss., Louisiana State University, 1980.

Watkins, Charles Alan. "The Blurred Image: Documentary Photography and the Depression South." Ph.D. diss., University of Delaware, 1982.

Woodruff, Nan E. "The Great Southern Drought of 1930-31: A Study in Rural Relief." Ph.D. diss., University of Tennessee, 1977.

9.5   WEST: Alaska, Arizona, California, Colorado, Hawaii, Idaho, Montana, Nevada, New Mexico, Oklahoma, Oregon, Texas, Utah, Washington, Wyoming

Books

Blumell, Bruce D. The Development of Public Assistance in the State of Washington during the Great Depression. New York: Garland, 1984.

Burke, Robert E. Olson's New Deal for California. Berkeley: University of California Press, 1953.

Clark, Norman H. The Dry Years: Prohibition and Social Change in Washington. Seattle: University of Washington Press, 1965.

Hillman, Arthur. The Unemployed Citizen's League of Seattle. Seattle: University of Seattle Press, 1934.

Karlin, Jules A. Joseph M. Dixon of Montana: Part 2, Governor Versus the Anaconda 1917-1934. Missoula: University of Montana, 1974.

Lowitt, Richard. The New Deal and the West. Bloomington: Indiana University Press, 1984.

Malone, Michael P. C. Ben Ross and the New Deal in Idaho. Seattle: University of Washington Press, 1970.

McKay, Seth Shepard. W. Lee O'Daniel and Texas Politics, 1938-1942. Lubbock: Texas Technological College Research Funds, 1944.

Ostrander, Gilman M. The Prohibition Movement in California, 1848-1933. Berkeley: University of California Press, 1957.

Patenaude, Lionel V. Texans, Politics and the New Deal. New York: Garland, 1983.

Stein, Walter J. California and the Dust Bowl Migration. Westport, Conn.: Greenwood, 1973.

Whisenhunt, Donald W. The Depression in Texas. Boston: American Press, 1982.

_____. The Depression in Texas: The Hoover Years. New York: Garland, 1983.

_____, ed. The Depression in the Southwest. Port Washington, N.Y.: Kennikat, 1980.

Wickens, James F. Colorado in the Great Depression. New York: Garland, 1979.

Articles

Allen, Howard W., and Erik W. Austin. "From the Populist Era to the New Deal: A Study of Partisan Realignment in Washington State, 1889-1950." Social Science History 3 (Winter 1979): 115-43.

Antognini, Richard. "The Role of A. P. Giannini in the 1934 California Gubernatorial Election." Southern California Quarterly 57 (Spring 1975): 53-86.

Arrington, Leonard J. "Arizona in the Great Depression Years." Arizona Review 17 (Dec. 1968): 11-19.

_____. "Idaho and the Great Depression." Idaho Yesterdays 13 (Summer 1969): 2-8.

_____. "The New Deal in the West: A Preliminary Statistical Inquiry." Pacific Historical Review 38 (Aug. 1969): 311-27.

_____. "The Sagebrush Resurrection: New Deal Expenditures in the Western States, 1933-1939." Pacific Historical Review 52 (Feb. 1983): 1-16.

_____. "Utah's Great Drought of 1934." Utah Historical Quarterly 54 (Summer 1986): 245-64.

_____ and Lowell Dittmer. "Reclamation in Three Layers: The Ogden River Project, 1934-1965." Pacific Historical Review 35 (Feb. 1966): 15-34.

Austin, Judith "The CCC in Idaho: An Anniversary View." Idaho Yesterdays 27 (Fall 1983): 13-18.

Barger, Bob "Raymond L. Haight and the Commonwealth Progressive Campaign of 1934." California Historical Society Quarterly 43 (Sept. 1964): 219-30.

Boyle, Robert D. "Chaos in the East Texas Oil Field, 1930-1935." Southwestern Historical Quarterly 69 (Jan. 1966): 340-52.

Bryant, Keith L., Jr. "Oklahoma and the New Deal." In The New Deal: The State and Local Levels ed. by John Braeman, Robert H. Bremner, and David Brody (Columbus: Ohio State University Press, 1975), pp. 166-97.

Burton, Robert E. "The New Deal in Oregon." In The New Deal: The State and Local Levels ed. by John Braeman, Robert H. Bremner, and David Brody (Columbus: Ohio State University Press, 1975), pp. 355-75.

Cannon, Brian Q. "Struggle Against Great Odds: Challenges in Utah's Marginal Agricultural Areas, 1925-39." Utah Historical Quarterly 54 (Fall 1986): 308-27.

Carroll, Eugene T. "John B. Kendrick's Fight for Western Water Legislation, 1917-1933." Annals of Wyoming 50 (Fall 1978): 319-33.

Chan, Loren B. "California during the Early 1930s: The Administration of Governor James Rolph, Jr., 1931-1934." Southern California Quarterly 63 (Fall 1981): 262-82.

Clark, Blue. "'To Preserve Local History:' The WPA Historical Records Survey in Oklahoma, 1936-1942." Chronicles of Oklahoma 61 (Summer 1985): 168-79.

Coombs, F. Alan. "The Impact of the New Deal on Wyoming Politics." In The New Deal: The State and Local Levels ed. by John Braeman, Robert H. Bremner, and David Brody (Columbus: Ohio State University Press, 1975), pp. 198-239.

Doerr, Arthur H. "Dry Conditions in Oklahoma in the 1930's and 1950's as Delimited by the Original Thornthwaite Climatic Classification." Great Plains Journal 2 (Spring 1963): 77-79.

_____ and Stephen M. Sutherland. "Humid and Dry Cycles in Oklahoma in the Period, 1920-1960." Great Plains Journal 5 (Spring 1966)): 84-94.

Donahue, Jim. "Drainage Districts and the Great Depression." Annals of Wyoming 53 (Fall 1981): 12-21.

Downing, Marvin. "The P.W.A. and the Acquisition of the Fort Worth Public Library Building, 1933-1939." Texas Libraries 27 (Fall 1965): 126-32.

Flynn, George Q. "The New Deal and Local Archives: The Pacific Northwest." American Archivist 33 (Jan. 1970): 41-52

Fossey, W. Richard. "'Talkin' Dust Bowl Blues': A Study of Oklahoma's Cultural Identity During the Great Depression." Chronicles of Oklahoma 55 (Spring 1977): 12-33.

Foster, Mark S. "Giant of the West: Henry J. Kaiser and Regional Industrialization, 1930-1950." Business History Review 59 (Spring 1985): 1-23.

Freidel, Frank. "Franklin D. Roosevelt in the Northwest: Informal Glimpses." Pacific Northwest Quarterly 76 (Oct. 1985): 122-31.

Hardeman, Nicholas P. "The Depression-Born Port of Stockton." Pacific Historian 27 (Winter 1983): 51-59.

Heath, Virgil, with John Clark Hunt. "Alaska CCC Days." Alaska Journal 2 (Spring 1972): 51-56.

Hendrickson, Gordon O. "The WPA Writers' Project in Wyoming: History and Collections." Annals of Wyoming 49 (Fall 1977): 175-92.

Hendrikson, Kenneth E., Jr. "Politics of Culture: The Federal Music Project in Oklahoma." Chronicles of Oklahoma 63 (Winter 1985-86): 361-75.

Henstell, Bruce. "When the Lid Blew Off Los Angeles." Westways 69 (November 1977): 32-35, 68.

Hinckley, Ted C. "Depression Anxieties Midst a Pasadena Eddy." Pacific Historian 27 (Winter 1983): 27-32.

Hine, Robert V. "Foreclosure in Los Angeles." Pacific Historian 27 (Winter 1983): 33-37.

Hinton, Wayne K. "The Economics of Ambivalence: Utah's Depression Experience." Utah Historical Quarterly 54 (Summer 1986): 268-85

Hoffman, Charles S. "Drought and Depression Migration into Oregon, 1930 to 1936." Monthly Labor Review 46 (Jan. 1938): 27-35.

Holland, Reid "Life in Oklahoma's Civilian Conservation Corps." Chronicles of Oklahoma 48 (Summer 1970): 224-34.

_____. "The Civilian Conservation Corps in the City: Tulsa and Oklahoma City in the 1930s." Chronicles of Oklahoma 53 (Fall 1975): 367-75.

Huffman, Roy E. "Montana's Contributions to New Deal Farm Policy." Agricultural History 33 (Oct. 1959): 164-67.

Johnson, William R. "Rural Rehabilitation in the New Deal: The Ropesville Project." Southwestern Historical Quarterly 79 (Jan. 1976): 279-95.

Kelly, William R. "Colorado-Big Thompson Initiation, 1933-1938: The Story of a Gigantic Irrigation Project in Embryo." Colorado Magazine 34 (Jan. 1957): 66-74.

Kirkendall, Richard S. "Social Science in the Central Valley of California: An Episode." California Historical Quarterly 43 (Sept. 1964): 195-218.

Koschmann, Fred. "Great Days in a Great Land." Alaska Journal 9 (Winter 1979): 90-93.

Lambert, C. Roger. "Slaughter of the Innocents in Oklahoma: The Emergency Hog Slaughter of 1933." Red River Valley Historical Review 7 (Fall 1982): 42-49.

Lane, James B. "Joseph B. Poindexter and Hawaii During the New Deal." Pacific Northwest Quarterly 62 (Jan. 1971): 7-15.

Larsen, Charles E. "The Epic Campaign of 1934." Pacific Historical Review 27 (May 1958): 127-47.

Larson, T. A. "The New Deal in Wyoming." Pacific Historical Review 38 (August 1969): 249-73.

Leiby, James. "State Welfare Administration in California, 1930-1945." Southern California Quarterly 55 (Fall 1973): 303-18.

Lotchin, Roger W. "The City and the Sword: San Francisco and the Rise of the Metropolitan-Military Complex, 1919-1941." Journal of American History 65 (March 1979): 996-1020.

Lovin, Hugh T. "The 'Farmer-Labor' Movement in Idaho, 1933-1938." Journal of the West 18 (April 1979): 21-29.

_____. "Toward a Farmer-Labor Party in Oregon, 1933-1938." Oregon Historical Quarterly 76 (June 1975): 135-51.

Malone, Michael P. "Montana Politics and the New Deal." Montana: The Magazine of Western History 21 (January 1971): 2-11.

_____. "Montana Politics at the Crossroads, 1932-1933." Pacific Northwest Quarterly 69 (Jan. 1978): 20-29.

_____. "The Montana New Dealers." In The New Deal: The State and Local Levels ed. by John Braeman, Robert H. Bremner, and David Brody (Coumbus: Ohio State University Press, 1975), pp. 240-68.

_____. "The New Deal in Idaho." Pacific Historical Review 38 (Aug. 1969): 293-310.

Maxwell, Margaret F. "The Depression in Tavapai County." Journal of Arizona History 23 (Summer 1982): 171-86.

McDean, Harry C. "The 'Okie' Migration as a Socio-Economic Necessity in Oklahoma." Red River Valley Historical Review 3 (Winter 1978): 77-92.

McGinty, Brian. "Shadows in St. James Park." California History 57 (Winter 1978-798): 290-307.

Mergen, Bernard. "Denver and the War on Unemployment." Colorado Magazine 47 (Fall 1970): 326-37.

Moehring, Eugene P. "Public Works and the New Deal in Las Vegas, 1933-1940." Nevada Historical Society Quarterly 24 (Summer 1981): 107-29.

Morris, James K. "Outpost of the Cooperative Commonwealth: The History of the Llano Del Rio Colony in Gila, New Mexico, 1932-1935." New Mexico Historical Review 56 (April 1981): 177-95.

Mullins, William H. "Self-Help in Seattle, 1931-1932: Herbert Hoover's Concept of Cooperative Individualism and the Unemployed Citizens' League." Pacific Northwest Quarterly 72 (Jan. 1981): 11-19.

Nash, Gerald D. "The American West in the Great Depression." In The Great Plains Experience ed. by James Wright and Sara Rosenberg (Lincoln: University of Mid-America, 1978), pp. 363-75.

Newbill, James G. "Yakima and the Wobblies, 1910-1936." In At the Point of Production: The Local History of the I.W.W. ed. by Joseph R. Conlin (Westport, Conn.: Greenwood Press, 1981), pp. 167-90.

_____. "Famers and Wobblies in the Yakima Valley, 1933." Pacific Northwest Quarterly 68 (April 1977): 80-87.

O'Neal, Bill. "The Personal Side of the Great Depression in East Texas." East Texas Historical Journal 18 (No. 2, 1980): 3-12.

Olson, James S., and Liz Byford. "Oasis in East Texas: Conroe and the Depression, 1929-1933." Texana 12 (No.2, 1974): 141-48.

Patenaude, Lionel "The New Deal: Its Effect on the Social Fabric of Texas Society, 1933-1939." Social Science Journal 14 (Oct. 1977): 51-60.

Patterson, James T. "The New Deal in the West." Pacific Historical Review 38 (Aug. 1969): 317-27.

Pew, Thomas W., Jr. "Route 66: Ghost Road of the Okies." American Heritage 28 (Aug. 1977): 24-33.

Pickens, William. "Bronson Cutting vs. Dennis Chavez: Battle of the Patrones in New Mexico, 1934." New Mexico Historical Review 47 (Jan. 1972): 337-59.

_____. "The New Deal in New Mexico." In The New Deal: The State and Local Levels ed. by John Braeman, Robert H. Bremner, and David Brody (Columbus: Ohio State University Press, 1975), pp. 311-54.

_____. "Cutting vs. Chavez: A Reply to Wolf's Comments." New Mexico Historical Review 47 (Oct. 1972): 357-59.

Powell, Charles Stewart. "Depression Days in Tobar." Northeastern Nevada Historical Society Quarterly 7 (Fall 1978): 126-41.

Pritchard, Robert L. "Orange County During the Depressed Thirties: A Study in Twentieth-Century California Local History." Southern California Quarterly 50 (Jan. 1968): 191-205.

Quinn, R. Thomas "Out of the Depression's Depths: Henry H. Blood's First Year as Governor." Utah Historical Quarterly 54 (Summer 1986): 216-39.

Richardson, Elmo R. "Federal Park Policy in Utah: The Escalante National Monument Controversy of 1935-1940." Utah Historical Quarterly 33 (Spring 1965): 109-33.

Rogers, Jane. "The WPA Statewide Library Project in Texas." Texas Libraries 34 (Winter 1972): 209-18.

Ruetten, Richard. "Burton K. Wheeler and the Montana Connection." Montana: The Magazine of Western History 27 (July 1977): 2-19.

_____. "Showdown in Montana, 1938: Burton Wheeler's Role in the Defeat of Jerry O'Connell." Pacific Northwest Quarterly 54 (Jan. 1963): 19-29.

Saindon, Bob, and Bunky Sullivan. "Taming the Missouri and Treating the Depression: Fort Peck Dam." Montana: The Magazine of Western History 27 (July 1977): 34-57.

Schwartz, Bonnie Fox. "Social Workers and New Deal Politicians in Conflict: California's Branion-Williams Case, 1933-1934." Pacific Historical Review 42 (Feb. 1973): 53-73.

Scott, George W. "The New Order of Cincinnatus: Municipal Politics in Seattle During the 1930's." Pacific Northwest Quarterly 64 (1973): 137-46.

Shinn, Paul L. "Eugene in the Depression, 1929-1935." Oregon Historical Quarterly 86 (Spring 1985): 341-69.

Singer, Donald L. "Upton Sinclair and the California Gubernatorial Campaign of 1934." Southern California Quarterly 56 (Winter 1974): 375-406.

Sonnichsen, C. L. "Hard Times in Tucson." Journal of Arizona History 22 (Spring 1981): 23-62.

_____ and M. G. McKinney. "El Paso--from War to Depression." Southwest Historical Quarterly 74 (Oct. 1970): 357-71.

Swanson, Merwin R. "Pocatello's Business Community and the New Deal." Idaho Yesterdays 21 (Fall 1977): 9-15.

_____. "The New Deal in Pocatello." Idaho Yesterdays 23 (Summer 1979): 53-57.

Swartout, Robert, Jr. "The Road over Neahkahnie Mountain, Oregon: A Case Study in Pacific Northwest Transportation History." Pacific Historian 21 (Fall 1977): 300-8.

Vindex, Charles. "Survival on the High Plains, 1929-1934." Montana: The Magazine of Western History 28 (Oct. 1978): 2-11.

Voeltz, Herman C. "Genesis and Development of a Regional Power Agency in the Pacific Northwest, 1933-1943." Pacific Northwest Quarterly 53 (April 1962): 65-76.

Wade, Michael G. "Back to the Land: The Woodlake Community, 1933-1943." East Texas Historical Journal 21 (No. 2, 1983): 46-56.

Ware, James. "The Sooner NRA: New Deal Recovery in Oklahoma." Chronicles of Oklahoma 54 (Fall 1976): 334-51.

Watson, Thomas. "The PWA Comes to the Red River Valley: Phase I, Non-Federal Projects in Texas, June 1933-February 1934." Red River Valley Historical Review 1 (Summer 1974): 146-64.

Whisenhunt, Donald. "The Texas Attitude Toward Relief, 1929-1933." Panhandle-Plains Historical Review 46 (1973): 94-112.

_____. "Depression in Tyler: A Labor View." Chronicles of Smith County, Texas 19 (Summer 1980): 19-22.

_____. "East Texas and the Stock Market Crash." East Texas Historical Journal 19 (Jan. 1981): 3-11.

_____. "Maury Maverick and the Diga Relief Colony, 1932-1933." Texana 9 (Summer 1971): 249-59.

_____. "The Bard in the Depression: Texas Style." Journal of Popular Culture 2 (Winter 1968): 370-86.

_____. "The Texan as a Radical, 1929-1933." Social Science Journal 14 (Oct. 1977): 61-72.

_____. "There is no Depression." Red River Valley Historical Review 5 (Fall 1980): 4-16.

_____. "'We've Got the Hoover Blues': Oklahoma Transiency in the Days of the Great Depression." In Hard Times in Oklahoma: The Depression Years ed. by Kenneth E. Hendrickson, Jr. (Oklahoma City: Oklahoma Historical Society, 1983).

_____. "West Texas and the Stock Market Crash of 1929." West Texas Historical Association Yearbook 15 (1979): 59-69.

Wickens, James F. "Depression and the New Deal in Colorado." In The New Deal:
   The State and Local Levels ed. by John Braeman, Robert H. Bremner, and
   David Brody (Columbus: Ohio State University Press, 1975), pp. 269-310.
   _____. "The New Deal in Colorado." Pacific Historical Review 38 (August
   1969): 275-291.
Wilson, William H. "Ahead of the Times: The Alaska Railroad and Tourism, 1924-
   1941." Alaska Journal 7 (Winter 1977): 18-24.
   _____. "The Alaska Railroad and Coal: Development of a Federal Policy, 1914-
   1939." Pacific Northwest Quarterly 73 (April 1982): 66-77.
Zimmerman, Tom. "'Ham and Eggs, Everybody!'" Southern California Quarterly 62
   (Spring 1980): 77-96.

Dissertations

Casey, Jack T. "Legislative History of the Central Valley Project, 1933-1949." Ph.D.
   diss., University of California, Berkeley, 1949.
Chinn, Ronald E. "Democratic Party Politics in California, 1920--56." Ph.D. diss.,
   University of California, Berkeley, 1958.
Delmatier, Royce D. "The Rebirth of the Democratic Party in California, 1928-1938."
   Ph.D. diss., University of California, Berkeley, 1955.
Gray, James. "The American Civil Liberties Union of Southern California and
   Imperial Valley Agricultural Labor Disturbances, 1930, 1934." Ph.D. diss.,
   University of California, Los Angeles, 1966.
Gregory, James Noble. "The Dust Bowl Migration and the Emergence of an Okie
   Subculture in California, 1930-1950." Ph.D. diss., University of California,
   Berkeley, 1983.
Huddleston, John David. "Good Roads for Texas: A History of the Texas Highway
   Department, 1917-1947." Ph.D. diss., Texas A & M University, 1981.
Kotlanger, Michael John. "Phoenix, Arizona: 1920-1940." Ph.D. diss., Arizona State
   University, 1983.
Malone Michael P. "C. Ben Ross and the New Deal in Idaho." Ph.D. diss.,
   Washington State University, 1966.
Manes, Sheila Goldring. "Depression Pioneers: The Conclusion of an American
   Odyssey. Oklahoma to California, 1930-1950, A Reinterpretation." Ph.D. diss.,
   University of California, Los Angeles, 1982.
Matthews, Glenna Christine. "A California Middletown: The Social History of San
   Jose in the Depression." Ph.D. diss., Stanford University, 1977.
Mullins, William Henry. "San Francisco and Seattle during the Hoover Years of the
   Depression: 1929-1933." Ph.D. diss., University of Washington, 1975.
Patenaude, Lionel V. "The New Deal and Texas." Ph.D. diss., University of Texas,
   1953.
Posner, Russell M. "State Politics and the Bank of America, 1920-1934." Ph.D. diss.,
   University of California, Berkeley, 1956.

Sherman, Jacqueline G. "The Oklahomans in California during the Depression Decade, 1931-1941." Ph.D. diss., University of California, Los Angeles, 1970.

Sitton, Thomas Joseph. "Urban Politics and Reform in New Deal Los Angeles: The Recall of Mayor Frank L. Shaw." Ph.D. diss., University of California, Riverside, 1983.

Stein, Walter J. "California and the 'Dust Bowl' Migration." Ph.D. diss., University of California, Berkeley, 1969.

Weber, Devra A. "The Struggle for Stability and Control in the Cotton Fields of California: Class Relations in Agriculture, 1919-1942." Ph.D. diss., University of California, Los Angeles, 1986.

Whisenhunt, Donald W. "Texas in the Depression, 1929-1933: A Study of Public Reaction." Ph.D. diss., Texas Technical College, 1966.

Wickens, James F. "Colorado in the Great Depression: A Study of New Deal Policies at the State Level." Ph.D. diss., University of Denver, 1964.

10

Thought & Culture

10.1 GENERAL

Books

Aaron, Daniel, and Robert Bendiner, eds. The Strenuous Decade: A Social and
    Intellectual Record of the 1930s. Garden City, N. Y.: Anchor Books, 1970.
Akin, William E. Technocracy and the American Dream: The Technocrat Movement,
    1900-1941. Berkeley: University of California Press, 1977.
Alexander, Charles. Nationalism in American Thought, 1930-1945. Chicago: Rand
    McNally, 1969.
Baker, Susan Stout. Radical Beginnings: Richard Hofstadter and the 1930s. Westport,
    Conn.: Greenwood, 1985.
Cantril, Hadley, and Mildred Strunk. Public Opinion, 1935-1946. Princeton: Princeton
    University Press, 1951.
Cargill, Oscar. Intellectual America: Ideas on the March. New York: Macmillan,
    1941.
Cooney, Terry A. The Rise of the New York Intellectuals: Partisan Review and Its
    Circle, 1934-1945. Madison: University of Wisconsin Press, 1986.
Crunden, Robert M. From Self to Society, 1919-1941: Transitions in American
    Thought. Englewood Cliffs, N.J.: Prentice-Hall, 1972.
Ekirch, Arthur A., Jr. Ideologies and Utopias: The Impact of the New Deal on
    American Thought. Chicago: Quadrangle, 1969.
Fermi, Laura. Illustrious Immigrants: The Intellectual Migration from Europe, 1930-
    41. Chicago: University of Chicago Press, 1968.
Fleming, Donald, and Bernard Bailyn, eds. The Intellectual Migration: Europe and
    America, 1930-1960. Cambridge: Harvard University Press, 1969.
Hearn, Charles R. The American Dream in the Great Depression. Westport, Conn.:
    Greenwood, 1977.
Hughes, H. Stuart. The Sea Change: The Migration of Social Thought, 1930-1965.
    New York: Harper & Row, 1965.

Jenkins, Thomas Paul. Reactions of Major Groups to Positive Government in the United States, 1930-1940: A Study in Contemporary Political Thought. Berkeley: University of California Press, 1945.

Marquis, Alice G. Hopes and Ashes: The Birth of Modern Times, 1929-1939. New York: Free Press, 1986.

Noggle, Burl. Working With History: The Historical Records Survey in Louisiana and the Nation. Baton Rouge: Louisiana State University Press, 1981.

Peeler, David P. Hope Among Us Yet: Social Criticism and Social Solace in Depression America. Athens: University of Georgia Press, 1987.

Pells, Richard H. Radical Visions and American Dreams: Culture and Social Thought in the Depression Years. New York: Harper & Row, 1973.

Stott, William. Documentary Expression and Thirties America. New York: Oxford University Press, 1973.

Susman, Warren I., ed. Culture and Commitment, 1929-1945. New York: George Braziller, 1973.

Waples, Douglas. People and Print: Social Aspects of Reading in the Depression. Chicago: University of Chicago Press, 1937.

Articles

Blayney, Michael S. "'Libraries for the Millions': Adult Public Library Services and the New Deal." Journal of Library History 12 (Summer 1977): 235-49.

Bordeau, Edward J. "John Dewey's Ideas about the Great Depression." Journal of the History of Ideas 32 (Jan.-March 1971): 67-84.

Braeman, John. "The Historian as Activist: Charles A. Beard and the New Deal." South Atlantic Quarterly 79 (Autumn 1980): 364-74.

Dugger, Ronnie. "Nobel Prize Winner Purged at the University of Texas." Southern Exposure 2 (Spring-Summer 1974): 67-70.

Farran, Don. "The Historical Records Survey in Iowa, 1936-1942." Annals of Iowa 42 (Spring 1975): 597-608.

Finison, Lorenz J. "An Aspect of the Early History of the Society for the Psychological Study of Social Issues: Psychologists and Labor." Journal of the History of the Behavioral Sciences 15 (Jan. 1979): 29-37.

Krueger, Thomas A., and Glidden, William. "The New Deal Intellectual Elite: A Collective Portrait." In The Rich, the Well Born, and the Powerful ed. Frederic Cople Jaher (Urbana; University of Illinois Press, 1973), pp. 338-74.

Leach, Eugene E. "Mastering the Crowd: Collective Behavior and Mass Society in American Social Thought, 1917-1939." American Studies 27 (Spring 1986): 99-114.

Matherly, Walter J. "The History of the Southern Economic Association, 1927-1939." Southern Economics Journal 7 (Oct. 1940): 225-40.

Mayer, Melton. "The Red Room." Massachusetts Review 16 (Summer 1975): 520-50.

McKinney, Fred. "Functionalism at Chicago--Memories of a Graduate Student, 1929-1931" Journal of the History of the Behavioral Sciences 14 (April 1978): 142-48.

Medhurst, Martin J., and Thomas W. Benson. "The City: The Rhetoric of Rhythm." Communication Mongraphs 48 (March 1981): 54-72.

Morrison, David E. "Kultur and Culture: The Case of Theodor W. Adorno and Paul F. Lazarsfeld." Social Research 45 (Summer 1978): 331-55.

Mottram, Eric. "Living Mythically: The Thirties." Journal of American Studies 6 (Dec. 1972): 267-87.

Norton, Paul F. "World's Fairs in the 1930s." Journal of the Society of Architectural Historians 24 (March 1965): 27-30.

Nye, Russel B. "The Thirties: The Framework of Belief." Centennial Review 19 (Spring 1975): 37-58.

Record, Wilson. "Intellectuals in Social and Racial Movements." Phylon 15 (3rd qtr. 1954): 231-42.

Remley, David A. "Upton Sinclair and H. L. Mencken in Correspondence: 'An Illustration of How Not to Agree.'" Southern California Quarterly 56 (Winter 1974): 337-58.

Shapiro, Edward S. "American Conservative Intellectuals, The 1930's, and the Crisis of Ideology." Modern Age 23 (Fall 1979): 370-80.

Shepardson, D. E. "In the Prime of his Time: H. L. Mencken." American History Illustrated. 9 (Jan. 1975): 10-19.

Shils, Edward. "Some Academics, Mainly in Chicago." American Scholar 50 (Spring 1981): 179-96.

Smith, T.V. "The New Deal as a Cultural Phenomenon." In Ideological Differences and World Order ed. by F. S. C. Northrup (New Haven: Yale University Press, 1949), pp. 208-28.

Trilling, Diana. "Lionel Trilling: A Jew at Columbia." Commentary 67 (March 1979): 40-46.

Turner, Fredrick. "'Just What the Hell Has Gone Wrong Here Anyhow?': Woody Guthrie and the American Dream." American Heritage 28 (Oct. 19770: 34-40.

Zucker, Bat-Ami. "Radical Jewish Intellectuals and the New Deal." In Bar-Ilan Studies in History ed. by Pinhas Artzi (Ramat-Gan, Israel: Bar-Iolan University Press, 1978), pp. 275-83.

Dissertations

Barrese, Edward Francis. "The Historical Records Survey: A Nation Acts to Save Its Memory." Ph.D diss., George Washington University, 1980.

Bloom, Alexander M. "The New York Intellectuals: The Formation of the Community." Ph.D diss., Boston College, 1979.

Carroll, Rosemary F. "The Impact of the Great Depression on American Attitudes toward Success: A Study of the Programs of Norman Vincent Peale, Dale Carnegie, and Johnson O'Connor." Ph.D diss., Rutgers University, 1969.

Corkern, Wilton C., Jr. "Architects, Preservationists, and the New Deal: The Historic American Buildings Survey, 1933-1942." Ph.D diss., George Washington University, 1984.

Davis, Robert L. "The Search for Values: The American Liberal Climate of Opinion in the Nineteen-Thirties and the Totalitarian Crisis of the Coming of the Second World War as Seen in the Thought of Charles Beard and Archibald MacLeish." Ph.D diss., Claremont, 1970.

Duffy, Bernard K. "The 1932 Technocracy Movement." Ph.D. diss., University of Pittsburgh, 1976.

Fagette, Paul Harvey, Jr. "Digging for Dollars: The Impact of the New Deal on the Professionalization of American Archaeology." Ph.D diss., University of California, Riverside, 1985.

Jones, Alfred H. "Roosevelt and Lincoln: The Political Uses of a Literary Image." Ph.D diss., Yale University, 1967.

Jones, Daniel Carroll. "H. L. Mencken: Critic of the New Deal, 1933-1936." Ph.D diss., West Virginia, 1977.

Lora, Ronald G. "Conservatism in American Thought, 1930-1950." Ph.D diss., Ohio University, 1967.

May, George S. "Ultra-Conservative Thought in the United States in the 1920's and 1930's." Ph.D diss., University of Michigan, 1954.

Nash, Anedith J. B. "Death on the Highway: The Automobile Wreck in American Culture, 1920-40." Ph.D diss., University of Minnesota, 1983.

Pells, Richard H. "Intellectuals and the Depression: American Thought in the 1930's." Ph.D diss., Harvard University, 1969.

Pulda, Arnold H. "'Better Todays': The American Public Culture in the 1930s." Ph.D diss., University of North Carolina, 1978.

Purcell, Edward A., Jr. "The Crisis of Democratic Theory: American Thought between the Wars, 1919-1941." Ph.D diss., University of Wisconsin, 1968.

Striner, Richard A. "The Machine as Symbol: 1920-1939." Ph.D diss., University of Maryland, 1982.

Sweeney, Eugene T. "The Ideal of the Good Citizen, 1920-1940, as Seen by Selected Major Groups." Ph.D diss., University of Chicago, 1961.

Trigg, Hugh L. "The Impact of a Pessimist: The Reception of Oswald Spengler in America, 1919-1939." Ph.D diss., George Peabody College, 1968.

Waugh, Thomas H. R. "John Ivens and the Evolution of the Radical Documentary, 1926-1946." Ph.D. diss., Columbia University, 1981.

Wilder, Robin G. "The Mind of Heywood Brown: 1921-1934." Ph.D. diss., University of Wisconsin, 1984.

10.2 ARTS

Books

Baigell, Matthew. The American Scene: American Painting of the 1930's. New
    York: Praeger, 1974.

Beach, Joseph Warren. American Fiction, 1920-1940. New York: Macmillan, 1941.

Blake, Nelson Manfred. Novelists' America: Fiction as History, 1910-1940.
    Syracuse: Syracuse University Press, 1969.

Bogardus, Ralph F., and Fred Hobson, eds. Literature at the Barricades: The
    American Writer in the 1930s. University: University of Alabama Press, 1982.

Brown, Milton W. American Painting: From the Armory Show to the Depression.
    Princeton: Princeton University Press, 1955.

Buttita, Tony, and Barry Witham. Uncle Sam Presents: A Memoir of the Federal
    Theatre, 1935-1939. Philadelphia: University of Pennsylvania Press, 1982.

Caldwell, Erskine, and Margaret Bourke-White. You Have Seen Their Faces. New
    York: Viking, 1937.

Craig, E. Quita. Black Drama of the Federal Theatre Era: Beyond the Formal
    Horizons. Amherst: University of Massachusetts Press, 1980.

Cutler, Phoebe. The Public Landscape of the New Deal. New Haven: Yale
    University Press, 1985.

Flanagan, Hallie. Arena. New York: Duell, Sloan and Pearce, 1940.

Garver, Thomas H., ed. Just Before the War: Urban America as Seen by
    Photographers of the Farm Security Administration. Los Angeles: Rapid
    Lithograph, 1968.

Geismar, Maxwell David. Writers in Crisis: The American Novel Between Two
    Wars. Boston: Houghton Mifflin, 1942.

Goldstein, Malcolm. The Political Stage: American Drama and Theater of the Great
    Depression. New York: Oxford University Press, 1974.

Gurko, Leo. The Angry Decade. New York: Dodd, Mead, 1947.

Himelstein, Morgan. Drama Was a Weapon: The Left Wing Theatre in New York,
    1929-1941. New Brunswick, N.J.: Rutgers University Press, 1963.

Hobson, Archie, ed. Remembering America: A Sampler of the WPA American Guide
    Series. New York: Columbia University Press, 1985.

Hurley, F. Jack. Portrait of a Decade: Roy Stryker and the Development of
    Documentary Photography in the Thirties. Baton Rouge: Louisiana State
    University Press, 1972.

Jones, Alfred Haworth. Roosevelt's Image Brokers: Poets, Playwrights, and the Use
    of the Lincoln Symbol. Port Washington, N.Y.: Kennikat, 1974.

Kazin, Alfred. On Native Grounds: An Interpretation of Modern American Prose
    Literature. New York: Reynal & Hitchcock, 1942.

Madden, David, ed. Proletarian Writers of the Thirties. Carbondale: Southern Illinois
    University Press, 1968.

_____. Tough Guy Writers of the Thirties. Carbondale: Southern Illinois University Press, 1968.

Maddox, Jerald C., ed. Walker Evans, Photographs for the Farm Security Administration, 1935-1938: A Catalog of Photographic Prints Available from the Farm Security Administration Collection in the Library of Congress. New York: DaCapo, 1973.

Mangione, Jerre. The Dream and the Deal: The Federal Writers' Project, 1935-1943. Boston: Little, Brown, 1972.

Marling, Karal A. Wall-to-Wall America: A Cultural History of Post-Office Murals in the Great Depression. Minneapolis: University of Minnesota Press, 1982.

_____ and Helen Harrison. 7 American Women: The Depression Decade: Rosalind Bengelsdorf, Lucienne Bloch, Minna Citron, Marion Greenwood, Doris Less, Elizabeth Olds, Concetta Scaravaglione: An Exhibition. Poughkeepsie, N.Y.: Vassar College Art Gallery, 1976.

Mathews, Jane D. The Federal Theatre: 1935-1939: Plays, Relief, and Politics. Princeton: Princeton University Press, 1965.

McDonald, William F. Federal Relief Administration and the Arts: The Origins and Administrative History of the Arts Projects of the Works Progress Administration. Columbus: Ohio State University Press, 1969.

McKinzie, Richard D. The New Deal for Artists. Princeton: Princeton University Press, 1973.

Mock, Elizabeth, ed. Built in USA, Since 1932. New York: Museum of Modern Art, 1945.

Owens, Louis. John Steinbeck's Re-Vision of America. Athens: University of Georgia Press, 1985.

Park, Marlene, and Gerald E. Markowitz. Democratic Vistas: Post Offices and Public Art in the New Deal. Philadelphia: Temple University Press, 1984.

_____. New Deal for Art: The Government Art Projects of the 1930's with Examples from New York City and State. Hamilton, N. Y.: Gallery Association of New York State, 1977.

Penkower, Monty N. The Federal Writers' Project: A Study in Government Patronage of the Arts. Urbana: University of Illinois Press, 1977.

Puckett, John Rogers. Five Photo-Textual Documentaries from the Great Depression. Ann Arbor: UMI Research Press, 1984.

Rothstein, Arthur. The Depression Years As Photographed by Arthur Rothstein. New York: Dover, 1978.

Salzman, Jack, ed. Years of Protest: A Collection of American Writing of the 1930s. New York: Pegasus, 1967.

Snyder, Robert L. Pare Lorentz and the Documentary Film. Norman: University of Oklahoma Press, 1968.

Swados, Harvey, ed. The American Writer and the Great Depression. Indianapolis: Bobbs-Merrill, 1966.

Weiss, Margaret R. Ben Shahn, Photographer: An Album from the Thirties. New York: DaCapo, 1973.

Whitman, Willson. Bread and Circuses: A Study of Federal Theatre. New York: Oxford University Press, 1937.

Wittler, C. J. Some Social Trends in WPA Drama. Washington: Catholic University of America Press, 1939.

Articles

Ahlander, Leslie Judd. "Mexico's Muralists and the New York School." Americas 31 (May 1979): 18-25.

Alter, Robert. "The Travels of Malcolm Cowley." Commentary 70 (Aug. 1980): 33-40.

Anonymous. "Reginald Marsh: Artist of the Depression Years." American History Illustrated 16 (Jan. 1982): 24-29.

Arner, Robert D. "'The Black, Memorable Year 1929': James Thurber and the Great Depression." Studies in American Humor 3 (Summer 1984): 237-52.

Baer, John W. "The Great Depression Humor of Galbraith, Leacock, and Mencken." Studies in American Humor 3 (Summer 1984): 220-27.

Baker, Howard. "The Gyroscope." Southern Review 17 (Oct. 1981): 735-57.

Beckh, Erica. "Government Art in the Roosevelt Era." Art Journal 20 (Fall 1960): 2-8.

Behar, Jack. "James Agee: Notes on the Man and the Work." Denver Quarterly 13 (Spring 1978): 3-15.

Benson, Jackson J., and Anne Loftis. "John Steinbeck and Farm Labor Unionization: The Background of In Dubious Battle." American Literature 52 (May 1980): 194-223.

Bernstein, Joel H. "The Artist and the Government: The P.W.A.P." Canadian Review of American Studies 1 (Fall 1970): 100-15.

Billington, Ray Allen. "Government and the Arts: The W.P.A. Experience." American Quarterly 13 (Winter 1961): 466-79.

Brooks, Cleanth. "Allan Tate and the Nature of Modernism." Southern Review 12 (Oct. 1976): 685-97.

Browne, Lorraine. "A Story Yet To Be Told: The Federal Theatre Research Project." Black Scholar 10 (July-Aug. 1979): 70-78.

_____. "Federal Theatre: Melodrama, Social Protest, and Genius." Quarterly Journal of the Library of Congress 36 (Winter 1979): 18-37.

Burden, Florence Canfield. "New Deal Artist Ernest E. Stevens." Nebraska History 66 (Fall 1985): 225-33.

Bystryn, Marcia N. "Variations in Artistic Circles." Sociological Quarterly 22 (Winter 1981): 119-32.

Christian, Henry A. "From Two Homelands to One World: Louis Adamic's Search for Unity." Papers in Slovene Studies (1975): 133-44.

Clark, William Bedford. "'Ez Sez'": Pound's 'Pithy Promulgations.'" Antioch Review 37 (Fall 1979): 420-27.

Clayton, Ronnie W. "Federal Writers' Project For Blacks in Louisiana." Louisiana History 19 (Summer 1978): 327-35.

Cole, John Y. "Amassing American 'Stuff': The Library of Congress and the Federal Arts Projects of the 1930s." Quarterly Journal of the Library of Congress 40 (Fall 1983): 356-89.

Coppock, Jane. "A Conversation with Arthur Berger." Partisan Review 48 (No. 3, 1981): 366-79.

Cosgrove, Stuart. "The Living Newspaper: Strikes, Strategies, and Solidarity." In Nothing Else to Fear: New Perspectives on America in the Thirties ed. by Stephen W. Baskerville and Ralph Willett (Manchester: Manchester University Press, 1985), pp. 238-57.

Culley, John J., and Peter L. Petersen. "Hard Times on the High Plains: FSA Photography during the 1930s." Panhandle-Plains Historical Review 52 (1979): 15-37.

Curtis, James C. "Dorothea Lange, Migrant Mother, and the Culture of the Great Depression." Winterthur Portfolio 21 (Spring 1986): 1-20.

_____ and Sheila Grannon. "Let Us Now Appraise Famous Photographs: Walker Evans and Documentary Photography." Winterthur Portfolio 15 (Spring 1980): 1-23.

Cutter, Charles R. "The WPA Federal Music Project in New Mexico." New Mexico Historical Review 61 (July 1986): 203-16.

Davidson, Marshall B. "The WPA's Amazing Artistic Record of American Design." American Heritage 23 (Feb. 1972): 65-80.

Dawson, Oliver B. "The Ironwork of Timberline." Oregon Historical Quarterly 76 (Sept. 1975): 258-68.

Day, Greg, and Jack Delano. "Folklife and Photography: Bringing the FSA Home." Southern Exposure 5 (No.2, 1977): 122-33.

Dayananda, Y. James. "Edmund Wilson and the Thirties." Lock Haven Review (No. 12, 1971): 1-23.

Deering, Catherine M. "The Poor of the World Are One Big Family: The Writings of Agnes Smedley." In Nothing Else to Fear: New Perspectives on America in the Thirties ed. by Stephen W. Baskerville and Ralph Willett (Manchester: Manchester University Press, 1985), pp. 134-45.

Dieterich, Herbert R. "The New Deal Cultural Projects in Wyoming: A Survey and Appraisal." Annals of Wyoming 52 (Fall 1980): 30-44.

_____ and Jacqueline Petravage. "New Deal Art in Wyoming: Some Case Studies." Annals of Wyoming 45 (Spring 1973): 53-67.

Douglas, Ann. "Studs Lonigan and the Failure of History in Mass Society: A Study in Claustrophobia." American Quarterly 29 (Winter 1977): 487-505.

Downs, Alexis. "George Milburn: Ozark Folklore in Oklahoma Fiction." Chronicles of Oklahoma 5 (Fall 1977): 309-23.

Eckey, Lorelei F. "Pilgrims of the Impossible." Palimpsest 61 (Jan.-Feb. 1980): 26-32.

Ewen, Frederic. "The Thirties, Commitment, and the Theatre." Science and Society 32 (Summer 1968): 300-6.

Eyster, Warren. "Conversations with James Agee." Southern Review 17 (April 1981): 346-57.

Faulkner, Jim. "Memories of Brother Will." Southern Review 16 (Oct. 1980): 907-20.
_____. "No Pistol Pocket." Southern Review 17 (April 1981): 358-365.

Fine, David M. "James M. Cain and the Los Angeles Novel." American Studies 20 (Spring 1979): 25-34.

Fox, Daniel M. "The Achievement of the Federal Writers' Project." American Quarterly 13 (Spring 1961): 3-32.

Gambrell, Jamey. "An Art of Protest and Despair." Art in America 71 (Dec. 1983): 92-99.

Garvey, Timothy J. "From 'God of Peace' to 'Onyx John': The Public Momument and Cultural Change." Upper Midwest History 1 (1981): 4-26.

Geller, Steven M. "Working to Prosperity: California's New Deal Murals." California History 58 (Summer 1979): 98-127.

Genauer, Emily. "An Art Deco Memory." Horizon 23 (Feb. 1980): 60-63.

Gerber, Philip L. "Dreiser: The Great Sloth of the Thirties." Old Northwest 11 (Spring/Summer 1985): 7-23.

Goodenow, Ronald K. "The Progressive Educator, Race and Ethnicity in the Depression Years: An Overview." History of Education Quarterly 15 (Winter 1975): 365-94.

Gordon, Caroline. "Life at Benfolly, 1930-1931: Letters of Caroline Gordon to a Northern Friend, Sally Wood." Southern Review 16 (April 1980): 301-36.

Gray, Ralph D. "Gas Buggy Revisited: A 'Lost' Novel of Kokomo, Indiana." Indiana Magazine of History 70 (March 1974): 24-43.

Hagerty, Donald J. "Hard Times, New Images: Artists and the Depression Years in California." Pacific Historian 27 (Winter 1983): 11-19.

Harrison, Helen A. "American Art and the New Deal." Journal of American Studies 6 (Dec. 1972): 289-96.

Hemenway, Robert. "Folklore Field Notes from Zora Neale Hurston." Black Scholar 7 (April 1976): 39-46.

Hightower, Paul. "A Study of the Messages in Depression Era Photos." Journalism Quarterly 57 (Autumn 1980): 495-97.

Hobbs, Glenda. "Starting Out in the Thirties: Harriette Arnouw's Literary Genius." In Literature at the Barracades: The American Writer in the 1930s ed. by Ralph F. Bogardus and Fred Hobson (University: University of Alabama Press, 1982), pp. 144-61.

Holcomb, Robert. "The Federal Theatre in Los Angeles." California Historical Society Quarterly 41 (June 1962): 131-48.

Holder, Alan. "Encounter in Alabama: Agee and the Tenant Farmer." Virginia Quarterly Review 42 (Spring 1966): 189-206.

Holman, C. Hugh. "Thomas Wolfe, Scribner's Magazine, and 'The Best Nouvelle'." In Essays Mostly on Periodocal Publishing in America: A Collection in Honor of Clarence Gohdes ed. by James Woodress (Durham: Duke University Press, 1973), pp. 205-20.

Hoopes, James. "Modernist Criticism and Trancendental Literature." New England Quarterly 52 (Dec. 1979): 451-66.

Howell, Elmo. "William Faulkner and the New Deal." Midwest Quarterly 5 (Summer 1964): 323-32.

Hundley, Patrick D. "People of the Cumberland (1937): An Attempt at Synthetic Documentary." Film and History 6 (Sept. 1976): 56-62.

Hux, Samuel. "The Necessity of Irrelevant Traditions." Antioch Review 38 (Winter 1980): 108-18.

Ikonne, Chidi. "Opportunity and Black Literature, 1923-1933." Phylon 40 (March 1979): 86-93.

Ivers, Louise H. "The Evolution of Modernistic Architecture in Long Beach, California, 1928-1937." Southern California Quarterly 68 (Fall 1986): 257-91.

Johnson, Abby Arthur and Ronald W. "Reform and Reaction: Black Literary Magazines in the 1930s." North Dakota Quarterly 46 (Winter 1978): 5-18.

Johnson, Glen M. "The Pastness of All The King's Men." American Literature 51 (Jan. 1980): 553-57.

Jordy, William H. "The International Style in the 1930s." Journal of the Society of Architectural Historians 24 (March 1965): 10-14.

Josephson, Matthew. "Leane Zugsmith: The Social Novel of the Thirties." Southern Review 11 (July 1975): 530-52.

Kaplan, Charles. "Two Depression Plays and Broadway's Popular Idealism." American Quarterly 15 (Winter 1963): 579-85.

Kaufman, Edgar, Jr. "Frank Lloyd Wright's Years of Modernism, 1925-1935." Journal of the Society of Architectural Historians 24 (March 1965): 31-33.

Kennedy, Richard S. "Thomas Wolfe's Last Manuscript." Harvard Library Bulletin 23 (April 1975): 203-11.

Key, Donald. "Milwaukee's Art of the Depression Era." Historical Messenger of the Milwaukee County Historical Society 31 (Summer 1975): 38-49.

Klein, Marcus. "The Roots of Radicals: Experience in the Thirties." In Proletarian Writers of the Thirties ed. by David Madden (Carbondale: Southern Illinois University Press), pp. 134-57.

Klug, Michael A. "James Agee and the Furious Angel." Canadian Review of American Studies 11 (Winter 1980): 313-26.

Kramer, Victor A. "Agee's Skepticism about Art and Audience." Southern Review 17 (April 1981): 320-31.

Landon, Brooks. "'Not Solve It But Be In It': Gertrude Stein's Detective Stories and the Mystery of Creativity." American Literature 53 (Nov. 1981): 487-498.

Linneman, William R. "Will Rogers and the Great Depression." Studies in American Humor 3 (Summer 1984): 237-52.

Lunden, Rolf. "Theodore Dreiser and the Nobel Prize." American Literature 50 (May 1978): 216-29.

Magnusson, Tor. "Fats Waller with Gene Austin on the Record." Journal of Jazz Studies 4 (Fall 1976): 75-83.

Marcus, Steven. "Dashiell Hammett and the Continental Op." Partisan Review 41 (No. 3, 1974): 362-77.

Mathews, Jane DeHart. "Arts and the People: The New Deal Quest for a Cultural Democracy." Journal of American History 62 (Sept. 1975): 316-39.

Maurer, Joyce C. "Federal Theatre in Cincinnati." Cincinnati Historical Society Bulletin 32 (Spring-Summer 1974): 29-45.

McDermott, Douglas. "Agitprop: Production Practice in the Workers' Theatre, 1932-1942." Theatre Survey 7 (Nov. 1966): 115ff.

_____. "The Theatre Knobdy Knows: Workers Theatre in America, 1926-1942." Theatre Survey 6 (May 1965): 65ff.

McGinty, Brian. "A Pinkerton Man in Spades. [Dashiell Hammett]" Westways 69 (March 1977): 28-31.

Meehan, James. "Seed of Destruction: The Death of Thomas Wolfe." South Atlantic Quarterly 73 (Spring 1974): 173-83.

Mehren, Peter. "San Diego's Opera Unit of the WPA Federal Music Project." Journal of San Diego History 18 (Summer 1972): 12-21.

Meixner, Mary L. "Lowell Houser and the Genesis of a Mural." Palimpsest 66 (Jan.-Feb. 1984): 2-13.

Melling, Philip H. "Samples of Horizon: Picaresque Patterns in the Thirties." In Nothing Else to Fear: New Perspectives on America in the Thirties ed. by. Stephen W. Baskerville and Ralph Willett (Manchester: Manchester University Press, 1985), pp. 106-31.

Miller, Jeanne-Marie A. "Successful Federal Theatre Dramas by Black Playwrights." Black Scholar 10 (July-Aug. 1970): 70-85.

Monroe, Gerald M. "The '30s: Art, Ideology and the WPA." Art in America 63 (Nov./Dec. 1975): 64-67.

Mottram, Eric. "Invention and the Collapse of Capitalism: American Poets in the Thirties." In Nothing Else to Fear: New Perspectives on America in the Thirties ed. by. Stephen W. Baskerville and Ralph Willett (Manchester: Manchester University Press, 1985), pp. 148-76.

Narber, Gregg R., and Lea Rosson DeLong. "The New Deal Murals in Iowa." Palimipsest 63 (May/June 1982): 86-96.

Nochlin, Linda. "Florine Stettheimer: Rococo Subversive." Art in America 68 (Sept. 1980): 64-83.

O'Connor, John. "'King Cotton': The Federal Theatre Project." Southern Exposure 6 (No.1, 1978): 74-81.

Orlin, Lena Cowen. "Night Over Taos: Maxwell Anderson's Sources and Artistry." North Dakota Quarterly 48 (Summer 1980): 12-25.

Peisch, Mark L. "Modern Architecture and Architectural Criticism in the U.S.A., 1929-1939." Journal of the Society of Architectural Historians 24 (March 1965): 78.

Perdue, Charles L, Jr. "Old Jack and the New Deal: The Virginia Writers' Project and Jack Tale Collecting in Wise County, Virginia." Appalachian Journal 14 (Winter 1987): 108-52.

Phillips, William. "How Partisan Review Began." Commentary 62 (Dec. 1976): 42-46.

Pommer, Richard. "The Architecture of Urban Housing in the United States during the Early 1930s." Journal of the Society of Architectural Historians 37 (Dec. 1978): 235-64.

Pratt, Linda Ray. "Imagining Existence: Form and History in Steinbeck and Agee." Southern Review 11 (Jan. 1975): 84-98.

Randle, Mallory B. "Texas Muralists of the PWAP." Southwestern Art 1 (Spring 1966): 51-69.

Redding, Mary Edrich. "Call It Myth: Henry Roth and The Golden Bough." Centennial Review 18 (Spring 1974): 180-95.

Reilly, John M. "Richard Wright's Apprenticeship." Journal of Black Studies 2 (June 1972): 434-60.

Rhoads, William B. "Franklin D. Roosevelt and Dutch Colonial Architecture." New York History 59 (Oct. 1978): 430-64.

_____. "Franklin D. Roosevelt and the Architecture of Warm Springs." Georgia Historical Quarterly 67 (Spring 1983): 70-87.

_____. "The Artistic Patronage of Franklin D. Roosevelt: Art as Historical Record." Prologue 15 (Spring 1983): 5-22.

Riggio, Thomas P. "Dreiser on Society and Literature: The San Francisco Exposition Interview." American Literary Realism 1870-1910 11 (Autumn 1978): 284-94.

Ross, Ronald. "The Role of Blacks in the Federal Theatre, 1935-1939." Journal of Negro History 59 (Jan. 1974): 38-50.

Rubenstein, Annette T. "The Radical American Theatre of the Thirties." Science and Society 50 (Fall 1986): 300-20.

Rubin, Louis D., Jr. "Trouble on the Land: Southern Literature and the Great Depression." Canadian Review of American Studies 10 (Fall 1979): 153-74.

Ruby, Christine Nelson. "Art for the Millions: Government Art During the Depression." Michigan History 66 (Jan. 1982): 17-20.

Salzman, Jack. "Conroy, Mencken, and 'The American Mercury'." Journal of Popular Culture 7 (Winter 1973): 524-28.

Sassner, John. "Social Realism and Imagination Theatre: Avant-Garde Stage Production in the American Social Theatre of the Nineteen-Thirties." Theatre Survey 3 (1962): 3-9.

Schrems, Suzanne H. "New Deal Culture in Oklahoma: The Federal Theatre and Music Projects." Heritage of the Great Plains 19 (Winter 1986): 1-13.

Scott, Robert L. "Diego Rivera at Rockefeller Center: Fresco Painting and Rhetoric." Western Journal of Speech Communication 41 (Spring 1977): 70-82.

Slade, Thomas M. "'The Crystal House' of 1934." Journal of the Society of Architectural Historians 29 (Dec. 1970): 350-53.

Smith, C. Zoe. "An Alternative View of the 30s: Hine's and Bouke-White's Industrial Photos." Journalism Quarterly 60 (Summer 1983): 305-10.

Snyder, Stephen. "From Words to Images: Five Novelists in Hollywood." Canadian Review of American Studies 8 (Fall 1977): 206-13.

Solomon, Eric. "Fiction and the New Deal." In The New Deal: The National Level ed. by John Braeman, Robert H. Bremner, and David Brody (Columbus: Ohio State University Press, 1975), pp. 310-25.

_____. "Notes towards a Definition of Robert Benchley's 1930s New Yorker Humor." Studies in American Humor 3 (Spring 1984): 34-55.

Taber, Ronald W. "Vardis Fisher and the 'Idaho Guide': Preserving Culture for the New Deal." Pacific Northwest Quarterly 59 (April 1968): 68-76.

_____. "Writers on Relief: The Making of the Washington Guide, 1935-1941." Pacific Northwest Quarterly 61 (Oct. 1970): 185-92.

Taylor, Joshua C. "A Poignant, Relevant Backward Look at Artists of the Great Depression." Smithsonian 10 (Oct. 1979): 44-53.

Teague, Frances. "Hamlet in the Thirties." Theatre Survey 26 (May 1985): 63-79.

Teichroew, Allan. "As Far as the Eye Can See: Some Depression Photographs of Mennonite Farmers." Mennonite Life 33 (Sept. 1978): 4-15.

Thomas, James W. "Lyle Saxon's Struggle with Children of Strangers." Southern Studies 16 (Spring 1977): 27-40.

Vacha, J. E. "Prosperity Was Just Around the Corner: The Influence of the Depression on the Development of the American Musical Theater in the Thirties." South Atlantic Quarterly 67 (Autumn 1968): 573-90.

_____. "The Case of the Runaway Opera: The Federal Theatre and Marc Blitzstein's The Cradle Will Rock." New York History 62 (April 1981): 133-52.

_____. "The Federal Theatre's Living Newspapers: New York's Docudramas of the Thirties." New York History 67 (Jan 1986): 67-88.

Vitz, Robert C. "Clubs, Congresses, and Unions: American Artists Confront the Thirties." New York History 54 (Oct. 1973): 425-47.

_____. "Struggle and Response: American Artists and the Great Depression" New York History 57 (Jan. 1976): 81-98.

Warren-Findley, Jannelle. "Musicians and Mountaineers: The Resettlement Administration's Music Program in Appalachia, 1935-37." Appalachian Journal 7 (Autumn/Winter 1979-80): 105-23.

Wasser, Henry H. "The New Deal and American Literature." Americana Norvegica: Norwegian Contributions to American Studies vol 1, ed. by Sigmund Skard and Henry H. Wasser (Philadelphia: University of Pennsylvania Press, 1966), pp. 331-38.

Webb, Max. "Ford Madox Ford and the Baton Rouge Writers' Conference." Southern Review 10 (Oct. 1974): 892-903.

Wheelock, Alan S. "Dark Mountain: H. P. Lovecraft and the 'Vermont Horror.'" Vermont History 45 (Fall 1977): 221-28.

Whitaker, Rosemary. "Violence in Old Jules and Slogum House." Western American Literature 16 (Fall 1981): 217-24.

Whitehead, James L. "John Albok's Record of the People of New York: 1933-45." Prologue 6 (Summer 1974): 100-17.

Wiles, Timothy J. "Tammanyite, Progressive, and Anarchist: Political Communities in The Iceman Cometh." Clio 9 (Winter 1980): 179-96.

Willett, Ralph. "'Naive, Human, Eager, and Alive': The Federal Art Project and the Response from Magazines." In Nothing Else to Fear: New Perspectives on America in the Thirties ed. by Stephen W. Baskerville and Ralph Willett (Manchester: Manchester University Press, 1985), pp. 179-93.

Wilmoth, Carol. "Heavenly Harmony: The WPA Symphony Orchestra, 1937-1942."
    Chronicles of Oklahoma 64 (Spring 1986): 34-51.
Woodward, Robert H. "John Steinbeck, Edith McGillicuddy and Tortilla Flat: A
    Problem in Manuscript Dating." San Jose Studies 3 (November 1977): 70-73.
Wurster, Catherine Bauer. "The Social Front of Modern Architecture in the 1930s."
    Journal of the Society of Architectural Historians 24 (March 1965): 48-52.
Yasko, Karel. "Treasures from the Depression." Historic Preservation 24 (July
    1972): 26-31.
York, Hildreth. "The New Deal Art Projects in New Jersey." New Jersey History
    98 (Fall-Winter 1980): 132-74.

Dissertations

Achter, Barbara A. Z. "Americanism and American Art Music, 1929-1945." Ph.D
    diss., University of Michigan, 1978.
Behringer, Fred D. "The Political Theatre of Elmer Rice, 1930-1943." Ph.D diss.,
    University of Texas, 1980.
Boddy, Julie M. "The Farm Security Administration Photographs of Marion Post
    Wolcott: A Cultural History." Ph.D diss., State University of New York at
    Buffalo, 1982.
Bongas, Pamela J. "The Woman's Woman on the American Stage in the 1930s."
    Ph.D diss., University of Missouri, 1980.
Boshoff, Willem Hendrik. "American Drama Between the World Wars (1919-1939):
    A Mirror of the Times." D. Litt. diss., University of South Africa, 1979.
Boyens, Charles W. "The WPA Mural Projects: The Effects of Constraints on
    Artistic Freedom." Ph.D. diss., Columbia University Teachers College, 1984.
Campbell, Russell D. "Radical Cinema in the United States, 1930-1942: The Work of
    the Film and Photo League, Nykino, and Frontier Films." Ph.D diss.,
    Northwestern University, 1978.
Connors, James J. "Poets and Politics: A Study of the Careers of C. Day Lewis,
    Stephen Spender, and W. H. Auden in the 1930's." Ph.D. diss., Yale University,
    1967.
Contreras, Belisario R. "The New Deal Treasury Department Art Programs and the
    American Artist, 1933 to 1943." Ph.D. diss., American University, 1967.
Cutrer, Thomas W. "'My Boys at LSU': Cleanth Brooks, Robert Penn Warren and the
    Baton Rouge Literary Community, 1934-1942." Ph.D. diss., University of Texas,
    1980.
Davis Thadious M. "Faulkner's 'Negro': Art and the Southern Context, 1926-1936."
    Ph.D. diss., Boston University, 1976.
DeVasto, Carl H. "The Poet of Demos: John Steinbeck's The Grapes of Wrath and
    Major Later Fiction." Ph.D. diss., University of Rhode Island, 1982.
Devore, Richard O. "Stylistic Diversity within the Music of Five Avant-Garde
    American Composers, 1929-1945." Ph.D. diss., University of Iowa, 1985.

Douglas, Krystan V. "Theater as Cultural Indicator: Broadway between World Wars." Ph.D. diss., University of New Mexico, 1978.

Ghirardo, Diane Yvonne. "Architecture and the State: Fascist Italy and New Deal America." Ph.D. diss., Stanford University, 1983.

Hirsch, Jerrold Maury. "Portrait of America: The Federal Writers' Project in an Intellectual and Cultural Context." Ph.D. diss., University of North Carolina, 1984.

Holder, Philancy N. "Sculpture as a Mirror of the American Experience 1918-1945: A Study in the Phenomenological Method of Art Criticism." Ph.D. diss., University of Georgia, 1981.

Johnson, Evamarii A. "A Production History of the Seattle Federal Theatre Project Negro Repertory Company: 1935-1939." Ph.D. diss., University of Washington, 1981.

Kahan, Mitchell D. "Subjective Currents in American Painting of the 1930s." Ph.D. diss., City University of New York, 1983.

Kahn, David Matthew. "The Federal Theatre Project in San Francisco: A History of an Indigenous Theatre." Ph.D. diss., University of California, Berkeley, 1984.

Koch, John Charles. "The Federal Theatre Project: Region IV--A Structural and Historical Analysis of How It Functioned and What It Acomplished." Ph.D. diss., University of Nebraska, 1981.

Lally, Kathleen A. "A History of the Federal Dance Theatre of the Works Progress Administration, 1935-1939." Ph.D. diss., Texas Women's University, 1978.

Levy, Robert J. "Art for the Public's Sake, 1920-1943." Ph.D. diss., University of Wisconsin, 1978.

Mathews, Jane D. "Art, Relief and Politics: The Federal Theatre, 1935-1939." Ph.D. diss., Duke University, 1966.

McKinzie, Kathleen H. "Writers on Relief, 1935-1942." Ph.D. diss., Indiana University, 1970.

McKinzie, Richard D. "The New Deal for Artists." Ph.D. diss., Indiana University, 1969.

Owens, Louis D. "A New Eye in the West: Steinbeck's California Fiction." Ph.D. diss., University of California, Davis, 1981.

Peeler, David P. "America's Depression Culture: Social Art and Literature of the 1930s." Ph.D. diss., University of Wisconsin, 1980.

Pollard, Leslie T. "The Grapes of Wrath and Native Son: Literary Criticism as Social Definition." Ph.D. diss., University of Kansas, 1983.

Prevots-Wallen, Naima. "The Hollywood Bowl and Los Angeles Dance, 1926-1941." Ph.D. diss., University of Southern California, 1983.

Ross, Theophil Walter, Jr. "Conflicting Concepts of the Federal Theatre Project: A Critical History." Ph.D. diss., University of Missouri, 1981.

Smith, Cynthia Z. "Emigre Photography in American: Contributions of German Photojournalism from Black Star Picture Agency to Life Magazine, 1933-1938." Ph.D. diss., University of Iowa, 1983.

Stein, Pauline Alpert. "A Vision of El Dorado: The Southern California New Deal Art Programs." Ph.D. diss., University of California, Los Angeles, 1984.

Swiss, Cheryl D. "Hallie Flanagan and the Federal Theatre Project: An Experiment in Form." Ph.D. diss., University of Wisconsin, 1982.

Tonelli, Edith A. "The Massachusetts Federal Art Project: A Case Study in Government Support for Art." Ph.D. diss., Boston University, 1980.

Townsend, Helen. "Ideology and Government Participation in the Arts: The WPA Federal Art Project in Tennessee." Ph.D. diss., Vanderbilt University, 1985.

Trainer, Kathleen M. "The Dissident Character in American Drama of the 1930's." Ph.D. diss., University of Notre Dame, 1983.

Wassmuth, Birgit L. J. "Art Movements and American Print Advertising: A Study of Magazine Advertising Graphics 1915-1935." Ph.D. diss., University of Minnesota, 1983.

Welburn, Ronald G. "American Jazz Criticism, 1914-1940." Ph.D. diss., New York University, 1983.

Williams, Elwood Pratt. "An Examination of Protagonists in Selected Federal Theatre Project Plays as a Reflection of New Deal Society and Politics." Ph.D. diss., Kent State University, 1984.

Willis, Wayne C. "A Fanfare for the Common Man: Nationalism and Democracy in the Arts of the American 1930's." Ph.D. diss., Brandeis University, 1977.

Wyman, Marilyn. "A New Deal for Art in Southern California: Murals and Sculpture under Government Patronage." Ph.D. diss., University of Southern California, 1982.

10.3   EDUCATION

Books

Adams, Frank, and Myles Horton. Unearthing Seeds of Fire, The Idea of Highlander. Winston-Salem, N.C.: John T. Blair, 1975.

Cook, Paul B. Academicians in Government from Roosevelt to Roosevelt. New York: Garland, 1892.

Duberman, Martin Black Mountain: An Exploration in Community. New York: E. P. Dutton, 1972.

Eagan, Eileen. Class, Culture, and the Classroom: The Student Peace Movement of the 1930s. Philadelphia: Temple University Press, 1981.

Koch, Raymond and Charlotte. Educational Commune: The Story of Commonwealth College. New York: Schocken, 1972.

Levine, David O. The American College and the Culture of Aspiration, 1915-1940. Ithaca: Cornell University Press, 1986.

Montalto, Nicholas V. A History of the Intercultural Education Movement, 1924-1941. New York: Garland, 1982.

Sargent, Porter. Between Two Wars: The Failure of Education, 1920-1940. Boston: Porter Sargent, 1945.

Tyack, David. Public Schools in Hard Times: The Great Depression and Recent Years. Cambridge: Harvard University Press, 1984.

Willey, Malcolm M., ed. Depression, Recovery, and Higher Education: A Report by Committee Y of the American Association of University Professors. New York: McGraw-Hill, 1937.

Articles

Barnard, Harry V., and John H. Best. "Growing Federal Involvement in American Education, 1918-1945." Current History 62 (June 1972): 290-92, 308.

Biebel, Charles D. "Private Foundations and Public Policy: The Case of Secondary Education during the Great Depression." History of Education Quarterly 16 (Spring 1976): 3-33.

Bowers, C. A. "Social Reconstructionism: Views from the Left and the Right, 1932-1942." History of Education Quarterly 10 (Spring 1970): 22-52.

Buerki, Robert A. "The George-Deen Act of 1936 and the 'Wisconsin Plan.'" Pharmacy in History 23 (No.1, 1981): 17-34.

Burbank, Lyman B. "Chicago Public Schools and the Depression Years of 1928-1937." Journal of the Illinois State Historical Society 64 (Winter 1971): 365-81.

Caliguire, Joseph A., Jr. "Union Township Schools and the Depression, 1929-1938." New Jersey History 93 (Autumn 1975): 115-27.

Clegg, Ambrose A., Jr. "Church Groups and Federal Aid to Education, 1933-1939." History of Education Quarterly 4 (Sept. 1964): 137-54.

Daniels, Roger. "Workers' Education and the University of California, 1921-1941." Labor History 4 (Winter 1963): 32-50.

Gower, Calvin W. "The Civilian Conservation Corps and American Education: Threat to Local Control?" History of Education Quarterly 7 (Spring 1967): 58-70.

Greet, Robert L. "The Plainfield School System in the Depression: 1930-1937." New Jersey History 90 (Summer 1972): 69-82.

Hawkes, James H. "Antimilitarism at State Universities: The Campaign Against Compulsory R.O.T.C.: 1920-1940." Wisconsin Magazine of History 49 (Autumn 1965-66): 41-54.

Hendrick, Irving G. "The Impact of the Great Depression on Public School Support in California." Southern California Quarterly 54 (Summer 1972): 176-95.

_____. "California's Response to the 'New Education' in the 1930's." California Historical Quarterly 53 (Spring 1974): 25-40.

Johnson, Oakley C. "Campus Battles for Freedom in the Thirties." Centennial Review 14 (Summer 1970): 341-67.

Kaufman, Menahem. "George Antonius and American Universities: Dissemination of the Mufti of Jerusalem's Anti-Zionist Propaganda, 1930-1936." American Jewish History 75 (June 1986): 386-96.

Margo, Robert A. "Race, Educational Attainment, and the 1940 Census." Journal of Economic History 46 (March 1986): 189-98.

Medary, Marjorie. "The History of Cornell College: Stalwart in Storms, 1915-1945." Palimpsest 34 (April 1953): 184-202.

Mehren, Peter. "The San Diego City Schools Curriculum Project of the W.P.A." Journal of San Diego History 18 (Spring 1972): 8-14.

Mesirow, David. "The AFT's Role in the Thirties." Changing Education 1 (Summer 1966): 28-33.

Quantz, Richard A. "The Complex Visions of Female Teachers and the Failure of Unionization in the 1930s: An Oral History." History of Education Quarterly 25 (Winter 1985): 439-58.

Ribson, David. "Federal Aid to Arkansas Education, 1933-1936." Arkansas Historical Quarterly 36 (Summer 1977): 192-200.

Rippa, S. Alexander. "Retrenchment in a Period of Defensive Opposition to the New Deal: The Business Community and the Public Schools, 1932-1934." History of Education Quarterly 2 (June 1962): 76-82.

Rise, Eric W. "Red Menaces and Drinking Buddies: Student Activism at the University of Florida, 1936-1939." Historian 48 (Aug. 1986): 559-71.

Roop, David D. "Collegiate Cavalry: R.O.T.C. at the University of Arizona, 1921-1941." Arizona and the West 27 (Spring 1985): 55-72.

Sheridan, Richard B. "The College Student Employment Project at the University of Kansas, 1934-1943." Kansas History 8 (Winter 1985-86): 206-16.

Soderbergh, Peter A. "Charles A. Beard and the Commission on the Social Studies, 1929-1933: A Reappraisal." Social Education 31 (Oct. 1967): 465-68, 477.

Swain, Martha H. "The Harrison Education Bills, 1936-1941." Mississippi Quarterly 31 (Winter 1977-78): 119-31.

Swanson, Merwin R. "Student Radicals at the 'Southern Branch': Campus Protest in the 1930's." Idaho Yesterdays 20 (Fall 1976): 21-26.

Thomas, H. Glyn. "The Highlander Folk School: The Depression Years." Tennessee Historical Quarterly 23 (December 1964): 358-71.

Thomas, William B. "Black Intellectuals, Intelligence Testing in the 1930's, and the Sociology of Knowledge." Teachers College Record 85 (Spring 1984): 477-501.

Valentine, Jerry W. "The WPA and Louisiana Education." Louisiana History 13 (Fall 1972): 391-95.

Violas, Paul C. "The Indoctrination Debate and the Great Depression." History Teacher 4 (May 1971): 25-35.

Dissertations

Connelly, Timothy D. "Education for Victory: Federal Efforts to Promote War-Related Instructional Activities by Public Schools Systems, 1940-1945." Ph.D. diss., University of Maryland, 1982.

Finn, Mary E. "Schools and Society in Buffalo, N.Y., 1918-1936: The Effects of Progressivism." Ph.D. diss., State University of New York at Buffalo, 1980.

Guyotte, Roland Lincoln, III. "Liberal Education and the American Dream: Public Attitudes and the Emergence of Mass Higher Education, 1920-1952." Ph.D. diss., Northwestern University, 1980.

Hilton, Ronald J. "The Short Happy Life of a Learning Society: Adult Education in American, 1930-39." Ph.D. diss., Syracuse University, 1981.

Hirsh, James B. "The Response of Selected Urban Private Universities to the Forces of the Economic Depression of the 1930s." Ph.D. diss., University of Denver, 1976.

Kornfeld, Paul I. "The Educational Program of the Federal Art Project." Ph.D. diss., Illinois State University, 1981.

Montalto, Nicholas V. "The Forgotten Dream: A History of the Intercultural Education Movement, 1924-1941." Ph.D. diss., University of Minnesota, 1977.

Moore, Colleen A. "The National Association of Manufacturers: The Voice of Industry and the Free Enterprise Campaign in the Schools, 1929-1949." Ph.D. diss., University of Akron, 1985.

Orr, Kenneth B. "The Impact of the Depression Years, 1929-39, on Faculty in American Colleges and Universities." Ph.D. diss., University of Michigan, 1978.

Palmquist, Eben O. "A History of the American Historical Association's Commission on the Social Studies, 1926-1934." Ph.D. diss., Loyola University of Chicago, 1981.

Pavlak, Raymond T. "The New Deal and Public Schooling in Connecticut, 1933-1939." Ph.D. diss., University of Connecticut, 1977.

Petty, Anne W. "Dramatic Activities and Workers' Education at Highland Folk School, 1932-1942." Ph.D. diss., Bowling Green State University, 1979.

Phelps, Marianne R. "The Response of Higher Education to Student Activism, 1933-1938." Ph.D. diss., George Washington University, 1980.

Pitkin, Royce S. "Public School Support in the United States during Periods of Economic Depression." Ph.D. diss., Columbia University, 1933.

Reeves, Mary Garwood. "Economic Depression in Higher Education: Emory University, the University of Georgia and Gorgia Tech, 1930-1940." Ph.D. diss., Georgia State University, 1985.

Smith, Mark Calvin. "Knowledge For What: Social Science and the Debate over its Role in 1930's America." Ph.D. diss., University of Texas, 1980.

10.4   MASS COMMUNICATION

Books

Barnouw, Eric. A History of Broadcasting in the United States, vol 1: A Tower in Babel: To 1933; vol 2: The Golden Web: 1933-1953. New York: Oxford University Press, 1966-68.

Carlisle, Rodney P. Hearst and the New Deal: The Progressive as Reactionary. New York: Garland, 1979.

Culbert, David H. News for Everyman: Radio and Foreign Affairs in Thirties America. Westport, Conn.: Greenwood, 1976.

Edwards, Jerome E. The Foreign Policy of Colonel McCormick's Tribune, 1929-1941. Reno: University of Nevada Press, 1971.

Elson, Robert T. Time, Inc.: The Intimate History of a Publishing Enterprise, 1923-1941. New York: Atheneum, 1968.

Hosley, David H. As Good As Any: Foreign Correspondence on American Radio, 1930-1940. Westport, Conn.: Greenwood, 1984.

Kneebone, John T. Southern Liberal Journalists and the Issue of Race, 1920-1944. Chapel Hill: University of North Carolina Press, 1985.

Lipstadt, Deborah E. Beyond Belief: The American Press and the Coming of the Holocaust, 1933-1945. New York: Free Press of Macmillan, 1986.

Marchand, Roland. Advertising the American Dream: Making Way for Modernity, 1920-1940. Berkeley: University of California Press, 1985.

Pease, Otis A. The Responsibilities of American Advertising: Private Control and Public Influence, 1920-1940. New Haven: Yale University Press, 1958.

Pollard, James E. The Presidents and the Press. New York: Macmillan, 1947.

Rosen, Philip T. The Modern Stentors: Radio Broadcasters and the Federal Government, 1920-1934. Westport, Conn.: Greenwood, 1980.

Rosten, Leo. The Washington Correspondents. New York: Harcourt, Brace, 1937.

Steele, Richard W. Propaganda in an Open Society: The Roosevelt Administration and the Media, 1933-1941. Westport, Conn.: Greenwood, 1985.

Swanberg, W. A. Luce and His Empire. New York: Scribner's, 1972.

Udelson, Joseph H. The Great Television Race: A History of the American Television Industry, 1925-1945. University: University of Alabama Press, 1982.

White, Graham J. FDR and the Press. Chicago: University of Chicago Press, 1979.

Articles

Beasley, Maurine. "Lorena A. Hickok: Woman Journalist." Journalism History 7 (Autumn-Winter 1980): 92-95, 113.

_____ and Paul Belgrade. "Eleanor Roosevelt: First Lady as Radio Pioneer." Journalism History 11 (Autumn-Winter 1984): 42-45.

Beddow, James B. "Midwestern Editorial Response to the New Deal." South Dakota History 4 (Winter 1973): 1-30.

Blanchard, Margaret A. "Freedom of the Press and the Newspaper Code: June 1933-February 1934." Journalism Quarterly 54 (Spring 1977): 40-49.

_____. "Press Criticism and National Reform Movements: The Progressive Era and the New Deal." Journalism History 5 (Summer 1978): 33-37, 54-55.

Bow, James. "The Times's Financial Markets Column in the Period around the 1929 Crash." Journalism Quarterly 57 (Autumn 1980): 447-50, 497.

Carlisle, Rodney P. "William Randolph Hearst: A Fascist Reputation Reconsidered." Journalism Quarterly 50 (Spring 1973): 125-33.

_____. "William Randolph Hearst's Reaction to the American Newspaper Guild: A Challenge to New Deal Labor Legislation." Labor History 10 (Winter 1969): 74-99.

Cornwell, Elmer E., Jr. "The Presidential Press Conference: A Study in Institutionalization." Midwest Journal of Poltical Science 4 (Feb. 1960): 370-89.

Culbert, David H. "U. S. Censorship of Radio News in the 1930s: The Case of Boake Carter." Historical Journal of Film, Radio and Television 2 (1982): 173-76.

_____. "'Croak' Carter: Radio's Voice of Doom." Pennsylvania Magazine of History and Biography 97 (July 1973): 287-317.

_____. "Radio's Raymond Gram Swing: "He Isn't the Kind of Man You Would Call Ray." Historian 35 (Aug. 1973): 587-606.

Eskola, Seikko. "The Objectivity of Foreign Crisis Reports in the American Press: News about Finland in 1941." American Studies in Scandinavia 14 (1982): 49-58.

Fang, Irving E. "Boake Carter, Radio Commentator." Journal of Popular Culture 12 (Fall 1979): 341-46.

Friendly, Fred W. "Censorship and Journalists' Privilege: The Case of Near versus Minnesota--A Half Century Later." Minnesota History 46 (Winter 1978): 147-51.

Goll, Eugene W. "Frank R. Kent's Opposition to Franklin D. Roosevelt and the New Deal." Maryland Historical Magazine 63 (June 1968): 158-71.

Havig, Alan R. "Critic from Within: Fred Allen Views Radio." Journal of Popular Culture 12 (Fall 1979): 328-40.

Jones, Alfred Haworth. "The Making of an Interventionist on the Air: Elmer Davis and CBS News, 1939-1941." Pacific Historical Review 42 (Feb. 1973): 74-93.

Libby, James K. "Liberal Journals and the Moscow Trials of 1936-38." Journalism Quarterly 52 (Spring 1975): 85-92.

Lichty, Lawrence W., and Thomas W. Bohn. "Radio's March of Time: Dramatized News." Journalism Quarterly 51 (Autumn 1972): 458-62.

Lipstadt, Deborah E. "The American Press and the Persecution of German Jewry: The Early Years, 1933-1935." Leo Baeck Institute Yearbook 29 (1984): 27-55.

Marquis, Alice Goldfarb. "Written on the Wind: The Impact of Radio during the 1930s." Journal of Contemporary History 19 (July 1984): 385-415.

Morrison, Joseph L. "The 'Tar Heel Editor' in North Carolina's Crisis, 1929-1932." North Carolina Historical Review 43 (Summer 1967): 270-82.

Mould, David H. "Historical Trends in the Criticism of the Newsreel and Television News, 1930-1955." Journal of Popular Film and Television 12 (Fall 1984): 118-26.

Norden, Margaret K. "American Editorial Response to the Rise of Adolph Hitler: A Preliminary Consideration." American Jewish Historical Quarterly 59 (March 1970): 290-301.

O'Rourke, James S. "The San Francisco Chronicle and the Air Mail Emergency of 1934: The Heisenberg Principle Exemplified in Journalism." Journalism History 6 (Spring 1979): 8-13.

Pfaff, Daniel W. "Joseph Pulitzer II and Advertising Censorship, 1929-1939."
Journalism Monographs 77 (1982): 1-38.
_____. "The Press and the Scottsboro Rape Cases, 1931-32." Journalism
History 1 (Autumn 1974): 72-76.
Ragland, James F. "Merchandisers of the First Amendment: Freedom and
Responsibility of the Press in the Age of Roosevelt, 1933-1940." Georgia
Review 16 (Winter 1962): 366-91.
Rudner, Lawrence S. "Born to a New Craft: Edward R. Murrow, 1938-1940."
Journal of Popular Culture 15 (Fall 1981): 97-105.
Skates, John Ray. "From Enchantment to Disillusionment: A Southern Editor Views
the New Deal." Southern Quarterly 5 (July 1967): 363-80.
Thorson, Winston B. "The American Press and the Munich Crisis in 1938." Research
Studies of the State College of Washington 18 (No. 1, 1950): 40-68.
_____. "The American Press and the Rhineland Crisis of 1936." Research
Studies of the State College of Washington 15 (No. 4, 1947): 233-57.
Weinrott, Lester A. "Chicago Radio: The Glory Days." Chicago History 3 (Spring-
Summer 1974): 14-22.
Wyche, Billy H. "Southern Newspapers View Organized Labor in the New Deal
Years." South Atlantic Quarterly 74 (Spring 1975): 178-96.

Dissertations

Bird, William L., Jr. "Order, Efficiency and Control: The Evolution of the Political Spot
Advertisement, 1936-1956." Ph.D. diss., Georgetown University, 1985.
Carlisle, Rodney P. "The Political Ideas and Influence of William Randolph Hearst,
1928-1936." Ph.D. diss., University of California, Berkeley, 1965.
Culbert, David Holbrook. "Tantalus' Dilemma: Public Opinion, Six Radio
Commentators, and Foreign Affairs, 1935-1941." Ph.D. diss., Northwestern
University, 1970.
Hosley, David H. "The Men, the Instrument, the Moment: The Development of Radio
Foreign Correspondence in the United States through 1940." Ph.D. diss.,
Columbia University, 1982.
Katzman, Murray. "News Broadcasting in the United States, 1920-1941." Ph.D. diss.,
New York University, 1968.
Keefe, Thomas M. "The Response of the American Journals of Opinion to the Rise
and Consolidation of National Socialism, 1930-1939." Ph.D. diss., Loyola
University, 1966.
Kneebone, John T. "Race, Reform, and History: Southern Liberal Journalists, 1920-
1940." Ph.D. diss., University of Virginia, 1981.
O'Rourke, Paul A. "Liberal Journals and the New Deal." Ph.D. diss., University of
Notre Dame, 1969.
Parmenter, William Q. "The News Control Explanation of News Making: The Case
of William Randolph Hearst, 1920-1940." Ph.D. diss., University of Washington,
1979.

Sayler, James Allen. "Window on an Age: Arthur Krock and the New Deal Era, 1929-1941." Ph.D. diss., Rutgers University, 1978.

Shapiro, Stephen R. "The Big Sell: Attitudes of Advertising Writers about Their Craft in the 1920's and 1930's." Ph.D. diss., University of Wisconsin, 1969.

Soukup, Paul A. "The Term 'Medium' in United States Communication Research, 1920-1940." Ph.D. diss., University of Texas, 1985.

White, Robert G. "Martin Block and WNEW: The Rise of the Recorded Music Radio Format, 1934-1954." Ph.D. diss., Bowling Green State University, 1981.

Winfield, Betty Houchin. "Roosevelt and the Press: How Franklin D. Roosevelt Influenced Newsgathering, 1933-1941." Ph.D. diss., University of Washington, 1978.

10.5 POPULAR CULTURE

Books

Bergman, Andrew. We're in the Money: Depression America and its Films. New York: New York University Press, 1971.

Denisoff, R. Serge. Great Day Coming: Folk Music and the American Left. Urbana: University of Illinois Press, 1971.

Roddick, Nick. A New Deal in Entertainment: Warner Brothers in the 1930s. London: British Film Institute, 1983.

Sklar, Robert. Movie-Made America: A Social History of American Movies. New York: Random House, 1975.

Articles

Alexander, William. "'The March of Time' and 'The World Today'." American Quarterly 29 (Summer 1977): 182-93.

Alley, Kenneth D. "High Sierra: Swan Song for an Era." Journal of Popular Film 5 (Nos. 3/4 1976): 248-62.

Ansley, Fran, Brenda Bell, and Florence Reece. "'Little David Blues': An Interview with Tom Lowry." Southern Exposure 1 (Winter 1974): 137-43.

Barra, Allen. "The Singing Brakeman [Jimmie Rodgers]." Horizon 22 (Sept. 1979): 70-73.

Barshay, Robert. "Ethnic Stereotypes in Flash Gordon." Journal of Popular Film 3 (Winter 1974): 15-30.

Benson, Edward. "Decor and Decorum from La Chienne to Scarlet Street: Franco-U.S. Trade in Film During the Thirties." Film and History 12 (Sept. 1982): 57-65.

Billington, Monroe. "The New Deal was a Joke: Political Humor during the Great Depression." Journal of American Culture 5 (Fall 1982): 15-21.

Brady, Gabriel. "Lou Gehrig: The Iron Man." Manuscripts 32 (Spring 1980): 84-89.

Brauer, Ralph A. "When the Lights Went Out: Hollywood, the Depression and the Thirties." Journal of Popular Film and Television 8 (Winter 1981): 18-29.

Brown, Sheldon. "The Depression and World War II as Seen through Country Music." Social Education 49 (Oct. 1985): 588-95.

Carpenter, Lynette. "'There's No Place Like Home': The Wizard of Oz and American Isolationism." Film and History 15 (May 1985): 37-45.

Carringer, Robert L. "The Scripts of Citizen Kane." Critical Inquiry 5 (Winter 1978): 369-400.

Coburn, Mark D. "America's Great Black Hope." American Heritage 29 (Oct./Nov. 1978): 82-91.

Crepeau, Richard C. "Urban and Rural Images in Baseball." Journal of Popular Culture 9 (Fall 1975): 315-24.

Cripps, Thomas R. "The Myth of the Southern Box Office: A Factor in Racial Stereotyping in American Movies, 1920-1940." In The Black Experience in America ed. by James C. Curtis and Lewis L. Gould (Austin: University of Texas Press, 1970), pp. 16-44.

Drew, Bernard A. "Alaska in the Pulps." Alaska Journal 8 (Autumn 1978): 342-43.

Dunaway, David King. "Unsung Songs of Protest: The Composers Collective of New York." New York Folklore 5 (Summer 1979): 1-19.

Edmonds, Anthony O. "The Second Louis-Schmeling Fight: Sport, Symbol, and Culture." Journal of Popular Culture 7 (Summer 1973): 42-50.

Fishbein, Leslie. "A Lost Legacy of Labor Films." Film and History 9 (May 1979): 33-40.

Garcia, Lois B. "H. Bedford Jones: King of the Woodpulps." Library Chronicle of the University of Texas 10 (1978): 73-75.

Geguld, Carolyn and Harry. "From Kops to Robbers: Transformation of Archetypal Figures in the American Cinema of the 20's and 30's." Journal of Popular Culture 1 (Spring 1968): 389-94.

Gehring, Wes D. "Frank Capra--In the Tradition of Will Rogers and Other Cracker-Barrel Yankees." Indiana Social Studies Quarterly 34 (Autumn 1981): 49-56.

_____. "McCarey vs. Capra: A Guide to American Film Comedy of the '30s." Journal of Popular Film and Television 7 (No. 1 1978): 67-84.

Gillette, Howard. "Film as Artifact: The City (1939)." American Studies 18 (Fall 1977): 71-85.

Gomery, Douglas. "Rethinking U.S. Film History: The Depression Decade and Monoply Control." Film and History 10 (May 1980): 32-38.

Gossard, Wayne H., Jr. "Three Ring Circus: The Zack Miller-Tom Mix Lawsuits, 1929-1934." Chronicles of Oklahoma 58 (Spring 1980): 3-16.

Gustafson, Richard. "The Vogue of the Screen Biography." Film and History 7 (Sept. 1977): 49-58.

Hausdorff, Don. "Topical Satire and the Temper of the Early 1930's." South Atlantic Quarterly 65 (Winter 1966): 21-33.

_____. "Magazine Humor and Popular Morality, 1929-34." Journalism Quarterly 41 (Autumn 1964): 509-16.

Hellerstein, Alice. "The 1936 Olympics: A U.S. Boycott That Failed." Potomac Review 1981: 1-9.

Hickey, Neil, and Edward Sorel. "The Warner Mob." American Heritage 35 (Dec. 1983): 32-39.

Hodgkinson, Anthony W. "'Forty-Second Street' New Deal: Some Thoughts About Early Film Musicals." Journal of Popular Film 4 (No. 1, 1975): 33-46

Hunter, John O. "Marc Blitzstein's 'The Cradle Will Rock' as a Document of America, 1937." American Quarterly 18 (Summer 1966): 227-33.

Isenberg, Michael T. "An Ambiguous Pacifism: A Retrospective on World War I Films, 1930-1938." Journal of Popular Film 4 (No. 2, 1975): 98-115.

Jackson, Charles. "The Night the Martians Came." In The Aspirin Age, 1919-1941 ed. by Isabel Leighton (New York: Simon and Schuster, 1949), pp. 431-43.

Jones, James P. "Nancy Drew, WASP Super Girl of the 1930's." Journal of Popular Culture 6 (Spring 1973): 707-17.

Karnes, David. "The Glamorous Crowd: Hollywood Movie Premiers between the Wars." American Quarterly 38 (Fall 1986): 553-72.

Kass, D. A. "The Issue of Racism at the 1936 Olympics." Journal of Sport History 3 (Winter 1976): 223-35.

Kehl, James A. "Defender of the Faith: Orphan Annie and the Conservative Tradition." South Atlantic Quarterly 76 (Autumn 1977): 454-65.

Kobol, John. "Hollywood Portraits." Society 18 (March-April 1981): 77-81.

Kruger, Arnd. "'Fair Play For American Athletes': A Study in Anti-Semitism." Canadian Journal of History of Sport and Physical Education 9 (May 1978): 42-57.

Leff, Leonard J. "David Selznick's Gone with the Wind: 'The Negro Problem'." Georgia Review 38 (Spring 1984): 146-64.

Levi, Steven C. "Sackcloth and Ashes of an Age: Wiley Post and Will Rogers at Barrow, August 15, 1935." Pacific Historian 29 (Spring 1985): 57-67.

Maland, Charles. "Mr. Deeds and the American Consensus." Film and History 8 (Feb. 1978): 10-15.

Marvin, Carolyn. "Avery Brundage and American Participation in the 1936 Olympic Games." Journal of American Studies 16 (April 1982): 81-105.

Meehan, James. "Bojangles of Richmond: 'His Dancing Feet Brought Joy to the World.'" Virginia Cavalcade 27 (Winter 1978): 100-13.

Melling, P. H. "The Mind of the Mob: Hollywood and Popular Culture in the 1930s." In Cinema, Politics, and Society in America ed. by Philip Davies and Brian Neve (New York: St. Martins, 1981), pp. 19-41.

Menig, Harry. "Woody Guthrie: The Columbia and the B.P.A. Documentary: Hydro." Film and History 5 (Feb. 1975): 1-10.

_____. "Woody Guthrie: The Oklahoma Years." Chronicles of Oklahoma 53 (Summer 1975): 239-65.

Montana, Patsy. "Portraits from the Most Popular Country Show on the Air, 1924-1939." Journal of Country Music 10 (No. 3, 1985): 33-56.

Moore, James Tice. "Depression Images: Subsistence Homesteads, 'Production-For-Use,' and King Vidor's Our Daily Bread." Midwest Quarterly 26 (Autumn 1984): 24-34.

Morson, Gary Saul. "The War of the Well(e)s." Journal of Communication 29 (1979): 10-20.

Morton, Marian J. "'My Dear, I Don't Give a Damn': Scarlett O'Hara and the Great Depression." Frontiers 5 (Fall 1980): 52-56.

Nelson, Joyce. "Mr. Smith Goes to Washington: Capra, Populism, and Comic-Strip Art." Journal of Popular Film 3 (Summer 1974): 245-55.

Neve, Brian. "The Screenwriter and the Social Problem Film, 1936- 38: The Case of Robert Rossen at Warner Brothers." Film and History 14 (Feb. 1984): 2-13.

Osgood, Richard. "The Birth of the Lone Ranger." Horizon 24 (March 1981): 52-55.

Otto, John Solomon. "Hard Times Blues (1929-40): Downhome Blues Recordings as Oral Documentation." Oral History Review 8 (1980): 73-80.

Otto, Solomon and John S. "I Played Against 'Satchel' for Three Seasons: Blacks and Whites in the 'Twilight' Leagues." Journal of Popular Culture 7 (Spring 1974): 797-803.

Pauly, Thomas H. "Gone With the Wind and The Grapes of Wrath as Hollywood Histories of the Depression." Journal of Popular Film 3 (Summer 1974): 202-22.

Pinto, Alfonso. "When Hollywood Spoke Spanish." Americas 32 (Oct. 1980): 3-8.

Powers, Richard Gid. "The Attorney General and the G-Man: Hollywood's Role in Hoover's Rise to Power." Southwest Review 62 (Autumn 1977): 329-46.

Rapf, Joanna E. "'What Do They Know in Pittsburgh?': American Comic Film in the Great Depression." Studies in American Humor 3 (Summer 1984): 187-200.

Rich, Carroll Y. "Clyde Barrow's Last Ford." Journal of Popular Culture 6 (Spring 1973): 631-41.

Rollins, Peter, and Harris J. Elder. "Environmental History in Two New Deal Documentaries." Film and History 3 (Feb. 1973): 1-7.

Rollins, Peter C. "Ideology and Film Rhetoric: Three Documentaries of the New Deal Era." Journal of Popular Film 5 (no. 2, 1976): 126-45.

Rosar, William H. "Music for the Monsters: Universal Pictures' Horror Film Scores of the Thirties." Quarterly Journal of the Library of Congress 40 (Fall1983): 390-421.

Schroeder, Fred E. H. "Radio's Home Folks, 'Vic and Sade': A Study in Aural Artistry." Journal of Popular Culture 12 (Fall 1979): 253-64.

Shout, John D. "The Film Musical and the Legacy of Show Business." Journal of Popular Film and Television 10 (Spring 1982): 23-26.

Sobchack, Vivian C. "'The Grapes of Wrath' (1940): Thematic Emphasis Through Visual Style." American Quarterly 31 (Winter 1979): 596-615.

Soderbergh, Peter A. "Moonlight and Shadows: The Big Bands, 1934-1974." Midwest Quarterly 16 (Oct. 1974): 85-96.

Solomon, Eric. "Eustace Tilley Sees the Thirties through a Glass Monocle, Lightly: New Yorker Cartoonists and the Depression Years." Studies in American Humor 3 (Summer 1984): 201-19.

Stewart, Garrett. "Modern Hard Times: Chaplin and the Cinema of Self-Reflection." Critical Inquiry 3 (Winter 1976): 295-314.

Stone, Edward. "Grocho and Adolf: or, The Summer of 1941." Journal of Popular Film 2 (Summer, 1973): 219-29.

Synott, Marcia G. "The 'Big Three' and the Harvard-Princeton Football Break, 1926-1934." Journal of Sport History 3 (Summer 1976): 188-202.

Telotte, J. P. "Dancing the Depression: Narrative Strategy in the Astaire-Rogers Films." Journal of Popular Film and Television 8 (Fall 1980): 15-24.

Tibbetts, John. "The Wisdom of the Serpent: Frauds and Miracles in Frank Capra's 'The Miracle Woman.'" Journal of Popular Film and Television 7 (No. 3, 1979): 293-309.

Walsh, Francis R. "The Films We Never Saw: American Movies View Organized Labor, 1934-1954." Labor History 27 (Fall 1986): 564-80.

Welsch, Roger L. "Straight from the Horse Trader's Mouth." Kansas Quarterly 13 (Spring 1981): 17-26.

Wertheim, Arthur Frank. "Relieving Social Tensions: Radio Comedy and the Great Depression." Journal of Popular Culture 10 (Winter 1976): 501-19.

Wilkinson, Dave. "'Wrong Way' Corrigan." American History Illustrated 12 (Jan. 1978): 24-33.

Wolfe, G. Joseph. "'War of the Worlds' and the Editors." Journalism Quarterly 57 (Spring 1980): 39-44.

Wolfenstein, Judith. "Okay Okie." Westways 71 (July 1979): 33-35.

Woll, Allen L. "Latin Images in American Films, 1929-1939." Journal of Mexican American History 4 (1974): 28-40.

Wollheim, Peter. "The Case of Bonnie and Clyde." Journal of Popular Culture 7 (Winter 1973): 602-5.

Young, William H., Jr. "That Indomitable Redhead: Little Orphan Annie." Journal of Popular Culture 8 (Fall 1974): 309-16.

_____. "The Serious Funnies: Adventure Comics During the Depression, 1929-1938." Journal of Popular Culture 3 (Winter 1969): 404-27.

Zimmerman, Paul. "L. A.'s Xth Olympiad." Westways 68 (August 1976): 54-57.

Dissertations

Bergman, Andrew L. "Depression America and Its Movies." Ph.D. diss., University of Wisconsin, 1970.

Bonora, Diane C. "The Hollywood Novel of the 1930's and 1940's." Ph.D. diss., State University of New York at Buffalo, 1983.

Byrge, Duane P. "A Critical Study of the Screwball Comedy Film, 1934-1941." Ph.D. diss., University of Southern California, 1985.

Colgan, Christine A. "Warner Brothers' Crusade against the Third Reich: A Study of Anti-Nazi Activism and Film Production, 1933 to 1941." Ph.D. diss., University of Southern California, 1985.

Doss, Erika L. "Regionalists in Hollywood: Painting, Film, and Patronage, 1925-1945." Ph.D. diss., University of Minnesota, 1983.

Ellery, Suzanne C. "From Sentimentalism to Sophistication: Best Sellers and Changing American Attitudes and Values, 1914-1945." Ph.D. diss., Johns Hopkins University, 1970.

Fine, Richard A. "Hollywood and the Profession of Authorship: 1928-1940." Ph.D. diss., University of Pennsylvania, 1979.

Gustafson, Robert W. "The Buying of Ideas: Source Acquisition at Warner Brothers 1930-1949." Ph.D. diss., University of Wisconsin, 1983.

Haralovich, Mary B. "Motion Picture Advertising: Industrial and Social Forces and Effects, 1930-1948." Ph.D. diss., University of Wisconsin, 1984.

Jacobs, Lea. "Reforming the Fallen Woman Cycle: Strategies of Film Censorship, 1930-1940." Ph.D. diss., University of California, Los Angeles, 1986.

McConnell, Robert L. "Hollywood and Political Issues: Three Films of the Depression Era." Ph.D. diss., University of Iowa, 1977.

Ward, Cynthia L. "Vanity Fair Magazine and the Modern Style, 1914-1936 (New York City)." Ph.D. diss., State University of New York, 1983.

10.6 POLITICAL IDEAS AND MOVEMENTS

Books

Aaron, Daniel. Writers on the Left: Episodes in American Literary Communism. New York: Harcourt, Brace & World, 1961.

Bell, Leland V. In Hitler's Shadow: The Anatomy of American Nazism. Port Washington, N.Y.: Kennikat, 1973.

Bennett, David. Demagogues in the Depression: American Radicals and the Union Party, 1932-1936. New Brunswick, N.J.: Rutgers University Press, 1969.

Bingham, Alfred M. Insurgent America: Revolt of the Middle-Classes. New York: Harper, 1935.

Bingham, Alfred M., and Seldon Rodman, eds. Challenge to the New Deal. New York: Falcon Press, 1934.

Brinkley, Alan. Voices of Protest: Huey Long, Father Coughlin, and the Great Depression. New York: Knopf, 1982.

[Carter, John Franklin] "The Unofficial Observer." American Messiahs. New York: Simon and Schuster, 1935.

Diamond, Sander A. The Nazi Movement in the United States, 1924-1941. Ithaca: Cornell University Press, 1974.

Diggins, John P. The American Left in the Twentieth Century. New York: Harcourt Brace Jovanovich, 1973.

Draper, Theodore. American Communism and Soviet Russia: The Formative Period. New York: Viking, 1960.

_____. The Roots of American Communism. New York: Viking, 1957.

Dyson, Lowell K. Red Harvest: The Communist Party and American Farmers. Lincoln: University of Nebraska Press, 1982.

Foster, William Z. History of the Communist Party of the United States. New York: International Publishers, 1952.

Gerber, Larry G. The Limits of Liberalism: Josephus Daniels, Henry Stimson, Bernard Baruch, Donald Richberg, Felix Frankfurter & the Development of the Modern American Political Economy. New York: New York University Press, 1985.

Glazer, Nathan. The Social Basis of American Communism. New York: Harcourt, Brace, 1961.

Holtzman, Abraham. The Townsend Movement: A Political Study. New York: Bookman, 1963.

Howe, Irving, and Lewis Coser, with Julius Jacobson. The American Communist Party: A Critical History (1919-1957). Boston: Beacon, 1957.

Iversen, Robert W. The Communists and the Schools. New York: Harcourt, 1959.

Jaffe, Philip J. The Rise and Fall of American Communism. New York: Horizon, 1975.

Johnpoll, Bernard K. Pacifist's Progress: Norman Thomas and the Decline of American Socialism. Chicago: Quadrangle, 1970.
_____ and Lillian. The Impossible Dream: The Rise and Demise of the American Left. Westport, Conn.: Greenwood, 1981.

Karl, Barry D. Charles E. Merriman and the Study of Politics. Chicago: University of Chicago Press, 1974.

Kempton, Murray. Part of Our Time: Some Ruins and Monuments of the Thirties. New York: Simon and Schuster, 1955.

Klehr, Harvey. The Heyday of American Communism: The Depression Decade. New York: Basic, 1984.

Latham, Earl. The Communist Controversy in Washington: From the New Deal to McCarthy. Cambridge: Harvard University Press, 1966.

Lawson, R. Alan. The Failure of Independent Liberalism, 1930-1941. New York: Putnam, 1971.

Lyons, Eugene. The Red Decade: The Stalinist Penetration of America. Indianapolis: Bobbs-Merrill, 1941.

Myers, Constance Ashton. The Prophet's Army: Trotskyists in America, 1928-1941. Westport, Conn.: Greenwood, 1977.

Naison, Mark. Communists in Harlem during the Depression. Urbana: University of Illinois Press, 1983.

Oneal, James, and G. A. Werner. American Communism: A Critical Analysis of Its Origins, Development and Programs. New York: E. P. Dutton, 1947.

Preston, William, Jr. Aliens and Dissenters: Federal Suppression of Radicals, 1903-1933. Cambridge: Harvard University Press, 1963.

Ribuffo, Leo P. The Old Christian Right: The Protestant Far Right from the Great Depression to the Cold War. Philadelphia: Temple University Press, 1983.

Rosenof, Theodore. Patterns of Political Economy in America: The Failure to Develop a Democratic Left Synthesis, 1933-1950. New York: Garland, 1983.

Roy, Ralph Lord. Communism and the Churches. New York: Harcourt Brace, 1960.

Saposs, David Joseph. Communism in American Politics. Washington, D.C.: Public Affairs Press, 1960.

Schonbach, Morris. Native American Fascism During the 1930s and 1940s: A Study of Its Roots, and Its Decline. New York: Garland, 1985.

Skotheim, Robert A. Totalitarianism and American Social Thought. New York: Holt, Rinehart, 1971.

Smith, Geoffrey S. To Save a Nation: American Countersubversives, the New Deal, and the Coming of World War II. New York: Basic Books, 1973.

Tobin, Eugene M. Organize or Perish: America's Independent Progressives, 1913-1933. Westport, Conn.: Greenwood, 1986.

Tull, Charles J. Father Coughlin and the New Deal. Syracuse: Syracuse University Press, 1965.

Warren, Frank A., III. An Alternative Vision: The Socialist Party in the 1930s. Bloomington: Indiana University Press, 1974.

_____. Liberals and Communism: The 'Red Decade' Revisited. Bloomington: Indiana University Press, 1966.

Wolfskill, George. The Revolt of the Conservatives: A History of the American Liberty League, 1934-1940. Boston: Houghton Mifflin, 1962.

Articles

Annuziata, Frank. "The Progressive as Conservative: George Creel's Quarrel with New Deal Liberalism." Wisconsin Magazine of History 57 (Spring 1974): 220-33.

Bell, Leland V. "The Failure of Nazism in America: The German American Bund, 1936-1941." Political Science Quarterly 85 (Dec. 1970): 585-99.

Bellush, Bernard and Jewel. "A Radical Response to the Roosevelt Presidency: The Communist Party (1933-1945)." Presidential Studies Quarterly 10 (Fall 1980): 645-61.

Bicha, Karel Denis. "Liberalism Frustrated: The League for Independent Poltiical Action, 1928-1933." Mid-America 48 (Jan. 1966): 19-28.

Brinkley, Alan. "Huey Long, The Share Our Wealth Movement, and the Limits of Depression Dissidence." Louisiana History 22 (Spring 1981): 117-34.

Bulkley, Peter B. "Townsendism as an Eastern and Urban Phenomenon: Chautauqua County, New York, as a Case Study." New York History 55 (April 1974): 179-98.

Burgchardt. Carl R. "Two Faces of American Communism: Pamphlet Rhetoric of the Third Period and the Popular Front." Quarterly Journal of Speech 66 (Dec. 1980): 375-91.

Dethloff, Henry C. "The Longs: Revolution or Populist Retrenchment?" Louisiana History 19 (Fall 1978): 401-12.

Diamond, Sander A. "The Years of Waiting: National Socialism in the United States, 1922-1933." American Jewish Historical Quarterly 59 (March 1970): 256-71.

Diggins, John P. "Flirtation with Fascism: American Pragmatic Liberals and Mussolini's Italy." American Historical Review 71 (Jan. 1966): 487-506.

Ferkiss, V. C. "Populist Influences on American Fascism." Western Political Quarterly 10 (June 1957): 350-73.

Gordon, Max. "The Communist Party of the Nineteen-Thirties and the New Left." Socialist Revolution 27 (Jan. 1976): 11-66.

_____. "The Party and the Polling Place: A Response [to Kenneth Waltzer]." Radical History Review 23 (1980): 130-35.

Hein, Virginia H., and Joseph O. Baylon. "American Intellectuals and the 'Red Decade.'" Studies in History and Society 2 (No.1, 1977): 40-59.

Homberger, Eric. "Proletarian Literature and the John Reed Clubs, 1929-1935." Journal of American Studies 13 (Aug. 1979): 221-44.

Hook, Sidney. "Letters from George Santayana." American Scholar 46 (Winter 1976-77): 76-84.

Jeansonne, Glen. "Challenge to the New Deal: Huey P. Long and the Redistribution of National Wealth." Louisiana History 21 (Fall 1980): 331-39.

_____. "Gerald L. K. Smith and the Share Our Wealth Movement." Red River Valley Historical Review 3 (Summer 1978): 52-65.

_____. "Partisan Parson: An Oral History Account of the Louisiana Years of Gerald L. K. Smith." Louisiana History 23 (Spring 1982): 149-58.

Johnson, Ronald W. "The German-American Bund and Nazi Germany: 1936-1941." Studies in History and Society 6 (Spring 1975): 31-45.

Karsh, Bernard, and Phillips L. Garman. "The Impact of the Political Left." In Labor and the New Deal ed. by Milton Derber and Edwin Young (Madison: University of Wisconsin Press, 1957), pp. 77-120.

Levenstein, Harvey. "Leninists Undone by Leninism: Communism and Unionism in the United States and Mexico, 1935-1939." Labor History 22 (Spring 1981): 237-61.

Leverette, William E., Jr., and Daniel E. Shi. "Herbert Agar and Free America: A Jeffersonian Alternative to the New Deal." Journal of American Studies 16 (Aug. 1982): 189-206.

Lovin, Hugh T. "The Fall of Farmer-Labor Parties, 1936-1938." Pacific Northwest Quarterly 62 (Jan. 1971): 16-26.

_____. "Thomas R. Amlie's Crusade and the Dissonant Farmers: A New Deal Windfall." North Dakota Quarterly 49 (Winter 1981): 91-105.

Mason, Bruce. "The Townsend Movement." Southwestern Social Science Quarterly 35 (June 1954): 36-47.

McCoy, Donald R. "Native Radicals in the Thirties." In The Roosevelt New Deal: A Program Assessment Fifty Years After ed. by Wilbur J. Cohen (Austin: Lyndon B. Johnson School of Public Affairs, 1986), pp. 53-66.

_____. "The National Progressives of America, 1938." Mississippi Valley Historical Review 44 (June 1957): 75-93.

_____. "The Progressive National Committee of 1936." Western Political Quarterly 9 (June 1956): 454-69.

McMillen, Neil R. "Pro-Nazi Sentiment in the United States, March, 1933 - March, 1934." Southern Quarterly 2 (Oct. 1963): 48-70.

Moore, John Hammond. "Communists and Fascists in a Southern City: Atlanta, 1930." South Atlantic Quarterly 67 (Summer 1968): 437-54.

Myers, Constance Ashton. "American Trotskyists: The First Years." Studies in Comparative Communism 10 (Spring/Summer 1977): 133-51.

Naison, Mark. "Lefties and Righties: The Communist Party and Sports during the Great Depression." Radical America 13 (July 1979): 47-59.

_____. "Richard Wright & the Communist Party." Radical America 13 (Jan.-Feb. 1979): 60-63.

Newton, Craig A. "Father Coughlin and His National Union for Social Justice." Southwestern Social Science Quarterly 41 (Dec. 1960): 341-49.

Pearson, Norman H. "The Nazi-Soviet Pact and the End of a Dream." In America in Crisis ed. by Daniel Aaron (New York: Knopf, 1952), pp. 327-48.

Petrusza, David A. "New Deal Nemesis." Reason 9 (Jan. 1978): 29-31.

Polenberg, Richard. "The National Committee to Uphold Constitutional Government, 1937-1941." Journal of American History 52 (Dec. 1965): 582-98.

Powell, David O. "The Union Party of 1936: Campaign Tactics and Issues." Mid-America 46 (April 1964): 126-41.

Rawick, George P. "From Faith to Dogma: The Development of the Communist Party Line, 1928-1939." South Atlantic Quarterly 53 (April 1954): 193-202.

Rosenof, Theodore. "The Political Education of an American Radical: Thomas R. Amlie in the 1930's." Wisconsin Magazine of History 58 (Autumn 1974): 19-30.

Rosenzweig, Roy. "Radicals and the Jobless: The Musteites and the Unemployed Leagues, 1932-1936." Labor History 16 (Winter 1975): 52-77.

_____. "'Socialism In Our Time': The Socialist Party and the Unemployed, 1929-1936." Labor History 20 (Fall 1979): 485-509.

Rudolph, Frederick. "The American Liberty League, 1934-1940." American Historical Review 56 (Oct. 1950): 19-33.

Ryan, James Gilbert. "The Making of a Native Marxist: The Early Career of Earl Browder." Review of Politics 39 (July 1977): 332-62.

Semes, Robert Louis. "Confrontation at Charlottesville: The American Liberty League and Its Critics, 1935." Magazine of the Albermarle County Historical Society 29 (1971): 33-48.

Shapiro, Edward S. "Decentralist Intellectuals and the New Deal." Journal of American History 58 (March 1972): 938-57.

Shenton, James. "The Coughlin Movement and the New Deal." Political Science Quarterly 73 (Sept. 1958): 352-73.

Skocpol, Theda. "Political Response to Capitalist Crisis: Neo-Marxist Theories of the State and the Case of the New Deal." Politics and Society 10 (No. 2, 1980): 155-201.

Skotheim, Robert Allen. "American 'Discoveries of Totalitarianism' in the Twentieth Century." Denver Quarterly 4 (Winter 1970): 19-33.

Smith, Arthur L., Jr. "The Kameradschaft USA." Journal of Modern History 34 (Dec. 1962): 398-408.

Stegner, Wallace. "The Radio Priest and His Flock." In The Aspirin Age, 1919-1941 ed. by Isabel Leighton (New York: Simon and Schuster, 1949), pp. 232-57.

Stephanson, Anders. "The CPUSA Conception of the Rooseveltian State, 1933-1939." Radical History Review 24 (Fall 1980): 160-76.

Stone, Albert E., Jr. "Seward Collins and the American Review: Experiment in Pro-Fascism, 1933-37." American Quarterly 12 (Spring 1960): 4-19.

Venkataramani, M. S. "Leon Trotsky's Adventure in American Radical Politics, 1935-37." International Review of Social History 1 (1964): 1-46.

Wald, Alan M. "The Menorah Group Moves Left." Jewish Social Studies 38 (Summer-Fall 1976): 289-320.

Waltzer, Kenneth. "The Party and the Polling Place: American Communism and an American Labor Party in the 1930's." Radical History Review 23 (Spring 1980): 104-35.

Whisenhunt, Donald W. "The Continental Congress of Workers and Farmers, 1933." Studies in History and Society 6 (Winter 1974-75): 1-14.

Williams, Elizabeth Evenson. "A South Dakota Agrarian's Views of Huey Long: A Rhetorical Approach to Emil Lorika." Midwest Review 8 (Spring 1986): 40-55.

Dissertations

Acena, Albert. "Washington Commonwealth Federation: Reform Politics and the Popular Front, 1935-1945." Ph.D. diss., University of Washington, 1975.

Annunziata, Frank A. "The Attack on the Welfare State: Patterns of Anti-Statism from the New Deal to the New Left." Ph.D. diss., Ohio University, 1968.

Bennett, David H. "The Demagogues' Appeal in the Depression: The Origins and Activities of the Union Party, 1932-1936." Ph.D. diss., University of Chicago, 1963.

Brinkley, Alan David. "The Long and Coughlin Movements: Dissident Voices in the Great Depression." Ph.D. diss., Harvard University, 1979.

Carlson, Lewis H. "J. Parnell Thomas and the House Committee on Un-American Activities, 1938-1948." Ph.D. diss., Michigan State University, 1967.

Comerford, Robert J. "The American Liberty League." Ph.D. diss., St. John's University, 1967.

Gerber, Larry G. "The Limits of Liberalism: A Study of the Careers and Ideological Development of Josephus Daniels, Henry Stimson, Bernard Baruch, Donald Richberg, and Felix Frankfurter." Ph.D. diss., University of California, Berkeley, 1979.

Karr, Albert S. "The Roosevelt Haters: A Study in Economic Motivation." Ph.D. diss., University of Southern California, 1956.

Kling, Joseph Milton. "Making the Revolution--Maybe. . . Deradicalization and Stalinism in the American Communist Party, 1928-1938." Ph.D. diss., City University of New York, 1983.

Kyvig, David E. "In Revolt Against Prohibition: The Association Against the Prohibition Amendment and the Movement for Repeal, 1919-1933." Ph.D. diss., Northwestern University, 1971.

Lawson, Richard A. "The Failure of Independent Liberalism, 1930-1941." Ph.D. diss., University of Michigan, 1966.

McCoy, Donald R. "New Party Politics in the New Deal Era: A Historical Study of Four Attempts to Form a New, National Political Party in the United States, 1929-1938." Ph.D. diss., American University, 1954.

Notaro, Carmen Anthony. "Franklin D. Roosevelt and the American Communists: Peacetime Relations, 1932-1941." Ph.D. diss., State University New York at Buffalo, 1969.

Powell, David O. "The Union Party of 1936." Ph.D. diss., Ohio University, 1962.

Prago, Albert. "The Organization of the Unemployed and the Role of the Radicals, 1929-1935." Ph.D. diss., Union Graduate School, 1976.

Rozakis, Laurie E. "How the Division within the Liberal Community Was Reflected in the Nation, 1930-1950." Ph.D. diss., State University of New York, Stony Brook, 1984.

Ryan, James G. "Earl Browder and American Communism at High Tide: 1934-1945." Ph.D. diss., University of Notre Dame, 1981.

Schonbach, Morris. "Native Fascism during the 1930's and 1940's: A Study of Its Roots, Its Growth, and Its Decline." Ph.D. diss., University of California, Los Angeles, 1958.

Schwartz, Lawrence H. "The C.P.U.S.A.'s Approach to Literature in the 1930's: Socialist Realism and the American Party's 'Line' on Literature." Ph.D. diss., Rutgers University, 1977.

Sokoll, Carl A. "The German-American Bund as a Model for American Fascism: 1924-1946." Ph.D. diss., Columbia University, 1974.

Sunness, Sheldon D. "American Radical Populism in the 1930s." Ph.D. diss., Columbia University, 1977.

Venkataramani, M.S. "Norman Thomas and the Socialist Party of America." Ph.D. diss., University of Oregon, 1955.

Waltzer, Kenneth Alan. "The American Labor Party: Third Party Politics in New Deal - Cold War New York." Ph.D. diss., Harvard University, 1978.

10.7 RELIGION

Books

Allen, Hugh. Roosevelt and the Will of God. New York: Lifetime Editions, 1950.

Carter, Paul A. The Decline and Revival of the Social Gospel: Social and Political Liberalism in American Protestant Churches, 1920-1940. Ithaca: Cornell University Press, 1956.

DeSaulniers, Lawrence B. The Response in American Catholic Periodicals to the
Crises of the Great Depression, 1930-1935. Lanham, Md.: University Press of
America, 1984.

Flynn, George Q. American Catholics and the Roosevelt Presidency, 1932-1936.
Lexington: University of Kentucky Press, 1968.

Meyer, Donald. The Protestant Search for Political Realism, 1919-1941. Berkeley:
University of California Press, 1960.

Miller, Robert Moats. American Protestantism and Social Issues, 1919-1939. Chapel
Hill: University of North Carolina Press, 1958.

O'Brien, David J. American Catholics and Social Reform: The New Deal Years.
New York: Oxford University Press, 1968.

Articles

Archer, J. Douglas. "Conscientious Objectors and the Northern Baptist Convention of
1940." Foundations 15 (Oct. 1972): 342-54.

Betten, Neil. "The Great Depression and the Activities of the Catholic Worker
Movement." Labor History 12 (Spring 1971): 243-58.

Billington, Monroe. "Roosevelt, the New Deal, and the Clergy." Mid-America 54
(Jan. 1972): 20-33.

_____. "The Alabama Clergy and the New Deal." Alabama Review 32 (July
1979): 214-25.

_____. "The Massachusetts Clergy and the New Deal." Historical Journal of
Massachusetts 8 (June 1980): 12-29.

_____ and Cal Clark. "Clergy Reaction to the New Deal: A Comparative
Study." Historian 48 (Aug. 1986): 509-24.

Burton, David H. "Robinson, Roosevelt, and Romanism: An Historical Reflection on
the Catholic Church and the American Ideal." Records of the American
Catholic Historical Society of Philadelphia 80 (March 1969): 3-16.

Cannistraro, Philip V., and Theodore P. Kovaleff. "Father Coughlin and Mussolini:
Impossible Allies." Journal of Church and State 13 (Autumn 1971): 427-43.

Carpenter, Joel A. "A Shelter in the Times of Storm: Fundamentalist Institutions and
the Rise of Evangelical Protestantism, 1929-1942." Church History 49 (March
1980): 62-75.

Cronin, E. David. "American Catholics and Mexican Anticlericalism, 1933-1936."
Mississippi Valley Historical Review 45 (Sept. 1958): 201-30.

Dorn, Jacob H. "Religion and Reform in the City: The Re-thinking Chicago Movement
of the 1930s." Church History 55 (Sept. 1986): 323-37.

Fox, Richard W. "Reinhold Niebuhr and the Emergence of the Liberal Realist Faith,
1930-1945." Review of Politics 38 (April 1976): 244-65.

Frost, Harlan M. "Impact of the Depression on the Work of the Local Council of
Churches." Niagra Frontier 17 (Winter 1970): 104-10.

Gallagher, Robert S. "The Radio Priest." American Heritage 23 (Oct. 1972): 38-41,
100-9.

Handy, Robert T. "The American Religious Depression, 1925-1935." Church History 29 (March 1960): 3-16.

Herrmann, Richard E. "Tennessee Churches During the 1930s." Tennessee Historical Quarterly 44 (Spring 1985): 59-71.

Kemper, Donald J. "Catholic Integration in St. Louis, 1935-1947." Missouri Historical Review 73 (Oct. 1978): 1-22.

Lankford, John "The Impact of the Religious Depression upon Protestant Benevolence, 1925-1935." Journal of Presbyterian History 42 (June 1964): 104-23.

Miller, Robert Moats. "The Attitudes of American Protestants Toward the Negro, 1919-1939." Journal of Negro History 41 (July 1956): 215-40.

_____. "The Protestant Churches and Lynching, 1919-1939." Journal of Negro History 42 (April 1957): 118-31.

Moellering, Ralph. "Lutherans on Social Problems, 1917 to 1940." Concordia Historical Institute Quarterly 42 (Feb. 1969): 27-40.

_____. "Some Lutheran Reaction to War and Pacifism, 1917 to 1941." Concordia Historical Institute Quarterly 41 (Aug. 1968): 121-30.

O'Brien, David. "American Catholics and Organized Labor in the 1930's." Catholic Historical Review 52 (Oct. 1966): 323-49.

Patterson, Michael S. "The Fall of a Bishop: James Cannon, Jr. versus Carter Glass, 1909-1934." Journal of Southern History 39 (Nov. 1973): 493-518.

Peterson, Keith. "Frank Bruce Robinson and Psychiana." Idaho Yesterdays 23 (Fall 1979): 9-15, 26-29.

Potter, Richard H. "Popular Religion of the 1930's as Reflected in the Best Sellers of Harry Emerson Fosdick." Journal of Popular Culture 3 (Spring 1970): 713-28.

Shapiro, Edward S. "Catholic Agrarian Thought and the New Deal." Catholic Historical Review 65 (Oct. 1979): 583-99.

_____. "The Catholic Rural Life Movement and the New Deal Farm Program." American Benedictine Review 28 (Sept. 1977): 307-32.

Shenton, James. "Fascism and Father Coughlin." Wisconsin Magazine of History 64 (Autumn 1960): 6-11.

Simms, Adam. "A Battle in the Air: Detroit's Jews Answer Father Coughlin." Michigan Jewish History 18 (June 1978): 7-13.

Wentz, Frederick K. "American Catholic Periodicals React to Nazism." Church History 31 (Dec. 1962): 400-20.

_____. "American Protestant Journals and the Nazi Religious Assault." Church History 23 (Dec. 1954): 321-38.

Dissertations

Athans, Mary C. "The Fahey-Coughlin Connection: Father Denis Fahey, C.S. Sp., Father Charles E. Coughlin, and Religious Anti-Semitism in the United States, 1938-1954." Ph.D. diss., Graudate Theological Union, 1982.

Betten, Neil B. "Catholicism and the Industrial Worker during the Great Depression." Ph.D. diss., University of Minnesota, 1968.

Carpenter, Joel A. "The Renewal of American Fundamentalism, 1930-1945." Ph.D. diss., Johns Hopkins University, 1984.

Carter, Paul A. "The Decline and Revival of the Social Gospel: Social and Political Liberalism in American Protestant Churches, 1920-1940." Ph.D. diss., Columbia University, 1954.

Darrow, Robert M. "Catholic Political Power--A Study of the American Catholic Church on Behalf of France, 1936-1939." Ph.D. diss., Columbia University, 1953.

Flynn, George Quitman. "Franklin D. Roosevelt and American Catholicism, 1932-1936." Ph.D. diss., Louisiana State University, 1966.

Herman, Douglas Edward. "Flooding the Kingdom: The Intellectual Development of Fundamentalism, 1930-1941." Ph.D. diss., Ohio University, 1980.

Klingbeil, Kurt A. "FDR and American Religious Leaders: A Study of President Franklin D. Roosevelt and His Relationship to Selected American Religious Leaders." Ph.D. diss., New York University, 1972.

McVicker, Eugene Robbins. "Social Christianity: A Study of Four Types of Protestant Reactions to New Deal Issues." Ph.D. diss., George Washington University, 1979.

Merkley, Paul C. "Reinhold Niebuhr, the Decisive Years, 1916-1941: A Study of the Interaction of Religious Faith and Political Commitment in an American Intellectual." Ph.D. diss., University of Toronto, 1966.

Meyer, Donald B. "The Protestant Social Liberals in America, 1919-1941." Ph.D. diss., Harvard University, 1953.

Miller, Robert M. "An Inquiry into the Social Attiudes of American Protestantism, 1919-1939." Ph.D. diss., Northwestern University, 1955

O'Brien, David J. "American Catholic Social Thought in the 1930's." Ph.D. diss., University of Rochester, 1965.

10.8 SCIENCE, MEDICINE, AND TECHNOLOGY

Books

Bromberg, Walter. Psychiatry Between the Wars, 1918-1945. Westport, Conn.: Greenwood, 1982.

Harden, Victoria A. Inventing the NIH: Federal Biomedical Research Policy, 1887-1937. Baltimore: Johns Hopkins University Press, 1986.

Jones, James H. Bad Blood: The Tuskegee Syphilis Experiment. New York: Free Press, 1981.

Meikle, Jeffrey L. Twentieth Century Limited: Industrial Design in America, 1925-1939. Philadelphia: Temple University Press, 1979.

Articles

Anderson, William D., and John Parascandolia. "American Concern over Marihuana in the 1930s." Pharmacy in History 14 (No.1, 1972): 25-35.

Auerbach, Lewis E. "Scientists in the New Deal: A Pre-War Episode in the Relations Between Science and Government in the United States." Minerva 3 (Summer 1965): 457-82.

Bauer, Gene. "On the Edge of Space: The Explorer Expeditions of 1934-1935." South Dakota History 12 (Spring 1982): 1-16.

Borell, Merriley. "Biologists and the Promotion of Birth Control Research, 1918-1938." Journal of the History of Biology 20 (Spring 1987): 51-87.

Busch, Jane. "Cooking Competition: Technology on the Domestic Market in the 1930's." Technology and Culture 24 (April 1983): 222-45.

Cole, Martin. "From Moscow to a Cow Pasture in America (in sixty-two hours and seventeen minutes!)" American West 12 (Jan. 1975): 10-13.

Corn, Joseph J. "An Airplane in Every Garage." American Heritage 32 (Aug./ Sept. 1981): 48-55.

_____. "'Making Flying 'Thinkable': Women Pilots and the Selling of Aviation, 1927-1940." American Quarterly 31 (Fall 1979): 556-71.

Dalrymple, Dana G. "American Technology and Soviet Agricultural Development, 1924-1933." Agricultural History 40 (July 1966): 187-206.

de Vries, John A. "Bill McMahon, the Monney 'Flivver' and the Gray Goose." American Aviation Historical Society Journal 24 (Winter 1979): 288-90.

Dunlap, Thomas R. "Values for Varmints: Predator Control and Environmental Ideas, 1920-1939." Pacific Historical Review 53 (May 1984): 141-61.

Glass, Bentley. "Geneticists Embattled: Their Stand against Rampant Eugenics and Racism in America during the 1920s and 1930s." Proceedings of the American Philosophical Society 130 (March 1986): 130-54.

Gleason, Robert J. "Pioneer Mail Flight to Siberia." Alaska Journal 4 (Spring 1974): 122-24.

Goodstein, Judith. "Science and Caltech in the Turbulent Thirties." California History 60 (Fall 1981): 228-43.

Inouye, Arlene, and Charles Susskind. "'Technological Trends and National Policy,' 1937: The First Modern Technology Assessment." Technology and Culture 18 (Oct. 1977): 593-621.

Kay, Lily E. "W. M. Stanley's Crystallization of the Tobacco Mosaic Virus, 1930-1940." Isis 77 (Sept. 1986): 450-72.

Knerr, Hugh J. "Washington to Alaska and Back: Memories of the 1934 U.S. Air Corps Test Flight." Aerospace Historian 19 (Spring 1972): 20-24.

Kohler, Robert E., Jr. "Rudolf Schoenheimer, Isotopic Tracers, and Biochemistry in the 1930's." Historical Studies in the Physical Sciences 8 (1977): 257-98.

Kusenda, Mike. "The Keith Rider R-6: Behind the Eight Ball." American Aviation Historical Society Journal 26 (Spring 1981): 15-25.

LaFaver, L. H. "Engineering and the Depression." Forest History 14 (Jan. 1971): 15.

Lockeretz, William. "The Lessons of the Dust Bowl." American Scientist 66 (Sept.-Oct. 1978): 560-69.

McCarthy, Charles J. "Naval Aircraft Design in the Mid-1930's." Technology and Culture 4 (Spring 1963): 165-73.

Meikle, Jeffrey L. "Norman Bel Geddes and the Popularization of Streamlining." Library Chronicle of the University of Texas 13 (1980): 91-110.

Prouty, L. Fletcher. "Jimmy Doolittle and the Gee Bee." Air Force Magazine 56 (Feb. 1973): 77-81.

Pursell, Carroll W. "The Administration of Science in the Department of Agriculture, 1933-1940." Agricultural History 42 (July 1968): 231-40.

_____. "The Farm Chemurgic Council and the United States Department of Agriculture, 1935-1939." Isis 60 (Fall 1969): 307-17.

_____. "Toys, Technology and Sex Roles in America, 1920-1940." In Dynamos and Virgins Revisited: Women and Technological Change in History: An Anthology ed. by Martha M. Trescott (Metuchen, N.J.: Scarecrow, 1979), pp. 252-67.

_____. "A Preface to Government Support of Research and Development: Research Legislation and the National Bureau of Standards, 1935-41." Technology and Culture 9 (April 1968): 145-64.

_____. "Government and Technology in the Great Depression." Technology and Culture 20 (Jan. 1979): 162-74.

_____. "The Anatomy of a Failure: The Science Advisory Board, 1933-1935." Proceedings of the American Philosophical Society 109 (1965): 342-51.

Reingold, Nathan. "History of Science Today, 1. Uniformity as Hidden Diversity: History of Science in the United States, 1920-1940." British Journal for the History of Science 19 (Nov. 1986): 243-62.

Ross, Davis R. B. "Patents and Bureaucrats: U.S. Synthetic Rubber Development Before Pearl Harbor." In Business and Government: Essays in 20th Century Cooperation and Confrontation ed. by Joseph R. Frese, S. J., and Jacob Judd (Terrytown, N.Y.: Sleepy Hollow Restorations, 1985), pp. 119-55.

Rydell, Robert W. "The Fan Dance of Science: American World's Fairs in the Great Depression." Isis 76 (Dec. 1985): 525-42.

Sageser, A. Bower. "I Remember When the Stratosphere Balloon Went Pfft." Kansas Quarterly 8 (Spring 1976): 55-58.

Schneider, Albert J. "'That Troublesome Old Cockkebur:' John R. Brinkley and the Medical Profession of Arkansas, 1937-1942." Arkansas Historical Quarterly 35 (Spring 1976): 27-46.

Smith, John K. "The Ten-Year Invention: Neoprene and Du Pont Research, 1930-1939." Technology and Culture 26 (Jan. 1985): 34-55.

Smith, Richard K. "The Intercontinental Airliner and the Essence of Airplane Performance, 1929-1939." Technology and Culture 24 (July 1983): 428-49.

Soule, William H. "The Green Mountain Boy: An Attempted Trans-Atlantic Flight from Vermont to Norway, 1932." Vermont History 42 (Fall 1974): 311-17.

Stepanek, Robert H. "The Rider R-3 at the Bradley Air Museum." American Aviation Historical Society Journal 24 (Summer 1979): 122-24.

Stern, Robert H. "Television in the Thirties: Emerging Patterns of Technical Development, Industrial Control and Governmental Concern." <u>American Journal of Economics and Sociology</u> 23 (July 1964): 285-301.

Stevens, Joseph E. "Building a Dream--Hoover Dam." <u>American West</u> 21 (July/Aug. 1984): 16-27.

Strong, Elizabeth. "Science and the Early New Deal: 1933-1935." <u>Synthesis</u> 5 (1982): 44-63.

Thomas, Donald W. "Amelia Earhart's Fatal Decision." <u>American Aviation Historical Society Journal</u> 22 (Summer 1977): 87-90.

Vincenti, Walter G. "Technological Knowledge without Science: The Innovation of Flush Riveting in American Airplanes, ca. 1930-ca. 1950." <u>Technology and Culture</u> 25 (July 1984): 540-76.

Walker, Forrest A. "Americanism versus Sovietism: A Study of the Reaction to the Committee on the Costs of Medical Care." <u>Bulletin of the History of Medicine</u> 53 (Winter 1979): 489-504.

Weiner, Charles. "A New Site for the Seminar: The Refugees and American Physics in the Thirties." In <u>The Intellectual Migration: Europe and America, 1920-1960</u> ed. by Donald Fleming and Bernard Bailyn (Cambridge: Harvard University Press, 1969), pp. 190-234.

_____. "Physics in the Great Depression." <u>Physics Today</u> 23 (Oct.1970): 31-38.

Williams, R. E. "The Aircraft of Donald Douglas." <u>American Aviation Historical Society Journal</u> 26 (Spring 1981): 72-79.

Wilson, Richard Guy. "Machine-Age Iconography in the American West: The Design of Hoover Dam." <u>Pacific Historical Review</u> 54 (Nov. 1985): 463-93.

Dissertations

Adams, Paul Langford. "Health of the State: British and American Public Health Policies in the Depression and World War II." D.S.W. diss., University of California, Berkeley, 1979.

Belfield, Robert Blake. "The Niagara Frontier: The Evolution of Electric Power Systems in New York and Ontario, 1880-1935." Ph.D. diss., University of Pennsylvania, 1981.

Hodes, Elizabeth. "Precedents for Social Responsibility among Scientists: The American Association of Scientific Workers and the Federation of American Scientists, 1938-1948." Ph.D. diss., University of California, Santa Barbara, 1982.

Kuznick, Peter Jeffrey. "Beyond the Laboratory: Scientists as Political Activists in 1930's America." Ph.D. diss., Rutgers University, 1984.

Meikle, Jeffrey L. "Technological Visions of American Industrial Designers, 1925-1939." Ph.D. diss., University of Texas, 1977

Swann, John P. "The Emergence of Cooperative Research between American Universities and the Pharamaceutical Industry, 1920-1940." Ph.D. diss., University of Wisconsin, 1985.
Williams, Bernard O. "Computing with Electricity, 1935-1945." Ph.D. diss., University of Kansas, 1984.

11

Constitutional & Legal

Books

Alsop, Joseph, and Turner Catledge. The 168 Days. Garden City, N. Y.: Doubleday, Doran, 1938.

Baker, Leonard. Back to Back: The Duel between FDR and the Supreme Court. New York: Macmillan, 1967.

_____. Brandeis and Frankfurter: A Dual Biography. New York: Harper & Row, 1984.

Biddle, Francis B. Justice Holmes, National Law and the Supreme Court. New York: Macmillan, 1961.

Brown, Francis J. The Social and Economic Philosophy of Pierce Butler. Washington, D.C.: Catholic University of America Press, 1945.

Cortner, Richard C. The Jones & Laughlin Case. New York: Knopf, 1970.

_____. The Wagner Act Cases. Knoxville: University of Tennessee Press, 1964.

Corwin, Edward S. Court over Constitution: A Study of Judicial Review as an Instrument of Popular Government. Princeton: Princeton University Press, 1938.

Daniel, Cletus E. The ACLU and the Wagner Act: An Inquiry into the Depression-Era Crisis of American Liberalism. Ithaca: New York State School of Industrial and Labor Relations, 1980.

Dawson, Nelson L. Louis D. Brandeis, Felix Frankfurter, and the New Deal. Hamden, Conn.: Archon, 1980.

Friendly, Fred W. Minnesota Rag: The Dramatic Story of the Landmark Supreme Court Case that Gave New Meaning to Freedom of the Press. New York: Random House, 1981.

Gerald, J. Edward. The Press and the Constitution, 1931-1947. Minneapolis: University of Minnesota Press, 1948.

Hendel, Samuel. Charles Evans Hughes and the Supreme Court. New York: King's Crown, 1951.

Irons, Peter. The New Deal Lawyers. Princeton: Princeton University Press, 1982.

Jackson, Robert H. The Struggle for Judicial Supremacy: A Study of a Crisis in
    American Power Politics. New York: Knopf, 1941.
Johnson, John W. American Legal Culture, 1908-1940. Westport, Conn.:
    Greenwood, 1981.
Konefsky, Samuel J. Chief Justice Stone and the Supreme Court. New York:
    Macmillan, 1945.
_____. The Legacy of Holmes and Brandeis: A Study in the Influence of Ideas.
    New York: Macmillan, 1956.
Kurland, Philip B., ed. Felix Frankfurter on the Supreme Court: Extrajudicial Essays
    on the Court and the Constitution. Cambridge: Harvard University Press, 1970.
Leonard, Charles A. A Search for a Judicial Philosophy: Mr. Justice Roberts and the
    Constitutional Revolution of 1937. Port Washington, N.Y.: Kennikat, 1971.
Levy, Beryl H. Cardozo and the Frontiers of Legal Thinking: with Selected Opinions.
    New York: Oxford University Press, 1938.
Mason, Alpheus T. The Supreme Court from Taft to Warren. Baton Rouge:
    Louisiana State University Press, 1968.
Mendolson, Wallace. Justices Black and Frankfurter: Conflict in the Court. Chicago:
    University of Chicago Press, 1961.
Murphy, Bruce A. The Brandeis/Frankfurter Connection: The Secret Political
    Activities of Two Supreme Court Justices. New York: Oxford University Press,
    1982.
Murphy, Paul L. The Constitution in Crisis Times, 1918-1969. New York: Harper &
    Row, 1972.
_____. The Meaning of Freedom of Speech: First Amendment Freedoms from
    Wilson to FDR. Westport, Conn.: Greenwood, 1972.
Paschel, Joel Francis. Mr. Justice Sutherland: A Man Against the State. Princeton:
    Princeton University Press, 1951.
Pearson, Drew, and Robert S. Allen. The Nine Old Men. Garden City, N. Y.:
    Doubleday, 1964.
Pritchett, C. Herman. The Roosevelt Court: A Study in Judicial Politics and Values,
    1937-1947. New York: Macmillan, 1948.
Silverstein, Mark. Constitutional Faiths: Felix Frankfurter, Hugo Black, and the
    Process of Judicial Decision Making. Ithaca: Cornell University Press, 1984.
Vose, Clement E. Constitutional Change: Amendment Politics and Supreme Court
    Litigation Since 1900. Lexington, Mass.: Lexington Books, 1972.

Articles

Abraham, Henry J. "Reflections on FDR's Appointees to the Supreme Court." In The
    Roosevelt New Deal: A Program Assessment Fifty Years After ed. by Wilbur
    J. Cohen (Austin: Lyndon B. Johnson School of Public Affairs, 1986), pp. 307-
    41.

Auerbach, Jerold S. "Lawyers and Social Change in the Depression Decade." In
The New Deal: The National Level ed. by John Braeman, Robert H. Bremner,
and David Brody (Columbus: Ohio State University Press, 1975), pp. 133-69.

_____ and Eugene Bardach. "'Born to an Era of Insecurity': Career Patterns of
Law Review Editors, 1918-1941." American Journal of Legal History 17
(1973): 3-26.

Berens, John F. "The FBI and Civil Liberties from Franklin Roosevelt to Jimmy
Carter: An Historical Overview." Michigan Academician 13 (1980): 131-44.

Bixby, David M. "The Roosevelt Court, Democratic Ideology, and Minority Rights:
Another Look at United States v. Classic." Yale Law Review 90 (March
1981): 741-85.

Chambers, John W. "The Big Switch: Justice Roberts and the Minimum Wage
Cases." Labor History 10 (Winter 1969): 43-73.

Cotroneo, Ross R. "United States v. Northern Pacific Railway Company: The Final
Settlement of the Land Grant Case, 1924-1941." Pacific Northwest Quarterly
71 (July 1980): 107-15.

Crouch, Barry A. "Dennis Chavez and Roosevelt's 'Court-Packing' Plan." New
Mexico Historical Review 42 (Oct. 1967): 261-80.

Dillard, Irving. "The Flag-Salute Cases." In Quarrels that Have Shaped the
Constitution ed. by John A. Garraty (New York: Harper & Row, 1962), pp.
222-42.

Divine, Robert. "The Case of the Smuggled Bombers." In Quarrels that Have Shaped
the Constitution ed. by John A. Garraty (New York: Harper & Row, 1962), pp.
210-21.

Duram, James C. "Constitutional Conservatism: The Kansas Press and the New Deal
Era as a Case Study." Kansas Historical Quarterly 43 (1977): 432-47.

_____. "Supreme Court Packing and the New Deal: The View From
Southwestern Michigan." Michigan History 52 (Spring 1968): 13-27.

_____. "The Farm Journals and the Constitutional Issues of the New Deal."
American Heritage 47 (Oct. 1973): 311-28.

_____. "The Labor Union Journals and the Constitutional Issues of the New
Deal: The Case For Court Restriction." Labor History 15 (1974): 216-38.

_____. "Thompson v. Auditor General: The Michigan Supreme Court and the
Depression Emergency." Michigan History 66 (Jan. 1982): 12-16.

_____ and Eleanor A. "Congressman Clifford Hope's Correspondence with his
Constituents: A Conservative View of the Court-Packing Fight of 1937."
Kansas Historical Quarterly 37 (Spring 1971): 64-80.

Fish, Peter Graham. "Crises, Politics, and Federal Judicial Reform: The
Administrative Office Act of 1939." Journal of Politics 32 (Aug.1970): 599-627.

Freidel, Frank. "The Sick Chicken Case." In Quarrels that Have Shaped the
Constitution ed. by John A. Garraty (New York: Harper & Row, 1962), pp.
191-209.

Freund, Paul A. "Charles Evans Hughes as Chief Justice." Harvard Law Review 81
(Nov. 1967): 4-43.

_____. "Justice Brandeis: A Law Clerk's Remembrance." American Jewish History 68 (1978): 7-18.

Galloway, Russell W., Jr. "The Roosevelt Court: The Liberals Conquer (1937-1941) and Divide (1941-1946)." Santa Clara Law Review 23 (Spring 1983): 491-542.

Gardner, Robert W. "Roosevelt and Supreme Court Expansion." Connecticut Review 3 (1969): 58-68.

Garvey, Gerald "Edward S. Corwin in the Campaign of History: The Struggle for Power in the 1930's." George Washington Law Review 34 (Dec. 1965): 219-31.

_____. "Scholar in Politics: Edward S. Corwin and the 1937 Court-packing Battle." Princeton University Library Chronicle 31 (Autumn 1969): 1-11.

Gressley, Gene M. "Joseph C. O'Mahoney, FDR, and the Supreme Court." Pacific Historical Review 40 (May 1971): 183-202.

Hartmann, John E. "The Minnesota Gag Law and the Fourteenth Amendment." Minnesota History 37 (Dec. 1960): 161-73.

Hastie, William H. "Toward an Equalitarian Legal Order: 1930-1950." Annals of the American Academy of Political and Social Science 1973: 18-31.

Hine, Darlene Clark. "The N.A.A.C.P. and the Supreme Court: Walter F. White and the Defeat of Judge John J. Parker, 1930." Negro History Bulletin 40 (Sept. 1977): 753-57.

Holsinger, M. Paul. "Mr Justice Van Devanter and the New Deal: A Note." Historian 31 (Nov. 1968): 57-63.

Jones, Alfred Haworth. "Ulysses' American Odyssey." American History Illustrated 17 (1982): 10-17.

Kenneally, James J. "Catholicism and the Supreme Court Reorganization Proposal of 1937." Journal of Church and State 25 (Autumn 1983): 469-89.

Knox, John. "Some Comments on Chief Justice Hughes." Supreme Court Historical Society Yearbook 1984: 34-44.

Lamb, Karl A. "The Opposition Party as Secret Agent: Republicans and the Court Fight, 1937." Papers of the Michigan Academy of Science, Arts and Letters 66 (1961): 539-50.

Leuchtenburg, William E. "FDR's Court-Packing Plan: A Second Life, A Second Death." Duke Law Journal 1985: 673-89.

_____. "Roosevelt's Supreme Court Packing Plan." In Essays on the New Deal ed. by Harold M. Hollingsworth and William F. Holmes (Austin: University of Texas Press, 1969), pp. 69-115.

_____. "The Case of the Chambermaid and the Nine Old Men." American Heritage 38 (Dec. 1986): 34-41.

_____. "The Case of the Contentious Commissioner: Humphrey's Executor v. U.S." In Freedom and Reform: Essays in Honor of Henry Steele Commager ed. by Harold M. Hyman and Leonard W. Levy (New York: Harper & Row, 1967), pp. 276-312.

_____. "The Case of the Wenatchee Chambermaid." In Quarrels that Have Shaped the Constitution ed. by John A. Garraty (New York: Harper & Row, 1987), pp. 266-84.

_____. "The Constitutional Revolution of 1937." Essays and Memoirs From Canada and the United States ed. by Victor Hoar (Toronto: 1969), pp. 31-83.

_____. "The Origins of Franklin D. Roosevelt's 'Court-Packing' Plan." Supreme Court Review 1966: 360-79.

Lowitt, Richard. "'Only God Can Change the Supreme Court'." Capitol Studies 5 (Spring 1977): 9-24.

Maidment, Richard. "The New Deal Court Revisited." In Nothing Else to Fear: New Perspectives on America in the Thirties ed. by. Stephen W. Baskerville and Ralph Willett (Manchester: Manchester University Press, 1985), pp. 38-69.

Mason, Alpheus T. "The Supreme Court: Instrument of Power or Revealed Truth, 1930-1937." Boston University Law Review 33 (June 1953): 279-336.

Morrison, Rodney J. "Franklin D. Roosevelt and the Supreme Court: An Example of the Use of Probability Theory in Political History." History and Theory 6 (No. 2, 1977): 137-46.

Murphy, Bruce Allen. "Brandeis, FDR, and the Ethics of Judicial Advising." In The Roosevelt New Deal: A Program Assessment Fifty Years After ed. by Wilbur J. Cohen (Austin: Lyndon B. Johnson School of Public Affairs, 1986), pp. 243-67.

Murphy, Paul L. "The New Deal Agricultural Program and the Constitution." Agricultural History 29 (1955): 160-68.

_____. "The New Deal and Judicial Activism." In The Roosevelt New Deal: A Program Assessment Fifty Years After ed. by Wilbur J. Cohen (Austin: Lyndon B. Johnson School of Public Affairs, 1986), pp. 287-306.

Nathanson, Nathaniel L. "Mr. Justice Brandeis: A Law Clerk's Recollections of the October Term, 1934." American Jewish Archives 15 (April 1963): 6-16.

O'Brien, David M. "Packing the Supreme Court." Virginia Quarterly Review 62 (Spring 1986): 189-212.

Parrish, Michael E. "The Hughes Court, the Great Depression, and the Historians." Historian 40 (Feb. 1978): 286-308.

Pusey, Merlo J. "F.D.R. vs. the Supreme Court." American Heritage 9 (April 1958): 24-27, 105-7.

_____. "Justice Roberts' 1937 Turnaround." Supreme Court History Society Yearbook 1983: 102-7.

Rippa, S. Alexander. "Constitutionalism: Political Defense of the Business Community During the New Deal Period." Social Studies 56 (Oct. 1965): 187-190.

Sherman, Richard B. "The Rejection of the Child Labor Amendment." Mid-America 45 (1963): 3-17.

Sherwood, Foster H. "Judicial Control of Administrative Discretion, 1932-1952." Western Political Quarterly 6 (1953): 750-61.

Siegan, Bernard H. "The Decline and Fall of Economic Freedom." Reason 12 (January 1981): 48-51.

Sirevag, Torbjorn. "Rooseveltian Ideas and the 1937 Court Fight: A Neglected Factor," Historian 33 (Aug. 1971): 578-95.

Skefos, Catherine Hetos. "The Supreme Court Gets a Home." Supreme Court Historical Society Yearbook 1976: 25-35.

Spaulding, Thomas M. "The Supreme Court--1937." Michigan Quarterly Review 2 (Winter 1963): 1-9.

Stern, Robert L. "The Commerce Clause and the National Economy, 1933-1946." Harvard Law Review Part I: 59 (May 1946): 645-93; Part II: 59 (July 1946): 883-947.

Ulmer, S. Sidney. "Supreme Court Behavior in Racial Exclusion Cases, 1935-1960." American Political Science Review 56 (June 1962): 325-30.

Vose, Clement E. "Repeal as a Political Achievement." In Law, Alcohol, and Order: Perspectives on National Prohibition ed. by David E. Kyvig (Westport, Conn.: Greenwood, 1985), pp. 97-121.

Watson, Richard L., Jr. "The Defeat of Judge Parker: A Study in Pressure Groups and Politics." Mississippi Valley Historical Review 50 (Sept. 1963): 213-34.

Weller, Cecil Edward, Jr. "Joseph Taylor Robinson: Keystone of Franklin D. Roosevelt's Supreme Court 'Packing' Plan." Southern Historian 7 (Spring 1986): 23-30.

Whisenhunt, Donald W. "Roosevelt, McReynolds, and the Court Fight." RE: Artes Liberales 4 (Fall 1977): 1-12.

Wrigley, Linda. "The Jerome N. Frank Papers." Yale University Library Gazette 48 (1974): 163-77.

Dissertations

Carrott, Montgomery B., Jr. "The Expansion of the Fourteenth Amendment to Include Personal Liberties, 1920-1941." Ph.D. diss., Northwestern University, 1966.

Dause, Charles Allan. "An Analysis of the 1937 Public Debate over Franklin D. Roosevelt's Court Reform Proposal." Ph.D. diss., Wayne State University, 1969.

Dawson, Nelson Lloyd. "Louis D. Brandeis, Felix Frankfurter, and the New Deal." Ph.D. diss., University of Kentucky, 1975.

Duram, James C. "Press Attitudes towards the Role of the Supreme Court in the 1930's." Ph.D. diss., Wayne State University, 1968.

Friedman, R. D. "Charles Evans Hughes as Chief Justice, 1930-41." Ph.D. diss., Oxford University, 1979.

Glennon, Robert Jerome. "The Iconoclast as Reformer: Jerome Frank's Impact on American Law." Ph.D. diss., Brandeis University, 1981.

Golembe, John Carter. "The Problem of Constitutional Reform, 1929-1940." Ph.D. diss., University of Maryland, 1981.

Kornberg, Harvey R. "Charles Evans Hughes and the Supreme Court: A Study in Judicial Philosophy and Voting Behavior." Ph.D. diss., Brown University, 1972.

MacColl, E. Kimbark. "The Supreme Court and Public Opinion: A Study of the Supreme Court Fight of 1937." Ph.D. diss., University of California, Los Angeles, 1953.

McCraw, John B. "Justice McReynolds and the Supreme Court, 1914-1941." Ph.D. diss., University of Texas, 1949.

Murphy, Bruce Allen. "Supreme Court Justices as Politicians: The Extrajudicial Activities of Justices Louis D. Brandeis and Felix Frankfurter." Ph.D. diss., University of Virginia, 1978.

Murphy, Paul L. "The New Deal and the Commerce Clause." Ph.D. diss., University of California, Berkeley, 1953.

Phelps, Bernard Fred. "A Rhetorical Analysis of the 1937 Addresses of Franklin D. Roosevelt in Support of Court Reform." Ph.D. diss., Ohio State University, 1957.

Schimmel, Barbara B. "The Judicial Policy of Mr. Justice McReynolds." Ph.D. diss., Yale University, 1964.

12

Foreign Relations

12.1 GENERAL

Books

Adler, Selig. The Isolationist Impulse: Its Twentieth-Century Reaction. New York: Free Press, 1966.

_____. The Uncertain Giant, 1921-1941: American Foreign Policy Between the Wars. New York: Macmillan, 1965.

Alsop, Joseph, and Robert Kintner. American White Paper: The Story of American Diplomacy and the Second World War. New York: Simon and Schuster, 1940.

Armstrong, Hamilton Fish. Peace and Counter-Peace: From Wilson to Hitler. New York: Harper & Row, 1971.

Bailey, Thomas A. The Man in the Street: The Impact of American Public Opinion on Foreign Policy. New York: Macmillan, 1948.

Baldwin, Hanson W. The Crucial Years, 1939-1941: The World at War. New York: Harper & Row, 1976.

Barnes, Harry Elmer. Perpetual War for Perpetual Peace: A Critical Examination of the Foreign Policy of Franklin Delano Roosevelt and Its Aftermath. Caldwell, Idaho: Caston Printers, 1953.

Barron, Gloria J. Leadership in Crisis: FDR and the Path to Intervention. Port Washington, N.Y.: Kennikat, 1973.

Beard, Charles A. A Foreign Policy for America. New York: Knopf, 1940.

_____. American Foreign Policy in the Making, 1932-1940: A Study in Responsibilities. New Haven: Yale University Press, 1946.

_____. President Roosevelt and the Coming of the War, 1941: A Study in Appearances and Realities. New Haven: Yale University Press, 1948.

_____. The Devil Theory of War: An Inquiry into the Nature of History and the Possibility of Keeping Out of War. New York: Vanguard, 1936.

Berger, Jason. A New Deal for the World: Eleanor Roosevelt and American Foreign
    Policy. New York: Social Science Mongraphs, 1981.
Bolt, Ernest C. Ballots before Bullets: The War Referendum Approach to Peace in
    America, 1914-1941. Charlottesville: University Press of Virginia, 1977.
Borchard, Edwin, and William P. Lage. Neutrality for the United States. New Haven:
    Yale Unversity Press, 1937.
Buell, Raymond L. Isolated America. New York: Knopf, 1940.
Chadwin, Mark L. The War Hawks of World War II. Chapel Hill: University of North
    Carolina Press, 1968.
Challener, Richard D., ed. From Isolation to Containment: Three Decades of
    American Foreign Policy from Harding to Truman, 1921-1951. New York: St.
    Martin's, 1970.
Chatfield, Charles. For Peace and Justice: Pacifism in America, 1914-1941.
    Knoxville: University of Tennessee Press, 1971.
Cohen, Warren I. The American Revisionists: The Lessons of Intervention in World
    War I. Chicago: University of Chicago Press, 1967.
Cole, Wayne S. America First: The Battle Against Intervention, 1940-1941. Madison:
    University of Wisconsin Press, 1953.
_____. Charles A. Lindbergh and the Battle against American Intervention in
    World War II. New York: Harcourt Brace Jovanovich, 1974.
_____. Roosevelt and the Isolationists, 1932-1945. Lincoln: University of
    Nebraska Press, 1983.
_____. Senator Gerald P. Nye and American Foreign Relations. Minneapolis:
    University of Minnesota Press, 1962.
Crabb, Cecil V., Jr., and Kevin V. Mulcahy. Presidents and Foreign Policy Making:
    From FDR to Reagan. Baton Rouge: Louisiana State University Press, 1984.
Curti, Merle E. Peace or War: The American Struggle, 1636-1936. New York: W.
    W. Norton, 1936.
Dallek, Robert. Franklin D. Roosevelt and American Foreign Policy, 1932-1945. New
    York: Oxford University Press, 1979.
Denovo, John A. American Interests and Policies in the Middle East, 1900-1939.
    Minneapolis: University of Minnesota Press, 1963.
Divine, Robert A. Foreign Policy and U.S. Presidential Elections, 1940-1948. New
    York: New Viewpoints, 1974.
_____. Roosevelt and World War II. Baltimore: Johns Hopkins University
    Press, 1969.
_____. The Illusion of Neutrality. Chicago: University of Chicago Press, 1962.
_____. The Reluctant Belligerent: American Entry into World War II. 2nd ed.;
    New York: Random House, 1979.
Drummond, Donald. The Passing of American Neutrality, 1937-41. Ann Arbor:
    University of Michigan Press, 1955.
Dulles, Allen W., and Hamilton Fish Armstrong. Can America Stay Neutral? New
    York: Harper, 1939.
_____. Can We Be Neutral? New York: Harper, 1936.

Dulles, Foster Rhea. America's Rise to World Power, 1898-1954. New York: Harper, 1955.

Durosell, E. Jean-Baptiste. From Wilson to Roosevelt: Foreign Policy of the United States, 1913-1945. Cambridge: Harvard University Press, 1963.

Ellis, L. Ethan. Republican Foreign Policy, 1921-1933. New Brunswick, N.J.: Rutgers University Press, 1968.

Esthus, Raymond A. From Enmity to Alliance: U.S.-Australian Relations, 1931-1941. Seattle: University of Washington Press, 1964.

Fehrenbach, T. R. F.D.R.'s Undeclared War, 1939-41. New York: David McKay, 1967.

Feis, Herbert. 1933: Characters in Crisis. Boston: Little, Brown, 1966.

Fenwick, Charles G. American Neutrality: Trial and Failure. New York: New York University Press, 1940.

Ferrell, Robert H.. American Diplomacy in the Great Depression: Hoover-Stimson Foreign Policy, 1929-1933. New Haven: Yale University Press, 1957.

Fleming, Denna Frank. The United States and the World Court. Garden City, N. Y.: Doubleday, 1945.

_____. The United States and World Organization, 1920-1933. New York: Columbia University Press, 1938.

Flynn, George Q. Roosevelt and Romanism: Catholics and American Diplomacy, 1937-1945. Westport, Conn.: Greenwood, 1976.

Guinsburg, Thomas N. The Pursuit of Isolationism in the United States Senate from Versailles to Pearl Harbor. New York: Garland, 1982.

Heinrichs, Waldo H., Jr. American Ambassador: Joesph C. Grew and the Development of the United States Diplomatic Tradition. Boston: Little, Brown, 1966.

Jablon, Howard. Crossroads of Decision: The State Department and Foreign Policy, 1933-1939. Lexington: University Press of Kentucky, 1983.

Johnson, Walter. The Battle Against Isolation. Chicago: University of Chicago Press, 1944.

Jonas, Manfred. Isolationism in America, 1935-1941. Ithaca: Cornell University Press, 1966.

Josephson, Harold. James T. Shotwell and the Rise of Internationalism in America. Rutherford, N.J.: Fairleigh Dickinson University Press, 1974.

Kennan, George F. American Diplomacy, 1900-1950. Chicago: University of Chicago Press, 1951.

Kennedy, Thomas C. Charles A. Beard and American Foreign Policy. Gainesville: University Presses of Florida, 1975.

Kimball, Warren. The Most Unsordid Act: Lend-Lease, 1939-1941. Baltimore: Johns Hopkins University Press, 1969.

Koenig, Louis W. The Presidency and the Crisis: Powers of the Office from the Invasion of Poland to Pearl Harbor. New York: King's Crown Press, 1944.

Langer, Robert. Seizure of Territory: The Stimson Doctrine and Related Principles in Legal Theory and Diplomatic Practice. Princeton: Princeton University Press, 1947.

Langer, William L, and S. Everett Gleason. The Challenge to Isolation, 1937-1940.
　　New York: Harper & Row, 1952.
　　_____. The Undeclared War, 1940-1941. New York: Harper & Row, 1953.
Leigh, Michael. Mobilizing Consent: Public Opinion and American Foreign Policy,
　　1937-1947. Westport, Conn.: Greenwood, 1976.
Liggio, Leonard P., and James J. Martin, eds. Watershed of Empire: Essays on New
　　Deal Foreign Policy. Colorado Springs: Ralph Myles, 1976.
Maddox, Robert James. William E. Borah and American Foreign Policy. Baton
　　Rouge: Louisiana State University Press, 1969.
Martin, James J. American Liberalism and World Politics, 1931-1941: Liberalism's
　　Press and Spokesmen on the Road Back to War between Mukden and Pearl
　　Harbor. New York: Devin-Adair, 1964.
Myers, William. The Foreign Policies of Herbert Hoover, 1929-1933. New York:
　　Scribners, 1940.
Nelson, John K. The Peace Prophets: American Pacifist Thought, 1919-1941. Chapel
　　Hill: University of North Carolina Press, 1967.
Nevins, Allan. The New Deal in World Affairs: A Chronicle of International Affairs,
　　1933-1945. New Haven: Yale University Press, 1950.
　　_____. The United States in a Chaotic World: A Chronicle of International
　　Affairs, 1918-1933. New Haven: Yale University Press, 1950.
　　_____ and Lewis M. Hacker, eds. The United States and Its Place in World
　　Affairs, 1918-1943. Boston: D.C. Heath, 1943.
O'Connor, Raymond G. Force & Diplomacy: Essays Military and Diplomatic. Coral
　　Gables: University of Miami Press, 1972.
　　_____. Perilous Equilibrium: The United States and the London Naval
　　Conference of 1930. Lawrence: University of Kansas Press, 1962.
Offner, Arnold A. The Origins of the Second World War: American Foreign Policy
　　and World Politics, 1914-1941. New York: Praeger, 1975.
Osgood, Robert E. Ideals and Self-Interest in America's Foreign Relations: The Great
　　Transformation of the Twentieth Century. Chicago: University of Chicago
　　Press, 1953.
Ostrower, Gary B. Collective Insecurity: The United States and the League of
　　Nations during the Early Thirties. Lewisburg, Pa.: Bucknell University Press,
　　1979.
Payne, Howard C., Raymond Callahan, and Edward M. Bennett. As the Storm Clouds
　　Gathered: European Perceptions of American Foreign Policy in the 1930s.
　　Durham, N.C.: Moore Publishing Co., 1979.
Pelz, Stephen E. Race to Pearl Harbor: The Failure of the Second London Naval
　　Conference and the Onset of World War II. Cambridge: Harvard University
　　Press, 1974.
Porter, David L. The Seventy-Sixth Congress and World War II, 1939-1940.
　　Columbia: University of Missouri Press, 1979.
Range, Willard. Franklin D. Roosevelt's World Order. Athens: University of Georgia
　　Press, 1959.

Rauch, Basil. Roosevelt: From Munich to Pearl Harbor: A Study in the Creation of a Foreign Policy. New York: Creative Age Press, 1950.

Russett, Bruce M. No Clear and Present Danger: A Skeptical View of the United States Entry into World War II. New York: Harper & Row, 1972.

Sontag, Raymond J. A Broken World, 1919-1939. New York: Harper, 1971.

Stenehjem, Michele Flynn. An American First: John T. Flynn and the America First Committee. New Rochelle: Arlington House, 1976.

Stromberg, Roland N. Collective Security and American Foreign Policy: From The League of Nations to NATO. New York: Praeger, 1963.

Tansill, Charles C. Back Door to War: The Roosevelt Foreign Policy, 1933-1941. Chicago: Henry Regnery, 1952.

Trask, Roger R. The United States Response to Turkish Nationalism and Reform, 1914-1939. Minneapolis: University of Minnesota Press, 1971.

Van Alstyne, Richard W. American Crisis Diplomacy: The Quest for Collective Security, 1918-1952. Stanford: Stanford University Press, 1952.

Williams, William Appleman. The Tragedy of American Diplomacy. Cleveland: World, 1959.

Wilson, Joan Hoff. American Business and Foreign Policy, 1920-1933. Lexington: University of Kentucky Press, 1971.

Wiltz, John Edward. From Isolation to War, 1931-1941. New York: Thomas Y. Crowell, 1968.

_____. In Search of Peace: The Senate Munitions Inquiry, 1934-36. Baton Rouge: Louisiana State University Press, 1963.

Articles

Accinelli, Robert D. "Militant Internationalists: The League of Nations Associations, the Peace Movement, and U.S. Foreign Policy, 1934-38." Diplomatic History 4 (Winter 1980): 19-38.

_____. "The Hoover Administration and the World Court." Peace and Change 4 (Fall 1977): 28-36.

_____. "The Roosevelt Administration and the World Court Defeat, 1935." Historian 40 (May 1978): 463-78.

Adams, D. K. "Messersmith's Appointment to Vienna in 1934: Presidential Patronage or Career Promotion?" Delaware History 18 (Spring 1978): 17-27.

Adler, Selig. "Hoover's Foreign Policy and the New Left." In The Hoover Presidency: A Reappraisal ed. by Martin L. Fausold and George T. Mazuzan (Albany: State University of New York Press, 1974), pp. 153-63.

_____. "United States Policy on Palestine in the FDR Era." American Jewish Historical Quarterly 62 (Sept. 1972): 11-29.

Allen, William R. "The Peace Movement." In Isolation and Security ed. by Alexander DeConde (Durham: Duke University Press, 1957), pp. 82-106.

Berg, Meredith W. "Admiral William H. Standley and the Second London Naval Treaty, 1934-1936." Historian 33 (Feb. 1971): 215-36.

Best, Gary Dean. "Totalitarianism or Peace: Herbert Hoover and the Road to War, 1939-1941." Annals of Iowa 44 (Winter 1979): 516-29..

Borg, Dorothy. "Notes on Roosevelt's Quarantine Speech." Political Science Quarterly 72 (Sept. 1957): 405-33.

Boyle, Peter G. "The Roots of Isolationism: A Case Study." Journal of American Studies 6 (No. 1, 1972): 41-50.

Brax, Ralph S. "When Students First Organized against War: Student Protest during the 1930s." New York Historical Society Quarterly 63 (July 1979): 228-55.

Bressler, Robert J. "The Ideology of the Executive State: Legacy of Liberal Internationalism." In Watershed of Empire: Essays on New Deal Foreign Policy ed. by Leonard P. Liggio and James J. Martin (Colorado Springs: Ralph Myles, 1976), pp. 1-18.

Brune, Lester H. "Considerations of Force in Cordell Hull's Diplomacy, July 26 to November 26, 1941." Diplomatic History 2 (Fall 1978): 389-405.

Burns, Richard Dean. "International Arms Inspection Policies Between World Wars, 1919-1934." Historian 31 (Aug. 1969): 583-603.

_____. "Regulating Submarine Warfare, 1921-41: A Case Study in Arms Control and Limited War." Military Affairs 35 (April 1971): 56-62.

_____. "Supervision, Control and Inspections of Armaments: 1919-1941 Perspective." Orbis 15 (Fall 1971): 943-52.

_____ and W. A. Dixon. "Foreign Policy and the 'Democratic Myth': The Debate on the Ludlow Amendment." Mid-America 47 (Oct. 1965)): 288-306.

Burt, Alfred L. "America and the Crisis of 1938-1939." In The United States and Its Place in World Affairs, 1918-1943 ed. by Allan Nevins and Louis M. Hacker (Boston: D.C. Heath, 1943), pp. 402-9.

_____. "Foreign Problems under Roosevelt, 1933-1935." In The United States and Its Place in World Affairs, 1918-1943 ed. by Allan Nevins and Louis M. Hacker (Boston: D.C. Heath, 1943), pp. 375-87.

_____. "The Isolationist Response to World Perils." In The United States and Its Place in World Affairs, 1918-1943 ed. by Allan Nevins and Louis M. Hacker (Boston: D.C. Heath, 1943), pp. 388-401.

Carleton, William G. "Isolationism and the Middle West." Mississippi Valley Historical Review 33 (Dec. 1946): 377-90.

Chatfield, Charles. "Alternative Antiwar Strategies of the Thirties." American Studies 13 (Spring 1972): 81-93.

Cherny, Robert W. "Isolationist Voting in 1940: A Statistical Analysis." Nebraska History 52 (Fall 1971): 293-310.

Clifford, J. Garry. "A Note on the Break between Senator Nye and President Roosevelt in 1939." North Dakota History 49 (Summer 1982): 14-17.

_____ and Robert Griffiths. "Senator John A. Danaher and the Battle Against American Intervention in World War II." Connecticut History 25 (Nov. 1984): 39-63.

Cole, Wayne S. "A Tale of Two Isolationists--Told Three Wars Later." Society for Historians of American Foreign Relations Newsletter 5 (March 1974): 2-16.

_____. "America First and the South, 1940-1941." Journal of Southern History 22 (Feb. 1956): 36-47.

Cook, Blanche Wisen. "'Turn toward Peace': ER and Foreign Affairs." In Without Precedent: The Life and Career of Eleanor Roosevelt ed. by Joan Hoff-Wilson and Marjorie Lightman (Bloomington: Indiana University Press, 1984), pp. 108-21.

Crownover, Donald A. "The Neutrality View from the Sunday News [1935-1939]," Lancaster County Historical Society Journal 70 (Trinity 1966): 163-78.

Current, Richard N. "The United States and 'Collective Security': Notes on the History of an Idea." In Isolation and Security ed. by Alexander DeConde (Durham, N.C.: Durke University Press, 1957): pp. 33-55.

Dallek, Robert. "Beyond Tradition: The Diplomatic Careers of William E. Dodd and George S. Messersmith, 1933-1938." South Atlantic Quarterly 66 (Spring 1967): 233-44.

Daniel, Robert L. "The United States and the Turkish Republic Before World War II: The Cultural Dimension." Middle East Journal 21 (Winter 1967): 52-63.

DeConde, Alexander. "The South and Isolationism." Journal of Southern History 24 (Aug. 1958): 332-46.

DeWitt, Howard A. "Hiram Johnson and Early New Deal Diplomacy, 1933-1934." California Historical Quarterly 53 (Winter 1974): 377-86.

Divine, Robert A. "Franklin D. Roosevelt and Collective Security, 1933." Mississippi Valley Historical Review 48 (June 1961): 42-59.

Doenecke, Justus D. "American Isolationism, 1939-1941." Journal of Libertarian Studies 6 (Summer/Fall 1982): 201-16.

_____. "Edwin M. Borchard, John Bassett Moore, and Opposition to American Intervention in World War II." Journal of Libertarian Studies 6 (Winter 1982): 1-34.

_____. "Explaining the Antiwar Movement, 1939-1941: The Next Assignment." Journal of Libertarian Studies 8 (Winter 1986): 321-25.

_____. "Isolationism of the Left: The Keep America Out of the War Congress, 1938-41." Journal of Contemporary History 12 (April 1977): 221-36.

_____. "Power, Markets, and Ideology: The Isolationist Response to Roosevelt Policy, 1940-1941." In Watershed of Empire: Essays on New Deal Foreign Policy ed. by Leonard P. Liggio and James J. Martin (Colorado Springs: Ralph Myles, 1976), pp. 132-61.

_____. "The Anti-Interventionist Tradition: Leaders and Perceptions." Literature of Liberty 4 (Summer 1981): 7-67.

_____. "The Isolationist as Collectivist: Lawrence Dennis and the Coming of World War II." Journal of Libertarian Studies 3 (Summer 1979): 191-207.

_____. "The Strange Career of American Isolationism." Peace and Change 3 (Summer 1975): 79-83.

_____. "Verne Marshall's Leadership of the No Foreign War Committee, 1940." Annals of Iowa 41 (Winter 1973): 1153-72.

Donnelly, James B. "Prentiss Gilbert's Mission to the League of Nations Council, October 1931." Diplomatic History 2 (Fall 1978): 373-87.

_____. "Prentiss Bailey Gilbert and the League of Nations: The Diplomacy of an Observer." In U.S. Diplomats in Europe, 1919-1941 ed. by Kenneth Paul Jones (Santa Barbara, Cal.: ABC-Clio, 1981), pp. 95-109.

Donovan, John C. "Congressional Isolationists and the Roosevelt Foreign Policy." World Politics 3 (April 1951): 299-316.

Dorwart, Jeffrey M. "The Roosevelt--Astor Espionage Ring." New York History 62 (July 1981): 307-22.

Dreier, John A. "Kenton County, Kentucky: Re-evaluating the Ethnic Origins of Isolationism." Filson Club History Quarterly 51 (July 1977): 262-75.

Dulles, Foster Rhea, and Gerald E. Ridinger. "The Anti-Colonial Policies of Franklin D. Roosevelt." Political Science Quarterly 70 (March 1955): 1-18.

Errico, Charles J. "The New Deal, Internationalism, and the New American Consensus, 1938-1940." Maryland Historian 9 (Spring 1978): 17-31.

Evans, William B. "Senator James E. Murray: A Voice of the People in Foreign Affairs." Montana: The Magazine of Western History 32 (Winter 1982): 24-36.

Fensterwald, Bernard, Jr. "The Anatomy of American 'Isolationism' and Expansionism." Journal of Conflict Resolution 2 (1958): 125-42, 280-307.

Fitzsimons, M. A. "Roosevelt: America's Strategist." Review of Politics 7 (July 1945): 280-96.

Fleisig, Heywood W. "The United States and the Non-European Periphery During the Early Years of the Great Depression." In The Great Depression Revisited ed. by H. van den Wee (The Hague: Martinus Nijhoff, 1973), pp. 145-81.

Gardner, Lloyd C. "New Deal Diplomacy: A View from the Seventies." In Watershed of Empire: Essays on New Deal Foreign Policy ed. by Leonard P. Liggio and James J. Martin (Colorado Springs: Ralph Myles, 1976), pp. 95-131.

Garlid, George W. "Minneapolis Unit of the Committee to Defend America by Aiding the Allies." Minnesota History 41 (No. 6, 1969): 267-83.

Goldberg, Joyce S. "FDR, Elbert D. Thomas, and American Neutrality." Mid-America 68 (Jan. 1986), 35-50.

Griffin, Walter R. "Louis Ludlow and the War Referendum Crusade, 1935-1941." Indiana Magazine of History 14 (Dec. 1968): 267-88.

Guinsburg, Thomas N. "The George W. Norris 'Conversion' to Internationalism, 1939-1941." Nebraska History 53 (Winter 1972): 477-90.

Haight, John McV., Jr. "Roosevelt and the Aftermath of the Quarantine Speech." Review of Politics 24 (April 1962): 233-59.

Halperin, Samuel, and Irwin Oder. "The United States in Search of a Policy: Franklin D. Roosevelt and Palestine." Review of Politics 24 (July 1962): 320-41.

Heinrichs, Waldo. "President Franklin D. Roosevelt's Intervention in the Battle of the Atlantic, 1941." Diplomatic History 10 (Fall 1986): 311-32.

Holsinger, M. Paul. "The I'm Alone Controversy: A Study in Inter-American Diplomacy, 1929-1935." Mid-America 50 (Oct. 1968): 305-13.

Jablon, Howard. "The State Department and Collective Security, 1933-34." Historian 33 (Feb 1971): 248-63.

Jacobs, Travis Beal. "Roosevelt's 'Quarantine Speech." Historian 24 (Aug. 1962): 483-502.

Jonas, Manfred. "Pro-Axis Sentiment and American Isolationism." Historian 29 (Feb. 1967): 221-37.

Kahn, David. "United States Views of Germany and Japan in 1941." In Knowing One's Enemies: Intelligence Assessment Before the Two World Wars ed. by Ernest R. May (Princeton: Princeton University Press, 1986), pp. 476-501.

Kahn, Gilbert N. "Presidential Passivity on a Nonsalient Issue: President Franklin D. Roosevelt and the 1935 World Court Fight." Diplomatic History 4 (Spring 1980): 137-59.

Kasurak, Peter. "American Foreign Policy Officials and Canada, 1927-1941: A Look through Bureaucratic Glasses." International Journal 32 (Summer 1977): 544-88.

Kennedy, Thomas C. "Beard vs. F.D.R. on National Defense and Rearmament." Mid-America 50 (Jan. 1968): 22-41.

Kinder, Douglas Clark, and William O. Walker. "Stable Force in a Storm: Harry J. Anslinger and United States Narcotics Foreign Policy, 1930-1962." Journal of American History 72 (March 1986): 908-27.

Kottman, Richard N. "Herbert Hoover and the St. Lawrence Seaway Treaty of 1932." New York History 52 (July 1975): 314-46.

_____. "Hoover and Canada Diplomatic Appointments." Canadian Historical Review 51 (Sept. 1970): 292-308.

_____. "The Hoover-Bennett Meeting of 1931: Mismanaged Summitry." Annals of Iowa 42 (Winter 1974): 205-21.

Kuehl, Warren F. "Midwestern Newspapers and Isolationist Sentiment." Diplomatic History 3 (Summer 1979): 283-306.

Lauderbaugh, Richard A. "Business, Labor, and Foreign Policy: U.S. Steel, the International Steel Cartel, and Recognition of the Steel Workers Organizing Committee." Politics and Society 6 (No. 4, 1976): 433-57.

Leopold, Richard W. "The Mississippi Valley and American Foreign Policy, 1890-1941: An Assessment and an Appeal." Mississippi Valley Historical Review 37 (March 1951): 625-42.

Loewenheim, Francis L. "An Illusion that Shaped History: New Light on the History and Historiography of American Peace Efforts before Munich." In Some Pathways in Twentieth Century History ed. by Daniel R. Beaver (Detroit, Wayne State University Press, 1969), pp. 177-220.

Lowenthal, Mark M. "Roosevelt and the Coming of the War: The Search for United States Policy, 1937-42." Journal of Contemporary History 16 (July 1981): 413-40.

Maddux, Thomas R. "Red Fascism, Brown Bolshevism: The American Image of Totalitarianism in the 1930s." Historian 40 (Nov. 1977): 85-103.

Margulies, Herbert F. "The Senate and the World Court." Capitol Studies 4 (Fall 1976): 37-52.

Marks, Frederick W., III. "Franklin Roosevelt's Diplomatic Debut: The Myth of the Hundred Days." South Atlantic Quarterly 84 (Summer 1985): 245-63.

Mazuzan, George H. "The Failure of Neutrality Revision in Mid-Summer 1939: Warren R. Austin's Memorandum of the White House Conference." Vermont History 42 (Summer 1974): 239-44.

Melosh, Barbara. "'Peace in Demand': Anti-War Drama in the 1930s." History Workshop Journal 22 (Autumn 1986): 70-88.

Neumann, William L. "Roosevelt's Options and Evasions in Foreign Policy Decisions, 1940-1945." In Watershed of Empire: Essays on New Deal Foreign Policy ed. by Leonard P. Liggio and James J. Martin (Colorado Springs: Ralph Myles, 1976), pp. 162-82.

Nichols, Jeannette P. "The Middle West and the Coming of World War II." Ohio State Archeological and Historical Quarterly 62 (April 1953): 122-45.

Norman, John. "Influence of Pro-Fascist Propaganda on American Neutrality, 1935-1936." In Essays in History and International Relations ed. by Dwight E. Lee and George E. McReynolds (Worcester, Mass.: Clark University Press, 1949), pp. 193-214.

Offner, Arnold A. "Appeasement and Aggression: The New Deal and the Origins of the Second World War." In Fifty Years Later: The New Deal Evaluated ed. by Harvard Sitkoff (New York: Knopf, 1985), pp. 187-210.

Ostrower, Gary B. "The American Decision to Join the International Labor Organization." Labor History 16 (Spring 1975): 495-504.

Papachristou, Judith. "An Exercise in Anti-Imperialism: The Thirties." American Studies 15 (Spring 1974): 61-77.

Partin, John W. "The Dilemma of "A Good, Very Good Man': Capper and Noninterventionism, 1936-1941." Kansas History 2 (Summer 1979): 86-95.

Patterson, James T. "Eating Humble Pie: A Note on Roosevelt, Congress, and Neutrality Revision in 1939." Historian 31 (May 1969): 407-14.

_____. "Robert A. Taft and American Foreign Policy, 1939-1945." In Watershed of Empire: Essays on New Deal Foreign Policy ed. by Leonard P. Liggio and James J. Martin (Colorado Springs: Ralph Myles, 1976), pp. 183-207.

Porter, David L. "Ohio Representative John M. Vorys and the Arms Embargo in 1939." Ohio History 83 (1974): 103-13.

_____. "Senator Warren R. Austin and the Neutrality Act of 1939." Vermont History 42 (Summer 1974): 228-38.

Pratt, Julius W. "The Ordeal of Cordell Hull." Pacific Historical Review 28 (Jan. 1966): 76-98.

Rhodes, Benjamin D. "Herbert Hoover and the War Debts, 1919-1933." Prologue 6 (Summer 1974): 130-44.

Roberts, Martha Byrd. "Reluctant Belligerent." American History Illustrated 17 (Nov. 1982): 20-29.

Rosenberg, Emily S. "The Invisible Protectorate: The United States, Liberia, and the Evolution of Neocolonialism, 1909-40." Diplomatic History 9 (Summer 1985): 191-214.

Ryant, Carl G. "From Isolation to Intervention: The Saturday Evening Post, 1939-1942." Journalism Quarterly 48 (1971): 679-89.

Sargent, James E. "F.D.R., Foreign Policy, and the Domestic-First Perspective, 1933-1936: An Appraisal." Peace and Change 3 (Spring 1975): 24-29.

Sbrega, John J. "The Anticolonial Policies of Franklin D. Roosevelt: A Reappraisal." Political Science Quarterly 101 (1986): 65-84.

Shapiro, Edward S. "The Approach of War: Congressional Isolationism and Anti-Semitism, 1939-1941." American Jewish History 74 (Sept. 1984): 45-65.

Shofner, Jerrell H. "Murders at Kiss-Me-Quick: The Underside of International Affairs." Florida Historical Quarterly 62 (Jan. 1984): 332-38.

Smith, Geoffrey S. "Isolationism, the Devil, and the Advent of WW II: Variations on a Theme." International History Review 4 (Feb. 1982): 55-89.

Smith, M. J. J. "F.D.R. and the Brussels Conference, 1937." Michigan Academician 14 (Fall 1981): 109-22.

Smith, Robert Freeman. "American Foreign Relations, 1920-1942." In Towards a New Past: Dissenting Essays in American History ed. by Barton J. Bernstein (New York: Pantheon, 1968), pp. 232-62.

Smuckler, Ralph H. "The Region of Isolationism." American Political Science Review 47 (June 1953): 386-401.

Sniegoski, Stephen J. "Unified Democracy: An Aspect of American World War II Interventionist Thought, 1939-1941." Maryland Historian 9 (Spring 1978): 33-48.

Sontag, Raymond J. "The Origins of the Second World War." Review of Politics 25 (Oct. 1963): 497-508.

Steele, Richard W. "Franklin D. Roosevelt and His Foreign Policy Critics." Political Science Quarterly 94 (Spring 1979): 15-32.

_____. "Preparing the Public for War: Efforts to Establish a National Propaganda Agency, 1940-41." American Historical Review 75 (Oct. 1970): 1640-53.

_____. "The Great Debate: Roosevelt, the Media, and the Coming of the War, 1940-1941." Journal of American History 71 (June 1984): 69-92.

Sternsher, Bernard. "The Stimson Doctrine: F.D.R. versus Moley and Tugwell." Pacific Historical Review 31 (Aug. 1962): 281-89.

Stromberg, Roland N. "American Business and the Approach of War, 1935-1941." Journal of Economic History 13 (Winter 1953): 58-78.

Stuhler, Barbara. "The One Man Who Voted 'Nay': The Story of John T. Bernard's Quarrel with American Foreign Policy, 1937-1939." Minnesota History 43 (Fall 1972-73): 83-92.

Swerczek, Ronald E. "Hugh Gibson and Disarmament: The Diplomacy of Gradualism." In U.S. Diplomats in Europe, 1919-1941 ed. by Kenneth Paul Jones (Santa Barbara, Cal.: ABC-Clio, 1981), pp. 75-90.

Thompson, Dean K. "World War II, Interventionism, and Henry Pitney Van Dussen." Journal of Presbyterian History 55 (Winter 1977): 327-45.

Tuttle, William M., Jr. "Aid-to-the-Allies Short-of-War versus American Intervention, 1940: A Reappraisal of William Allen White's Leadership." Journal of American History 56 (March 1970): 840-58.

Utley, Jonathan G. "The U.S. Enters World War II." In Modern American Diplomacy ed. by John M. Carroll and George C. Herring, Jr. (Wilmington: Scholarly Resources, 1986), pp. 91-105.

Van Alstyne, Richard W. "Papers Relating to the Foreign Relations of the United States, 1931: A Review." Pacific Historical Review 16 (Nov. 1947): 429-36.

Vinson, John C. "War Debts and Peace Legislation: The Johnson Act of 1934." Mid-America 50 (July 1968): 206-22.

Vieth, Jane Karoline. "The Diplomacy of the Depression." In Modern American Diplomacy ed. by John M. Carroll and George C. Herring, Jr. (Wilmington: Scholarly Resources, 1986), pp. 71-89.

Walker, Samuel. "Communists and Isolation: The American Peace Mobilization, 1940-1941." Maryland Historian 4 (Spring 1973): 1-12.

Wallace, Benjamin J. "How the United States 'Led the League' in 1931." American Political Science Review 30 (1961): 165-78.

Weiss, Stuart L. "American Foreign Policy and Presidential Power: The Neutrality Act of 1935." Journal of Politics 30 (Aug. 1968): 672-95.

Wilkins, Robert P. "Middle Western Isolationism: A Re-Examination." North Dakota Quarterly 25 (Summer 1957): 69-76.

_____. "The Nonpartisan League and Upper Midwest Isolationism." Agricultural History 39 (April 1965): 102-9.

Williams, William Appleman. "A Note on the Isolationism of Senator William E. Borah." Pacific Historical Review 22 (Nov. 1953): 391-92.

Wilson, Joan Hoff. "A Reevaluation of Herbert Hoover's Foreign Policy." In The Hoover Presidency: A Reappraisal ed. by Martin L. Fausold and George T. Mazuzan (Albany: State University of New York Press, 1974), pp. 164-86.

_____. "'Peace is a Woman's Job . . .' Jeannette Rankin's Foreign Policy." Montana: The Magazine of Western History 20 (Jan. and April 1980): 28-41, 38-53.

Wiltz, John E. "The Nye Committee Revisited." Historian 23 (Feb. 1961): 211-33.

Winkler, Fred H. "Disarmament and Security: The American Policy at Geneva, 1926-1935." North Dakota Quarterly 38 (Autumn 1971): 21-33.

_____. "The War Department and Disarmament, 1926-1935." Historian 28 (May 1966): 426-46.

Young, Lowell T. "Franklin D. Roosevelt and American Islets: Acquisition of Territory in the Carribean and in the Pacific." Historian 35 (Feb. 1973): 205-20.

Zeitzer, Glen. "The Fellowship of Reconciliation on the Eve of the Second World War: A Peace Organization Prepares." Peace and Change 3 (Summer-Fall 1975): 46-51.

Dissertations

Alexander, Robert J. "The Disarmament Policy of the United States, 1933-1934." Ph.D. diss., Georgetown University, 1953.

Anderson, John Thomas. "Senator Burton K. Wheeler and United States Foreign Relations (Montana)." Ph.D. diss., University of Virginia, 1982.

Berg, Meredith W. "The United States and the Breakdown of Naval Limitation, 1934-1939." Ph.D. diss., Tulane University, 1966.

Berger, Jason. "A New Deal for the World: Eleanor Roosevelt and American Foreign Policy, 1920-1962." Ph.D. diss., City University of New York, 1979.

Bowers, Robert E. "The American Peace Movement, 1933-41." Ph.D. diss., University of Wisconsin, 1949.

Brandenburg, Earnest S. "An Analysis and Criticism of Franklin D. Roosevelt's Speeches on International Affairs Delivered between September 3, 1939 and December 7, 1941." Ph.D. diss., University of Iowa, 1949.

Burns, Richard D. "Cordell Hull: A Study in Diplomacy--1933-1941." Ph.D. diss., University of Illinois, 1960.

Chadwin, Mark L. "Warhawks: The Interventionists of 1940-1941." Ph.D. diss., Columbia University, 1965.

Chatfield, E. Charles, Jr. "Pacifism and American Life, 1914 to 1941." Ph.D. diss., Vanderbilt University, 1965.

Cleary, Charles R. "Congress, the Executive, and Neutrality: 1935 to 1940." Ph.D. diss., Fordham University, 1953.

Cleary, Robert E. "Executive Agreements in the Conduct of United States Foreign Policy: A Case Study: The Destroyer-Base Deal." Ph.D. diss., Rutgers University, 1969.

Cohen, Warren I. "Revisionism between World Wars: A Study in American Diplomatic History." Ph.D. diss., Washington University, 1962.

Conway, Maurice B. "The Intellectual Origins of the Cold War: American Policymakers and Policy, 1933-1945." Ph.D. diss., University of California, Santa Barbara, 1974.

Crollman, Catherine A. "Cordell Hull and His Concept of a World Organization." Ph.D. diss., University of North Carolina, 1965.

DeBoe, David C. "The United States and the Geneva Disarmament Conference, 1932-1934." Ph.D. diss., Tulane University, 1969.

Dohse, Michael A. "American Periodicals and the Palestine Triangle, April, 1936 to February, 1947." Ph.D. diss., Mississippi State University, 1966.

Downing, Marvin L. "Hugh R. Wilson and American Relations with the League of Nations, 1927-1937." Ph.D. diss., University of Oklahoma, 1970.

Dreier, John A. "The Politics of Isolation: A Quantitative Study of Congressional Foreign Policy Voting, 1937-1941." Ph.D. diss., University of Kentucky, 1977.

Dressler, Thomas Herbert Bernhard. "The Foreign Policies of American Individualism: Herbert Hoover, Reluctant Internationalist." Ph.D. diss., Brown University, 1973.

Eagen, Eileen M. "The Student Peace Movement in the U.S., 1930-1941." Ph.D. diss., Temple University, 1979.

Edwards, Jerome E. "Foreign Policy Attitudes of the Chicago Tribune, 1929-1941." Ph.D. diss., University of Chicago, 1966.

Ehrenreich, Dixie L. W. "Newspapers, Public Opinion, and Neutrality: 1935-1939." Ph.D. diss., University of Idaho, 1977.

Fedyszyn, Thomas R. "Liberal America and War Entry: A Study of the Propaganda Campaign Conducted Prior to the American Intervention in World War II." Ph.D. diss., Johns Hopkins University, 1978.

Ferguson, Robert B. "The Southern Baptist Response to International Affairs and Threats to Peace, 1931-1941." Ph.D. diss., Carnegie-Mellon University, 1981.

Fitzgerald, Paul A. "American Neutrality and the Italo-Ethiopian Conflict." Ph.D. diss., Georgetown University, 1953.

Frank, Catherine M. "Franklin D. Roosevelt and His Conference Advisers: The Determination of the Influence of Certain Men and Institutions on Franklin D. Roosevelt from August 1941 to April 1945, Particularly in Making Certain Conference Decisions and Agreements." Ph.D. diss., Fordham University, 1955.

Gardner, Lloyd C. "American Foreign Policy in a Closed World: 1933-1945." Ph.D. diss., University of Wisconsin, 1960.

Guinsberg, Thomas N. "Senatorial Isolationism in America, 1919-1941." Ph.D. diss., Columbia University, 1969.

Herring, George C., Jr. "Experiment in Foreign Aid: Lend-Lease, 1941-1945." Ph.D. diss., University of Virginia, 1965.

Holtzclaw, Harold W. "The American War Referendum Movement, 1914-1941." Ph.D. diss., University of Denver, 1965.

Irvin, Thomas C. "Norman H. Davis and the Quest for Arms Control, 1931-1938." Ph.D. diss., Ohio University, 1963.

Jablon, Howard. "Cordell Hull, the State Department, and the Foreign Policy of the First Roosevelt Administration, 1933-1936." Ph.D. diss., Rutgers University, 1967.

Jaffe, Joseph L. "Isolationism and Neutrality in Academe, 1938-1941." Ph.D. diss., Case Western Reserve University, 1979.

Jonas, Manfred. "The Isolationist Viewpoint, 1935-1941: An Analysis." Ph.D. diss., Harvard University, 1959.

Kanawada, Leo Vincent, Jr. "The Ethnic Factor in American Diplomacy during the Presidency of Franklin D. Roosevelt: 1933-1939." Ph.D. diss., St. John's University, 1980.

Kasurak, Peter C. "The United States Legation at Ottawa, 1927-1941: An Institutional Study." Ph.D. diss., Duke University, 1976.

Kennedy, Thomas Crawford. "Charles A. Beard and American Foreign Policy." Ph.D. diss., Stanford University, 1961.

Kinsella, William Edward, Jr. "Franklin D. Roosevelt and the Necessity of War." Ph.D. diss., Georgetown University, 1974.

Kosberg, Roberta Louise. "Executive-Legislative Rhetoric Regarding American Participation in an Association of Nations, 1916-1920 and 1935-1945." Ph.D. diss., Pennsylvania State University, 1982.

Lauderbaugh, Richard A. "American Steel Makers and the Coming of the Second World War." Ph.D. diss., Washington University, 1979.

Leach, David M. "The American Approach to Neutrality: A Study in the Evolution of an Idea with Special Emphasis upon the 'New Neutrality' of the 1930's." Ph.D. diss., University of Rochester, 1959.

Lindley, Christopher. "Franklin D. Roosevelt and the Politics of Isolationism, 1932-1936." Ph.D. diss., Cornell University, 1963.

Little, John Michael. "Canada Discovered: Continentalist Perceptions of the Roosevelt Administration, 1939-1945." Ph.D. diss., University of Toronto, 1975.

Loebs, Bruce Duane. "A Study of Franklin D. Roosevelt's Rhetorical Strategies in Pursuing his Prewar Goals in 1940 and 1941." Ph.D. diss., University of Oregon, 1968.

Marabell, George P. "Frederick Libby and the American Peace Movement, 1921-1941." Ph.D. diss., Michigan State University, 1975.

Miller, Jean-Donald. "The United States and Colonial Sub-Saharan Africa, 1939-1945." Ph.D. diss., University of Connecticut, 1981.

Moore, Jamie W. "The Logic of Isolation and Neutrality: American Foreign Policy 1933-1935." Ph.D. diss., University of North Carolina, 1970.

Moss, Kenneth B. "Bureaucrat as Diplomat: George S. Messersmith and the State Department's Approach to War, 1933-1941." Ph.D. diss., University of Minnesota, 1978.

Muresiano, John M. "War of Ideas: American Intellectuals and the World Crisis, 1938-1945." Ph.D. diss., Harvard University, 1982.

Norris, Parthenia E. "United States and Liberia: The Slavery Crisis, 1929-1935." Ph.D. diss., Indiana University, 1961.

Norton, Nile B. "Frank R. McCoy and American Diplomacy, 1929-1932." Ph.D. diss., University of Denver, 1966.

O'Connor, Raymond G. "The United States and the London Naval Conference of 1930." Ph.D. diss., Stanford University, 1957.

Ostrower, Gary B. "The United States, the League of Nations, and Collective Security, 1931-1934." Ph.D. diss., University of Rochester, 1970.

Papachristou, Judith R. "American-Soviet Relations and United States Policy in the Pacific, 1933-1941." Ph.D. diss., University of Colorado, 1968.

Range, Willard. "Franklin D. Roosevelt's Theory of International Relations." Ph.D. diss., University of North Carolina, 1958.

Reuter, Paul H., Jr. "William Phillips and the Development of American Foreign Policy, 1933-1947." Ph.D. diss., University of Southern Mississippi, 1979.

Rhodes, Benjamin D. "The United States and the War Debt Questions, 1917-1934." Ph.D. diss., University of Colorado, 1965.

Roberds, Elmo M., Jr. "The South and the United States Foreign Policy, 1933-1952." Ph.D. diss., University of Chicago, 1954.

Robinson, Peter E. "The United States and the World Court, 1930-1946." Ph.D. diss., Mississippi State University, 1964.

Sallach, David L. "Enlightened Self-Interest: The Congress of Industrial Organizations' Foreign Policy, 1935-1955." Ph.D. diss., Rutgers University, 1983.

Shulman, Holly C. "The Voice of Victory: The Development of American Propaganda and the Voice of America, 1920-1942." Ph.D. diss., University of Maryland, 1984.

Silverman, Sheldon A. "At the Water's Edge: Arthur Vandenberg and the Foundations of American Bipartisan Foreign Policy." Ph.D. diss., University of California, Los Angeles, 1967.

Smith, Glenn H. "Senator William Langer: A Study of Isolationism." Ph.D. diss., University of Iowa, 1968.

Sniegoski, Stephen J. "The Intellectual Wellsprings of American World War II Interventionism, 1939-1941." Ph.D. diss., University of Maryland, 1977.

Spooner, Ward A. "United States Policy toward South Africa, 1919-1941, Political and Economic Aspects." Ph.D. diss., St. John's University, 1979.

Stiller, Jesse Herbert. "George S. Messersmith: A Diplomatic Biography." Ph.D. diss., City University of New York, 1980.

Towne, Ralph Louis, Jr. "Roosevelt and the Coming of World War II: An Analysis of the War Issues Treated by Franklin D. Roosevelt in Selected Speeches, October 5, 1937 to December 7, 1941." Ph.D. diss., Michigan State University, 1961.

Trask, Roger R. "The Relations of the United States and Turkey, 1927-1939." Ph.D. diss., Pennsylvania State University, 1959.

Trotter, Agnes Anne. "The Development of the Merchants of Death Theory of American Intervention in the First World War, 1914-1937." Ph.D. diss., Duke University, 1966.

Viault, Birdsall S. "The Peace Issue, 1939-1940." Ph.D. diss., Duke University, 1963.

Weiss, Stuart L. "The New Deal and Collective Security, 1933-1936: The Origins and Development of a Foreign Policy." Ph.D. diss., University of Chicago, 1961.

Winkler, Fred H. "The United States and the World Disarmament Conference, 1926-1935: A Study of the Formulation of Foreign Policy." Ph.D. diss., Northwestern University, 1957.

Young, Lowell T. "Franklin D. Roosevelt and Imperialism." Ph.D. diss., University of Virginia, 1970.

12.2   ASIA

Books

Anderson, Irvine H., Jr. The Standard-Vacuum Oil Company and United States East Asian Policy, 1933-1941. Princeton: Princeton University Press, 1975.

Baker, Leonard. Roosevelt and Pearl Harbor. New York: Macmillan, 1970.

Borg, Dorothy. The United States and the Far Eastern Crisis of 1933-1938: From the Machurian Incident through the Initial Stage of the Undeclared Sino-Japanese War. Cambridge: Harvard University Press, 1964.

_____ and Shumpei Okamoto, eds. Pearl Harbor as History: Japanese-American Relations, 1931-1941. New York: Columbia University Press, 1973.

Buhite, Russell D. Nelson T. Johnson and American Policy Toward China, 1925-1941. East Lansing: Michigan State University Press, 1968.

Burns, Richard D., and Edward M. Bennett, eds. Diplomats in Crisis: United States-Chinese-Japanese Relations, 1919-1941. Santa Barbara, Cal.: ABC-Clio, 1974.

Doenecke, Justus D. The Diplomacy of Frustration: The Manchurian Crisis of 1931-1933 as Revealed in the Papers of Stanley K. Hornbeck. Stanford, Cal.: Hoover Institution Press, 1981.

_____. When the Wicked Rise: American Opinion-Makers and the Manchurian Crisis, 1931-1933. Lewisburg, Pa.: Bucknell University Press, 1984.

Fairbank, John King. The United States & China. 4th, enlarged ed.; Cambridge: Harvard University Press, 1983.

Farago, Ladislas. The Broken Seal: The Story of "Operation Magic" and the Pearl Harbor Disaster. New York: Random House, 1967.

Feis, Herbert. The Road to Pearl Harbor: The Coming of War between the United States and Japan. Princeton: Princeton University Press, 1950.

Friedman, Donald J. The Road from Isolation: The Campaign of the American Committee for Non-Participation in Japanese Agression, 1938-1941. Cambridge: Harvard University Press, 1968.

Herzog, James H. Closing the Open Door: American and Japanese Diplomatic Relations, 1936-1941. Annapolis, Md.: Naval INstitute Press, 1973.

Hoehling, Adolph A. The Week before Pearl Harbor. New York: Norton, 1963.

Koginos, Manny T. The Panay Incident: Prelude to War. Lafayette: Purdue University Press, 1967.

Lord, Walter. Day of Infamy. New York: Holt, Rinehart & Winston, 1957.

Melosi, Martin V. The Shadow of Pearl Harbor: Political Controversy over the Surprise Attack, 1941-1946. College Station: Texas A&M University Press, 1977.

Millis, Walter. This Is Pearl: The United States and Japan, 1941. New York: Morrow, 1947.

Neu, Charles E. The Troubled Encounter: The United States and Japan. New York: Wiley, 1975.

Neumann, William L. America Encounters Japan: From Perry to MacArthur. Baltimore: Johns Hopkins University Press, 1963.

Perry, Hamilton D. The Panay Incident: Prelude to Pearl Harbor. New York: Macmillan, 1969.

Prange, Gordon W. At Dawn We Slept: The Untold Story of Pearl Harbor. New York: McGraw Hill, 1981.

Rappaport, Armin. Henry L. Stimson and Japan, 1931-1933. Chicago: University of Chicago Press, 1963.

Schaller, Michael. The U.S. Crusade in China, 1938-1945. New York: Columbia University Press, 1979.

Schroeder, Paul. The Axis Alliance and Japanese-American Relations, 1941. Ithaca: Cornell University Press, 1958.

Smith, Sara R. The Manchurian Crisis, 1931-1932: A Tragedy in International Relations. New York: Columbia University Press, 1948.

Taylor, Sandra C. Advocate of Understanding: Sidney Gulick and the Search for Peace with Japan. Kent, Ohio: Kent State University Press, 1984.

Theobold, Robert A. The Final Secret of Pearl Harbor: The Washington Contribution to the Japanese Attack. New York: Devin-Adair, 1954.

Tuchman, Barbara. Stillwell and the American Experience in China, 1911-1945. New York: Macmillan, 1971.

Utley, Jonathan G. Going to War with Japan, 1937-1941. Knoxville: University of Tennessee Press, 1985.

Varg, Paul A. The Closing of the Door: Sino-American Relations, 1936-1946. East Lansing: Michigan State University Press, 1973.

Wohlstetter, Roberta. Pearl Harbor: Warning and Decision. Stanford: Stanford University Press, 1962.

Articles

Adams, Frederick C. "The Road to Pearl Harbor: A Reexamination of American Far Eastern Policy, July 1937-December 1938." Journal of American History 58 (June 1971): 73-92.

Anderson, Irvine H., Jr. "The 1941 De Facto Embargo on Oil to Japan: A Bureaucratic Reflex." Pacific Historical Review 44 (May 1975): 201-31.

Barclay, Glen St. John. "Singapore Strategy: The Role of the United States in Imperial Defense." Military Affairs 39 (April 1975): 54-59.

Barnhart, Michael A. "Planning the Pearl Harbor Attack: A Study in Military Politics." Aerospace Historian 29 (Winter 1982): 246-59.

Bennett, Edward M. "Joseph C. Grew: The Diplomacy of Pacification." In Diplomats in Crisis: United States-Chinese-Japanese Relations, 1919-1941 ed. by Richard Dean Burns and Edward M. Bennett (Santa Barbara, Cal.: ABC-Clio, 1974), pp. 65-89.

Ben-Zvi, Abraham. "American Preconceptions and Policies toward Japan, 1940-1941: A Case Study in Misperception." International Studies Quarterly 19 (June 1975): 228-48.

Boyle, John A. "The Drought-Walsh Mission to Japan." Pacific Historical Review 34 (May 1965): 141-61.

Bratzel, John F., and Leslie B. Rout, Jr. "Pearl Harbor, Microdots, and J. Edgar Hoover." American Historical Review 87 (Dec 1982): 1342-51.

Breslin, Thomas A. "Trouble Over Oil: America, Japan, and the Oil Cartel, 1934-1935." Bulletin of Concerned Asian Scholars 7 (July 1975): 41-50.

Buckley, Thomas. "John Van Antwerp MacMurray: The Diplomacy of an American Mandarin." In Diplomats in Crisis: United States-Chinese-Japanese Relations, 1919-1941 ed. by Richard Dean Burns and Edward M. Bennett (Santa Barbara, Cal.: ABC-Clio, 1974), pp. 27-48.

Burns, Richard Dean. "Inspection of the Mandates, 1919-1941." Pacific Historical Review 37 (Nov. 1968): 445-62.

_____. "Stanley K. Hornbeck: The Diplomacy of the Open Door." In Diplomats in Crisis: United States-Chinese-Japanese Relations, 1919-1941 ed. by Richard Dean Burns and Edward M. Bennett (Santa Barbara, Cal.: ABC-Clio, 1974), pp. 91-117.

Burt, Alfred L. "The United States and the League in the Far East, 1931-1932." In The United States and Its Place in World Affairs, 1918-1943 ed. by Allan Nevins and Louis M. Hacker (Boston: D.C. Heath, 1943), pp. 330-46.

Butow, R. J. C. "Backdoor Diplomacy in the Pacific: The Proposal for a Konoye-Roosevelt Meeting, 1941." Journal of American History 59 (June 1972): 48-72.

_____. "The Hull-Nomura Conversations: A Fundamental Misconception." American Historical Review 65 (July 1960): 822-36.

Castle, Alfred L. "William R. Castle and Opposition to U.S. Involvement in an Asian War, 1939-1941." Pacific Historical Review 54 (Aug. 1985): 337-51.

Clauss, Errol MacGregor. "The Roosevelt Administration and Manchukuo, 1933-1941." Historian 32 (Aug. 1970): 595-611.

Clifford, Nicholas R. "Britain, America and the Far East, 1937-1940." Journal of British Studies 3 (Nov. 1963): 137-54.

Clyde, Paul H. "The Diplomacy of 'Playing no Favorites': Secretary Stimson and Manchuria, 1931." Mississippi Valley History Review 35 (Sept. 1948): 187-202.

Cole, Wayne S. "Senator Key Pittman and American Neutrality Policies, 1933-1940." Mississippi Valley Historical Review 46 (March 1960): 644-62.

Current, Richard N. "How Stimson Meant to 'Maneuver' the Japanese." Mississippi Valley Historical Review 40 (June 1953): 67-74.

_____. "The Stimson Doctrine and the Hoover Doctrine." American Historical Review 59 (April 1954): 513-42.

Daniels, Jonathan. "Pearl Harbor Sunday: The End of an Era." In The Aspirin Age, 1919-1941 ed. by Isabel Leighton (New York: Simon and Schuster, 1949), pp. 476-91.

Dingman, Roger. "Farewell to Friendship: The U.S.S. Astoria's Visit to Japan, April 1939." Diplomatic History 10 (Spring 1986): 121-39.

Doenecke, Justus D. "The Debate Over Coercion: The Dilemma of America's Pacifists and the Machurian Crisis." Peace and Change 11 (Spring 1974): 265-76.

Dupuy, T. N. "Pearl Harbor: Who Blundered?" American Heritage 13 (Feb. 1962): 64-81.

Eismeier, Dana L. "U.S. Oil Policy, Japan, and the Coming of War in the Pacific, 1940-1941." Michigan Academician 14 (Spring 1982): 359-67.

Ferrell, Robert H. "Pearl Harbor and the Revisionists." Historian 17 (Spring 1955): 215-33.

Graebner, Norman A. "Japan: Unanswered Challenge, 1931-1941." In Essays on American Foreign Policy ed. by David G. DeBoe, et al. (Austin: University of Texas Press, 1974), pp. 117-44.

Haight, John McVickar, Jr. "Franklin D. Roosevelt and a Naval Quarantine of Japan." Pacific Historical Review 40 (May 1971): 203-26.

Harrington, Daniel F. "A Careless Hope: American Air Power and Japan, 1941." Pacific Historical Review 48 (May 1979): 217-38.

Harris, Ruth R. "The 'Magic' Leak of 1941 and Japanese-American Relations." Pacific Historical Review 50 (Feb. 1981): 77-96.

Herzog, James H. "Influence of the United States Navy in the Embargo of Oil to Japan, 1940-1941." Pacific Historical Review 35 (Aug. 1966): 317-28.

Hill, Norman. "Was There an Ultimatum before Pearl Harbor?" American Journal of International Law 42 (April 1948): 355-67.

Hoffer, Peter C. "American Business and the Japan Trade, 1931-1941: A Case Study of Attitude Formation." Pacific Historical Review 41 (May 1972): 189-205.

Honan, William H. "Japan Strikes: 1941." American Heritage 22 (Dec. 1970): 12-15, 91-95.

Howard, Woodford. "Frank Murphy and the Philippine Commonwealth." Pacific Historical Review 33 (Feb. 1964): 45-68.

Hoyt, Frederick B. "The Summer of '30: American Policy and Chinese Communism." Pacific Historical Review 46 (May 1977): 229-49.

Hsu, Immanuel C. Y. "Kurusu's Mission to the United States and the Abortive Modus Vivendi." Journal of Modern History 24 (Sept. 1952): 301-7.

Jablon, Howard. "Cordell Hull, His 'Associates', and Relations with Japan, 1933-1936." Mid-America 56 (July 1974): 160-74.

Kent, Charles R. "American Articulate Opinion of the Chinese Communist Movement, 1918-1937." Lock Haven Review 9 (1967): 48-57.

LaFeber, Walter. "Before Pearl Harbor." Current History 57 (Aug. 1969): 65-70, 114.

Lawrence, James R. "The American Federation of Labor and the Philippine Independence Question, 1920-1935." Labor History 7 (Winter 1966): 62-69.

Leary, William M., Jr. "Wings for China: The Jouet Mission, 1932-1935." Pacific Historical Review 38 (Nov. 1969): 447-62.

Libby, Justin H. "American-Japanese Relations and the Coming War in the Pacific: A Congressional View." Pacific Historian 22 (Winter 1978): 379-402.

_____. "Anti-Japanese Sentiment in the Pacific Northwest: Senator Schwellenbach and Congressman Coffee Attempt to Embargo Japan." Mid-America 58 (Oct. 1972):167-74.

_____. "The Irreconcilable Conflict: Key Pittman and Japan During the Interwar Years." Nevada Historical Society Quarterly 18 (Fall 1975): 129-40.

Liu, Daniel T. J. "A Review of Diplomatic Relations Between the Republic of China and the United States of America: The Sino-Japanese Conflicts, 1931-1936." Chinese Culture 15 (Sept. 1974): 43-75.

_____. "A Study of Diplomatic Relations Between China and the United States of America: The Sino-Japanese War, 1937-1941." Chinese Culture 15 (Dec. 1974): 11-38.

Maga, Timothy P. "Democracy and Defense: The Case of Guam, U.S.A., 1918-1941." Journal of Pacific History 20 (July 1985): 156-72.

Masland, John W. "Commercial Influence Upon American Far Eastern Policy, 1937-1941." Pacific Historical Review 2 (Sept. 1942): 281-90.

McCarthy, Kenneth G., Jr. "Stanley K. Hornbeck and the Manchurian Crisis." Southern Quarterly 10 (July 1972): 305-24.

Neumann, William L. "Franklin D. Roosevelt and Japan, 1913-1933." Pacific Historical Review 22 (May 1953): 143-53.

Okumiya, Masotoka. "How the Panay was Sunk." U.S. Naval Institute Proceedings 79 (June 1955): 587-96.

Pearson, Alden B., Jr. "A Christian Moralist Responds to War: Charles C. Morrison, The Christian Century and the Manchurian Crisis, 1931-33." World Affairs 139 (No. 4, 1977): 296-307.

Perkins, Ernest Ralph. "The Non-application of Sanctions against Japan, 1931-1932." In Essays in History and International Relations ed. by Dwight E. Lee and George E. McReynolds (Worceser, Mass.: Clark University Press, 1949), pp. 215-32.

Perry, Darby. "Rehearsal for World War II." American Heritage 18 (April 1967): 40-45, 76-81.

Pratt, Lawrence. "The Anglo-American Naval Conversations on the Far East of January 1938." International Affairs 47 (Oct. 1971): 745-63.

Ray, Deborah Wing. "The Takoradi Route: Roosevelt's Prewar Venture beyond the Western Hemisphere." Journal of American History 62 (Sept. 1975): 340-58.

Ross, Gary. "W. Cameron Forbes: The Diplomacy of a Darwinist." In Diplomats in Crisis: United States-Chinese-Japanese Relations, 1919-1941 ed. by Richard Dean Burns and Edward M. Bennett (Santa Barbara, Cal.: ABC-Clio, 1974), pp. 49-64.

Sewall, Arthur F. "Key Pittman and the Quest for the China Market, 1933-1940." Pacific Historical Review 44 (Aug. 1975): 351-71.

Shewmaker, Kenneth E. "The American Liberal Dream: Evans F. Carlson and the Chinese Communists, 1937-1947." Pacific Historical Review 38 (May 1969): 207-16.

Smith, M. J. J. "Henry L. Stimson and the Philippines: American Withdrawal from Empire, 1931-1935." Michigan Academician 5 (Winter 1973): 335-48.

Swanson, Harlan J. "The Panay Incident: Prelude to Pearl Harbor." Proceedings of the United States Naval Institute 93 (December 1967): 26-37.

Tuchman, Barbara W. "Japan Strikes: 1937: Part Two of a Series on General Joseph W. Stilwell in China." American Heritage 22 (Dec. 1970): 4-11, 79-90.

Utley, Jonathan G. "Diplomacy in a Democracy: The United States and Japan, 1937-1941." World Affairs 139 (Fall 1976): 130-40.

_____. "Japanese Exclusion from American Fisheries, 1936-1939: The Department of State and the Public Interest." Pacific Northwest Quarterly 65 (Jan. 1974): 8-16.

_____. "Upstairs, Downstairs at Foggy Bottom: Oil Exports and Japan, 1940-41." Prologue 8 (Spring 1976): 17-28.

Wheeler, Gerald E. "Isolated Japan: Anglo-American Diplomatic Co-operation, 1927-1936." Pacific Historical Review 30 (May 1961): 165-78.

_____. "Republican Philippine Policy, 1921-1933." Pacific Historical Review 28 (Nov. 1959): 377-90.

Wood, Herbert J. "Nelson Trusler Johnson: The Diplomacy of Benevolent Pragmatism." In Diplomats in Crisis: United States-Chinese-Japanese Relations, 1919-1941 ed. by Richard Dean Burns and Edward M. Bennett (Santa Barbara, Cal.: ABC-Clio, 1974), pp. 7-26.

Dissertations

Bader, Ernest Birny. "Some Aspects of American Public Reaction to Franklin D. Roosevelt's Japanese Policy, 1933-1941." Ph.D. diss., University of Nebraska, 1957.

Bibber, Joyce K. "The Chinese Communists as Viewed by the American Periodical Press, 1920-1937." Ph.D. diss., Stanford University, 1969.

Buhite, Russell D. "Nelson T. Johnson and American Policy toward China, 1925-1941." Ph.D. diss., Michigan State University, 1965.

Burke, Robert Louis. "Franklin D. Roosevelt and the Far East, 1913-1941." Ph.D. diss., Michigan State University, 1969.

Doenecke, Justus D. "American Public Opinion and the Manchurian Crisis, 1931-1933." Ph.D. diss., Princeton University, 1966.

Donnelly, James B. "Prentiss Bailey Gilbert, the League Council, and the Manchurian Crisis of 1931." Ph.D. diss., University of Virginia, 1969.

Douglas, Donald E. "American Education in the Creation of an Independent Philippines: The Commonwealth Period 1935-1941." Ph.D. diss., University of Michigan, 1979.

Graa, Frederick A. "The Open Door Policy of the United States: A Fundamental Cause of War between the United States and Japan." Ph.D. diss., St. John's University, 1948.

Grunfeld, Adalbert T. "Friends of the Revolution: American Supporters of China's Communists, 1926-1939." Ph.D. diss., New York University, 1985.

Hamilton, Thomas T. "The Impact of the Shanghai Incident of 1932 upon the United States and the League of Nations." Ph.D. diss., Duke University, 1953.

Hecht, Robert A. "Britain and America Face Japan, 1931-1933: A Study of Anglo-American Far Eastern Diplomacy during the Manchurian and Shanghai Crisis." Ph.D. diss., City University of New York, 1970.

Herzberg, James R. "American Economic Policies towards Japan, 1931-1941." Ph.D. diss., University of Texas, 1977.

Iriye, Akira. "American Diplomacy and Sino-Japanese Relations, 1926-1931." Ph.D. diss., Harvard University, 1961.

Ishi, Osamu. "Cotton-Textile Diplomacy: Japan, Great Britain, and the United States, 1930-1936." Ph.D. diss., Rutgers University, 1977.

Koginos, Emmanuel T. "The Panay Incident: Prelude to War." Ph.D. diss., American University, 1965.

Kubek, Anthony N. "Japanese-American Relations, 1937-1945." Ph.D. diss., Georgetown University, 1956.

McReynolds, George E. "American Sentiment regarding Japan, 1924-1934." Ph.D. diss., Clark University, 1937.

Nolan, William F. "America's Participation in the Military Defense of Shanghai, 1931-1941." Ph.D. diss., Saint Louis University, 1978.

Pearson, Alden B. "The American Christian Press and the Sino-Japanese Crisis of 1931-1933: An Aspect of Public Response to the Breakdown of World Peace." Ph.D. diss., Duke University, 1968.

Rodney, Robert M., Jr. "Reaching Out For Solutions: American Diplomacy during the Manchurian Crisis, 1931-1933." Ph.D. diss., University of Hawaii, 1985.

Smith, Sara R. "The Manchurian Crisis, 1931-1932: A Tragedy in International Relations." Ph.D. diss., Columbia University, 1945.

Stevens, Donald G. "The United States and the League of Nations during the Machurian Crisis, September-December, 1931." Ph.D. diss., St. John's University, 1967.

Towell, William P. "Cognitive Complexity of a Foreign Policy Decision-Maker under Conditions of Rising Threat: Joseph Grew and U.S.-Japan Relations, 1938-1941." Ph.D. diss., University of Illinois, 1975.

12.3 EUROPE

Books

Bailey, Thomas A., and Paul B. Ryan. Hitler vs. Roosevelt: The Undeclared Naval War. New York: Free Press, 1979.

Bennett, Edward M. Franklin D. Roosevelt and the Search for Security: American Soviet Relations, 1933-1939. Wilmington, Del.: Scholarly Resources, 1985.

_____. Recognition of Russia: An American Foreign Policy Dilemma. Waltham, Mass.: Blaidell, 1970.

Blumenthal, Henry. Illusion and Reality in Franco-American Diplomacy, 1914-1945. Baton Rouge: Louisiana State University Press, 1986.

Bishop, Donald G. The Roosevelt-Litvinov Agreements: The American View. Syracuse: Syracuse University Press, 1965.

Compton, James V. The Swastika and the Eagle: Hitler, the United States, and the Origins of World War II. Boston: Houghton Mifflin, 1967.

Dawson, Raymond H. The Decision to Aid Russia, 1941: Foreign Policy and Domestic Politics. Chapel Hill: University of North Carolina Press, 1959.

DeBedts, Ralph F. Ambassador Joseph Kennedy, 1938-1940: An Anatomy of Appeasement. New York: Peter Lang, 1985.

Diggins, John P. Mussolini and Fascism: The View from America. Princeton: Princeton University Press, 1972.

Dizikes, John. Britain, Roosevelt, and the New Deal: British Opinion, 1932-1938. New York: Garland, 1979.

Dulles, Foster Rhea. The Road to Teheran: The Story of Russia and America, 1781-1943. Princeton: Princeton University Press, 1944.

Eagles, Keith David. Ambassador Joseph E. Davies and American-Soviet Relations, 1937-1941. New York: Garland, 1985.

Farnsworth, Beatrice. William C. Bullitt and the Soviet Union. Bloomington: Indiana University Press, 1967.

Filene, Peter G. Americans and the Soviet Experiment, 1917-1933. Cambridge: Harvard University Press, 1967.

Friedlander, Saul. Prelude to Downfall: Hitler and the United States, 1939-1941. New York: Knopf, 1967.

Frye, Alton. Nazi Germany and the American Hemisphere, 1933-1941. New Haven: Yale University Press, 1967.

Gerassi, John. The Premature Antifascists: North American Volunteers in the Spanish Civil War, 1936-39: An Oral History. New York: Praeger, 1986.

Goodhart, Philip. Fifty Ships that Saved the World: The Foundation of the Anglo-American Alliance. Garden City, N. Y.: Doubleday, 1965.

Guttmann, Allen. The Wound in the Heart: America and the Spanish Civil War. New York: Free Press, 1962.

Haight, John McVickar, Jr. American Aid to France, 1938-1940. New York: Atheneum, 1970.

Harris, Brice, Jr. The United States and the Italo-Ethiopian Crisis. Stanford: Stanford University Press, 1964.

Hearden, Patrick J. Roosevelt Confronts Hitler: America's Entry into World War II. DeKalb: Northern Illinois University Press, 1987.

Jacobs, Travis Beal. America and the Winter War, 1939-1940. New York: Garland, 1981.

Jones, Kenneth Paul, ed. U.S. Diplomats in Europe, 1919-1941. Santa Barbara, Cal.: ABC-Clio, 1981.

Jones, Robert H. The Roads to Russia: United States Lend-Lease to the Soviet Union. Norman: University of Oklahoma Press, 1969.

Kennan, George F. Russia and the West Under Lenin and Stalin. Boston: Little, Brown, 1961.

Landis, Arthur H. The Abraham Lincoln Brigade. New York: Citadel, 1967.

Lash, Joseph P. Roosevelt and Churchill, 1939-1941: The Partnership that Saved the World. New York: Norton, 1976.

Leffler, Melvyn P. The Elusive Quest: America's Pursuit of European Stability and French Security, 1919-1933. Chapel Hill: University of North Carolina Press, 1970.

Leutze, James R. Bargaining for Supremacy: Anglo-American Naval Collaboration, 1937-1941. Chapel Hill: University of North Carolina Press, 1977.

Libby, James K. Alexander Gumberg and Soviet-American Relations, 1917-1933. Lexington: University Press of Kentucky, 1977.

Lochner, Louis P. Herbert Hoover and Germany. New York: Macmillan, 1960.

Lovenstein, Meno. American Opinion of Soviet Russia. Washington, D.C.: American Council on Public Affairs, 1941.

Meiburger, Anne Vincent. Efforts of Raymond Robins toward the Recognition of Soviet Russia and the Outlawry of War, 1917-1933. Washington, D.C.: Catholic University of America Press, 1958.

Offner, Arnold A. American Appeasement: United States Foreign Policy and Germany, 1933-1938. Cambridge: Harvard University Press, 1969.

Reynolds, David. The Creation of the Anglo-American Alliance, 1937-1941: A Study in Competitive .Cooperation. Chapel Hill: University of North Carolina Press, 1982.

Rosenstone, Robert A. Crusade of the Left: The Lincoln Battalion in the Spanish Civil War. New York: Pegasus, 1969.

Rowland, Benjamin M. Commercial Conflict and Foreign Policy: A Study in Anglo-American Relations, 1932-1938. New York: Garland, 1975.

Schwartz, Andrew. America and the Russo-Finnish War. Washington, D.C.: Public Affairs Press, 1960.

Smith, Arthur L., Jr. The Deutschtum of Nazi Germany and the United States. The Hague: Nijhoff, 1965.

Sobel, Robert. The Origins of Interventionism: The United States and the Russo-Finnish War. New York: Bookman, 1961.

Taylor, F. Jay. The United States and the Spanish Civil War. New York: Bookman Associates, 1956.

Traina, Richard P. American Diplomacy and the Spanish Civil War. Bloomington: Indiana University Press, 1968.

Trefousse, Hans L. Germany and American Neutrality, 1939-1941. New York: Bookman Associates, 1951.

Williams, William Appleman. American-Russian Relations, 1781-1947. New York: Octagon, 1952.

Wilson, Joan Hoff. Ideology and Economics: U.S. Relations with the Soviet Union, 1918-1933. Columbia: University of Missouri Press, 1974.

Wilson, Theodore A. The First Summit: Roosevelt and Churchill at Placentia Bay, 1941. Boston: Houghton Mifflin, 1969.

Articles

Adler, Les K., and Thomas G. Paterson. "Red Fascism: The Merger of Nazi
  Germany and Soviet Russia in the American Image of Totalitarianism, 1930's-
  1950's." American Historical Review 75 (April 1970): 1046-64.

Bowers, Robert E. "American Diplomacy, the 1933 Wheat Conference, and
  Recognition of the Soviet Union." Agricultural History 40 (Jan. 1966): 39-52.

_____. "Hull, Russian Subversion of Cuba, and Recognition of the U.S.S.R."
  Journal of American History 53 (Dec. 1966): 542-54.

Braddick, Henderson B. "A New Look at American Policy During the Italo-Ethiopian
  Crisis, 1935-36." Journal of Modern History 34 (March 1962): 64-73.

Browder, Robert P. "Soviet Far Eastern Policy and American Recognition, 1932-
  1934." Pacific Historical Review 21 (Aug. 1952): 263-73.

Burt, Alfred L. "European Relations under Hoover." In The United States and Its
  Place in World Affairs, 1918-1943 ed. by Allan Nevins and Louis M. Hacker
  (Boston: D.C. Heath, 1943), pp. 323-37.

Crosby, Donald F. "Boston's Catholics and the Spanish Civil War: 1936-1939." New
  England Quarterly 44 (March 1971): 82-100.

Dewey, Donald O. "America and Russia, 1939-1941: The Views of the New York
  Times." Journalism Quarterly 44 (Spring 1967): 62-70.

Doenecke, Justus D. "Germany in Isolationist Ideology, 1939-1941: The Issue of a
  Negotiated Peace." In Germany and American: Essays on Problems of
  International Relations and Immigration ed. by Hans L. Trefousse (New York:
  Brooklyn College Press, 1980), pp. 215-26.

Esthus, Raymond A. "President Roosevelt's Commitment to Britain to Intervene in a
  Pacific War." Mississippi Valley Historical Review 50 (June 1963): 28-38.

Evans, Ellen L., and Joseph O. Baylen. "History as Propaganda: The German Foreign
  Office and the 'Enlightenment of American Historians on the War Guilt
  Question, 1930-1933." Canadian Journal of History 10 (Aug. 1975): 185-207.

Feuer, Lewis S. "American Travelers to the Soviet Union, 1917-32: The Formation of
  a Component of New Deal Ideology." American Quarterly 14 (Summer 1962):
  119-49.

Flynn, George Q. "Franklin Roosevelt and the Vatican: The Myron Taylor
  Appointment." Catholic Historical Review 58 (July 1972): 171-94.

Friedlander, Robert A. "New Light on the Anglo-American Reaction to the Ethiopian
  War, 1935-1936." Mid-America 45 (April 1963): 115-25.

Gottlieb, Moshe. "In the Shadow of War: The American Anti-Nazi Boycott
  Movement in 1939-1941." American Jewish Historical Quarterly 62 (Dec.
  1972): 146-61.

_____. "The American Controversy Over the Olympic Games." American
  Jewish Historical Quarterly 61 (March 1972): 181-213.

_____. "The Berlin Riots of 1935 and Their Repercussions in America."
  American Jewish Historical Quarterly 59 (March 1970): 302-30.

Greenberg, Daniel S. "U.S. Destroyers for British Bases--Fifty Old Ships Go to War."
  Proceedings of the United States Naval Institute 88 (November 1962): 70-83.

Hachey, Thomas E., ed. "Profiles in Politics: British Embassy Views of Prominent Americans in 1939." Wisconsin Magazine of History 54 (Autumn 1970): 3-22.
_____. "Winning Friends and Influencing Policy: British Strategy to Woo America in 1937." Wisconsin Magazine of History 55 (Winter 1971): 120-29.

Haglund, David G. "George C. Marshall and the Question of Military Aid to England, May-June 1940." Journal of Contemporary History 15 (Oct. 1980): 745-60.

Haight, John McVickar, Jr. "Roosevelt as Friend of France." Foreign Affairs 44 (April 1966): 518-26.

Harrison, Richard A. "A Presidential Demarche: Franklin D. Roosevelt's Personal Diplomacy and Great Britain, 1936-37." Diplomatic History 5 (Summer 1981): 245-72.
_____. "The Runciman Visit to Washington in January 1937: Presidential Diplomacy and the Non-Commercial Implications of Anglo-American Trade Negotiations." Canadian Journal of History 19 (April 1984): 217-39.

Hecht, Robert A. "Great Britain and the Stimson Note of January 7, 1932." Pacific Historical Review 38 (May 1969): 177-91.

Herwig, Holger H. "Miscalculated Risks: The German Declaration of War against the United States, 1917 and 1941." Naval War College Review 39 (Autumn 1986): 88-100.
_____. "Prelude to Weltblitzkrieg: Germany's Naval Policy Toward the United States of America, 1939-1941." Journal of Modern History 43 (Dec. 1971): 649-68.

Hillmer, Norman. "Defense and Ideology: The Anglo-American Military 'Alliance' in the 1930s." International Journal 33 (Summer 1978): 588-612.

Hilton, Stanley E. "The Welles Mission to Europe, February-March 1940: Illusion or Realism?" Journal of American History 58 (June 1971): 93-120.

Hoff-Wilson ,Joan. "American Business and the Recognition of the Soviet Union." Social Science Quarterly 52 (Sept. 1971): 349-68.

Jablon, Howard. "Franklin D. Roosevelt and the Spanish Civil War." Social Studies 56 (Feb. 1965): 59-69.

Jonas, Manfred. "Prophet without Honor: Hans Heinrich Dieckhoff's Reports from Washington." Mid-America 47 (July 1965): 222-33.

Kimball, Warren F. "Dieckhoff and America: A German's View of German-American Relations, 1937-1941." Historian 27 (Feb. 1965): 218-43.
_____. "Lend-Lease and the Open Door: The Temptation of British Opulence, 1937-1942." Political Science Quarterly 86 (June 1971): 232-59.

Kimball, Warren F., and Bruce Bartlett. "Roosevelt and Prewar Commitments to Churchill: The Tyler Kent Affair." Diplomatic History 5 (Fall 1981): 291-311.

Kolko, Gabriel. "American Business and Germany, 1930-1941." Western Political Quarterly 15 (Dec. 1962): 713-28.

Kulevsky, Shirley G. "Facets of Isolationism: North Dakota's Reaction to the Spanish Civil War, 1936-1939." North Dakota Quarterly 46 (Autumn 1978): 5-20.

Langenberg, William H. "Destroyers for Naval Bases: Highlights of an Unprecedented Trade." Naval War College Review 22 (May 1970): 80-92.

Leffler, Melvyn P. "American Policy Making and European Stability, 1921-1933." Pacific Historical Review 46 (May 1977): 207-28.

_____. "Political Isolationism, Economic Expansion, or Diplomatic Realism: American Foreign Policy Toward Western Europe, 1921-1933." Perspectives in American History 8 (1974): 413-61.

Leutze, James. "Technology and Bargaining in Anglo-American Naval Relations, 1938-1946." U.S Naval Institute Proceedings 103 (June 1977): 50-66.

_____. "The Secret of the Churchill-Roosevelt Correspondence September 1939_May 1940." Journal of Contemporary History 10 (No. 3, 1975): 465-91.

Lindley, William R. "The Atlantic Charter: Press Release or Historic Document?" Journalism Quarterly 41 (Summer 1964): 375-79, 394.

Little, Douglas. "Claude Bowers and His Mission to Spain: The Diplomacy of a Jeffersonian Democrat." In U.S. Diplomats in Europe, 1919-1941 ed. by Kenneth Paul Jones (Santa Barbara, Cal.: ABC-Clio, 1981), pp. 129-46.

Lukas, Richard C. "Aircraft Commitments to Russia: The Moscow Conference, September-October 1941." Air University Review 16 (Aug. 1965): 44-53.

_____. "The Impact of 'Barbarossa' on the Soviet Air Force and the Resulting Commitment of United States Aircraft, June-October, 1941." Historian 29 (Nov. 1966): 60-80.

Maddux, Thomas R. "American Diplomats and the Soviet Experiment: The View from the Moscow Embassy, 1934-1939." South Atlantic Quarterly 74 (Autumn 1975): 468-87.

_____. "Loy W. Henderson and Soviet-American Relations: The Diplomacy of a Professional." In U.S. Diplomats in Europe, 1919-1941 ed. by Kenneth Paul Jones (Santa Barbara, Cal.: ABC-Clio, 1981), pp. 149-61.

_____. "United States-Soviet Naval Relations in the 1930's: The Soviet Union's Efforts to Purchase Naval Vessels." Naval War College Review 29 (Fall 1976): 28-37.

_____. "Watching Stalin Maneuver between Hitler and the West: American Diplomats and Soviet Deplomacy, 1934-1939." Diplomatic History 1 (Spring 1977): 140-54.

Marks, Frederich W., III. "Six between Roosevelt and Hitler: America's Role in the Appeasement of Nazi Germany." Historical Journal 28 (Dec. 1985): 969-82.

_____. "The Origins of FDR's Promise to Support Britain Militarily in the Far East--A New Look." Pacific Historical Review 53 (Nov. 1984): 447-62.

Morris, Robert L. "A Reassessment of Russian Recognition." Historian 24 (Aug. 1962): 470-82.

Moss, Kenneth. "George S. Messersmith: An American Diplomat and Nazi Germany." Delaware History 17 (Fall-Winter 1977): 236-49.

_____. "George S. Mesersmith and Nazi Germany: The Diplomacy of Limits in Central Europe." In U.S. Diplomats in Europe, 1919-1941 ed. by Kenneth Paul Jones (Santa Barbara, Cal.: ABC-Clio, 1981), pp. 113-26.

_____. "The United States, the Open Door, and Nazi Germany, 1933-1938." South Atlantic Quarterly 78 (Autumn 1979): 489-506.

Muir, Malcolm, Jr. "American Warship Construction for Stalin's Navy Prior to World War II: A Study in Paralysis of Policy." Diplomatic History 5 (Fall 1981): 337-51.

Murray, G. E. Patrick. "'Under Urgent Consideration': American Planes for Greece, 1940-1941." Aerospace Historian 24 (Summer 1977): 61-69.

Offner, Arnold A. "Appeasement Revisited: The United States, Great Britain, and Germany, 1933-1940." Journal of American History 64 (Sept. 1977): 373-93.

Pollack, Fred E. "Roosevelt, the Ogdensburg Agreement, and the British Fleet: All Done with Mirrors." Diplomatic History 5 (Summer 1981): 203-19.

Propas, Frederic L. "Creating a Hard Line Toward Russia: The Training of State Department Soviet Experts, 1927-1937." Diplomatic History 8 (Summer 1984): 209-26.

Remak, Joachim. "'Friends of the New Germany': The Bund and German-American Relations." Journal of Modern History 29 (March 1957): 38-41.

Reynolds, David. "FDR's Foreign Policy and the British Royal Visit to the U.S.A., 1939." Historian 45 (Aug.1983): 461-72.

_____. "Roosevelt, the British Left, and the Appointment of John G. Winant as U.S. Ambassador to Britain in 1941." International History Review 4 (Aug. 1982): 393-413.

Rhodes, Benjamin D. "The British Royal Visit of 1939 and the 'Psychological Approach' to the United States." Diplomatic History 2 (Spring 1978): 197-211.

_____. "The Origins of Finnish-American Friendship, 1919-1941." Mid-America 54 (Jan. 1972): 3-29.

Ribuffo, Leo. "Fascists, Nazis, and American Minds: Perceptions and Preconceptions." American Quarterly 26 (December 1974): 417-32.

Rosenstone, Robert A. "American Commissars in Spain." South Atlantic Quarterly 67 (Autumn 1968): 688-702

_____. "The Men of the Abraham Lincoln Battalion." Journal of American History 54 (Sept. 1967): 327-38.

Shafir, Shlomo. "George S. Messersmith: An Anti=Nazi Diplomat's View of the German-Jewish Crisis." Jewish Social Studies 35 (Jan. 1973): 32-41.

Singerman, Robert. "American Jewish Reaction to the Spanish Civil War." Journal of Church and State 19 (Spring 1977): 261-78.

Smith, Truman. "An American Estimate of the German Air Force: November 1937." Aerospace Historian 10 (April 1963): 54-56.

Szajkowski, Zosa. "Relief for German Jewry: Problems of American Involvement." American Jewish Historical Quarterly 62 (Dec. 1972): 111-45.

Timberlake, Charles E. "Russian American Contacts, 1917-1937: A Review Article." Pacific Northwest Quarterly 61 (Oct. 1970): 217-21.

Trefousse, Hans L. "Failure of German Intelligence in the United States, 1935-1945." Mississippi Valley Historical Review 42 (June 1955): 84-100.

Ullman, Richard H. "The Davies Mission and United States-Soviet Relations, 1937-1941." World Politics 9 (Jan. 1957): 220-39.

Valaik, John D. "American Catholic Dissenters and the Spanish Civil War." Catholic Historical Review 53 (Jan. 1968): 537-55.

_____. "American Catholics and the Second Spanish Republic, 1931-1936." Journal of Church and State 10 (Winter 1968): 13-27.

_____. "Catholics, Neutrality, and the Spanish Embargo, 1937-1939." Journal of American History 54 (June1967): 73-85.

_____. "In the Days Before Ecumenism: American Catholics, Anti-Semitism, and the Spanish Civil War." Journal of Church and State 13 (Autumn 1971): 465-77.

Vieth, Jane Karoline. "The Donkey and the Lion: The Ambassadorship of Joseph P. Kennedy at the Court of St. James, 1938-1940." Michigan Academician 10 (Winter 1978): 23-82.

_____. "Joseph P. Kennedy and British Appeasement: The Diplomacy of a Boston Irishman." In U.S. Diplomats in Europe, 1919-1941 ed. by Kenneth Paul Jones (Santa Barbara, Cal.: ABC-Clio, 1981), pp. 165-82.

Wallace, William V. "Roosevelt and British Appeasement, 1938." Bulletin of the British Association for American Studies 5 (December 1962): 4-30.

Watt, Donald C. "Roosevelt and Chamberlain: Two Appeasers." International Journal 28 (No. 1, 1972/1973): 185-204.

Weinberg, Gerhard L. "Hitler's Image of the United States." American Historical Review 69 (July 1964): 1006-21.

Whitaker, W. Richard. "Outline of Hitler's 'Final Solution' Apparent by 1933." Journalism Quarterly 58 (Summer 1981): 192-200.

Wilson, J. H. "American Business and the Recognition of the Soviet Union." Social Science Quarterly 52 (Sept. 1971): 349-68.

Dissertations

Bauer, Wolfred. "The Shipment of American Strategic Raw Materials to Nazi Germany: A Study in United States Economic Foreign Policy, 1933-1939." Ph.D. diss., Washington University, 1964.

Beck, Alfred M. "The Ambivalent Attaché: Friedrich von Boetticher in America, 1933-1941." Ph.D. diss., Georgetown University, 1977.

Bell, John B. "The Non-Intervention Committee and the Spanish Civil War, 1936-1939." Ph.D. diss., Duke University, 1958.

Bengal, Saint Callista, Sister. "The United States and Spain, 1939-1946: A Study in Press Opinion and Public Reaction" Ph.D. diss., Fordham University, 1959.

Boe, Jonathan E. "American Business: The Response to the Soviet Union, 1933-1947." Ph.D. diss., Stanford University, 1979.

Burke, Bernard V. "American Diplomats and Hitler's Rise to Power, 1930-1933: The Mission of Ambassador Sackett." Ph.D. diss., Washington University, 1966.

Butler, Michael Anthony. "The Neutrals, 1933-1940: The United States, The Oslo Nations and the Response to Hitler." Ph.D. diss., University of Virginia, 1980.

Buzzell, Rolfe G. "The Eagle and the Fasces: The United States and Italy, 1935-1939." Ph.D. diss., University of California, Santa Barbara, 1977.

Dahlheimer, Harry. "The United States, Germany and the Quest for Neutrality, 1933-1937." Ph.D. diss., University of Iowa, 1976.

Day, Daniel S. "American Opinion of German National Socialism, 1933-1937." Ph.D. diss., University of California, Los Angeles, 1958.

DeCola, Thomas G. "Roosevelt and Mussolini: The Critical Years, 1938-1941." Ph.D. diss., Kent State University, 1967.

Dizikes, John. "Britain, Roosevelt and the New Deal, 1932-1938." Ph.D. diss., Harvard University, 1964.

Eagles, Keith D. "Ambassador Joseph E. Davies and American-Soviet Relations, 1937-1941." Ph.D. diss., Washington University, 1966.

Fithian, Floyd J. "Soviet-American Economic Relations, 1918-1933: American Business in Russia during the Period of Nonrecognition." Ph.D. diss., University of Nebraska, 1964.

Francese, Carl James. "United States Policy toward Italy on Arms Limitation and War Debts, 1929-1933." Ph.D. diss., University of Houston, 1982.

Gerberding, William P. "Franklin D. Roosevelt's Conception of the Soviet Union in World Politics." Ph.D. diss., University of Chicago, 1959.

Gilman, E. "Economic Aspects of Anglo-American Relations in the Era of Roosevelt and Chamberlain." Ph.D. diss., University of London, 1976.

Gottsacker, M. Hugh, Sister. "German-American Relations, 1938-1941, and the Influence of Hans Thomsen." Ph.D. diss., Georgetown University, 1968.

Gurney, Ramsdell, Jr. "From Recognition to Munich: Official and Historiographical Views of Soviet-American Relations, 1933-1938." Ph.D. diss., State University of New York, Buffalo, 1969.

Haight, John M., Jr. "The Paris Press and the Neutrality Policy of the United States (1935-1939)." Ph.D. diss., Northwestern University, 1953.

Linder, Doris H. "The Reaction of Norway to American Foreign Policy, 1918-1939." Ph.D. diss., University of Minnesota, 1961.

Litsky, Elliott Burton. "The Murphy-Weygand Agreement: The United States and French North Africa (1940-1942)." Ph.D. diss., Fordham University, 1986.

Little, Douglas J. "Malevolent Neutrality: The United States, Great Britain, and the Revolution in Spain, 1931-1936." Ph.D. diss., Cornell University, 1978

Maddux, Thomas R. "American Relations with the Soviet Union, 1933-1941." Ph.D. diss., University of Michigan, 1969.

Magden, Ronald E. "Attitudes of the American Religious Press toward Soviet Russia, 1939-1941." Ph.D. diss., Washington University, 1964.

Manning, Donald J. "Soviet-American Relations, 1929-1941: The Impact of Domestic Considerations on Foreign Policy Decision-Making." Ph.D. diss., Michigan State University, 1978.

McClelland, Robert C. "The Soviet Union in American Opinion, 1933-1942." Ph.D. diss., West Virginia University, 1951.

McMullen, Aidan C. "The Diplomtic Background of the Munich Agreement of 1938: A Re-Examination." Ph.D. diss., Georgetown University, 1952.

McNeil, William C. "American Money and the German Economy: Economics and Politics on the Eve of the Great Depression." Ph.D. diss., University of California, Berkeley, 1981.

Offner, Arnold A. "American Diplomacy and Germany, 1933-1938." Ph.D. diss., Indiana University, 1964.

Parry, Hugh J. "The Spanish Civil War, 1936-1939: A Study in American Public Opinion, Propaganda, and Pressure Groups." Ph.D. diss., University of Southern California, 1949.

Propas, Frederic Lewis. "The State Department, Bureaucratic Politics and Soviet-American Relations, 1918-1938." Ph.D. diss., Universiaty of California, Los Angeles, 1982.

Reges, Stephen G. "Diplomatic Relations between the United States and Norway, 1933-1944." Ph.D. diss., Georgetown University, 1959.

Reynolds, D. J. "Competitive Co-operation: The Creation of the Anglo-American Alliance, 1938-1941." Ph.D. diss., Cambridge University, 1980.

Rosenberg, Joseph L. "America and the Neutrality of Ireland, 1939-1941." Ph.D. diss., University of Iowa, 1976.

Schmitz, David F. "United States Foreign Policy toward Fascist Italy, 1922-1940." Ph.D. diss., Rutgers University, 1985.

Shanley, Kevin M. "Reinhold Niebuhr and Relations betweeen Germany and America (1916-1956)." Ph.D. diss., State University of New York at Albany, 1984.

Sigel, Roberta S. "Opinions of Nazi Germany: A Study of Three Popular American Magazines, 1933-1941." Ph.D. diss., Clark University, 1950.

Sobel, Robert. "The United States and the Russo-Finnish War of 1939-1940." Ph.D. diss., New York University, 1957.

Stern, Sheldon M. "The American Perception of the Emergence of Adolf Hitler and the Nazis, 1923-1934." Ph.D. diss., Harvard University, 1970.

Susser, Marc Jonathan. "The 'Eternal Question Mark': The United States and British Foreign Policy in the Early Nineteen-Thirties." Ph.D. diss., Harvard University, 1982.

Taylor, Foster J. "The United States and the Spanish Civil War, 1936-1939." Ph.D. diss., Tulane University, 1952.

Traina, Richard P. "American Diplomacy and the Spanish Civil War, 1936-1939." Ph.D. diss., University of California, Berkeley, 1964.

Valaik, John D. "American Catholics and the Spanish Civil War, 1931-1939." Ph.D. diss., University of Rochester, 1964.

Van Everen, Brooks. "Franklin D. Roosevelt and the German Problem: 1914-1945." Ph.D. diss., University of Colorado, 1970.

Wilson, Joan H. "The Role of the Business Community in American Relations with Russia and Europe, 1920-1933." Ph.D. diss., University of California, Berkeley, 1966.

12.4   LATIN AMERICA

Books

Bemis, Samuel F. The Latin American Policy of the United States: An Historical Interpretation. New York: Harcourt, Brace, 1943.

Callcott, Wilfrid Hardy. The Western Hemisphere: Its Influence on United States Policies to the End of World War II. Austin: University of Texas, 1968.

Clark, Truman R. Puerto Rico and the United States, 1917-1933. Pittsburgh: University of Pittsburgh Press, 1975.

Cronon, Edmund David. Josephus Daniels in Mexico. Madison: University of Wisconsin Press, 1960.

Curry, Earl R. Hoover's Dominican Diplomacy and the Origins of the Good Neighbor Policy. New York: Garland, 1979.

DeConde, Alexander. Herbert Hoover's Latin-American Policy. Stanford: Stanford University Press, 1951.

Dozer, Donald M. Are We Good Neighbors? Three Decades of Inter-American Relations, 1930-1960. Gainesville: University of Florida Press, 1959.

Fitzgibbon, Russell H. Cuba and the United States, 1900-1935. Menasha, Wis.: George Banta, 1935.

Gellman, Irwin F. Good Neighbor Policy: United States Policies in Latin America, 1933-1945. Baltimore: Johns Hopkins University Press, 1979.

_____. Roosevelt and Batista: Good Neighbor Diplomacy in Cuba, 1933-1945. Albuquerque: University of New Mexico Press, 1973.

Green, David. The Containment of Latin America: A History of the Myths and Realities of the Good Neighbor Policy. Chicago: Quadrangle, 1971.

Guerrant, Edward O. Roosevelt's Good Neighbor Policy. Albuquerque: University of New Mexico Press, 1950.

Kamman, William. A Search for Stability: United States Diplomacy Toward Nicaragua, 1925-1933. Notre Dame: University of Notre Dame Press, 1968.

McCann, Frank D., Jr. The Brazilian-American Alliance, 1937-1945. Princeton: Princeton University Press, 1973.

Meyer, Lorenzo. Mexico and the United States in the Oil Controversy, 1917-1942. Austin: University of Texas Press, 1977.

Munro, Dana G. The United States and the Caribbean Republics, 1921-1933. Princeton: Princeton University Press, 1974.

Parks, E. Taylor. Colombia and the United States, 1765-1934. Durham, N.C.: Duke Univeristy Press, 1935.

Randall, Stephen J. The Diplomacy of Modernization: Colombian-American Relations, 1920-1940. Toronto: University of Toronto Press, 1978.

Schmidt, Hans. The United States Occupation of Haiti, 1915-1934. New Brunswick, N.J.: Rutgers University Press, 1971.

Smith, Robert Freeman. The United States and Revolutionary Nationalism in Mexico, 1916-1932. Chicago: University of Chicago Press, 1972.

Spector, Robert M. W. Cameron Forbes and the Hoover Commissions to Haiti (1930). Lanham, Md.: University Press of America, 1985.

Steward, Dick. Trade and Hemisphere: The Good Neighbor Policy and Reciprocal Trade. Columbia: University of Missouri Press, 1975.

Wood, Bryce. The Making of the Good Neighbor Policy. New York: Columbia University Press, 1961.

_____. The United States and Latin-American Wars, 1932-1942. New York: Columbia University Press, 1966.

Articles

Cooper, Donald B. "The Withdrawal of the United States from Haiti, 1928-1934." Journal of Inter-American Studies and World Affairs 5 (Jan. 1963): 83-102.

Cronon, E. David. "Interpreting the New Good Neighbor Policy: The Cuban Crisis of 1933." Hispanic American Historical Review 39 (Nov. 1959): 538-67.

Davies, Thomas M. "The Rio Grande Treaty of 1933: A Prelude to Settlement." New Mexico Historical Review 40 (Oct. 1965): 277-92.

Ferrell, Robert H. "Repudiation of a Repudiation." Journal of American History 51 (March 1965): 669-73.

Gellman, Irwin F. "Prelude to Reciprocity: The Abortive United States-Columbian Treaty of 1933." Historian 32 (Nov. 1969): 52-68.

Grayson, George W., Jr. "The Era of the Good Neighbor." Current History 56 (June 1969): 327-32, 365, 370.

Grieb, Kenneth J. "Negotiating a Reciprocal Trade Agreement with an Underdeveloped Country: Guatemala as a Case Study." Prologue 5 (Spring 1973): 22-29.

_____. "The United States and Genral Jorge Ubicas's Retention of Power." Revista de Historia de America 71 (1971): 119-35.

Griffin, Charles C., ed. "Welles to Roosevelt: A Memorandum on Inter-American Relations, 1933." Hispanic American Historical Review 34 (May 1954): 190-92.

Koppes, Clayton R. "The Good Neighbor Policy and the Nationalization of Mexican Oil: A Reinterpretation." Journal of American History 69 (June 1982): 62-81.

Langley, Lester D. "Negotiating New Treaties with Panama: 1936." Hispanic American Historical Review 48 (May 1968): 220-33.

_____. "The World Crisis and the Good Neighbor Policy in Panama, 1936-1941." Americas 24 (Oct. 1967): 137-52.

McCann, Frank D., Jr. "Aviation Diplomacy: The United States and Brazil, 1939-1941." Inter-American Economic Affairs 21 (Spring 1968): 35-50.

Munro, Dana G. "The American Withdrawal from Haiti, 1929-1934." Hispanic American Historical Review 49 (Feb. 1969): 1-26

Parker, James R., and Terry G. Simmons. "The Rise and Fall of the Good Neighbor Policy: The North American View." Maryland Historian 1 (Spring 1970): 31-44.

Pulley, Raymond H. "The United States and the Trujillo Dictatorship, 1933-1940: The High Price of Caribbean Stability." Caribbean Studies 5 (Oct. 1965): 22-31.

Randall, Stephen James. "Columbia, the United States, and Interamerican Aviation Rivalry, 1927-1940." Journal of Interamerican Studies of World Affairs 14 (Aug. 1972): 297-323.

Smith, Robert Freeman. "The Good Neighbor Policy: The Liberal Paradox in United States Relations with Latin America." In Watershed of Empire: Essays on New Deal Foreign Policy ed. by Leonard P. Liggio and James J. Martin (Colorado Springs: Ralph Myles, 1976), pp. 65-94.

Snyder, J. Richard. "William S. Culbertson in Chile: Opening the Door to a Good Neighbor, 1928-1933." Inter-American Economic Affairs 26 (Summer 1972): 81-96.

Spector, Robert M. "W. Cameron Forbes in Haiti: Additional Light on the Genesis of the 'Good Neighbor' Policy." Caribbean Studies 6 (July 1966): 28-45.

Tierney, John J., Jr. "U.S. Intervention in Nicaragua, 1927-1933: Lessons for Today." Orbis 14 (Winter 1971): 1012-28.

Varg, Paul A. "The Economic Side of the Good Neighbor Policy: The Reciprocal Trade Program and South America." Pacific Historical Review 45 (Feb. 1976): 47-71.

Walker, William O., III. "Control Across the Border: The United States, Mexico, and Narcotics Policy, 1936-1940." Pacific Historical Review 47 (Feb. 1978): 91-106.

Yerxa, Donald A. "The Special Service Squadron and the Caribbean Region, 1920-1940: A Case Study in Naval Diplomacy." Naval War College Review 39 (Autumn 1986): 60-72.

Dissertations

Beck, Robert T. "Cordell Hull and Latin America, 1933-39." Ph.D. diss., Temple University, 1977.

Bennett, Edward Moore. "Franklin D. Roosevelt and Russian-American Relations, 1933-1939." Ph.D. diss., University of Illinois, 1961.

Berger, Henry W. "Union Diplomacy: American Labor's Foreign Policy in Latin America, 1932-1955." Ph.D. diss., University of Wisconsin, 1966.

Bodayla, Stephen D. "Financial Diplomacy: The United States and Mexico, 1919-1933." Ph. D. diss., New York University, 1975.

Coleman, George C. "The Good Neighbor Policy of Franklin D. Roosevelt with Special Reference to Three Inter-American Conferences, 1933-1938." Ph.D. diss., University of Iowa, 1951.

Cronon, Edmund D., Jr. "Good Neighbor Ambassador Josephus Daniels in Mexico." Ph.D. diss., University of Wisconsin, 1953.

Curry, Earl R. "The United States and the Dominican Republic, 1924-1933: Dilemma in the Caribbean." Ph.D. diss., University of Minnesota, 1966.

DeConde, Alexander. "Herbert Hoover and Latin America." Ph.D. diss., Stanford University, 1949.

Dodd, Thomas J., Jr. "The United States in Nicaraguan Politics: Supervised Elections, 1927-1932." Ph.D. diss., George Washington University, 1966.

Elsasser, Edward O. "The Export-Import Bank and Latin America, 1934-1945." Ph.D. diss., University of Chicago, 1954.

Faust, George H. "Economic Relations of the United States and Colombia, 1920-40." Ph.D. diss., University of Chicago, 1946.

Fejes, Fred Allan. "Imperialism, Media, and the Good Neighbor: New Deal Foreign Policy and United Sttes Shortwave Broadcasting to Latin America." Ph.D. diss., University of Illinois, 1982.

Gellman, Irwin F. "Good Neighbor Diplomacy and the Rise of Batista, 1933-1945." Ph.D. diss., Indiana University, 1970.

Giffin, Donald W. "The Normal Years: Brazilian-American Relations, 1930-1939." Ph.D. diss., Vanderbilt University, 1962.

Guerrant, Edward Owings. "The Foreign Policy of the Roosevelt Administration in Latin America, 1933-1941." Ph.D. diss., University of Southern California, 1942.

Haglund, David George. "The Battle of Latin America: Franklin D. Roosevelt and the End of Isolation, 1936-1941." Ph.D. diss., Johns Hopkins University. 1978.

Harris, Sally Ann. "The Inter-American Conferences of the 1930's." Ph.D. diss., University of Missouri, 1967.

Kesler, John C. "Spruille Braden as a Good Neighbor: The Latin American Policy of the United States, 1930-1947." Ph.D. diss., Kent State University, 1985.

Langley, Lester D. "The United States and Panama, 1933-1941: A Study in Strategy and Diplomacy." Ph.D. diss., University of Kansas, 1965.

Morgan, Hugh J. "The United States Press Coverage of Mexico during the Presidency of Lazaro Cardenas, 1934-1940." Ph.D. diss., Southern Illinois University, 1985.

Plummer, Brenda Gayle. "Black and White in the Caribbean: Haitian-American Relations, 1902-1934." Ph.D. diss., Cornell University, 1981.

Randall, Stephen James. "Good Neighbours in Depression: The United States and Colombia, 1928-1938." Ph.D. diss., University of Toronto, 1972.

Rohr, Mary Ann. "The Inter-American Coffee Agreement of 1940." Ph.D. diss., University of Toledo, 1981.

Schultegann, Mary Annunciata, Sister. "Henry L. Stimson's Latin American Policy, 1929-1933." Ph.D. diss., Georgetown University, 1967.

Steward, Dick H. "In Search of Markets: The New Deal, Latin America, and Reciprocal Trade." Ph.D. diss., University of Missouri, 1969.

Yeilding, Thomas David. "United States Lend-Lease Policy in Latin America." Ph.D. diss., North Texas State University, 1983.

12.5 MILITARY

Books

Abbazia, Patrick. Mr. Roosevelt's Navy: The Private War of the U.S. Atlantic Fleet, 1939-1942. Annapolis: Naval Institute Press, 1976.

Clifford, J. Garry, and Samuel R. Spencer, Jr. The First Peacetime Draft. Lawrence: University Press of Kansas, 1986.

Davis, George T. A Navy Second to None: The Development of Modern American Naval Policy. New York: Harcourt, Brace, 1940.

Griffith, Robert K., Jr. Men Wanted for the U.S. Army: America's Experience with an All-Volunteer Army Between the World Wars. Westport, Conn.: Greenwood, 1982.

Huzar, Elias. The Purse and the Sword: Control of the Army by Congress Through Military Appropriations, 1933-1950. Ithaca: Cornell University Press, 1950.

Killigrew, John W. The Impact of the Great Depression on the Army. New York: Garland, 1979.

Pogue, Forrest C. George C. Marshall: Ordeal and Hope, 1939-1942. New York: Viking, 1966.

Rutkowski, Edwin H. The Politics of Military Aviation Procurement, 1926-1934: A Study in the Political Assertion of Consensual Values. Columbus: Ohio State University Press, 1966.

Watson, Mark Skinner. Chief of Staff: Prewar Plans and Preparations. Washington, D. C.: GPO, 1950.

Articles

Anders, Leslie. "The Watershed: Forrest Harding's Infantry Journal, 1934-1938." Military Affairs 40 (Feb. 1976): 12-16.

Blum, Albert A., and J. Douglas Smyth. "Who Should Serve: Pre-World War II Planning for Selective Service." Journal of Economic History 30 (June 1970): 379-404.

Conn, Stetson. "Changing Concepts of National Defense in the United States, 1937-1947." Military Affairs 28 (Spring 1964): 1-7.

Cooling, B. Franklin, III. "The Arkansas Maneuvers, 1941." Arkansas Historical Quarterly 26 (Summer 1967): 103-22.

_____. "The Tennessee Maneuvers, June, 1941." Tennessee Historical Quarterly 24 (Fall 1965): 265-80.

Doherty, Thomas. "Blitzkrieg for Beginners: The Maneuvers of 1940 in Central Wisconsin." Wisconsin Magazine of History 68 (Winter 1984): 83-107.

Downs, Eldon W. "Army and the Airmail--1934." Aerospace Historian 9 (Jan. 1962): 35-51.

Doyle, Michael K. "The U.S. Navy and War Plan Orange, 1933-1940: Making Necessity a Virtue." Naval War College Review 33 (May 1980): 49-63.

_____. "The United States Navy--Strategy and Far Eastern Foreign Policy, 1931-1941." Naval War College Review 29 (Winter 1977): 52-60.

Gale, Henry G. "War Planning at the War College of the Mid-1930s." Parameters 15 (Spring 1985): 52-64.

Greene, Fred. "The Military View of American National Policy, 1904-1940." American Historical Review 66 (Jan. 1961): 354-77.

Greene, Murray. "The Alaskan Flight of 1934: A Spectacular Official Failure." Aerospace Historian 24 (Spring 1977): 15-19.

Hamilton, Virginia Van Der Veer. "Barnstorming the U. S. Mail." American Heritage 25 (Aug. 1974): 32-36.

Hays, Robert E., Jr. "Civil-Military Cooperation on the Threshold of World War II, 1938-1940." Rocky Mountain Social Science Journal 4 (1967): 100-13.

Hone, Thomas C. "Battleships vs. Aircraft Carriers: The Patterns of the U.S. Navy Operating Expenditures, 1932-1941." Military Affairs 41 (Oct. 1977): 133-41.

LaPlante, John B. "The Evolution of Pacific Policy and Strategic Planning: June 1940 - July 1941." Naval War College Review 25 (May-June 1973): 57-72.

Millett, Richard. "The State Department's Navy: A History of the Special Service Squadron, 1930-1940." American Neptune 35 (April 1975): 118-38.

Morton, Louis. "War Plan Orange: Evolution of a Strategy." World Politics 11 (Jan. 1959): 221-50.

Nastri, Anthony D. "An Ordinary Joe." U.S. Naval Institute Proceedings 104 (November 1978): 71-77.

O'Connor, Raymond G. "The American Navy, 1939-1941: The Enlisted Perspective." Military Affairs 50 (Oct. 1986): 173-78.

Petersen, Barbara Bennett. "FDR's 'Quarterbacking' of U.S. Naval Policy in the Pacific, 1933-39." Pacific Historian "Part One" 16 (Winter 1972): 44-53; "Part Two" 17 (Spring 1973): 61-72; "Part Three." 17 (Summer 1973): 60-73.

Rader, Frank J. "The Works Progress Administration and Hawaiian Preparedness, 1935-1940." Military Affairs 43 (Feb. 1979): 12-17.

_____. "Work Relief and National Defense: Some Notes on WPA in Alaska." Alaska Journal 6 (Winter 1976): 54-59.

Roberts, Stephen S. "The Decline of the Overseas Station Fleets: The United States Asiatic Fleet and the Shanghai Crisis, 1932." American Neptune 32 (July 1977): 185-202.

Rosenberg, David Alan. "Officer Development in the Interwar Navy: Arleigh Burke-- The Making of a Naval Professional, 1919-1940." Pacific Historical Review 44 (Nov. 1975): 503-26.

Schaffer, Ronald. "The War Department's Defense of RPTC, 1920-1940." Wisconsin Magazine of History 53 (Winter 1969-70): 108-20.

Schaller, Michael. "American Air Strategy in China, 1939-1941: The Origins of Clandestine Air Warfare." American Quarterly 28 (Spring 1976): 3-19.

Shiner, John. "General Benjamin Foulois and the 1934 Air Mail Disaster." Aerospace Historian 25 (Winter 1978): 221-30.

Symonds, Craig L. "William Veazie Pratt as CNO: 17 September 1930-3 June 1933." Naval War College Review 33 (March 1980): 17-33.

Talbott, J. E. "Weapons Development, War Planning and Policy: The U.S. Navy and the Submarine, 1917-1941." Naval War College Review 37 (May 1984): 53-71.

Vinson, J. Chalmers. "Military Force and American Policy, 1919-1934." In Isolation and Security ed. by Alexander DeConde (Durham: Duke University Press, 1957), pp. 56-81.

Vlahos, Michael. "Wargaming, an Enforcer of Strategic Realism: 1919-1942." Naval War College Review 39 (March 1986): 7-22.

Walter, John C. "Congressman Carl Vinson and Franklin D. Roosevelt: Naval Preparedness and the Coming of World War II, 1932-40." Georgia Historical Quarterly 64 (Fall 1980): 294-305.

Wheeler, Gerald E. "The United States Navy and War in the Pacific, 1919-1941." World Affairs Quarterly 30 (Spring: 1959): 199-225.

Dissertations

Andrade, Ernest, Jr. "United States Naval Policy in the Disarmament Era, 1921-1937." Ph.D. diss., Michigan State University, 1968.

Bohman, Eric J. "Rehearsals for Victory: The War Department and the Planning and Direction of Civil Affairs, 1940-1943." Ph.D. diss., Yale University, 1984.

Doyle, Michael K. "The U.S. Navy: Strategy, Defense, and Foreign Policy, 1932-1941." Ph.D. diss., University of Washington, 1977.

Dunn, James Ward. "President Franklin D. Roosevelt and the United States Army, 1933-1940." Ph.D. diss., University of Hawaii, 1977.

Dwan, John Edmund, II. "Franklin D. Roosevelt and the Revolution in the Strategy of National Security: Foreign Policy and Military Planning before Pearl Harbor." Ph.D. diss., Yale University, 1954.

Gabel, Christopher R. "The U.S. GHQ Maneuvers of 1941." Ph.D. diss., Ohio State University, 1981.

McClain, Linda. "The Role of Admiral W. D. Leahy in U.S. Foreign Policy." Ph.D. diss., University of Virginia, 1984.

McFarland, Keith D. "Secretary of War Harry H. Woodring and the Problems of Readiness, Rearmament and Neutrality, 1936-1940." Ph.D. diss., Ohio University, 1969.

Oyos, Lynwood E. "The Navy and the United States Far Eastern Policy, 1930-1939." Ph.D. diss., University of Nebraska, 1958.

Reynolds, Charles V. "America and a Two-Ocean Navy, 1933-1941." Ph.D. diss., Boston University, 1978.

Steele, Richard W. "Roosevelt, Marshall, and the First Offensive: The Politics of Strategy Making, 1941-1942." Ph.D. diss., Johns Hopkins University, 1969.

Tuleja, Thaddeus V. "United States Naval Policy in the Pacific, 1930-1941." Ph.D. diss., Fordham University, 1961.

West, Michael Allen. "Laying the Legislative Foundation: The House Naval Affairs Committee and the Construction of the Treaty Navy, 1926-1934." Ph.D. diss., Ohio State University, 1980.

Yoshino, Ronald. "A Doctrine Destroyed: The American Fighter Offensive, 1917-1939." Ph.D. diss., Claremont Graduate School, 1985.

12.6 REFUGEES

Books

Feingold, Henry L. The Politics of Rescue: The Roosevelt Administration and the Holcaust, 1938-1945. New Brunswick, N.J.: Rutgers University Press, 1970.

Friedman, Saul S. No Haven for the Oppressed: United States Policy Toward Jewish Refugees, 1938-1945. Detroit: Wayne State University Press, 1973.

Maga, Timothy P. America, France, and the European Refugee Problem, 1933-1947. New York: Garland, 1985.

Stewart, Barbara McDonald. United States Government Policy on Refugees from Nazism, 1933-1940. New York: Garland, 1982.

Wyman, David S. Paper Walls: America and the Refugee Crisis, 1938-1941. Amherst: University of Massachusetts Press, 1968.

Articles

Brody, David. "American Jewry, the Refugees and Immigration Restriction (1932-1942)." Publications of the American Jewish Historical Society 45 (No. 4, 1955/1956): 219-47.

Gellman, Irwin F. "The St. Louis Tragedy." American Jewish Historical Quarterly 5 (No. 2, 1971): 144-56.

Genizi, Haim. "New York is Big--America is Bigger: The Resettlement of Refugees from Nazism, 1936-1945." Jewish Social Studies 46 (Winter 1984): 61-72.

Kraut, Alan M., Richard Breitman, and Thomas W. Imhoof. "The State Department, the Labor Department, and German Jewish Immigration, 1930--1940." Journal of American Ethnic History 3 (Spring 1984): 5-38.

Maga, Timothy P. "The United States, France, and the European Refugee Problem, 1933-1940." Historian 46 (Aug. 1984): 503-19.

Dissertations

Friedman, Saul S. "Official United States Policy toward Jewish Refugees, 1938-1945." Ph.D. diss., Ohio University, 1969.

Stewart, Barbara M. "United States Government Policy on Refugees from Nazism, 1933-1940." Ph.D. diss., Columbia University, 1969.

Wetzel, Charles J. "The American Rescue of Refugee Scholars and Scientists from Europe, 1933-1945." Ph.D. diss., University of Wisconsin, 1964.

Wyman, David S. "American Policy toward Immigration of Refugees from Nazism, 1938-1941." Ph.D. diss., Harvard University, 1966.

12.7   TRADE AND ECONOMIC RELATIONS

Books

Adams, Frederick C. Economic Diplomacy: The Export-Import Bank and American Foreign Policy, 1934-1939. Columbia: University of Missouri Press, 1976.

Anderson, Irvine H. ARAMCO, the United States, and Saudi Arabia: A Study of the Dynamics of Foreign Oil Policy, 1933-1950. Princeton: Princeton University Press, 1981.

Beckett, Grace L. The Reciprocal Trade Agreements Program. New York: Columbia University Press, 1941.

Buell, Raymond L. The Hull Trade Program and the American System. New York: Foreign Policy Association, 1938.

Feis, Herbert. The Diplomacy of the Dollar: First Era, 1919-1932. Baltimore: Johns Hopkins University Press, 1950.

Gardner, Lloyd C. Economic Aspects of New Deal Diplomacy. Madison: University of Wisconsin Press, 1964.

Hasib, Abdul. Monetary Negotiations in the World Economic Conference, 1933. Aligarh, India: Muslim University, 1958.

Kottman, Richard N. Reciprocity and the North Atlantic Triangle, 1932-1938. Ithaca: Cornell University Press, 1968.

Pearson, James C. The Reciprocal Trade Agreements Program: The Policy of the United States and its Effectiveness. Washington, D.C.: Catholic University of America Press, 1942.

Tasca, Henry J. The Reciprocal Trade Policy of the United States: A Study in Trade Philosophy. Philadelphia: University of Pennsylvania Press, 1938.

Taylor, Alonzo E. The New Deal and Foreign Trade. NewYork: Macmillan, 1935.

Articles

Allen, William R. "Cordell Hull and the Defense of the Trade Agreements Program, 1934-1940." In Isolation and Security: Ideas and Interests in Twentieth-Century American Foreign Policy ed. by Alexander DeConde (Durham. N.C.: Duke University Press, 1957), pp. 107-32.

Beckett, Grace L. "The Effect of the Reciprocal Trade Agreements upon the Foreign Trade of the United States." Quarterly Journal of Economics 54 (Nov. 1939): 80-94.

Benjamin, Jules R. "The New Deal, Cuba, and the Rise of a Global Foreign Economic Policy." Business History Review 51 (Spring 1977): 57-78.

Burke, Robert. "Reciprocal Trade in the New Deal." Current History 42 (June 1962): 350-55, 364.

Costigliola, Frank. "The Other Side of Isolationism: The Establishment of the First World Bank, 1929-1930." Journal of American History 59 (Dec. 1972): 602-20.

Ferrell, Robert H. "Cordell Hull and the Defense of the Trade Agreements Program, 1934-1940." In Isolation and Security ed. by Alexander DeConde (Durham: Duke University Press, 1957), pp. 107-32.

Ghosh, Partha Sarathy. "Passage of the Silver Purchase Act of 1934: The China Lobby and the Issue of China Trade." Indian Journal of American Studies 6 (Jan./June 1976): 18-29.

Goldstein, Judith. "The Political Economy of Trade: Institutions of Protection." American Political Science Review 80 (March 1986): 161-84.

Huber, J. Richard. "The Effects of German Clearing Agreements and Import Restrictions on Cotton, 1934-1939." Southern Economic Journal 6 (April 1940): 419-39.

Kimball, Warren F. "'Beggar My Neighbor': America and the British Interim Finance Crisis, 1940-1941." Journal of Economic History 29 (Dec. 1969): 758-72.

Kottman, Richard N. "Herbert Hoover and the Smoot-Hawley Tariff: Canada, A Case Study." Journal of American History 62 (Dec. 1975): 609-35.

_____. "The Canadian-American Trade Agreement of 1935." Journal of American History 52 (Sept. 1965): 275-96.

McHale, James M. "National Planning and Reciprocal Trade: The New Deal Origins of Government Guarantees for Private Exporters." Prologue 6 (Fall 1974): 189-99.

Nichols, Jeannette P. "Roosevelt's Monetary Diplomacy in 1933." American Historical Review 56 (Jan. 1951): 295-317.

Porter, David L. "Senator Pat Harrison of Mississippi and the Reciprocal Trade Act of 1940." Journal of Mississippi History 36 (Nov. 1974): 363-76.

Repko, Allen F. "The Failure of Reciprocal Trade: United States-Germany Commerical Rivalry in Brazil, 1934-1940." Mid-America 60 (Jan. 1978): 3-20.

Schatz, Arthur W. "The Anglo-American Trade Agreement and Cordell Hull's Search for Peace, 1936-38." Journal of American History 57 (June 1970): 85-103.

_____. "The Reciprocal Trade Agreements Program and the 'Farm Vote,' 1934-1940." Agricultural History 46 (Oct. 1972): 498-514.

Dissertations

Adams, Frederick C. "The Export-Import Bank and American Foreign Policy, 1934-1939." Ph.D. diss., Cornell University, 1968.

Beddow, James B. "Economic Nationalism or Internationalism: Upper Midwestern Response to New Deal Tariff Policy, 1934-1940." Ph.D. diss., University of Oklahoma, 1969.

Casillas, Rex J. "Oil and Diplomacy: The Evolution of American Foreign Policy in Saudi Arabia, 1933-1945." Ph.D. diss., University of Utah, 1983.

Lewis, James Andrew. "Diplomacy and Gold: American Attitudes toward the Role of Government In World Recovery from Versailles to the First New Deal." Ph.D. diss., University of Chicago, 1984.

McHale, James M. "The New Deal and the Origins of Public Lending for Foreign Economic Development, 1933-1945." Ph.D. diss., University of Wisconsin, 1970.

Nairab, Mohammad M. "Petroleum in Saudi-American Relations: The Formative Period, 1932-1948." Ph.D. diss., North Texas State University, 1978.

Schatz, Arthur W. "Cordell Hull and the Struggle for the Reciprocal Trade Agreements Program, 1932-1940." Ph.D. diss., University of Oregon, 1965.

Smith, Daniel Bennett. "Toward Internationalism: New Deal Foreign Economic Policy, 1933-1939." Ph.D. diss., Stanford University, 1984.

Snyder, John R. "Edward P. Costigan and the U.S. Tariff Commission." Ph.D. diss., University of Colorado, 1966.

13

Aftereffects

Books

Gordon, Lincoln. A New Deal for Latin America: The Alliance for Progress. Cambridge: Harvard University Press, 1963.

Graham, Otis L., Jr. Toward a Planned Society: From Roosevelt to Nixon. New York: Oxford University Press, 1976.

Hamby, Alonzo L. Beyond the New Deal: Harry S. Truman and American Liberalism. New York: Columbia University Press, 1973.

_____. Liberalism and Its Challengers: F.D.R. to Reagan. New York: Oxford University Press, 1985.

Leuchtenburg, William E. In the Shadow of FDR: From Harry Truman to Ronald Reagan. Ithaca: Cornell University Press, 1983.

Saint-Etienne, Christian. The Great Depression, 1929-1938: Lessons for the 1980s. Stanford, Cal.: Hoover Institution Press, 1984.

Sirevag, Torbjorn. The Eclipse of the New Deal. New York: Garland, 1985.

Smith, Fred. The Growth and Decline of the New Deal, 1933-1970. Greenwich, Conn.: Devin-Adair, 1970.

Tugwell, Rexford G. Off Course: From Truman to Nixon. New York: Praeger, 1971.

Articles

Freidel, Frank B. "The New Deal: Laying the Foundation for Modern America." In The Roosevelt New Deal: A Program Assessment Fifty Years After ed. by Wilbur J. Cohen (Austin: Lyndon B. Johnson School of Public Affairs, 1986), pp. 3-18.

Graham, Otis L., Jr. "The Planning Idea from Roosevelt to Post-Reagan." In The New Deal Viewed from Fifty Years ed. by Lawrence E. Gelfand and Robert J. Neymeyer (Iowa City: Center for the Study of Recent History of the United States. 1983), pp. 1-19.

Hamby, Alonzo L. "The Liberals, Truman, and FDR as Symbol and Myth." Journal of American History 56 (March 1970): 859-67.

Horowitz, Irving Louis. "From the New Deal to the New Federalism: Presidential Ideology in the U.S. from 1932 to 1982." American Journal of Economics and Sociology 92 (April 1983): 129-48.

Johnson, Lyndon B. "In Commemoration of the 82nd Anniversary of the Birth of Franklin Delano Roosevelt." Centennial Review 9 (Spring 1965): 153-55.

Kyvig, David E. "Sober Thoughts: Myths and Realities of National Prohibition after Fifty Years." In Law, Alcohol, and Order: Perspectives on National Prohibition ed. by David E. Kyvig (Westport, Conn: Greenwood, 1985), pp. 3-20.

Ladd, Everett Carl, Jr. "Liberalism Upside Down: The Inversion of the New Deal Order." Political Science Quarterly 91 (Winter 1976-77): 577-600.

Lawson, Alan. "The Cultural Legacy of the New Deal." In Fifty Years Later: The New Deal Evaluated ed. by Harvard Sitkoff (New York: Knopf, 1985), pp. 155-86.

Leuchtenburg, William E. "The Achievement of the New Deal." In Fifty Years Later: The New Deal Evaluated ed. by Harvard Sitkoff (New York: Knopf, 1985), pp. 211-31.

_____. "The Legacy of FDR." Wilson Quarterly 6 (Spring 1982): 77-93.

Polenberg, Richard. "Roosevelt, Carter, and Executive Reorganization: Lessons of the 1930's." Presidential Studies Quarterly 9 (Winter 1979): 35-46.

Temin, Peter. "Lessons for the Present from the Great Depression." American Economic Review 66 (May 1976): 40-45.

Author Index

Entries indicate the chapter and section in which the author's work may be found and whether the work is a book (b), article (a), or dissertation (d).

Aaron, Daniel 1b, 3.3b, 3.3a, 10.1b, 10.2b, 10.6b
Abbazia, Patrick 12.5b
Abbott, Edith 7.1b
Abbott, Grace 6.3b
Abegglen, James C. 7.4b
Abraham, Henry J. 11a
Abrahams, Paul 7.2a
Abramowitz, Mildred W. 6.1a
Abrams, Douglas Carl 9.4d
Accinelli, Robert D. 12.1a
Acena, Albert 10.6d
Acheson, Dean 3.3b
Achter, Barbara A. Z. 10.2d
Adamic, Louis 3.3b
Adams, D. K. 12.1a
Adams, Frank 10.3b
Adams, Frederick C. 12.2a, 12.7b, 12.7d
Adams, Grace 7.1b
Adams, Henry H. 4b
Adams, J. W. 9.4a
Adams, John Clifford 7.2d
Adams, Paul Langford 10.8d
Adler, Les K. 12.3a

Adler, Selig 12.1b, 12.1a
Adubato, Robert A. 8.2d
Aeschbacher, William D. 7.2d
Agee, James 8.1b
Agee, Steven Craig 7.1d
Ahearn, Daniel J., Jr. 7.5b
Ahlander, Leslie Judd 10.2a
Ajay, Abe 3.3a
Akin, William E. 10.1b
Akins, Bill 9.4b
Albertson, Dean 4b, 4d
Albjerg, Victor L. 5.1a
Albright, Horace M. 6.1a
Alchom, Guy 7.1d
Alderfer, Harold F. 9.2b
Alexander, Albert 6.1a
Alexander, Charles 10.1b
Alexander, Donald Crichton 9.4b
Alexander, Robert J. 12.1d
Alexander, William 10.5a
Alford, B. W. E. 7.4a
Alinsky, Saul David 4b
Allan, Arnold A. 5.2d
Allen, Donald R. 1b
Allen, Frederick Lewis 1b

About the Compilers

DAVID E. KYVIG is Professor of History at the University of Akron. He is the author of *Law, Alcohol, and Order* (Greenwood Press, 1985), *Repealing National Prohibition,* and *FDR's America* and the coauthor of *Nearby History* and *Your Family History.*

MARY-ANN BLASIO is a doctoral student in History at the University of Akron.